Ngũgĩ wa Thiong'o

Interviews with the Kenyan Writer

Edited by
Reinhard Sander
&
Bernth Lindfors

With the assistance of
Lynette Cintrón

James Currey
OXFORD

EAEP
NAIROBI

James Currey Ltd
73 Botley Road
Oxford OX2 OBS
www.jamescurrey.co.uk

East African Educational Publishers (EAEP)
P.O.Box 45314
00100 Nairobi
www.eastafricanpublishers.com

First published in the United States of America
by Africa World Press 2006
First published in Britain
by James Currey 2006

British Library Cataloguing in Publication data applied for

ISBN 10: 0-85255-580-6 (James Currey paper)
ISBN 13: 978-0-85255-580-4 (James Currey paper)

Printed and bound in Britain by
Woolnough, Irthlingborough

Books by Ngũgĩ wa Thiong'o

Weep Not, Child. London & Ibadan: Heinemann, 1964; New York: Collier, 1969.

The River Between. London: Heinemann, 1965.

A Grain of Wheat. London: Heinemann, 1967.

The Black Hermit. Nairobi, London & Ibadan: Heinemann, 1968.

This Time Tomorrow: Three Plays. Nairobi: East African Literature Bureau, 1970.

Homecoming: Essays on African and Caribbean Literature, Culture and Politics. London: Heinemann, 1972; New York: Lawrence Hill, 1973.

Secret Lives, and Other Stories. London: Heinemann; New York: Lawrence Hill, 1975.

The Trial of Dedan Kimathi. By Ngugi and Micere Githae Mugo. London : Heinemann, 1976.

The Independence of Africa and Cultural Decolonisation. Lagos: Afrografica, 1977 (published with *The Poverty of African Historiography* by A. E. Afigbo).

Petals of Blood. London: Heinemann, 1977; New York: Dutton, 1978.

Caitaani Mutharaba-ini. Nairobi: Heinemann, 1980. Trans. as *Devil on the Cross.* London: Heinemann, 1982.

Ngaahika Ndeenda: Ithaako ria Ngerekano. By Ngugi & Ngugi wa Mirii. Nairobi: Heinemann, 1980. Trans. as *I Will Marry When I Want.* London & Exeter, NH: Heinemann, 1982.

Detained: A Writer's Prison Diary. London, Nairobi & Exeter, NH: Heinemann, 1981.

Writers in Politics: Essays. London & Exeter, NH: Heinemann, 1981. Rev. & enlarged as *Writers in Politics: A Re-Engagement with Issues of Literature & Society.* Oxford, Oxfordshire: J. Currey; Portsmouth, NH: Heinemann, 1997.

Education for a National Culture. Harare: Zimbabwe Pub. House, 1981.

Njamba Nene na Mbaathi i Mathagu. Nairobi: Heinemann, 1982. Trans. as *Njamba Nene and the Flying Bus.* Nairobi: Heinemann, 1986; Trenton, NJ: Africa World Press, 1994.

Barrel of a Pen: Resistance to Repression in Neo-Colonial Kenya. London: New Beacon; Trenton, NJ: Africa World Press, 1983.

Bathitoora ya Njamba Nene. Nairobi: Heinemann, 1984. Trans. as *Njamba Nene's Pistol.* Nairobi: Heinemann, 1986; Trenton, NJ: Africa World Press, 1994.

Decolonising the Mind: The Politics of Language in African Literature. London: J. Currey; Portsmouth, NH: Heinemann, 1986.

Matigari ma Njiruungi. Nairobi: Heinemann, 1986. Trans. as *Matigari.* Oxford: Heinemann, 1989; Trenton, NJ: Africa World Press, 1998.

Writing against Neocolonialism. Wembley, Middlesex: Vita, 1986.

Njamba Nene na Cibu King'ang'i. Nairobi: Heinemann, 1986.

The First Walter Rodney Memorial Lecture, 1985. London: Friends of Bogle, 1987.

Moving the Centre: The Struggle for Cultural Freedoms. London: J. Currey; Nairobi: East African Educational Publishers; Portsmouth, N.H.: Heinemann, 1993.

Penpoints, Gunpoints, and Dreams: Towards a Critical Theory of the Arts and the State in Africa. Oxford: Clarendon Press; New York: Oxford University Press, 1998.

Mũrogi wa Kagogo. Vol. 1 (Bks. 1 & 2). Nairobi, Kampala, Dar es Salaam: East African Educational Publishers, 2004. Vol. 2 (Bks. 3 & 4) and Vol. 3 (Bks. 5 & 6) forthcoming. Trans. as *Wizard of the Crow.* New York: Knopf/Pantheon Books, forthcoming 2006.

Contents

Introduction

Ngugi wa Thiong'o is one of Africa's most famous writers. His novels, plays, essays and speeches have earned him an international reputation as an articulate spokesman not just for Africa but for the entire Third World as well. His writings, rooted in historical and material realities, have always been politically engaged, arguing a case for the poor and oppressed who, as victims of economic exploitation and cultural domination by the West, have sought to liberate themselves by resisting the forces that hold them down. He has become a champion of the dispossessed, an inspiring advocate for freedom, justice and human rights for all the downtrodden peoples of the world.

His evolution as a thinker can be discerned in the interviews collected here. The earliest, recorded forty years ago, reflect his interest in exploring events in Kenya's colonial past that had a profound impact on his own people, the Kikuyu, and ultimately on his own life. One of these was the Kikuyu independent schools movement, the other the emergence of the Mau Mau insurrection against British rule. Ngugi wrote his first two novels on these themes while an undergraduate at Makerere University in Uganda. His literary education at that time consisted of a heavy dose of British curricular classics (Shakespeare to T.S. Elliot, with special emphasis on D.H. Lawrence and Joseph Conrad) moderated to some extent by his independent discovery of such early African and West Indian authors as Peter Abrahams, Chinua Achebe, Cyprian Ekwensi and George Lamming. When he sat down to write, he sought to put on record the specific historical experience of his own kinsmen, just as these others had done.

When he moved on to postgraduate studies at Leeds University in England, he was exposed to a wider range of reading that included theoretical works by Marx, Engels, Lenin and Fanon. These books influenced his thinking about colonialism and imperialism, and his next two novels, set in contemporary times in Kenya, contained radical ideas about the plight of peasants and workers trapped in a neo-colonial society that, on the eve of independence and even afterward, continued to oppress them.

The third phase of Ngugi's writing career began when he was invited to participate in a literacy project by co-authoring a play for the Kamiriithu Community Education and Cultural Centre in Limuru, his home village. To do this, he had to write for the first time in his mother tongue, which required seeking appropriate cultural and linguistic input from members of the community. The play, which dealt with poor, landless people being exploited by wealthy landowners, was enormously popular in the countryside but was shut down by Kenyan authorities who then arrested Ngugi and, without ever pressing charges against him, kept him in detention in a maximum security prison for almost a year. It was this bitter experience that led Ngugi to resolve to do all his future creative writing in his mother tongue so he could continue to communicate with his target audience—the proletariat who were at the mercy of a parasitic bourgeoisie and a corrupt, avaricious ruling class.

A few years later, unable to resume his teaching career at the University of Nairobi and prevented from continuing his theatrical work in Kenya, Ngugi went into exile, first in Britain, then in America where he accepted teaching positions at Yale University, New York University, and most recently at the University of California at Irvine. During this period he has continued to write prolifically and to speak at conferences and campuses throughout the world. Yet despite becoming an international public intellectual, he has persisted in expressing himself creatively solely in Kikuyu, addressing his message first to his own people, from whom he has been physically separated for more than the past twenty years.

The interviews reproduced here trace the trajectory of his intellectual engagement with his times, showing what he had in mind and how he chose to deal with the challenges confronting him. By eavesdropping on what he says, we can learn a lot not only about what Ngugi was thinking and doing at various stages of his career but also about what was happening in Africa before, during and after independence. Ngugi's words lead us to a deeper understanding of colonial and postcolonial history.

The Editors
June 2004

Acknowledgments

First, we wish to thank Ngugi wa Thiong'o for allowing us to collect and publish these interviews.

We also thank the following individuals for granting us permission to reprint their interviews with Ngugi: Tami Alpert, Katebaliirwe Amooti wa Irumba, Charles Cantalupo, Reed Way Dasenbrock, Raoul Granqvist, Feroza Jussawalla, Mandla Langa, Nonqaba Msimang, Lee Nichols, Essop Pahad, D. Venkat Rao, Dianne Schwerdt, Anita Shreve, Carol Sicherman, Bettye Parker Smith, Harish Trivedi, Wangui wa Goro, Maureen Warner-Lewis and Jane Wilkinson.

In addition, we express our gratitude to the following publishers for enabling us to reprint material from their books: Africa World Press, James Currey, Duke University Press, Hans Zell Publishers, Heinemann Educational Publishers, Indiana University Press, University of Mississippi Press, and the W.E.B. DuBois Institute, Harvard University.

We are also grateful to the editors of the following journals and newspapers for permitting us to reprint interviews that first appeared in their pages: *African Communist*, *African Literature Association Bulletin*, *Ba Shiru*, *BBC Arts and Africa*, *Commonwealth: Essays and Studies*; *CRNLE Reviews Journal*, *East African Standard*, *Glendora Review*, *Ife Studies in African Literature and the Arts*, *Kunapipi*, *Left Curve*, *Meanjin*, *Research in African Literatures*, *Span*, *Sunday Nation*, *Third World Quarterly*, *Transition*, *Wasafiri*, and *The Weekly Review*.

We have made a concerted effort to contact all parties holding rights to these interviews, even the editors of defunct publications. We would like to hear from anyone we may have missed.

We want to thank the University of Puerto Rico for granting Reinhard Sander several *descargues* (course reductions) and graduate assistants to help with the collecting, scanning, word processing, and proofreading of the interviews. The impeccable work of Liza Rivera Hudders, Mae Teitelbaum and Narielys Márquez Carrasquillo is greatly appreciated. Thanks also to the secretaries of the UPR Department of English for their advice on various practical matters concerning the production of the manuscript. Special thanks go to our assistant editor, Lynette Cintrón, sponsored by both the UPR and the Puerto Rican government's *Juvempleo* program, for her invaluable contribution throughout all stages of the project and for preparing camera-ready copy of the collection.

The Editors

Chronology

1938	Born in Kamiriithu, Limuru on 5 January to Thiong'o wa Nduucu and Wanjiku wa Ngugi.
1947-48	Attends Church of Scotland Mission at Kamaandura, Limuru.
1948-55	Attends Manguu Karinga (Gikuyu independent) school.
1952	Governor Baring declares State of Emergency.
1954	Manguu school moves to Kinyogoori, becoming Kinyogoori District Education Board school; English is the medium of instruction.
1955-59	Studies at Alliance High School, Kikuyu.
1955	Returns home to find his family house and village razed to the ground and being rebuilt in villagization project as a result of the anti-Mau Mau campaign.
1956	Capture of Dedan Kimathi.
1957	Execution of Dedan Kimathi; publication of "I Try Witchcraft," in Allliance High School magazine.
1959	Teaches briefly at Kahuguini Primary School in Gatundu; enters Makerere U College, Uganda.
1959-64	Studies at Makerere U College; revives *The Undergraduate*, a magazine dealing with intellectual and cultural matters.

1960	Publication of "The Fig Tree" in *Penpoint*, the literary magazine of the English Department at Makerere; Kenyan Emergency officially ends.
1961	Marriage partnership with Nyambura begins; birth of first child, Thiong'o.
1961-64	Columnist first for *Sunday Post* and then for *Daily Nation* and *Sunday Nation*.
1962	Writes *Weep Not, Child*; *The Rebels* is broadcast on Uganda Broadcasting Service; wins Shell Exhibition (scholarship) for outstanding academic performance; production of *The Black Hermit* at the Ugandan National Theatre, Kampala; attends the Makerere Conference of African Writers of English Expression.
1962-64	On Editorial Board of *Penpoint*.
1963	Kenya gains Independence within British Commonwealth; on staff of *Makererean*, student newspaper; publication of *The Black Hermit* by Makerere UP; wins Shell Exhibition a second time; birth of second child, Kimunya.
1963-64	Assists David Cook in making selections from *Penpoint* for *Origin East Africa: A Makerere Anthology*.
1964	Graduates from Makerere, B. A.; enters Leeds U where he begins writing *A Grain of Wheat*; publication of *Weep Not, Child*; Kenya is declared republic within the Commonwealth.
1965	Publication of *The River Between*; assistant editor of the magazine *Africa: Tradition and Change* at Leeds to which he contributes section of *Grain* under the

	title "The Trench"; publication of *Origin East Africa*; birth of third child, Nduucu.
1966	*Weep Not, Child* wins first prize for anglophone novel at first World Festival of Negro Arts at Dakar; attends International PEN Conference in the United States; completes *A Grain of Wheat*; speaks at the Africa Centre, London.
1967	Attends Third Afro-Asian Writers Conference in Beirut, Lebanon; returns to Kenya; *This Time Tomorrow* is broadcast on BBC Africa Service; publication of *A Grain of Wheat*; attends first African-Scandinavian Writers' Conference, Stockholm; although not credited edits *Zuka* no. 1, a journal of East African creative writing
1967-69	Special Lecturer in English at University College, Nairobi.
1968	Guest editor of special creative-writing issue of *East Africa Journal*; edits *Zuka* no. 2; along with members of the African Studies Program, proposes abolition of the Department of English and its replacement by Department of African Literature and Languages; speaks at Ife Conference on African Writing in English, Ife, Nigeria; visiting lecturer, University College, Dar es Salaam.
1969	Resigns from his teaching position to protest violations of academic freedom at the University; co-edits *Zuka* no. 3; writes "Towards a National Culture" for UNESCO conference on "Cultural Policy in Africa" in Dakar, Senegal; speaks at Institute of African Studies, U of Ghana.
1969-70	Fellow in Creative Writing, Makerere U; works on *Homecoming*.

1970	Publication of *This Time Tomorrow*, containing *The Rebels*, *The Wound in the Heart*, and the title play; organizes writers' workshop at Makerere; at University College, Nairobi the Department of English becomes the Department of Literature, and the Department of Linguistics and African languages is formed.
1970-71	Visiting Associate Professor at Northwestern U; starts writing *Petals of Blood*; lectures at Rice U, U of Houston and Texas Southern U, Texas.
1971	Returns to U of Nairobi (during the next year or two supervises final renovation of literature syllabus); on editorial board of *Busara* (3.3 and 3.4), magazine of Department of Literature, U of Nairobi; birth of fourth child, Mukoma.
1972	Publication of *Homecoming*; birth of fifth child, Wanjiku.
1973	Promoted to Senior Lecturer and Head of the Department of Literature at the U of Nairobi; awarded the Lotus Prize in literature at 5th Afro-Asian Writers Conference in Alma Ata, Khazakhstan; on editorial board of *Busara* (5.1) and advisor to issue 5.2; with Taban lo Liyong and Okot p'Bitek, launches Writers' Sessions in Nairobi.
1974	Editorial adviser to *Busara* (6.1, 6.2); with Micere Githae Mugo begins *The Trial of Dedan Kimathi*.
1975	Publication of *Secret Lives*; editorial adviser, *Busara* (7.1, 7.2); completes *Petals of Blood*, during month-long stay at Yalta.
1976	Becomes chairman of Kamiriithu Community Education and Cultural Centre's cultural committee; attends International Emergency Conference on

Korea in Tokyo; portions of *The Trial of Dedan Kimathi* are performed at Kamiriithu and elsewhere; the play is performed at the Kenya National Theatre, Nairobi; along with Ngugi wa Mirii is commissioned by Kamiriithu Centre to write the script which becomes *Ngaahika Ndeenda* (*I Will Marry When I Want*); becomes Associate Professor at U of Nairobi; begins writing *Devil on the Cross* in English.

1977 — *The Trial of Dedan Kimathi* is performed at FESTAC 1977 in Lagos, Nigeria; publication of *Petals of Blood*; legally changes name to Ngugi wa Thiong'o; *Ngaahika Ndeenda* is performed at Kamiriithu; license for further performances of the play is withdrawn; Ngugi is detained at Kamiti Maximum Security Prison; *This Time Tomorrow* broadcast in Germany.

1978 — The drama group of African Students Association of Sussex U tours Britain with *The Trial of Dedan Kimathi* as part of the widespread international responses against his detention; in detention writes *Caitaani Mutharaba-ini* and parts of *Detained*; adopted as prisoner of conscience by Amnesty International; birth of sixth child, Njooki; death of Jomo Kenyatta; released from detention; denied position at U of Nairobi.

1979 — His family receives death threats; along with Ngugi wa Mirii is arrested under false charges for drinking after hours; charges are dismissed; some 400 academics sign a petition asking for his reinstatement at U of Nairobi.

1979-82 — Initiates study group led by Karega Mutahi to revise inconsistent and inaccurate Gikuyu orthography established by missionaries.

1980	Kiswahili production of *The Trial of Dedan Kimathi* is performed at U of Nairobi; gives talk at Africa Centre, London; participates in 75th anniversary celebration of Danish Library Association, Denmark; publication of Gikuyu editions of *Caitaani Mutharaba-ini* and *Ngaahika Ndeenda* in Nairobi.
1981	*Mzalendo Kimathi* (Kiswahili translation of *The Trial*) is performed at U of Nairobi; *Caitaani* receives Special Commendation in Noma Awards for Publishing in Africa; rehearsals begin at Kamiriithu Community Education and Cultural Centre for *Maitu Njugira*; publication of *Detained: A Writer's Prison Diary* and *Writers in Politics*.
1982	Denied permission to produce *Maitu Njugira* at the Kenya National Theatre; issues public statement on suppression of the play; government de-registers the Kamiriithu Centre and bans all theater in the region; publication of English editions of *Devil on the Cross* and *I Will Marry When I Want* in London; attends launch of *Devil on the Cross* in London; after attempted coup is suppressed in Kenya, remains in exile in London while his family remains in Limuru; publication of *Njamba Nene na Mbaathi i Mathagu* in Nairobi; with other Kenyan exiles in London forms Committee for the Release of Political Prisioners in Kenya; in Sweden speaks at four universities; delivers keynote address at annual U of Calabar International Conference on African Literature and English Language, Calabar, Nigeria.
1983	*Njamba Nene na Mbaathi i Mathagu* receives Special Commendation in the Noma Award for Publishing in Africa; publication of *Barrel of a Pen*; writes *Matigari ma Njiruungi* in London.

1984	Guest Professor, U of Bayreuth; delivers Robb Lectures, U of Auckland, New Zealand; in Zimbabwe delivers papers at U of Zimbabwe and Institute for Development Studies, Harare; a production of *The Trial* tours England; delivers keynote address at African Writers' Conference; *I Will Marry When I Want* performed in Japanese in Japan; publication of *Bathitoora ya Njamba Nene.*
1985	Delivers keynote address at the African Literature Association, Northwestern U.
1985-86	Studies film-making in Sweden; along with two other African students, makes the documentary *Africa in Sweden*; by himself he completes the twenty-minute film, *Blood-Grapes and Black Diamonds.*
1986	Participates in Second African Writers' Conference, Stockholm; joins boycott of Commonwealth arts festival in Edinburgh to protest the policies of South African government; participates in conference at Commonwealth Institute, London; participates in conference at Duke U, North Carolina, and goes on a three-week speaking tour of the United States; publication of *Matigari ma Njiruungi*; Kenya government confiscates all available copies from the publisher; delivers paper in Gikuyu at Institute Marie Haps, Brussels, with simultaneous translation into English and French; publication of *Decolonising the Mind*, *Writing Against Neo-Colonialism* and *Njamba Nene na Cibu King' ang' i.*
1987	Delivers address at the opening of the 6th International Book Fair of Radical, Black and Third World Books, London; chairman of Umoja, umbrella organization of Kenyan dissident groups in exile; publication of *The First Walter Rodney Memorial Lecture, 1985.*

1988	Speaks at the BBC World Service Seminar on "English: A Language for the World"; in Africa collaborates on film on Ousmane Sembène.
1989	Publication of *Matigari*, the English translation of *Matigari ma Njiruungi*.
1990-92	Visiting Professor at Yale U.
1991	Visiting Professor at Amherst and Smith colleges.
1992	Receives the Paul Robeson award for Artistic Excellence, Political Conscience and Integrity; marries Njeeri wa Ndung'u.
1993	Appointed Professor of Comparative Literature and Performance Studies at New York U where he serves as the Erich Maria Remarque Chair in Languages; publication of *Moving the Centre: The Struggle for Cultural Freedoms*; receives the Zora Neale Hurston-Paul Robeson Award of the Council for Black Studies, Accra, Ghana.
1994	Edits and publishes *Mũtiiri*, a Gikuyu journal of culture; Honorary Doctorate in Humane Letters from Albright College, Reading, Pennsylvania; receives Contributor's Arts Award of Chicago State U's Gwendolyn Brooks Center; birth of daughter, Mumbi.
1995	Birth of son, Thiong'o Kimathi.
1996	Delivers the Clarendon Lectures in English, Oxford U; receives the Fonlon-Nichols Prize for Artistic Excellence and Human Rights; receives the Distinguished Africanist Award of the New York African Studies Association.

1997	Publication of revised edition of *Writers in Politics*; lectures at the Center for Hawaiian Studies, U of Hawaii.
1998	Publication of *Penpoints, Gunpoints, and Dreams: Towards a Critical Theory of the Arts and the State in Africa*; keynote speaker at African Literature Association conference, Austin, Texas.
1999	Delivers Ashby Lecture at Clare Hall, Cambridge. Mentions that he has "just finished the fourth draft of a one thousand one hundred and forty-two page novel in the Gikuyu language tentatively titled *Murogi wa Kagogo*, in English *The Wizard of the Crow*."
2000	Presiding chairman of the conference "Against All Odds: African Languages and Literatures into the 21st Century," Asmara, Eritrea.
Since 2001	Distinguished Professor of English and Comparative Literature and Director, International Center for Writing and Translation at U of California, Irvine.
2002	Mwai Kibaki's National Rainbow Coalition (NARC) wins the December elections.
2003	Conducts the 6th Annual William H. Matheson Seminar in Comparative Arts, Washington U, St. Louis; in South Africa at the invitation of the Steve Biko Foundation, to commemorate the deaths of Steve Biko and Robert Sobukwe.
2004	Returns to Kenya, after twenty-two years of exile, for a one-month visit. The first of three projected volumes of the Gikuyu novel *Murogi wa Kagogo* is launched in Nairobi. Pantheon Books of the Knopf Publishing Group in New York announces plans to

publish the novel's English translation, *Wizard of the Crow*.

1 Ngugi wa Thiong'o: James Ngugi

Dennis Duerden / 1964 (1972)

This interview with James Ngugi was made by Dennis Duerden in January 1964. Ngugi had by then published in 1963 a play, The Black Hermit, *in a small edition by Makerere University Press. This had been produced in November 1962 at the Uganda National Theatre as part of the Independence Celebrations in Kampala. In December 1970 his radio play,* This Time Tomorrow, *adapted for stage presentation, was published with two others by the East African Literature Bureau. Stories of his had already appeared in* Penpoint *and* The New African *and stories, articles, and criticism were to appear widely in the next six or seven years. Some have now been collected and will be published as* Homecoming *(Heinemann, 1972). In 1964 Ngugi had published his first novel,* Weep Not, Child *(Heinemann), which is referred to in the following interview. Heinemann were subsequently to publish in 1965 and 1967 respectively,* The River Between *and* A Grain of Wheat.

Actually in the novel I have tried to show the effect of the Mau Mau war on the ordinary man and woman who were left in the villages. I think the terrible thing about the Mau Mau war was the destruction of family life, the destruction of personal relationships. You found a friend betraying a friend, the father suspicious of the son, a brother doubting the sincerity or the good intentions of a brother, and above all these things the terrible fear under which all these people lived. Some people in the novel, for instance, think that this is no ordinary calamity. That this, in fact, is the second coming of Christ. They go back to the Old Testament and the New Testament and they find that their fears are confirmed.

Does this mean that your first novel is linked to your second novel, because I believe that the title of your second novel is The Black Messiah*?*

In a way, yes, because *The Black Messiah* deals with a situation in the thirties when there was a clash between the Kikuyu and the missionaries and also between the Kikuyu and the government. The result of that is that we saw the beginnings of the political movement in Kenya and also the beginning of Kikuyu independent schools. Well, my second novel, *The Black Messiah,* deals with this clash; so in a way you might say that *Weep Not, Child* is one more step after *The Black Messiah.* As a matter of fact, I wrote *The Black Messiah* first and *Weep Not, Child* one year later.

When did you start writing? When would you say you first began work on The Black Messiah*?*

I can't quite remember, but I think it was in March 1961. I was writing *The Black Messiah* for a novel writing competition which was organized by the East African Literature Bureau; the closing date was December 1961; and around January 1962 I began my second novel, *Weep Not, Child.*

What started you to write, have you always written or were you set off by the novel competition?

I have not always written, but I have always been interested in writing. When I finished primary school, I was wondering why in fact people who were highly educated and knew the English language—I thought, for instance, that they knew everything about English!—could not write stories like those I read, e.g. by R. L. Stevenson. He is the one who really set my imagination flying and I thought that one day I would like to write stories like those which he himself had written. For instance, *Treasure Island* had made a big impression on me and I thought that if ever I got enough education I would like to write a story like that one. That was around 1955.

Can you talk about other writers, or other novels which have influenced you in your writing?

When I went to Makerere in 1959, I was very much taken up with Peter Abrahams.[*] I found his stories very moving and I tried to read as many of his novels as I could, and then, just soon after Peter Abrahams, I discovered D. H. Lawrence, and again his way of entering into the spirit of things, as it were, influenced me quite a lot.

Presumably you have read Things Fall Apart. *At what part or time in your career would you say that this took place?*

I think it was soon after D. H. Lawrence. I began ploughing into African writers and I began with, I think, yes, with Achebe—*Things Fall Apart.*

So you had read a number of African writers before you started on your own work?

I think so, yes. I had read Chinua Achebe, I had read Ekwensi and I think some of the West Indian writers, and I think these people set my imagination flying.

Would you say that you had two sets of influences, one from African writers and one from English writers, and if so, can you distinguish between them?

I do not think that I can easily distinguish between them. What the African writers did for me in a way that no other English writer could do for me was to make me feel that they were really speaking to me: The situation about which they were writing was one which was immediate to me, and also I found for the first time I was talking with my own people. I was talking with characters whom I knew, in a way, who had agonies which I had seen with our own people in Kenya, and at that point I felt that if there could be Africans who could write such stories, I could write as well. I felt with D. H. Lawrence, although the situation, the geographical situation and even the moral situations he is writing about, are in some ways remote to me, that he is able to go into the spirit of things. You know I felt as if he was entering into the soul of the people, and not only of the people, but even of the land, of the countryside, of things like plants, of the atmosphere.

This sort of theme of identification with land seems to be quite a strong one in your work. I mean somehow the relationship between the European farmer and the man he has replaced in this first novel of yours, which has been published, is somehow tied up with the land. Would you say that this was a principle, a preoccupation, or even a principal preoccupation of yours?

Not mine, but more of the people at home. I know that the land, the soil, has got a lot of effect on the people who come to Kenya, those people who have lived in Kenya, both African and European—I do not know very much about the Asian community, but I think they are also affected by the land. It is more than the material; it is not just because of its economic possibilities, it is something almost akin to spiritual.

I think it makes it easier to understand why you find this kind of kinship with Lawrence. I mean his sort of identification between the people and the land and some kind of natural forces. Would you say there are other European writers who have struck you in the same way?

No, I wouldn't say in the same way. I know Conrad, whom at present I am reading, has, I think, affected me in a different way, but not because he is able to enter into the soul of things in the same way as D. H. Lawrence. When I am reading D. H. Lawrence, I feel the spirituality of things very near me as if I am touching the very spirit of things. With Conrad, I'm impressed by the way he questions things, requestions things like action, the morality of action, for instance.

Doesn't he question man's ability to have any control over his own destiny?

No; yes and no, because while he questions man's ideas and man's ability to control his destiny, at the heart of Conrad is a feeling that man is great, and reading Conrad one feels struck by man's capacity for bearing suffering, but much more than this, he questions what appears on the surface. He questions what I would call "the morality of action." What is "success," for instance, what we would normally call success? What is "action"? Is failure to make a decision a moral action or not? So you find that some characters in Conrad fail to do something, but their failure to do something is a moral decision with Conrad. This kind of questioning has impressed me a lot because with Conrad I have felt I have come into contact with another whose questioning to me is much more important than the answers which he gives.

---

* By 1959, Peter Abrahams had published one book of stories, *Dark Testament* (London: Allen & Unwin, 1942), five novels: *Song of the City* (London: D. Crisp, 1945), *Mine Boy* (London: Crisp, 1946; New York: Knopf, 1955), *The Path of Thunder* (New York: Harper, 1948; London: Faber & Faber, 1952), *Wild Conquest* (New York: Harper, 1950; London: Faber, 1951) and *A Wreath for Udomo* (London: Faber, 1956; New York: Knopf, 1956) as well as *Return to Goli* (London: Faber, 1953—impressions of Johannesburg and South Africa on a visit after living abroad—and the autobiographical *Tell Freedom* (London: Faber, 1954; New York: Knopf, 1954).

2 The Birth of a New East African Author

John de Villiers / 1964

Slightly built James Ngugi spoke slowly, earnestly. Only his hands were restless, seeming to flay the air in frustration when his command of the English language, as spoken, left him groping for the word or phrase that would express exactly his meaning. "I was trying," he said, "to express the feelings of a small village community in Kenya during the Emergency. The terror, the fear of the unknown in which so many of the little people lived. The setting is a local one, which I know and have lived in, but the feeling, I think, is universal: the feeling of the little man, a child, in a world at war. He is caught in a situation he cannot control; he can only live it...." He was talking about his book, Weep Not, Child, *which is being published in Britain this week by William Heinemann.*

Was this your first novel?

No, my first was *The Black Messiah*, which I wrote in 1961 for the competition organized by the East African Literature Bureau.

How did it fare?

It won the top prize in the English section which, of course, pleased and encouraged me a great deal. But I was not really satisfied with it; I'm not yet satisfied with my work....I feel when I see the finished product that I did not really get to grips with the subject or, perhaps, the language; I feel I want to go back and do it all over again—properly.

But I understand this first novel is also due to be published?

Yes, that is what seems to happen when you have your first book accepted; the publishers are prepared to take a look at the things you have written before. *The Black Messiah* is due to be published later this year or early next year, but we will probably make changes. There may even be a different title.

Who is your favorite writer?

Joseph Conrad. Perhaps it is because English was for him a second language. He only really started using it when he was nineteen and yet he beat it into a particular shape to express himself; the anguish and agony of a community. For me he had an awareness of the loneliness of man...but he did not reject society; he believed in it and was a part of it.

Has his work made any significant impression on your own?

That sort of thing is very difficult to pin down. I think everything you read and enjoy, every writer you admire must leave a small impression somewhere. I'm a great admirer of Conrad, but it's possible that D. H. Lawrence, if anyone, may have made the deepest impression on me.

Which of his works impressed you most?

Possibly *The Rainbow*, but when I discovered him for myself the way one does, I just read everything of his that I could lay my hands on. I was touched by his closeness to the soil; for me he captured the rhythm of life, be it in a small village or in an industrial area.

Which brings us to the controversial Lady Chatterley's Lover*...?*

It is a great pity that he should be *known* for this book; he has written so much that is so much better; books like *The Rainbow* and *Women in Love*.

Have you been influenced by any of the growing school of new African authors?

Not only influenced but also in many cases helped and encouraged.

The West African writer Chinua Achebe (*Things Fall Apart*) attended a conference at Makerere in 1962. He took a very kind interest in some of my work and it was he who introduced me to his publishers, William Heinemann. There was also the South African writer Peter Abrahams (*Tell Freedom*) who made a strong impression on me.

You were educated at the Alliance High School, Kikuyu, and later went on to Makerere to study literature and English. You wrote your final examinations for B.A. Honors in March. Do you think you passed well?

I don't think I failed, but anything can happen with examinations. I should know within the next few days.

When did you actually start writing—I mean professionally?

I started writing short stories in 1960, and the first ones were published in the *Kenya Weekly News*. I then started feature writing to bring in some ready cash. I wrote first for the *Sunday Post* and then started writing for the *Sunday Nation* and other newspapers and magazines. But I was advised a long time ago by Jack Ensoll, who was the editor of the *Sunday Post*, that I should concentrate on writing for hard covers.

He was right of course?

I sincerely hope so; there's still a long way to go—but I think I'm learning and I feel I have something to say.

3 Ngugi wa Thiong'o: James Ngugi

Aminu Abdullahi / 1964 (1972)

The interview that follows was made in October 1964 with Aminu Abdullahi of Nigeria—then working as a script-writer, interviewer, and program director for the Transcription Centre at Dover Street. Ngugi was doing a post-graduate degree in literature at Leeds University.

Mr. Ngugi, your first novel, Weep Not, Child, *which was published by Heinemann this year, was the first novel in English to be written by an East African. The theme of the novel is set against the background of the Mau Mau uprising. Well now, have you any idea what your next novel is going to be about?*

If I write another one—I'm not doing it now—but if I write another one, it is going to be set against the Emergency because the Kenya Emergency or the Mau Mau war in Kenya is a very important factor in the creation of the present individuals in Kenya. It was a very formative factor in nation building.

This reminds me of something that somebody told me—I think it was Mr. Mphahlele—namely, that before Weep Not, Child, *you had already written a first novel, that in fact* Weep Not, Child *was not your first book.*

Yes, I had written what I then called *The Black Messiah*, which I have now changed to *The River Between*; it is being published by Heinemann, I think early next year.

And what's the theme of that?

That one's set against the background of the clash between the Kikuyu of Kenya and the missionaries in the thirties. You know at that time, or about 1930 or so, the Kikuyu quarreled with the missionaries because of the circumcision of women.

I see, and I believe this was the time when we had the first independent Kikuyu schools, as a result of this clash.

Yes, they clashed. Some of the missionary churches would not allow boys and girls to go to their schools if their fathers had not renounced circumcision. So the Kikuyu, or a majority of the Kikuyu, sort of broke away from the churches and established their own churches and started their own independent schools run by the independent churches.

I see. Why The River Between *as a title for this work?*

The river between: In the novel itself there is physically a river between two hills that house two communities which keep quarreling, but I maintain, you know, that the river between can be a factor which brings people together as well as being a factor of separation. It can both unite and separate.

Quite. Incidentally, before you yourself started writing, were there any authors that made a particular impression on you?

Yes. I would say Peter Abrahams, not so much because of his style as the subject matter, and he gave you the feeling that you also could write. After reading him, you felt that he also wanted us to go and write. I read Ekwensi, *People of the City*, and I read Chinua Achebe, *Things Fall Apart*, and all these writings were an inspiration, but of course from the body of English literature I also read quite a lot; I read especially Conrad.

That's most interesting because I suppose English is not your first language. When did you first begin to speak English?

I first went to school in 1946 or 1947; I started learning English four or five years later.

I see. At what age would that be? About?

Thirteen, fourteen, fifteen, thereabouts.

I see, I asked this because Conrad himself was not English-speaking until he was an adult.

Well, I understand he knew his first word of English at nineteen; that may be an exaggeration but I think what is interesting about Conrad is this very factor: that he was able to beat a language which was not his own into various shapes to give...well...meaning to the physical and moral world around him.

Quite. One other thing. I wonder if you ever read Mugo Gatheru's book, Child of Two Worlds*?*[1]

Yes, I read it: It's thrilling, in its own way: a straightforward account of the experiences of a Kikuyu searching for education; in fact, probably, the title should have been "A Fight for Education." I think it is important because of this very quality, this quality of fighting in the Kikuyu; you know that schools have always associated education with advancement, with political freedom, with even economic freedom. The Kikuyu have always seen education as a means to greater prosperity, and when the white man came to Kenya and took away the land and ruled the people, they said to themselves: "The white man can do this because he has got education, now if we also can get education, then we can get the things which he has."

I see. Now then, Mr. Ngugi, coming back to Mugo Gatheru's Child of Two Worlds, *I wonder if you could tell me what sort of reaction it received in Kenya?*

I don't know what reaction it received from Kenya, because I think it was not extensively reviewed in Kenya,[2] and it's a pity actually it wasn't because I think it's a very important book. Certain qualities do emerge from the book, for instance the quality of endurance, the quality of perseverance and more: This fight for education is a classic example, the Kikuyu's fight for education generally. I know one person whom I met, who after reading Gatheru's book said, "This is just like me."

But this was also, as far as I can recall, the first time that an African had sat down and become absolutely frank about the most intimate details of his tribal background.

Oh no! Not exactly: Kenyatta's book *Facing Mount Kenya* I think of as going into Kikuyu rituals much more....

Well, perhaps I was talking about people of our generation?

Oh, I see. Yes, certainly he's the first of the new generation.

Incidentally, now that we have you and Mugo Gatheru writing in English, do you foresee the possibility of having an East African school of literature?

Well, I wouldn't use the word school exactly but I would say that what has been done in East Africa so far is bound to have an effect on the oncoming writers, it's bound to encourage a few people in their endeavors, and I know at present there are a few people in Kenya who are doing a lot of short stories actually.

I see. To what extent does the Chemchemi Centre which is being run by Mr. Ezekiel Mphahlele help in this way?

This Chemchemi is playing a very important role in the creation of literature in Kenya, or in East Africa generally. For instance, Chemchemi has been holding exhibitions of African artists, and then you get very many African people in Nairobi asking, "When is the next exhibition?" It is one of the interesting features about Chemchemi because normally you just say that Africans don't like art and so on, but many of them are going to Chemchemi, and to see what is happening there could belie this kind of general comment.

Quite. I understand that you gave some lectures to one or two classes at Chemchemi. What were the lectures about?

Chemchemi has also been holding a writers' workshop; this is being attended by people who hope to or are writing fiction, short stories, novels and so on, and I only talked to them once about the problems of the African writer.

What would you say are those problems?

Well, I told them that I thought the problem of the African writer was actually himself.

But surely this is a problem with any writer, whether he is an American, a Pole, or a Chilean.

Precisely, that is the point I was trying to make, but in the African context or in the Kenyan context, the geographical or racial situation adds a special problem which makes it even more difficult for the African writer to really confess what's in his heart of hearts.

I see. A little while ago you mentioned the fact that you had read Ekwensi and Achebe; now then, I wouldn't have thought that Achebe in particular had this problem.

I should have been more particular and said in Kenya, where we have got three communities: We have got Asians, we have got Africans and we have got Europeans, and you know the history of Kenya has been one of racial tensions, racial quarrels: African people feeling they have been rejected, or feeling they have been subjugated to a certain class or position. Now the problem with the African writer in Kenya is surely one of being able to stand a little bit detached; and see the problem, the human problem, the human relationship, in its proper perspective.

Well, what is he supposed to do then, stand outside of the problem and write purely as a spectator and observer, or else...?

Not exactly. I wouldn't use the word "observer" plain and simple. He has got to be an observer, and at the same time a part of him is committed, committed to the situation. Let me put it this way: He must be wholly involved in the problems of Kenya; at the same time he mustn't allow the involvement in that particular social situation to impinge on his judgment or on his creative activities. A little while ago I talked about confession, let me now say a little bit about it. Writing, I take to be a kind of confession where the writer is almost confessing his own private reactions to various individuals, to various problems; you know the feeling of shame here, the feeling of inadequacy there, the love-hatred. But in a place like Kenya you might feel inclined to want to say only the good things about your community and pass over the other communities because you see you are fighting for your community, and I tell you, this tendency is very, very strong indeed; after being in that place in your country, you know, you might feel compelled to want to justify your position and your people, and only say the good things about them. Or necessarily take the other communities as mere illustrations of an attitude; when you take these characters from the Asian community, or the European community, you might tend to use them as mere pieces of wood.

I see. This is most interesting. Now you are here to read literature at Leeds University. What particular branch of literature do you want to concentrate on?

I am hoping that I may be able to do something on West Indian literature. Probably this sounds strange.

No, it doesn't. I can see the reason why. For instance, the West Indies is also a mixed community.

Yes. The West Indies is a mixed community, and also the literature is just emerging, and there would be interesting parallels and contrasts and comparisons between this emergent West Indian literature and the new literature from Africa.

What sort of writers from the Caribbean do you particularly enjoy reading?

I must confess I have not read very many, simply because their books are not available in Kenya, but I was overwhelmed by George Lamming. I read him uncritically—almost everything he wrote, uncritically—from cover to cover. He really overwhelmed me. The other person whom I like is Naipaul.

But Naipaul insists that he must not be labeled as a West Indian writer. He claims that he is a writer, period, of no particular school. The mere fact that all of his works to date—excepting his latest book, An Area of Darkness, *which is about his journey to India—all his previous efforts were based on or were set in the Caribbean, he claims, does not make him a West Indian writer.*

As far as he physically comes from the West Indies and the fact that he's written about West Indians and himself, he can't help but be a West Indian writer.

This is most interesting. To take up your other point, his best known work, A House for Mr. Biswas, *is a good case to support the point you made earlier: that he has chosen the Indian community and painted them white, and he has used other people in the West Indian community as pieces of wood to support some of the ideas he wanted to put forward.*

Yes. This is a great tendency from people who are writing from plural communities. I must say I don't blame him. I can explain them without excusing them. In a place like Kenya you really don't know about the other communities. You don't know how the children play, you don't know the talk that goes on at breakfast, at lunchtime, at night; you rarely meet on such occasions. You must officially meet at parties, but then people are normally quite official at parties. That is, you do not know the European character in his own home, which is very important.

Quite. How long are you going to be in Leeds?

About two years, I hope. I have been given a scholarship by the British Council, initially for one year, but I am hoping that I may be able to get some further grant to stay for two years.

During your stay are you proposing to continue with your writing, or do you intend solely to devote your time to your academic work, and then take up creative writing later?

I am expecting the two to exist side by side and live together! All my writing so far I did when I was at Makerere College in Uganda. Anyway, I see my intellectual activity as contributing towards my creative activity. So that when I am at Leeds I am hoping to write at least a novel and dive into the "Kenya Emergency."

I see, this promises to be a most interesting work. But, coming back to the West Indian writers, do you realize that all the established West Indian writers are in fact resident overseas, with one or two, or, at most, very few exceptions?

I understand so, though I have not met any of them so far. What, for me, is very important, is that I like reading them; I like George Lamming, for instance.

Well, for instance, Lamming: He has been in Britain for about ten years now, and people like Dathorne are working in West Africa.

This does not upset me at all because they are not writing about their exile, they are writing about the West Indies, they are writing about human characters, about human relationships, and as long as their stay away does not falsify their image, or does not falsify their writing, I am....

Wouldn't you find it extremely difficult after being away for ten years? Supposing you were out of Kenya for ten years, and you base a novel on the Kenyan situation, surely there are bound to be certain areas where you have to draw on your imagination very hard?

I agree with you but it depends on the period in which you are writing. We don't know as yet how the quality of imagination works. The quality of the imagination is the synthetic factor which makes the work of art. It depends on the period, you know. Whether your exile will falsify the image you make, would, I think, depend on the geographical and social situations you take. For instance if George Lamming were writing a book after ten years in Britain and away from the West Indies and he sets it in a social situation prevailing during his childhood somewhere in the West Indies, surely for me this seems to be quite good background material for his creative work. However, personally, I wouldn't want to stay away from Kenya for so long and still write about Kenya.

Incidentally there is also another point to be taken into consideration. To most Africans, English is a second language, but with the West Indians it's their only language.

Yes, I think that's another interesting point because, yes, the African writer in fact has got this added problem—you've just reminded me of it. Whereas people like George Lamming or an English English writer can get narrative value from the "slang," from twists of language from his community, we have got to get the slangs and the twists of language in a different language and then try to put that into English. You have visited Kenya; not many Africans speak English anyway and even those who speak it don't use it as their normal language. It is not what they use every day, at breakfast, lunch, when they make jokes and so you're getting nourishment, linguistic nourishment, in a different medium and then trying to use the English medium to create.

Do you think first in Kikuyu and then transpose your thoughts into English, or do you first automatically write straightaway in English?

I think I write straightaway...I think...I never really know what really happens, but I am not aware of thinking first in another language. I think when I come to write, I just write.

---

[1] New York: Praeger, 1964; London: Routledge & Kegan Paul, 1964; Heinemann (A.W.S. No. 20), 1966.

[2] We have not been able to trace Kenyan reviews—only one in Britain (*Times Literary Supplement*, March 1964) and one in the U.S.A. (*Africa Report*, October 1965).

4 Excerpt from: A Discussion between James Ngugi, Author of *The River Between* (Heinemann), Who Is Studying at Leeds University, John Nagenda, a Writer from Uganda Who Has Just Spent Some Time in the United States of America and Is Now on His Way Back to Uganda, and Robert Serumaga from Uganda Who Is Studying at Trinity College, Dublin

1966

Serumaga: *James Ngugi, I would like to ask you this question: When you write a book like* The River Between, *with the two ridges of the hills and the different tribes on each, are you using these things allegorically, or are you using them as historical social truths?*

Ngugi: They are all those things actually, both allegorical and historical. I mean there isn't a historical river called the Honia River, but allegorically, it's true, and even factually, it's true. I'm using it both as a symbol to illustrate a social truth and....

Serumaga: *What is this social truth you are trying to illustrate?*

Ngugi: The social truth is the fact that as a result of the missionary enterprise in East Africa, there were people who followed the missionaries' truth and there were those who were not convinced by their activities. And these divisions did bring about conflicts.

Serumaga: *I see the conflict as going deeper than just as between two groups of a society living on two different ridges. I see the conflict as going right to the individual having to choose between one way and the other, and not being able to choose, but rather getting something from here and something from the other side, to form a sort of unity. Do you agree with this?*

Ngugi: I agree with it in so far as any kind of conflict operates on a number of levels, on the individual level, on the political level and even on a religious level—and the individual, man the individual, is involved in all these levels.

Nagenda: *What really interests me here is the symbolism in writing. I haven't read* The River Between, *but even generally, I think, I can ask this question. Do you, when you are writing, consciously make a symbol? Do you consciously say, "I will write about two ridges and a river in between so that it can suggest a truth?" Or do you in fact write about a place you know which has two ridges and a river, and which then at two levels is known to you, both in the physical sense and in the other sense, and almost as an accident the symbol then becomes inbuilt? You haven't formed it as a symbol, but it is there and spontaneously, almost by accident, working.*

Ngugi: I really think a symbol operates at all those levels. You've got a central image which drives you to write a book. And then as you go developing the central image, other things begin to suggest themselves, so that in fact you can say the intellect is operating at the same time as the intuition—you are operating at all those levels at any one given moment.

[....]

Serumaga: *There is a conflict in the person of Muthoni, in the book: She wants to embrace Christianity, but at the same time she wants to be circumcised in the way of the tribe, and she dies in the attempt. [....] Do you think she is defeated, or is this a comment on the activities of the Christians? Is she the one who wins, or Joshua who goes entirely to Christianity, or the other man who stays entirely with the tribe?*

Ngugi: Obviously I would like the reader to decide for himself who wins in the book. But personally, I think the person who undergoes a martyrdom is not the loser. In the book, for instance, the people who apparently lose and die as persons, in fact, leave an effect, and their work is carried on by other people who come after them. In the same way, you might say, Christ, as a person, lost, in that when he was thirty years old he was crucified and died on the cross (maybe he rose to Heaven, but in fact physically he ceased to exist), but people like Peter and the other disciples carried on his work. So that an individual's importance is not only the life he leads in this world, but the effect of his work on other people after he's gone.

Nagenda: *I would like to ask James a question. Listening to you speak, I would say that you look the writer, the creative person. Now, every man is a social animal in the sense that he cannot opt out of society. Neither can he do actions that refer only to himself. Applying it to yourself, I think that you would not feel it enough to be a dilettante writer—a writer of romantic poetry, unless this poetry had definite social implications; that you feel your duty as being to society, that what you create must in some way improve society? Rather than a writer who only writes for himself, and if people understand it and like it, good; if they don't, too bad!*

Ngugi: I agree with you here. I think that any writer who is dealing with serious problems that confront an individual must write about the whole social and political society. I can even go further and say that I believe in the socialist vision. I believe that a writer must write not only to entertain people, but also to change society for the better. And as far as I am concerned, only if you are working towards a socialist vision, can you be working for the better. Of course there are many writers who are only concerned with reflecting the realities behind a society—writers who are not concerned with what is going to happen tomorrow, but who are prepared to accept the *status quo*, so long as they can reflect the reality behind it. In Africa today, no matter who you are, you cannot be content with simply reflecting the conflict—you must be prepared to suggest. People who write in the West escape their social responsibilities by writing about space and that kind of thing, when there's so much to write about in Britain about the relationships between individuals. I believe the African writer has not time to write about space. There is so much to write about in the actual society—a society which is changing all the time. [....] Creative writing must mean creative writing—I mean really exploring. But at the same time I do think that beauty must be related to social realities, in the sense that if a man is starving, he has no time for jazz or poetry, or novels or Beethoven. In other words, an African writer should have social responsibilities to society as it is now—not necessarily as it ought to be, but as it is now.

Serumaga: *Now in this context, James, what is your message? What would you like society to become?*

Ngugi: Frankly as a citizen, and as a person, I would like to see a socialist East Africa. [...] I would say that as far as I am concerned there is no question of art for art's sake. I'm concerned with the social and political problems as they are in Africa now—I want to see a change in Africa now.

5 James Ngugi Interviewed by Fellow Students at Leeds University

Alan Marcuson, Mike González and Dave Williams / 1967

Marcuson: *James, where were you born?*

Ngugi: I was born in Limuru, Kenya, in 1938. I come from a large peasant family. My father had four wives. I was the fifth child of the third wife. In all there were about twenty-eight children. My father was a tenant farmer on the farm of an African landowner.

Marcuson: *At what age did you go to school?*

Ngugi: Nine, to a primary school near our village for about two years. Then I moved to another primary school, part of what was called Gikuyu Independent Schools. These were schools which belonged to people who had rebelled against missionary influence, so they wanted the kind of education that belonged to the people.

Marcuson: *What did you think of the missionary schools?*

Ngugi: As I see them, you know, in their historical role, they have been the forerunners of colonialism—the John the Baptists preparing the way for Christ—the colonial administration.

Marcuson: *At school, did you find that they were pumping into you colonialist ideas?*

Ngugi: They didn't brainwash you so directly. Can I give you an example? After the Gikuyu primary school, I went to a missionary secondary school. Here I found white people, missionaries, and they were very kind, very peaceful, and they wanted to help you, but in a very patronizing manner. The Headmaster was said to be pro-African but he believed, and often told us so, that there was not a single African in the whole of Kenya, who on the basis of merit could qualify to Cambridge. As an African you could be taken in Cambridge, but not on the basis of merit, more as a gesture. Of course we protested, but inwardly we believed it, and unconsciously had a high regard for white boys.

Marcuson: *After that, where did you go?*

Ngugi: To take a degree in English Literature at Makerere University College.

Marcuson: *Can you tell us about the University—the political atmosphere, the student activity?*

Ngugi: You must see universities in Africa in their colonialist missionary setting. They didn't want you to question things, or compare Western institutions with other systems. For instance, those who studied political science heard of Karl Marx only as an incidental, rather eccentric figure. You would never have thought he was one of the people whose doctrine has influenced two-thirds of the world. African History was taught merely as an extension of Europe. One or two of the lecturers were enlightened, but they nearly all believed that the only real education was to be found in Britain. Literature had nothing or very little to do with what was happening in Africa. So in novels and plays we learnt about British people. And even then we learnt about them not in terms of social issues, but in terms of universal values and the tragedy of a human being caught in a situation whose conditions he cannot control.

Marcuson: *When did you start writing and what moved you to do so?*

Ngugi: I wanted to write when I was in school, but I never actually got down to it until I got to the university. I wrote, I suppose, because I had been moved by the bloodshed and violence during the Mau Mau uprising. Apart from that I have always believed that a student at university should not measure himself against the standards set by their departments and their professors, but against those of life and his own experience. This is the spirit in which I wrote my two books and plays.

Marcuson: *To what extent are your books autobiographical?*

Ngugi: Every writer's books are autobiographical—that is, you write about your experience, your immediate experience.

Marcuson: *Your hero and his family in* Weep Not, Child *place tremendous importance on education. One gets the impression that they feel that with education comes freedom. Did you feel this?*

Ngugi: You have hit on a very important point. Education in Africa has always been regarded as the tool with which you can attain the white man's wisdom. Again you have got to see this in the colonial context. The white man has conquered you and within a short space of forty years has brought buildings that scrape the sky, motor-cars, razor blades, needles, railways and other buildings that walk on water. "Fear the white man," says the peasant. But at the same time he wonders: "How come the white man has achieved all this? Through education!" Therefore get education and you'll get all the benefits of the white man's world. The gospel of the peasant has always been: "Get ye first education and all other things will be added unto you."

Marcuson: *Does this imply that the peasants aspire to the European way of life?*

Ngugi: No, they are very critical of the Western way of life. They want to maintain the traditional set-up but at the same time, they want to gain the material benefits which the white man has introduced.

Marcuson: *Can you tell us something about your trade as a writer?*

Ngugi: My trade as a writer? I wrote *The River Between* first. I had come from a missionary school and I was deeply Christian. I used to go to church at 5 o'clock in the morning, and I was quite sure my destiny lay in heaven, not hell. In school I was concerned with trying to remove the central Christian doctrine from the dress of Western culture, and seeing how this might be grafted onto the central beliefs of our people. *The River Between* was concerned with this process. In my second book, *Weep Not, Child*, I was primarily interested in [developing] what a simple village community felt caught between forces which they could not quite understand. I lived through that period myself, and I know what it means to live under guns and bombs almost every day for about seven years.

Marcuson: *Are you still a Christian?*

Ngugi: No, I gave up the Christian faith at the university. But it was not that I woke up one day and decided that I was no longer a Christian. It just gradually lost its appeal to me as I began to see what it stood for.

Marcuson: *From Makerere you came straight to Leeds?*

Ngugi: Yes, I came here to do an MA in West Indian Literature. In between I worked as a junior reporter for a daily newspaper in Kenya for about eight months. As a student I had been writing a Sunday column for *The Sunday Nation* in East Africa

Marcuson: *I believe this was the first time you had left Africa. What were your impressions of England and of Leeds University?*

Ngugi: Well, that's rather a complicated question. First there is what I physically felt when I arrived here. It was winter and London was quite nice, but I found Leeds absolutely depressing. All those houses crouching like old men and women hidden in the mist! Then there is the question of what I had expected. I told you before about the way colonial education made you think of England as the ideal. Well, I was not here for long before I realized that things were not so rosy, that all this idle talk about freedom of the press and freedom of speech, etc., has to be seen in the context of an economic and political life dominated by a few rich men. The whole system is basically wrong. Just a small thing—I would never have believed before I came here that policemen in Britain could be violent and that they could manhandle peaceful students demonstrating in the streets of Leeds (the Stewart Demonstration). We always believed in the traditional view of the English bobby.

González: *Does it make the struggle in Africa easier when you find out what England is really like?*

Ngugi: I think so—especially before independence. You see decolonization has three stages. The first is one of acceptance—the colored people more or less recognize the superiority of the colonizer, at any rate they don't question it very much. The second stage is what Philip Mason calls the stage of rivalry and challenge.

The colored people begin to challenge the political assumptions of the colonizer. During this period you get Africans and Asians who have come to Britain and go back home really dissatisfied. And they begin to organize the restive peasants and urban workers into mass movements with one name—Independence. Then you come to the third stage where the colonizer realizes the game is up. So he quickly makes arrangements with the nationalist elite and he gives them independence. But for the peasants, who are really the base of the whole struggle, this is not real independence but a realization that they are still exploited and the struggle has got to start all over again.

Williams: *What is your view of the English student?*

Ngugi: On the whole very disappointing. Some of them are so naive that they believe everything they are told in the *Daily Express*, *Daily Telegraph* or *Daily Mirror* about Africa, Russia or China. But the few who are active are really active and broad-minded. In this respect I am glad I came to Leeds. There is a strong radical tradition here which of course helps almost every "colonial" student who comes to Leeds in a way that places like Oxford or Cambridge cannot do. I went to Oxford last term, and some students I met there! Lord! They were worse than they ever were before coming to England. But invariably a colonial student who comes to Leeds goes back with a disturbed state of mind.

Marcuson: *You went to the USA last June as a guest of honor at the international P.E.N. Conference. What did you think of America?*

Ngugi: Well, I was impressed by the actual material progress. But in the streets of New York, one of the richest cities in the world, I found beggars crawling in the streets and people who had nowhere to sleep. I couldn't believe it. This progress soon sickens you when you go to a place like Harlem and see how rundown they really are—in fact, worse than I somehow expected. In Chicago I found some of the worst slums that surely exist anywhere in the world. These slums stand side by side with some of the wealthiest areas in the world. Some friends of mine who took me round these slums—they were white—would never come to the same area after 6 p.m. because they were afraid of being murdered. So it did not surprise me that there were riots in this area a few days after I left. The Negro in America has been exploited for over three hundred years and yet people still try and explain racialism as a psychological phenomenon. It is surely the economic aspect of racialism which is of prime importance. The Negro community in America is part of the exploited working class. The color of the skin is a convenient excuse for using state economic and political machinery to continue this kind of ruthless exploitation. I am disappointed with James Baldwin because I think that he panders to all the talk of love-hate relationships and guilt complexes. The white liberals love this: It enables them to maintain the system which they hold so dear, and which is the root-cause and the very condition of racialism, and at the same time to feel good inside—you know, pure and holy—because they "really are fighting color prejudice." Take the two arguments side by side: "You must not be nasty to Negroes, we must accept them with love, because they are human beings" (Liberals) and "We are going to organize ourselves, we must change the system, we must change the social conditions so that Negroes can be equal in education, wealth, power, status" (Black Power group)—I think you can see which is more likely to eradicate racialism.

Marcuson: *I would like to return to the question of African literature. Firstly, I would like to ask what your attitude is to the fact that for a long time, and in fact still now, European critics regard African art as a sociological and political phenomenon, as an oddity but not as literature. They look at it in the light of "Africans are beginning to write."*

Ngugi: Art in Europe has always been the property of those who have; how can those who do not have aspire to this glorious thing? European critics and the middle classes have often said that Africa has no art because art can only be produced by those who have civilization. So they are struck with the historical freak of finding Africans who can produce plays or novels, as good as, if not better than, theirs.

Marcuson: *Jean-Paul Sartre said that the only committed artists in the world today are those in Africa.*

Ngugi: I would not say that they are only to be found in Africa. But I think on the whole everyone was committed during the struggle for independence. But what do you say about people like Sédar Senghor who used to be so vocal, and yet now that they are in power do not want to change anything? Such artists were only committed to the color of their skin.

Marcuson: *What do you consider your responsibility as an author to be? Before you answer I would like to read you a remark made by Sékou Touré and quoted in Frantz Fanon's* The Wretched of the Earth*: "To take part in the African revolution, it is not enough to write a revolutionary song. You must fashion the revolution with the people, and if you fashion it with the people, the songs will come by themselves and of themselves. In order to achieve real action you must yourself be a living part of Africa and of their thought. You must be an element of that popular energy which is entirely poured forth for the freeing, the progress and happiness of Africa. There is no place outside that fight for the artists or for the intellectual who is not himself concerned with and completely at one with the people in the great battle and with suffering humanity."*

Ngugi: Of course I agree. It is not enough to talk about culture. It is more important to create the conditions necessary for that culture to be enjoyed.

Marcuson: *Are you a pacifist?*

Ngugi: I am not a pacifist. I do not condemn violence indiscriminately. For the oppressed have no option but to use violence.

Marcuson: *Do you feel that African literature today subscribes for the most part to the sentiments expressed by Sékou Touré?*

Ngugi: I don't know how to answer your question. I don't know the political sentiments of every individual African artist. But in their work, people like Wole Soyinka and Chinua Achebe have exposed corruption and social injustices in Nigeria. In his last novel, *A Man of the People*, Chinua Achebe has made a brilliant analysis of the character and workings of the present African regime. In South Africa, artists and writers like Ezekiel Mphahlele, Alex La Guma, Dennis Brutus have been exiled, shot or imprisoned.

González: *In Latin America there are moments when literature reaches tremendous peaks, usually in moments of fantastically vital struggle when the issues are more direct. But afterwards, when the* *bourgeois regime sets in, there seems to come a point where the artists, even if they don't lose their commitment, lose their energy, and become so disillusioned that art is no longer a form directly concerned with the people. They stop producing and they stop creating. Do you think this is likely to happen in Africa?*

Ngugi: I think this is a danger. It is very easy to become cynical and withdraw into oneself—or else to lose faith in the possibilities of life.

González: *I think a bourgeois regime tends to alienate the artist from the people by giving him a position of privilege. Do you agree?*

Ngugi: This is a very important point in relationship to Africa because artists alone with the educated few are in an exceptionally privileged position. The temptation to remain in an ivory tower is therefore great. But writers must reject this false position or else they will be alienated from the living source of their inspiration: truth and life in the struggle.

Marcuson: *Could you tell us something about your new novel?*

Ngugi: In *A Grain of Wheat*, I look at the people who fought for independence—I see them falling into various groups. There were those who thought the white man was supreme. They saw no point in opposing that which was divinely willed. Your best chance, they argued, was to work, to cooperate with the master. There were others who supported the independence movement and who took the oath. Of these some fought to the last but others, when it came to the test, did not live up to their faith and ideals. They gave in. Finally, there were those whom we might call neutrals—the uncommitted. But these soon find that in a given social crisis they can never be uncommitted. You know the saying: He who is not with us is against us.

Marcuson: *Do you have any plans for other books?*

Ngugi: No plans at present. You see I have reached a point of crisis. I don't know whether it is worth any longer writing in English.

González: *Would you not be playing up to narrow nationalism? Would you not be limiting your audience?*

Ngugi: It is very difficult to say. I am very suspicious about writing about universal values. If there are universal values, they are always contained in the framework of social realities. And one important social reality in Africa is that ninety percent of the people cannot read or speak English. The problem is this: I know whom I write about, but whom do I write for?

González: *Do you intend returning to Africa?*

Ngugi: Certainly, this year in fact. I sincerely believe that everybody's struggle, except in very special circumstances, lies in his own country where that struggle is taking place. I don't believe in exile, although there are situations where this is unavoidable.

Marcuson: *James Ngugi, thank you very much.*

6 Problems Confronting African Writers

E. C. Ndonde / 1968

Mr. James Ngugi, Lecturer at the University College, Nairobi, and a celebrated East African novelist, is currently a visiting lecturer at the University College, Dar es Salaam. In the following interview, Mr Ngugi answers some questions on various problems confronting African writers when he met our college special correspondent, Mr. E. C. Ndonde.

Mr. Ngugi, what do you think are the problems of an African writer today?

The most obvious problem is one of language. The fact that you are writing in a foreign language means that you are operating in a foreign cultural framework. This often leads African writers standing as referees between the common man and the elite.

What do you think is the audience of an African writer and what should it be?

The African writer has a limited audience—that is, it is limited only to those who can read and write English.

And how best can he reach a wider, more African audience?

There should be more people writing not only in English but in other languages like Swahili. In Tanzania where Swahili is a national language, writers should look at Swahili as an instrument for reaching their audience. The same should be the case in Uganda and Kenya.

Why is it that there are more novelists in West Africa than in East

Africa?

They started earlier for one thing, and they have had many more years of education than we have had. But East Africa is catching up very quickly, especially with the setting up of local publishing houses like the East African Publishing House in Nairobi.

African writers in East and West Africa have sometimes been criticized for writing mainly on cultural conflicts between the past and the present. Is it a fair criticism?

That is the kind of thing said by people who have not read carefully what African writers say. The African writer is concerned with people, with the society, and the cultural conflict happens to be a very lively issue. But writers are not simply concerned with a simple pull between the present and the past, but they are trying to look at society as it is: What has been happening, what is happening, what is going to happen.

And now coming to your three novels, some people have criticized you that you can't write about anything but "Emergency in Kenya."

Again, I think this is a kind of mistaken attitude because I think the person who said this was not concerned with what each of my books had to say. He should have asked whether the third book said anything different from the second or the first book. Secondly, you cannot understand Kenya at the present or Kenyan people without understanding the Emergency. Thirdly, the Mau Mau movement is the one single important political event in East Africa and its revolutionary implications have only been scratched on the surface. The critics who said such a thing were operating within a philosophy of forgetting the past.

What of the accusation that you very much imitated Chinua Achebe in your style of writing and you are trying to be to the Kikuyu in Kenya what Chinua Achebe is to the Igbo?

I admire Chinua Achebe very much. He is a very fine novelist. But I don't try to imitate him and I could not do it even if I tried.

Furthermore, I am not writing for the Kikuyu exclusively, I am writing for the people of Kenya using the only experience I know.

Mr. Ngugi, what do you think is the role of a writer in the nation-building endeavors of the particular country in which he lives?

It depends upon which country he is living in. Each country has its own problems and a writer must respond accordingly. I think, however, his real job is to raise the consciousness of the people. Obviously his job is more compelling in a socialist context in the sense that in order to build a socialist society you need a high degree of consciousness so that people know where they are coming from and where they are going.

Are you suggesting that he should be a reformist?

Obviously, in a capitalist set-up the writer should raise the consciousness of the people to the extent that the overthrow of that set-up is possible. One of the sad things is that the African writer, apart from South Africa, tends to follow the politicians. Look at Cuba. It is said that the revolution was very much influenced by early writers like José Martí. These early Cuban writers were committed to the people—they wrote for Cuba, for Cuban people.

In trying to raise the consciousness of the people, don't you think the writer runs the risk of ending up in jail like Wole Soyinka?

This is one of the risks which an African writer runs. But it is a risk which everybody runs if one wants changes. If a writer is imprisoned, he is imprisoned like any other citizen.

You have read Odinga's book Not Yet Uhuru. *How do you like it?*

It is very good! It is one of the most significant books to have been written since Jomo Kenyatta's book *Facing Mount Kenya.*

And what about Cry, the Beloved Country *by Alan Paton?*

You know some European writers have tended to create an African character who, as it were, had no choice but to be content with his environment. Thus the African character in European fiction tends to be merely at the mercy of his social environment. Alan Paton is no exception.

Do you think English literature as taught in schools and universities in East Africa has any African content, and is it geared to producing African writers?

Literature should be completely African oriented. A start in that direction should be: (a) to make African literature compulsory in schools and universities; (b) to give Swahili its true role in East Africa; (c) African traditions and songs should have their rightful place in the teaching. The old traditions are not something of the past—they are living. Indeed you cannot separate, for example, TANU songs from TANU.

Mr. Ngugi, are you thinking of writing another novel—say on Tanzania?

I would like to write one or two books but I don't have time now. I would like to write on Zanzibar. It interests me most.

7 Kenyan Writer James Ngugi Interviewed in Nairobi

Heinz Friedberger* / 1969

The phase when African writers were seen as some kind of exotic novelty finally seems to belong to the past. Some people feel that there was too much uncritical adulation during that period. Do you agree?

I think partly what happened was that as African writers emerged from obscurity there was at first reluctant acceptance of African writers by Western publishing firms. Then there was a change in the tide and African writers were really accepted, especially when the market for African books rose. But then people did not know what critical standards to adopt. And this was the real difficulty. They did not know whether this African novel was great or whether it was promising or whether it was nonsense. So the tendency on the whole, I think, was to pat African writers on the back.

But now a number of African writers have established themselves, and quite a lot of publishing is going on in Africa and overseas. The subjects, however, which the African writers are largely dealing with, seem to be preoccupied either with the colonial past or the clash between tribal and modern life. Why do you think—with certain exceptions—there has been so much avoidance of treatment of post-independence developments?

The African writer emerged as a reaction to what I might call the white presence in Africa or rather this simplistic European response to the African experience. For a long time African writers were seen—or Africans as a whole—were seen as having no vital culture and having no history. So the African writer's first job was, I think, to see the African society in the perspective of history. Of course, a few African writers tended to react to the extreme and say that the African past was all innocence, simplicity and beauty. But what I might call the "school of realism" in African writing arose when Chinua Achebe in Nigeria tried to show that an African society was not wholly simplistic, wholly beautiful, wholly serene, but in fact was a mixture of beauty and ugliness, or virtue and vice. But at the same time, in a way, the African writer was outstripped by events. He was a little bit too fascinated by the past, and he forgot about the modern problems. But the modern problems in themselves were complex. For instance, there was the problem of the alienated African, educated out of his own society. Let's say the African student who has been abroad; he has "been to"—as they say in Nigeria—and comes back to find that he no longer fits into his society. He has become a little bit too Westernized as it were, a part of Western society. So the African novelist turned to that problem, and again to cite Chinua Achebe, his book *No Longer at Ease* deals with that kind of problem. But at the same time the African writer forgot that certain other seeds of present conflicts were already developing in his formerly colonial society. And because of this fascination with the past, because of the fascination with alienation, he forgot, I think, about the conflicts arising out of the emergent bourgeoisie in Africa and what they call the aspirations of the masses. The African writer of course now is turning slowly to the modern African society. And people like Wole Soyinka in his novel *The Interpreters*, Chinua Achebe in *A Man of the People*, and some writers in Kenya like Leonard Kibera are sort of addressing themselves to the African society and telling us: "All of you, the elite and the masses, are responsible for the present crisis in our society and our lives."

James, to summarize, do you yourself feel that there is a need for new themes and new treatment in African writing?

Yes, what I would like to see is a treatment of the African society as a whole—that is, the African society not only in space, but also in time, so that the great African novel, when it comes, will not only have to embrace the precolonial past. It will also include the colonial past and the post-independence period with a pointer to the future. Of course that is the ideal. Meanwhile, I think, the African writers ought to be addressing themselves more and more fully to the present needs, especially what I call the crisis or conflict between the emergent African bourgeoisie and the African masses.

Those novels by African writers which have been published during the past few years were still the beginning of novel writing on this continent anyway. Who are the authors who have already proved that they can write novels?

This is a very difficult question that I would not quite answer in the sense that I am what I might call an interested party. But people like Chinua Achebe have, you know, proved that they are novelists of outstanding merit. In South Africa we also have some prominent novelists, for example Peter Abrahams and Alex La Guma. There are of course also great short story writers and autobiographers in South Africa like Ezekiel Mphahlele, Bloke Modisane, Arthur Maimane, Richard Rive. And all of them are trying to establish a firm basis for the great African literature of the future.

And in East Africa, it is you who has become the idol of the younger writers. What is your opinion about the attempts of East African writers such as Grace Ogot, David Rubadiri and so on?

We in East Africa of course have been rather late in the field. But already there is a lot of great creative intensity here. We can find the beginnings in people like Grace Ogot who is, I think, a great short story writer, not so good a novelist at present. David Rubadiri again in his novel *No Bride Price* has laid the foundation for an East African novel, but the foundation needs to be stronger. To me the strongest East African writer that has emerged of late is Leonard Kibera and his brother Samuel Kahiga who have recently published a volume of short stories called *Potent Ash*. I think they are generally trying to grapple with the problem of themes, of new themes in African writing, but also with the problem of language to meet, as it were, the needs of their present preoccupations.

---

* A longer version of this interview was published in *Afrika Heute* (15 October 1970): 309-12. The name Heinz Berger appeared

instead of Heinz Friedberger.

8 "Tolstoy in Africa": An Interview with Ngugi wa Thiong'o

Reinhard Sander and Ian Munro / 1971 (1973)

The interview which follows has been taken from Ngugi's answers to questions following his lectures on West Indian literature at Rice University and the University of Houston, and from a videotaped discussion at Texas Southern University.

Our thanks are due to Father Salisbury for the use of the videotape facilities of Newman Hall at Texas Southern University, and to Professor Robert Wren, Director of the Houston Inter-University African Studies Program, for his consideration and aid during the preparation of this interview.

Until recently critics of African literature have considered East Africa a "literary desert." Now one can notice a slight shift in opinion. You yourself have published three novels and a number of short stories and plays, which were received favorably by literary critics and have largely contributed to the awakening of interest in East Africa. Who else is writing in East Africa now?

Yes, there was a time when people used to say East Africa was a "literary desert" and most of us used to believe it. But in fact even then it was not really true. For instance, Swahili has had a very rich literature, dating about two or three centuries back. And even in terms of modern writing, by 1962 or 1964 Shaaban Robert had already established himself as a great poet in Swahili, a great contemporary poet. In 1954 Okot p'Bitek had produced a modern novel in Luo, called *Lak Tar*, about the same time that Ekwensi and Tutuola were producing modern novels in Nigeria, using the English language. So the image of East Africa as a "literary desert" in 1960 was not quite correct. What they meant by "desert," I think, was that there were very few East African writers using English or French or whatever the colonial language was. And even on this level the situation has really changed radically, so much so that you can't really recognize the East African literary scene. In the field of the novel, for instance, and the short story there is a voice which will be heard in the future: Leonard Kibera. He and his brother Kahiga produced a volume of short stories called *Potent Ash*, which dealt with the same kinds of institutions I deal with in my novels, although in a slightly different way. Leonard Kibera has now produced a novel about the past; from a quick glance I think he's trying to experiment with the form of the novel. Okello Oculi, from Uganda, has produced a novel called *Prostitute*, which deals with the post-independence era in East Africa. He also tries to experiment with the form of the novel, mixing prose with poetry. Perhaps the most interesting thing in East Africa is the development in poetry. The most remarkable poet, whom I mentioned earlier, is Okot p'Bitek, with his long poem *Song of Lawino*. It is a lament by Lawino, a village woman, married to someone who is educated and trying to get away from African values and adopt a style of life which is patterned on the West. This poem is being read everywhere, in villages, in schools, in universities. And this was followed up by Oculi's long poem *The Orphan*.

Didn't Okot p'Bitek himself write a response to Song of Lawino*?*

Yes, in *Song of Ocol*. But he has many more songs now: *Song of Malaya, Song of a Prisoner,* and others. The situation has really so changed that even now it is very difficult to contain what is happening in East Africa within this kind of interview. There are creative magazines in East Africa—*Zuka, Penpoint, East African Journal,* and so on. All these magazines are getting material from within East Africa. If you go to East Africa, you'll find that even the simple schoolteacher somewhere in the countryside now feels that he can write. School children now feel that they can write because they know there are publishing houses near or next door. Writing is no longer something so remote. It is no longer something to be done in London or Paris. It is something there with the people. There are about five publishing houses in East Africa. And all of these have done a tremendous job.

I know the role of the East African publishing houses has been pretty significant. Why have you never published in an East African publishing house?

This is really a tendency of a writer wanting to stay with the same publisher unless he sees there is something radically wrong. So it's really a matter of simply continuing, because I don't see anything wrong so far. Maybe tomorrow or the next day I'll switch to another publisher. Incidentally, *This Time Tomorrow* is published by the East African Literature Bureau in East Africa. I support what they mean.

You are doing research in West Indian literature, focusing especially on the work of the Barbadian writer George Lamming. What would you say is the major difference between West Indian and African literature?

First of all there's the difference in language, I would say, a very crucial difference in their use of language. For the African, English is a second language, so that when someone like Chinua Achebe or Leonard Kibera, from Kenya, is writing, there's a kind of tension in their work which arises out of the fact that they're using the English language created by one cultural environment to capture a rhythm of life, a rhythm of speech, created by a totally different cultural environment. And this I find very, very fascinating. Whereas for the West Indian writer, English is not a second language. It is his own language with which he has grown, but a language which he has completely assimilated, as it were, and which is now different from what you might call standard or normal English. As for the themes they deal with, on the whole, I find the West Indian writer is much more interested in his roots and his state of alienation in a way that the African writer is not interested. The African writer is much more interested in the encounter between the West and Africa, the encounter between the two traditions. So the difference is really on the linguistic level and also in certain of their thematic concerns.

You write in English, but you have not written anything after A Grain of Wheat, *which was published in 1967. When asked about future plans in an interview you gave a couple of years ago in Leeds, you said, "I have reached a point of crisis. I don't know whether it is worth any longer writing in English." Have you resolved your crisis?*

I have not really resolved the crisis, although maybe I don't feel quite as strongly about it as I used to. The crisis arose out of the writing of *A Grain of Wheat*. I felt I dealt with the Kenyan or African institutions so intimately. Then I felt that people who fed the novel, that is the peasantry as it were, will not be in a position to read it. And this is very painful. So I really didn't see the point of writing anything at all. Maybe in two years' time I might write in Kikuyu or in Swahili. Or I might continue with the English—maybe as an escape. I don't know.

When reading your novels one notices that you are using predominantly Standard English. Why don't East African writers, including yourself, write in the fashion of Chinua Achebe or Gabriel Okara?

These writers are fed linguistically from below. They are fed by the idiom of speech, the rhythm of speech of the people about whom they are writing. You find that, on the whole, West Africans have been in a lot more contact with the English language than the East Africans. And you find that West Africans have even developed a form of English that is peculiar to the West African scene—the Pidgin English. So that somebody like Chinua Achebe finds it easy when he's portraying a character to fall back on Pidgin English as a form of characterization. We don't, on the whole, have an East African English yet, although it may come into being. So the kind of English we have in East Africa is very much the sort of school English with correct grammar, etc. But maybe in a few years' time in East Africa, there will be a variation of English that can be used as a form or method of characterization. Meanwhile we shall be content merely to capture everything of ordinary life and speech, using the so-called Standard English.

I mentioned another West African writer—Gabriel Okara. What do you think of his experiment in the use of English?

Yes, I have seen very well what he has done with *The Voice*. He has tried to reproduce the syntax of Ijaw into English, and whereas on the whole he's very poetic and very, very good indeed, I don't think it's something which he can repeat, and I don't think it's something which I can emulate. I don't think there's any use in trying to reproduce the syntax of Kikuyu or Swahili into an entirely different language with a different kind of syntax. A more admirable thing as far as I'm concerned is what Chinua Achebe tries to do. Even when he writes in Standard English, I am able to feel that there is an old man talking, or I feel that a child's talking, or I feel that's an old woman talking in the village. That kind of thing I find much more successful and, in fact, much closer to the African situation than in the case of Gabriel Okara.

The first novel you wrote was The River Between, *which was actually published as your second in 1965. Can you tell us something about the circumstances under which it was written? You were a student at Makerere College in Uganda, weren't you?*

Yes, I was at Makerere College. This was in 1961, and I was writing my novel for a competition. It was really financially motivated. They were not offering very much money—$70 prize money. But the main thing is that we were a small group of students who were interested in writing, and we just met and encouraged one another. And I remember this friend of mine. He's a poet from East Africa, Joe Muhiga. We were very poor students, so we met together and he said, "You know, James, after this competition, we shall not get the first prize, but we shall certainly get the consolation prizes"—these worth about $10.50. So I started writing and then one day I got stuck. He came and beseeched me, "Please go on! Please go on! The consolation prize! The consolation prize is there!" So I went on. Then he himself stopped. So I came and said "Please go on! Please go on! There is a consolation prize! There is a consolation prize!" But unfortunately I was not as persuasive as he was, and he did not actually finish.

One of the main themes in The River Between *seems to be the theme of education—education as a sort of weapon against the whites in Kenya.*

Yes, I was trying to capture what I believe people thought about education or about other problems at this time in Kenya's history, in the 1930s, when the missionaries and the colonial government and the African people were struggling for power. Education was really seen as a tool, education was a weapon, and you used this weapon to wrench your independence from the colonial regime. And even now, I think, education is still seen as a tool, maybe as a means of bettering oneself, maybe economically, but nevertheless, as a tool. But in the 1930s, education was definitely a political weapon. It was seen as such by the colonial government. It was seen as such by the African peoples. Because with an education you could conform with or deny your cultural roots. So the missionaries really started the fight by saying that denying one's cultural roots is necessary before you can get a Western kind of education. But African people said, "We're going to get that Western education, but within our own cultural soil. We're going to get that education without having to accept the religion, without having to accept the colonial government."

How did the independent schools, the creation of which is portrayed fictionally in The River Between, *differ in practice from the missionary schools?*

They didn't really differ very much, but they did differ in their cultural emphasis. For instance, if you went to an independent school, you didn't have to renounce your customs. You didn't have to say: "I am against the circumcision of boys and girls." You didn't have to renounce your religion. You didn't have to renounce your beliefs. Now, with the missionary schools, you had to renounce your beliefs and your customs, and in fact, I think, you had to embrace Christianity. In the independent schools, the educational system took into account people's values or cultural assumptions. Their approach, I think, is still valid today.

Waiyaki, the main character in The River Between, *is contrasted with Joshua and Kabonyi. His aim, the reconciliation between European and Kikuyu ways of life, is destroyed by his people when they put him to death at the end of the novel. Politically he appears to be blind to future developments in Kenya. But you arouse sympathy for him with your reader. Did you actually intend this?*

If I wrote this book today, I don't know if I'd write it in exactly the same way. I wouldn't have been as sympathetic to Waiyaki as I probably was. But nevertheless, I still think a person who tries to interweave certain experiences has done quite a good job. After all, when society is changing all the time, you have to assimilate the best and reject the dead, and I think someone like Waiyaki is trying to assimilate only the best and reject the dead. I'd look at the role of Kabonyi, though, much more deeply and seriously than I did at the time.

He would become the major character now, perhaps?

I don't know. I would look at Kabonyi slightly different now, because in some ways he is much more aware politically than Waiyaki.

Could he be considered as a forerunner of Mau Mau fighters who later appear in your two novels Weep Not, Child *and* A Grain of Wheat*?*

I don't think I treated him deeply enough for me to see how he might have developed. By the time I wrote *Weep Not, Child*, I don't know if I was more aware of various forces or if I was more aware of people, individuals being at the center, expressive of social forces of which they themselves may not be aware consciously. *A Grain of Wheat* was much more self-explicit, much more expressive of the symbolic nature of action or the business of people being agents of social forces.

In Weep Not, Child *there are numerous allusions to Jomo Kenyatta as the savior, the black messiah. How do you reconcile this with your last statement—that people are agents of social forces?*

I don't think individuals as such are saviors as such. They are more symbols of certain social forces which are started, and the individuals are mere agents of those forces which are already in society. So I don't think there is any one individual who is a savior as such. But he can be an active agent of liberation, or he can be an active agent of change. So it is the people who invest someone with this symbolic significance, but he himself is not inherently a savior—he is invested to be so symbolically. I'd be more in line with Tolstoy when he sees in the country the social forces creating certain individuals—individuals as such do not create situations, situations create these individuals. Of course, certain individuals are very important too. But the people create the individual.

Taking the Mau Mau fighters as a pervasive symbol in Weep Not, Child *and* A Grain of Wheat, *do you regard them as representative of African resistance to colonialism?*

When one is writing this kind of novel, which is based on historical events, one is guided more by the nature of the historical event. In this case I was guided more by the experience of the Mau Mau resistance movement. But in my approach to the novel you use even a small village as a symbol of a larger concern. So the Mau Mau movement represented a subject that was not confined to Kenya, but which went beyond the borders of Kenya, because it is an African theme, as opposed to its being primarily a Kenyan theme. I use a small village as a guide for the whole African struggle for identity.

How do you see the role of the artist vis-à-vis *his society—in your case,* vis-à-vis *African society?*

I'd say he is trying to probe into society, to probe into the kinds of tensions and conflicts in society. He might indicate areas of past conflict, and areas of possible development. He might give moral guidance in a struggle. And I see the artist trying to get people to come more together and with society's struggle, to create a different type of society from the one which we've inherited from the colonial set-up.

How much of your own experience did get into a novel like Weep Not, Child*? Njoroge, the school boy, is not very much aware of what was going on during the Emergency.*

As a child growing up during this period, it would be silly and not true to say one was aware of all implications of even the struggle itself. But one did get the impressions. You are so young. You see your uncles being killed. British soldiers come to collect your uncles. You see some of your friends being taken from their homes. These things stay with you. You see an old man you respected being emasculated as a condition of war. These things leave you with an impression though you take those things for granted and just go on. In *Weep Not, Child* I just wanted to capture as much as possible the atmosphere of the situation, what it felt like to actually live in a small village at this time. So I wasn't trying to capture anything that was very deep, but I was trying to capture what it felt like to live in a civil war. So that even if I didn't use my experience in many of the episodes, there are things which I may have seen or heard or felt at the time.

In A Grain of Wheat *it seemed to me you started a new departure, a way of looking at the events that seemed to me to be rather different from your two earlier novels. I thought perhaps this was going to define a new direction. Could you talk about* A Grain of Wheat *in this respect?*

I don't know if it was a new departure or a combination of my several previous preoccupations. The only really different thing in *A Grain of Wheat* was my preoccupation with the time structure and the problem of judgment. I asked myself: "Is an event an isolated phenomenon, an act in a particular moment of time? Is it isolated from what has gone on previously in history, is it separated from what goes on in the same time in space?" So in the problem of judging an action, you have to take into account the spatial and also the historical dimensions. It's a complex thing—the problem of time and judgment and space. I was at this time much more interested in capturing this movement of history, the way things change from previous moments—the way there is this progressive movement forward.

Recently there has been fairly strong expression in the U.S. that the time for African writing which is a reaction to the colonial experience is at an end. It is now time for writing of the African experience itself. Do you agree?

No. I think this is a mistaken notion—that something is not an African experience. Obviously a reaction to colonialism is an experience. It's part of one's contemporary understanding. People seem to think colonialism has been exhausted as a theme in literature. But a form of colonialism still does exist even though formal independence has been granted. But much more important, any experience which affects Africa is an African experience. However, concerning the "second round" which you allude to: People here know *A Man of the People*, but they are not really seeing things like *Song of Lawino*, which is not really a reaction against colonial rule—it's a reaction against the colonial effect in Africa. They've not seen things like *The Orphan*. Even *A Grain of Wheat* is not a reaction. They've not seen the works like that of Wole Soyinka, *The Interpreters*, that just recently came out.

You use Kikuyu and Christian mythology quite frequently in your novels. Don't you think there are a large number of your readers who are unable to understand your allusions?

I don't actually do this as much as, for instance, Chinua Achebe. He uses a lot of African stories, African folklore, African sayings—much more effectively than I do. What I try to do is to use the Christian or African mythology merely as a frame of reference, as the only body of assumptions I can take for granted, especially in the area I come from. I think most people will be familiar with stories from the Old Testament in one form or another because of the missionaries in Africa. On the other hand, I see the problem with the particular African mythology with which most readers, non-African and even African, will not be acquainted. This is a problem which writers face—how do you create a common body of assumptions to which you can allude without having to explain the significance?

I have found that some of the short stories resemble vignettes which you utilize again very similarly in your novels. Do you regard your short stories primarily as experiments to be later integrated into novels?

I think short stories are a form in themselves. I don't think I'm particularly good at them myself. You see, you cannot really separate your moods or your preoccupations if you write in a certain period. If you write a short story and then a play and a novel at about the same time, you'll find that they tend to be preoccupied with the same kind of things. That's why you find that some of the themes that are in my plays or short stories in a certain period reappear in the novel. It's not really something which one thinks about—it happens. A short story is not like an experiment, not like a visual artist might draw a sketch of something he's going to use later on. For me, when I write a short story, I want it to be as good a short story as possible when I'm writing it. Later, I may want to return to the same theme in a novel or a play when I feel I've not exhausted that particular theme.

I got very interested in the theme of return—I mean the detainee's return in a play like This Wound of My Heart, *in a story like* "The Return" *and in* A Grain of Wheat. *Do you see any further literary possibilities in this theme?*

This is a very crucial theme which has not been exhausted yet. There are so many people who have been detained and come back. It's a traumatic experience for them to come back and find the world has changed. It might be interesting, in fact, to write a short story or a novel about how the people who remain in the village see the ones who return. It's a dramatic theme and also an actual theme. There are people who did return, who found their homes broken; they found all their children seriously affected by the colonial regime. That's why it's such an important theme in my work—and you also find it in the works of Kibera and his brother Kahiga, and I think we'll read more about it in the future of Kenya.

The end of your play The Black Hermit *puzzled me. Remi, the main character, is working towards an inter-tribalist movement on his return to the village; then he loses his own wife who could be symbolic of his own tribe.*

The play is very confused, and I don't like to comment on it very much. I suppose I was trying to get to the problem of what does it matter if he condemns tribalism when he doesn't really care about the sensibilities of the individuals. I was probably trying to show the relationship on the level of caring. It's not enough to care only on the level of group and never care on the level of individuals. But this was written in 1962. Maybe if I did it now, I would do it differently—I don't know.

What do you think of Robert Ruark's novel Something of Value, *which deals with one of your major subjects, the Mau Mau uprising?*

It is made from a very European, colonial point of view. Ruark was a liberal who was very uptight in spirit, in practice, and in various other things. The mood of the portrayal is very vicious and conforms more with the colonialists' image of Africa. Ruark is very anti-Mau Mau. I think he is a false liberal.

Ezekiel Mphahlele, in a section of his latest novel, The Wanderers, *also deals with Kenya—with post-independence Kenya. Do you think his picture of modern Kenya is a fair one?*

Nairobi is. But I come from a village, and so can look at things differently. I look at things from below. I don't look as someone who is just passing through or someone who is most of the time with degenerates. This is true especially as it relates to European advisors. I never know what to think about that particular section. I think it depends on the particular type of society in Nairobi.

How do you see the present political situation in East Africa? And do you have any visions of the future?

I don't really know. I write about politics on the subconscious level, not the conscious level. As for the future of East Africa, I've really got a lot of faith. I'm really very optimistic about the possibilities. I think there will probably be a period of pain—a very difficult period, what one might call birth pains. Every young nation has it. And the main question in East Africa is where shall we go from here? We've got our formal independence. But what do we do with all of these institutions which we have inherited? How are we going to organize our economic life? How are we going to organize the land system? What shall we do about the differences between the educated or elite class and the masses of peasants and workers? What is the best form of social organization which might release this tremendous energy in the people of East Africa?

What struck me in A Grain of Wheat *was that in the events around independence day there was a kind of disillusionment. Some of the peasants were even worse off—they didn't gain anything through independence. It was the new bourgeoisie that gained something. Do you feel that one way of progress for Africa is to get rid of the black bourgeoisie?*

I think that we're striving for a form or organization that will release this tremendous energy. I think there is the danger of the black bourgeoisie blocking this energy of the people. This is not a problem of just the black bourgeoisie, but of the middle class everywhere, trying to block the energy of the people. But even more important in Africa, there is the problem of sheer economic development—the colonial governments left Africa, especially Kenya or Uganda, in a state of sheer primitive underdevelopment. So the problem is clearer in these countries because of the smallness of the bourgeoisie and because of the enormous underdevelopment of the countries. And also, on the whole, the economy of the country is not always in the control of the people inside. So there are a lot of troubles in East Africa.

In the interview you gave in Leeds you talked about a socialist vision for East Africa. What did you mean?

The socialist system is the only system which stresses interdependence and the only system which encourages cooperation. The more I think about it, the more I believe this is the only salvation for Africa. The point, though, is to look at things, not in terms of labels, but in terms of reality. African societies were most communal in those countries that had organized their own communal business—in those societies where material life was organized on a communal basis or where the means of production had been communalized. I can't see where communal values can exist when the material wealth is in a few hands. It would simply be a contradiction.

What are your impressions of the American political scene, especially of the black liberation groups in this country?

I've found myself a bit confined, and I haven't come into as much contact with these people as I would have liked to. I'm very much in sympathy with the preoccupations of the black people here—definitely I am in sympathy with the actual struggle of the black people here. And obviously since I find it difficult to make judgments on the East African scene, I find it even harder to make clear judgments where I do not understand the situation sufficiently. In the case of Kenya, as in the case here, I'm in sympathy with the struggle of the people to get a place in the sun. But as to what form—I'm in no position to pass judgment.

9 BBB Interviews Ngugi wa Thiong'o

Bettye J. Parker / 1975 (1978)

In the winter of 1975, just after he had completed Petals of Blood, *Ngugi wa Thiong'o, formerly known as James Ngugi, wrote the following statement to Dr. Bettye J. Parker:*

"I was away for the month of September in the Soviet Union at the invitation of the Soviet Writers' Union who kindly gave me the use of their rest house at Yalta on the Black Sea to finish my novel Petals of Blood. *It was, I suppose, my contribution to 'détente' since the novel was really started in Evanston, Illinois and completed at Yalta where Roosevelt and Churchill and Stalin met after the Second World War."*

This statement is symbolic of the political fervor and sensitivity present in all of Ngugi's novels: Weep Not, Child, The River Between, A Grain of Wheat *and* Petals of Blood. *A play,* Ngaahika Ndeenda, *written and performed in Kikuyu, critically addresses the problems from pre-independence to present Kenya.*

Currently, Professor Ngugi is being detained under Kenya's Public Security Act. He was arrested recently by Kenyan police and many of his books were seized.

The following interview was conducted by Dr. Parker with Ngugi in 1975 at the University of Nairobi.

Let us begin this discussion with your own fiction. What kind of impact do you see your writing having on the growth and development of African people, especially since the past figures very prominently in your work?

From my writing one can see that the past, present and future are bound and interrelated. My interest in the past is because of the present and there is no way to discuss the future or present separate from the past.

There is a tendency among students and literary scholars in the United States to compare your first novel, Weep Not, Child, *with James Baldwin's* Go Tell It on the Mountain *and Richard Wright's* Black Boy. *Were you consciously aware of any specific antecedents when you wrote* Weep Not, Child*?*

Not particularly, although I did not write in a vacuum. I have read literature, listened to stories and have seen boys and girls growing up, and it was important that I had all these experiences behind me when I began to write. I cannot isolate and say that one particular thing influenced me because many factors came into play. However, I am not aware of any specific text that I may have read at that time that specifically influenced the origins and growth of *Weep Not, Child.*

The poem by Walt Whitman at the beginning of Weep Not, Child *serves as the source of the title of the book.* Does that poem generate some specific inspiration within you and do you accord any specific significance to Walt Whitman?*

Not particularly, except that the poem I used seemed to express the mood of the people that I was trying to express in the novel. I think that Whitman was saying, in that section of the poem anyway, that although there are clouds in the sky, they will pass away and sunshine will come. It is a long night that will not find the light of day. So, *Weep Not, Child* expresses a similar type of mood. Now, in the context of the Kenyan struggle for independence, this became very important because underlying the people's experiences was the element of hope and optimism that things would change and something positive would emerge.

In the United States students easily compare Weep Not, Child *to the struggle of black people in America. At the time that you wrote the book, were you familiar with the struggles of African Americans?*

No. I can say quite categorically that in 1962 in Makerere, it was very unlikely that one could have heard much about the struggle of African people in the United States. Langston Hughes was the first black writer that I met from the United States. In 1962 we had a conference of African writers and Langston Hughes came to Makerere. It was an interesting experience.

What specific role did Hughes play at that conference?

He talked and read from one of his collections. However, he was more at home in the streets of Kampala than he was at the formal sessions of the conference. Meeting Hughes was a very interesting experience.

I can only imagine the excitement you must have felt. Tell me, do you find the time now to get together with other writers in East Africa on a formal or informal basis?

We have just formed a Kenyan writers' organization here. Though we have not yet met formally, important informal meetings have been held. We are lucky that many of our writers are here at the University. This has meant two things. One, we have what one may call a creative jealousy where one may say, "Oh, I have just been writing a poem," and the response may be, "Oh!" or, it may generate some new idea. It has reached the point where we celebrate a new book every month or so. Secondly, younger writers have access to older writers. They not only have the opportunity to read their works but to discuss their own works with them. They can meet Okot p'Bitek or Grace Ogot, for example, and discuss their writing informally.

Is there a particular scholar of African literature that you would recommend for those of us studying African literature in the context of the diaspora?

Yes, Frantz Fanon, although he doesn't write as a critic in this sense. But I always think that he is very important background to the study of African literature because he describes the conditions against which most of our writers are now writing. If you take the writings of Okot p'Bitek, my own writings, the writings of Achebe and so on, you will find that all of these works are being written against a specific background of certain social and political movements and pressures. So, although we have different personalities and use different approaches, the issues against which our imagination is working is very much the same. These are described by Fanon in *The Wretched of the Earth*.

Those of us who study and teach African literature in the United States generally take this approach—beginning with the concepts Fanon explores and moving to the text of the writing. You are cognizant, of course, of the developing concept among black scholars, particularly in the United States, of a black aesthetics. What directions do you see the black aesthetics taking here on the continent?

Interestingly enough, we have just instituted a course here at the University of Nairobi called "The Black Aesthetics." It is a first-year course and the approach we use is specifically to study the movement of ideas and politics beginning with the Harlem Renaissance and moving to the West Indies, to West Africa, and then to East Africa. Our approach begins with the question: What are the conditions of life—colonial, historical, political experiences—that prevent the realization of a black aesthetics? Black people have been evolving against a background of colonialism, political oppression, and economic deprivation. We realize that an aspect of black humanity has been deprived. But against this background, there is also another aspect of the struggle: the struggle to transform these conditions. And we see the two sides as being very important. So that while we still sing about our oppression, we must sing beautifully. A death dance must be danced beautifully.

How do you distinguish the good dancer from the poor dancer, the good black writer from the poor black writer?

No writer writes in the same way or has the same attitude. Even in our own popular culture, people are able to distinguish between a good dancer and a poor dancer, a good singer and a poor singer, a sweet song and a not-so-sweet song, and so on. Discrimination is part and parcel of the Black Aesthetics.

But how does one make the distinction between a sweet singer and a sour singer?

One must listen to the beat of the drums. If a singer is out of tune with the drums, he is a poor singer. He is a sweet singer when everybody joins in. The sweet songs last longer, too. They have more meaning and more emotion.

This brings me to the critical question of criticism of black literature. Often the concerns of black critics are no different from those of white critics. Is this because these critics have no sensitivity to the struggle?

This is a growing problem. So often we find African critics who evaluate African literature in the same way, using the same words and types of judgments as those seen by white Western critics. That kind of criticism becomes dangerous. We don't want the kind of critic who insults people's involvement in the struggle by calling those people who are really struggling for our liberation by derogatory names—thugs, terrorists, and so on. Many of our critics are on this level.

How do you define the black critic?

We want the kind of critic who can really see the significance of those involved in the struggle. In other words, we want someone who is on the side of the people. To me this seems to be fundamental and basic. The critic should review, comment on every work from the point of view of how far it is to a particular point of the struggle of the people for the full realization of themselves as a people and how far that work returns that realization. Because no matter how beautiful a work is, if it is not returning the people's struggle or march towards self-realization as a people, then the work cannot be good. We cannot go on praising the works of critics who are cutting our people's throats.

Speaking of critics, I understand that George Lamming, the West Indian novelist and critic, recently visited the University of Nairobi. What was the nature of his visit and how do you view him as a critic?

He had been to the University of Dar es Salaam as a visiting professor for three months in Black Literature and we invited him here for another fourteen days. He made a very important impact on our students by his approach to literature and especially Caribbean literature. He is very fond of Richard Wright and some of the more revolutionary writers. His approach is very much in keeping with the kind of approach that we are trying to encourage. So, he fitted in very beautifully with the whole structure here as well as in Dar es Salaam. George Lamming is definitely on the side of the people—on the side of the struggle. His writing is revolutionary and illustrates the struggle of the people. One of the most sensible comments that I ever read about black writing was written by George Lamming when he was writing about what he called "The Position of the Negro Writer." That was approximately 1956 when he said that the commitment of the black writer was first to know the black world very intimately, and then, fundamentally, to know the world. He starts with the black world and then moves outwardly, something which was then before his time. This is very important. If you take his novels, for example, *In the Castle of My Skin* and even down to this latest work, you find his commitment to a continuous struggle. He is one of the people who is very harsh in his writing about the black bourgeoisie. He is very contemptuous because he sees this class as being counter-revolutionary.

He spends a great deal of time away from the Caribbean, in London, for example. There always seems to be the necessity for some kind of exile among black artists. We are especially aware of it in the United States, as specifically in the cases of Wright, Baldwin, Himes, and others. How do you explain this?

The stupidity and insensitivity of the ruling classes oftentimes cause people to run away.

Is this attitude rampant among the writers here in Kenya? Do they feel the need to get away from the existing situation and write?

Not really. At this point I think most of our writers want to stay home in the struggle, but I can see the time is coming when more of them will probably go away. However, it has not come to that yet.

You see, right now they are stimulated by the people. After all, if we are not stimulated by the people, then we cannot truly be writers.

On some rare occasions, prominent African writers have denounced Negritude and have made negative comments to the white press in the United States. As a writer on the continent do you find this defeating?

The problem here is that sometimes one can say something outside one's own country which is really based on specific differences. For example, when Soyinka denounces Negritude he is not objecting to everything about Negritude, but he is reacting to certain aspects of Negritude that he reacts to even when he is home. There is the tendency when you are away for things to be taken out of context. This can sometimes be damaging.

What are your own feelings about Negritude?

There was a time when people reacted against Negritude because it was expected that all writers should write the same way and use the same kind of phrases. Some people reacted to this harshly. I think that there was somewhat of an overreaction. Of course, I also think that there are some very reactionary tendencies in Negritude as well as revolutionary tendencies in Negritude. One has to distinguish between the reactionary and the revolutionary, and this is very important. What comes out of this is a great challenge for all of us to understand each other a little more. If this is not done, if little statements as those made by Soyinka are used to divide us, then that is very bad.

How do you propose that we begin to close the gaps of misunderstanding and misinformation that are present among us?

More visits need to be arranged. We need to get more writers to black college campuses in the United States, not so much to teach formal courses but to just be around for discussion. We must also get teachers from the United States to come here for longer visits. We have had African-American professors here at the university and some of our experiences have been similar to yours in terms of them making dangerous statements about African-American life and history. I am thinking particularly of an African-American history professor who was here recently and was denounced by our students and called an "Uncle Tom." He was very unhappy because he said that he had never been called an Uncle Tom before. He said to come to Africa to be called an Uncle Tom was an insult.

What prompted this name calling by the students?

When he came here he was talking about Malcolm X, Martin Luther King Jr., and some other black leaders and movements in the same terms. He told the students that he was going to write a book where he would give equal credit to all of the leaders and movements. They questioned how he could give equal credit to reactionary and revolutionary leaders alike.

In terms of Malcolm and King, which did the students view as the revolutionary leader?

We see Malcolm X as a revolutionary leader. You read the *Autobiography of Malcolm X* and you see three definite stages of movement: the first stage is the rebel who internalizes violence in Harlem and so on. We see him in the second stage as a cultural nationalist which is the Black Muslim stage and which is very important. It emphasizes certain aspects of black history, black awareness, and creates a mythology that may or may not be scientifically or historically correct, but nevertheless it is a mythology that emphasizes certain positive aspects of black culture and black people. Then the third important stage which one can especially get from his speeches is when he sees the black struggle in a definite political, social, and economic category. In other words, it is the stage where he begins to assume a definite anti-imperialist position which is a very crucial position to most of the people here. The moment any black writer or black leader begins to see the problems as Malcolm does in this stage, when he sees the similarities between the problems of the chap in Mississippi and the chap in the Congo, he begins to see that imperialism is a worldwide phenomenon and he can get to the root of the problem.

In exactly what terms is Martin Luther King seen here?

Martin Luther King is seen here as symbolizing certain tendencies of accommodation, except for some things he said toward the end of his life about Vietnam. Here, he is seen as trying to get a share within American capitalism. Black people here cannot see how black people in America, in London, or wherever can really find a place within capitalism because all you are going to get is a few black people moving up and joining the exploiters.

What are the dimensions of black exploitation?

Because racism does not emanate from some biological arrangement, I must assume that it can be changed. We can see racism as a phenomenon that has social, political, and economic bases and origins, and is thus subject to social, political, and economic solutions. Black people have been victims of double exploitation. They have been exploited on the level of class because they constitute the majority of the working class and the laboring masses. They have also been exploited on the dimension of race because of the whole colonial context in which black and white people have met. Thus, black people must realize themselves on the level of class and take anti-capitalist and anti-imperialist positions. Also, they must proclaim their color with pride, their culture with pride, their history with pride, their whole past with pride!

At this juncture in history what is the struggle of black people?

The struggle of black people is a collective struggle against imperialism. Here, Nairobi is the center of exploitation. This is where American capitalists are—Shell, Esso, Kentucky Fried Chicken, Woolworths, First National Bank of Chicago, etc. All of these are international in character and America is at the helm of it all. When I go to America or Nigeria or other places, I see certain similarities. I cannot isolate and see a Chicago Hilton or a Nigerian Hilton or a Kenyan Hilton. I see exploitation! And we must all be concerned about this exploitation.

* The title of the poem is "On the Beach at Night."

10 *BBC Arts and Africa* Interview with Ngugi wa Thiong'o about *Petals of Blood*

Charles Harrison / 1977

The well-known Kenyan novelist Ngugi wa Thiong'o--perhaps better known by his previous name, James Ngugi--recently published a new book called Petals of Blood. *His previous work includes novels such as* The River Between, A Grain of Wheat *and* Weep Not, Child, *and he was one of the first African writers to attain world recognition. Charles Harrison spoke with him in Nairobi, where he teaches literature at the University, and first asked him what the significance of the title of his new book was.*

The new book is called *Petals of Blood* and the title is taken from a poem by the West Indian poet Derek Walcott who pictures a situation: a very huge tree prevents little flowers from reaching out to the light.* So I was really comparing the social system of capitalism and imperialism as being equivalent to this huge tree that prevents plants from reaching out into the light.

Now what briefly is the story about?

Well, the novel is really set in a small village somewhere in Kenya. The village is imaginary and what we do see is a village which has been underdeveloped because most of its wealth has gone into the big cities and also into foreign countries. A village which is suffering from drought and so on. And what we do see is the kind of development that occurs in the village as a result of the combination, if you like, of foreign financial capital and a class of local property-owners, and the development is seen not as development but really as some kind of underdevelopment. We see the peasants eventually being ousted from the land they have always occupied as a result of this incursion of foreign financial capital.

So this is not necessarily simply a Kenyan story. It could, in fact, I suppose, have its setting anywhere in Africa?

Yes. This could be set anywhere in Africa or, for that matter, in most parts of the Third World, but as a novelist I try to be very particular and localize the situation as much as one can, following, I suppose, in the footsteps of William Blake, the English poet, who once said that we must try and see the world in a grain of sand. So I was trying to see the world through a grain of sand in a small village in Kenya.

I think pretty well all your other books, Mr. Ngugi, have been very closely aligned with the Kikuyu country. Now, does this book follow that pattern?

As I said, it is set in a small village, which is regionally set in Central Province but, in terms of movement of characters, it tends to traverse all over Kenya from Mombasa to the Lakes. But much of the action, and the actual disintegration, if you like, takes place in this small Kikuyu village or imaginary Kikuyu village somewhere in Central Province.

It seems to me that you are moving a long way ahead from the themes which you developed in your earlier books. They were definitely about the pre-Independence struggle. Now this seems to mean that you are moving into a new era in your creative writing.

Yes. As I said, this particular novel, *Petals of Blood,* is much more contemporary and it really looks at, if you like, imperialism at the stage of neo-colonialism. In other words, where before my other novels were set, as you correctly say, during the struggle against imperialism but during the *colonial* stage, now it looks at the phenomenon of neo-colonialism or rather it looks at the phenomenon of post-independence, of postcolonial struggles in Africa. I've also changed slightly in the sense that where before I tended to look at the character of the conflicts, as if they were isolated from political and economic conflicts, I think this time the novel is much more firmly in a definite economic and political setting, so that the cultural and psychological conflicts are seen as, if you like, reflections of the material reality under which the peasants and the workers in Kenya are living.

Can we then regard this as perhaps the start of a new pattern in your writing? You are moving into a new and, shall we say, somewhat broader field?

In a sense, yes. But the problem really is that one does not know what one is going to write next. So that maybe the next novel might be very, very different. But whatever the case, I think I move into a new era where I look at social forces much more closely, I think, without illusions.

---

* The poem is "The Swamp," and it appears in Derek Walcott's *The Castaway and Other Poems* (1965).

11 *Petals of Blood*

Anita Shreve / 1977

Ngugi wa Thiong'o has written a remarkable book. In a moving and sympathetic portrayal of the alienation of four central characters who come together in the fictional town of Ilmorog, Petals of Blood *is a strong, incisive critique of the struggle of the worker and peasant classes in a society which has been dominated by colonial interests. Imperialism, tourism, and a lust for the shilling are the evils on a battlefield, where barmaids, teachers, peasant women and rural shopkeepers are the victims. Although the four main characters are well-drawn and detailed, in the end they remain as symbols for a much larger population.*

The framework of the novel is a detective story. Three big shots have been murdered in a fire in Ilmorog, and four residents of Ilmorog have been arrested and detained. The four characters are: Munira, a schoolteacher whose family background and whose own inner conflict contribute to an ideological indecisiveness; Wanja, a beautiful and pragmatic prostitute, whose essential innocence remains intact despite circumstances which force her to kill her child and slip into the role of a barmaid; Abdullah, a Freedom Fighter who lost his leg in the struggle for Independence, and who now runs a shop in Ilmorog; and Karega, the enigmatic drifter, searcher for truth, who at the end of the book becomes something of a prophet. The characters come together in old Ilmorog, work on each other in varying degrees of intimacy, and watch the town and its people undergo an inevitable and brutal change when the trans-Africa highway transforms life there forever. The book encompasses twelve years of reminiscences of the four characters—their personal hopes and illusions, struggles and delusions, and finally a tentative optimism at the end.

This optimism is important, for without it, the book would be a catalog of despair, paralyzing in its message. Munira finds a personal salvation in the Christianity he has rejected all his life.

Wanja is given the child for whom she has pined for twelve years. Abdullah finds his illusions renewed by the love of a woman. And Karega, in the strongest and truest voice of the four characters, finds hope in the growing political awareness of the workers of Ilmorog. "Tomorrow, tomorrow," he says at the end of the book, echoing the voice of the secondary school student, Joseph, who speaks a different language from the students of the previous generation. "This time we are going to demand that the school should be run by a committee of students, staff, and workers....And that all our studies should be related to the liberation of our people...."

Ngugi wa Thiong'o's book is heavy, serious reading, though often lyrical and beautiful in its descriptions. Petals of Blood *is not meant as entertainment, but as an education for all of us who have a tendency to forget that most of the peoples of the world are poor and struggling.*

We interviewed Ngugi wa Thiong'o at the University of Nairobi where he is the Chairman of the Department of Literature. We began by asking him about Wanja, one of the strongest characters in his book.

Do you think the things that happened to Wanja were typical, or did you intend her to be an exception?

I don't think she is an exception. The things that have happened to her have happened to many other women. A barmaid is a woman without a fixed means of income. She is not a prostitute, strictly speaking, nor is she a straight girl. Her salary is not regulated; it is paid according to the whim of her employer. She has little chance of marrying. I believe that barmaids are the most ruthlessly exploited category of women. Barmaids came into being after Independence, and were a result of the many bars that sprang up after 1963. Drinking, alcohol, and sexism are part of our national pastime.

Do you think that women are any more exploited or oppressed than men?

Yes. Let me explain it this way. Capitalism and imperialism are the root causes of evil. Our economy is dependent on international capitalism. And capitalism can never bring about equality of peoples. The exploitation of one group by another is the very essence of capitalism. The peasants and workers are very much exploited in this country. They get very low pay, very poor housing, and unemployment affects them more than anyone else. Now, women form the majority in this category of peasants. Women are doubly exploited and oppressed. It's a general Third-World problem. Workers and peasants and women form the most important element in this country. They are the true producers of wealth. They produce all the wealth that feeds, clothes, houses everyone in the society. They also produce all the wealth that goes out of the country. Yet they do not get even the barest minimum of that which they produced. The middle class that feeds on the workers and peasants is a superfluous, parasitic class.

How do you feel, then, about the university women that you teach?

Given the system of capitalism, how can they change? Given the domination of our economy by imperialism, all these men and women are going to be involved in contradictions. As for myself, I often think of a phrase by Bertolt Brecht, which goes something like this: "How can I eat and sleep peacefully, when I know that my food has been taken from the hungry."

Then you personally experience a lot of anxiety about contradictions in your own life.

I have already answered that.

How do you feel about the double standard that exists in sexual relationships between men and women? For instance, the general acceptance that it's all right for a man to sleep around, but not all right for a woman.

The double standard is a result of the present system. The woman is seen as property. The problem of men and women cannot be satisfactorily solved under the present system. Sexual relations are a reflection of an unequal economic system.

At the end of the book, you reward Wanja with a child, even though for twelve years she has thought herself infertile. Why?

There are always possibilities of renewal and growth. But only in a different kind of system. I believe that change is inevitable. Change is an eternal theme in nature and in human society. For instance, there was a time not so long ago when the whole earth was ruled by imperialism. Today imperialism is retreating, as seen by the number of African countries which gained independence through the struggle of the workers. In the postcolonial era, we saw the retreat of U.S. imperialism from southeast Asia. The whole American effort was defeated by peasant workers. That was a tremendous thing. Here, we saw the British forces being routed by Mau Mau. And women were the most important elements in Mau Mau. All these things indicate possibilities of change, possibilities of creating a new world through a united peoples' determined resistance against imperialism, against foreign domination, against all other social forces that diminish men and women.

Do you think that fiction, Petals of Blood, *can change anything?*

Fiction cannot be the agent of change. The people are the agent of change. All writers can do is really try to point out where things went wrong. They can do no more than that. But fiction should be firmly on the side of the oppressed. Fiction should firmly embody the aspirations and hopes of the majority—of the peasants and workers.

Is that why some of the characters in the novel seem like stereotypes? All the European characters, for instance, and all the middle-class or upper-class characters?

In this novel, there are individual characters that are not fully explored. They are supposed to stand as class types, as typical of a class that has come to be completely indifferent to the cry of the people. I see no value whatever in the middle class.

Have you ever thought of examining middle-class women? I notice in the book that none of the "bad" middle-class characters are women.

I think it's something I might look into in the future.

What is the future? What is your next project?

I'm working on another novel, but I don't think it's a good idea to talk about that now. Beyond that, I want to write some things in Kikuyu. Our languages are in need of development. Our languages have been oppressed.

How does Petals of Blood *relate to your other works?*

I feel that I have changed in terms of outlook. But I see this book as a continuation of some of the basic concerns that motivated this country in the earlier novels.

12 "Open Criticism Is Very Healthy in Any Society"

John Esibi / 1977

You have once again come out with yet another controversial contemporary novel based on Kenya's political set-up. Would you care to summarize what message you were trying to convey to readers[in Petals of Blood*]?*

It is difficult for a writer to comment about his book. It is equally dangerous for him to try and indicate what message he was trying to convey to readers. A writer would try and leave it to his readers to try and dig out what message (if any) he is trying to convey to readers. The problem is a writer tries to use fictional forms where he employs the use of many characters with conflicting views and outlooks on the said society. He tries not to side emphatically with any of the characters mentioned in the book.

With due respect, Mr. Ngugi, you will agree that there must have been an idea you conceived in your mind before embarking on writing Petals of Blood*? It is this idea that you may wish to explain to readers. Just exactly what are you expressing in the book?*

Maybe the word "message" is a wrong one.... Perhaps I could try and give the background. The novel was really meant to look at the different aspects of Kenyan society: contemporary society, that is, looking at the whole picture, say, starting from bar life in Kenya right up to the question of foreign ownership of property here and the devastating effects of tourism on our national life. In other words, I look at contemporary society but in a historical perspective. I examine the different social forces that are encroaching on the minds and lives of Kenyan people today and also their historical roots. For instance, I have moved back to the time during the wars waged by our people against British imperialism, I have gone through the struggle waged by our people in the 1930s, 1950s, and so on, so that a glance at contemporary society has been at the same time a glance at our history.

You talk of "grabbers of fruits" of Independence in the countryside. Whom did you have in mind at the time you wrote the book?

Really it is not a question of names...and it is very, very important for people to realize that it is not a question of one or two names.... It is not a question of one or two people being this or that. It is to do with the nature, with the system that we have opted for. In other words, if we have opted for certain ways of organizing the production and distribution of wealth, then this way has certain logical, inevitable consequences. It does not matter who is running that system as each one (system) has its own logic. So the novel tries to look at the structure of our society as the root of our social evils, rather than at one or two individuals. It looks at things like social inequalities, what is at the root of unequal distribution of wealth, unemployment, etc.

*How about the title of the book—*Petals of Blood. *What did you have in mind and to what exactly does it refer?*

Actually this title is taken from a poem by a West Indian writer, Derek Walcott, in which he sees a huge tree preventing a little flower from reaching out into the light. So I took that as a symbol of the contemporary African situation where imperialism and foreign interests are preventing little flowers (the workers and peasants in Africa) from reaching out into the light. In the novel, I show imperialism as a monster preventing all our authentic Kenyan and African flowers from reaching out into the light...flowering in glory and dignity.

In the book you talk of foreign ownership of industries within our society, yet, amazingly, you chose a foreign publisher. Why did you have to do that?

In a sense I had no choice in the matter. This question must be seen in relation to the whole problem of publishing in Kenya and the rest of Africa. In my own case, it is because I had a long association with Heinemann Publishers. All the same, I would say that the publishing situation in the country and in Africa as a whole leaves a lot to be desired, because you find that most of the firms which we say are local are branches of the foreign ones. I would say that the publishing houses and businesses are more or less in the same situation as other industries. Often what we do get is a combination of foreign firms with, if you like, local branches and local directors and so on. As far as I know, we don't as yet have what one might term national publishing firms in Kenya. It is only one or two firms you can say are just beginning...but often these publishers themselves come up against foreign domination in the local publishing business. Some fold up even before they have started. In a nutshell I would say that there are no national publishing houses in Kenya other than just branches of foreign ones. So as a writer, I am caught up in the same contradiction that many others in Kenya are caught up in. We are all caught up in having most of our industries dominated by foreigners.

Are those "one or two" local firms you have in mind below the standard or in which way will they also end up folding up due to foreign ownership domination?

No, it is not a question of being below the standard because one or two are trying very hard, but at the time I finished writing my novel, I think there were practically no such local firms established here. In fact, even today we cannot meaningfully talk of a Kenyan national publishing industry.

Also in the book you talk of a few African elites holding top positions in Kenya.... Now whichever way one looks at it, you are one of those few Africans with top positions in our country. That being so, how do you explain yourself out of this anomalous situation?

You see, as a writer I try not to talk from a holier-than-thou position. I think it is wrong for writers to try and talk of themselves as if they are angels and so on. You see, even if all the angels in Heaven were running this social system, we would still have the same ills. As I said earlier, the novel is all about the structure of our society so that even when talking about the so-called few Africans in top positions, this is not the issue really. The issue is having our own national life dominated by foreigners. Grabbing is a direct consequence of our economy being dominated by imperialism. The book tries to look at all those social forces that are preventing the possibilities of a national economic and national cultural personality.

You talk of "national cultural personality" and so on.... By the way, do we still have to use foreign languages like English in expressing ourselves culturally? Hasn't the time come when people like you ought to be writing in vernaculars so that our people can probably understand you better?

I quite agree with you, especially the sentiments behind the question. But once again when you go back to what I said about foreign domination, you see how it is clearly reflected in our language situation: that is, our national cultural life tends to be dominated by the need of the use of the English language. This cuts off about seventy to ninety percent of our people from the written words (books and newspapers). Once again we still see foreign forces (in this case linguistic forces) dominating our national culture. In the same way as I have been caught up in a contradiction between writing about a national situation and being published by a foreign firm, which I find unsatisfactory, I also find myself in the same contradiction in writing about Kenya, but in a foreign language. After seventeen years of writing, I have come to the realization that if we want to develop Kenyan literature, then it must be in the Kenyan national languages such as Kikuyu, Luo, Kamba, Somali, Giryama, etc., and of course, Kiswahili. I do not think that there is a language too small to have its right to exist. If we have to successfully express ourselves culturally, then it has to be in our various national languages. So I should say that English should be seen as one among several foreign languages and that we should have Kiswahili as our main national language, supported by other various national languages.

As head of the Literature Department at the University of Nairobi, what are you doing to achieve what you have just expressed?

Well, this has to do with the educational policy which we have adopted as far as our national languages are concerned. The fact is that there has been a very wrong national policy, which tends to emphasize the primacy of the English language from nursery schools right up to university level. This is so bad that you still find some of our children unable to read and write in any of our national languages. So the solution can only be found in our national educational policy. That is, the Ministry of Education should come out with a new national language policy which should be reflected in our education system and curricula from primary to university level.

Is there any other African language that you express yourself in better than English?

Well, I think every Kenyan can express himself in at least one or two African languages. In my case I can at least express myself in Kikuyu. In fact, a friend of mine and I have begun to experiment in writing in Kikuyu, and we have come across very interesting possibilities. We have seen that Kikuyu, for instance, has more innovative possibilities than English. You find that there are many [more] ways one can express oneself than there are possibly in English.

Back to the foreign ownership of industries in Kenya, there have been feelings here and there that one of the reasons you chose a foreign publishing house is that your novel itself was too hot to have been published locally. Is that correct?

No, that is incorrect. To be fair, I did not think of that. As I said at the time I completed my book, there wasn't a single Kenyan national publishing house. It is not correct that I tried several national firms and that they rejected my manuscripts as such. The fact is there were no national firms to even try.

How about the book itself? How many copies have arrived from London, and if they haven't arrived, when are you expecting them?

Some have already arrived, and I am told they have all been grabbed by readers. But I think Heinemann Educational Books (EA) Ltd. are expecting some more copies, and I should think that the book should be on the shelves any time from now.

Since the book itself centers on political life in Kenya, do you have any fears of being in trouble with the authorities?

No, I have no such fears because I do believe that criticism of our social institutions and structures is a very healthy thing for our society. I do believe that we can move forward only through open and healthy criticisms; writers must sincerely examine all aspects of our national life.... If writers do not do this anywhere in the world, they would be failing in their duties. I believe that open criticism is a very healthy thing in any society.

Do you think that most African writers possess the same feelings?

I should think that most African writers have played a very important role in critically examining our national ills and problems.

Since you have tried to expose the ills and problems facing our nation, what sort of suggestions would you recommend to end such problems?

In a sense this is one of the problems a writer faces very often, because a writer tends to raise more questions than he can offer answers to, because answers can only be found by the collective "we," us Kenyans. In other words, the role of a writer is only to pose uncomfortable questions. But the answers to those questions can only be found by the masses of Kenya. Of course, sometimes solutions are implied in the questions. For instance, when talking about foreign ownership of our industries, I don't believe that imperialism has ever developed any country nor will it ever develop any country. This is because imperialism tries to serve its own interests. So posing the question of foreign interests implies the need for total resistance and opposition to imperialism as the only way through which we can develop our own national life economically, socially, politically and culturally. I believe that many countries in Africa (Kenya included) are poor not because they are poor themselves, but because the wealth from these countries goes to developed countries like America, Britain, West Germany and other Western countries. The product of their people's sweat has gone to develop a privileged few in other cities like New York, Bonn, London, Paris, etc.

How much time do you normally devote to a novel, Mr. Ngugi, and how would you advise would-be writers to develop their talents?

It took me between five to six years to compose *Petals of Blood*. That is a fairly long time for a novel. However, writers must try to remain patient when it comes to writing books. One should not be in a rush while working over a book. Also writers must try and seize every opportunity they have. As for me, I seized these moments anytime I was free—during lunch, in the evenings and even during the mornings. This is because I am not a professional writer—that is, I do not write full time for my living as I have other responsibilities. I do scribble a few things in my notebook while riding in a *matatu* or in a bus, even while sitting at table with my friends.[*]

[*] *Matatu*: originally an unlicensed "pirate" taxi; now a recognized form of transport.

13 An Interview with Ngugi

***The Weekly Review* / 1978**

Shortly after his latest novel, Petals of Blood, *was published last year, Ngugi wa Thiong'o granted* The Weekly Review *the following interview.*

A Grain of Wheat *was your last major novel, written in 1967.* Petals of Blood *comes ten years later. What happened to you as a writer during that interim time and what kinds of changes do you see yourself having gone through?*

Well, I started writing *Petals of Blood* in 1970, although the idea had been conceived a year before. So between 1970 and 1976 I was fully engaged in writing that novel so that my development as a writer is related to the development of *Petals of Blood* in that period. It was not a very easy novel to write. It kept changing all the time. I grew with it all the time. And that is why it took so long to write. In that period I don't think I wrote much else in the way of creative writing, except occasional articles and occasional public lectures in which I tried to define my outlook on literature. But, in short, I can say that this period was dominated by my writing *Petals of Blood.*

Talking about Ilmorog, and its transformation, do you think of it as a village which is particularly Kenyan or is it a village anywhere in Africa or in the Third World?

Ilmorog is a fictional village, but within that fictional setting, I have tried to be as particular as I can in terms of details. A novelist must be always very, very particular even when he's trying to make a general statement. At the same time I hope Ilmorog is as applicable to Kenya, as it is applicable to East Africa, Africa, and the Third World. This is because some of the problems raised in the novel affect not only Kenya but the whole world. For instance, the issues of national identity and foreign domination: I'm thinking, for instance, of the exploitation of workers and peasants by a combination of foreign capital and its local allies, and this is something I think is true of most countries in the world which are dominated by imperialism.

I found Karega to be a kind of character who himself goes through many different changes. I feel some of his ideas are some of your own, and that he, as a character, reflects most closely your own development as a thinker and actor in history. Could you discuss some of those ideas and clarify whether they do mirror any of your own?

First, I want to say that it is not fair to identify a writer with any one of his characters since he is trying to make the novel as a whole have an impact, taking all the factors into consideration. Nevertheless, you might say that there are one or two characters with whose ideas a writer may be in basic sympathy. But as with the other characters in the novel, I am more interested in their development from the stage of black cultural nationalism to the stage of class consciousness—from a stage when (a character) sees oppression in terms of culture alone, to the stage when he can see oppression and exploitation as being total, that is, as being economic, political, and cultural. From a stage where he can talk about African people *en masse* to a situation where he can see African societies as differentiated between the peasantry and the workers on the one hand, and imperialism and its allies on the other. I think it is an important development in the growth of the character.

History seems to be a very dominant theme and motif in the novel. Why does history play such a prevalent role in your thinking and in the novel itself?

History is very important in any people. How we look at our past is very important in determining how we look at and how we evaluate the present. A distorted view of a people's past can very easily distort our views and evaluation of the present as well as the evaluation of our present potentials and our future possibilities as a people. Our history up to now has been distorted by the cultural needs of imperialism; that is, it was in the interest of the imperialists to distort Kenyan history with the view of showing that Kenyan people had not struggled with nature and with other men to change their natural environment and create a positive social environment. It was also in the interests of the imperialists to show that the Kenyan people had not resisted foreign domination. It was also in the interests of imperialism to depict missionaries and other agents of imperialism in bright colors, and they did all these things using the terms of apparent objectivity. Now I feel that Kenyan writers, intellectuals, historians, political scientists, must be able to show us Kenya's past which correctly evaluates Kenyan people's achievements in the past, in the present, and at the same time, pointing out their creative potential in the future.

Sometimes when I look at Kenya's history, I ask myself what about all those Kenyans who so resisted the Portuguese intrusion into Kenya in the sixteenth century to the extent that the Portuguese were forced to build one of the strongest forts in the world, Fort Jesus? Or rather put it this way: Isn't the strength of Fort Jesus a comment on the ferocity of the resistance by the Kenyan people? What about all the Kenyan people that fought against Arab slave owning and slave hunting classes, and for many years successfully made sure that the Arabs were unable to penetrate into the interior of Kenya? What about all the fierce wars of resistance by Kenyan people in the nineteenth century against British imperialism? What about the wars fought by heroes like Waiyaki and others? What about all the fierce wars fought by Kenyan people around Mount Elgon?

We, as writers, as historians, as Kenyan intellectuals must be able to tell these stories, or histories, or history of heroic resistance to foreign domination by Kenyan people. Doing so, we shall not be looking at ourselves as people who were weak in the face of foreign domination, threats, aggression, but as a people whose history shines with the grandeur, if you like, of heroic resistance and achievement of the Kenyan people. That's why I think history dominates *Petals of Blood* so much. I feel that Kenyan history, either precolonial or colonial, has not yet been written.

Why do you feel that it is important this story be told in terms of the implications that it has for the present and for the future?

It is important because we are still not yet free of imperialist domination and exploitation. The Kenyan people must know their history in order to face up to the challenges of imperialism.

You talk a lot about Christianity in the lives of Kenyan people. What is the role that you feel Christianity plays in Ilmorog and in Kenya? And also why do you use biblical imagery yourself throughout the novel?

First of all, I would say I have not used biblical imagery throughout the novel. I have also used imagery drawn from national songs and national stories and what they might call national literature, oral literature. But I have also drawn from the Bible in the sense that the Bible was for a long time the only literature available to Kenyan people that has been available to them in their national languages. I have always thought of Christianity itself as part and parcel of cultural imperialism. Christianity, in the past, has been used to rationalize imperialist domination and exploitation of peasants and workers. It has been used to blind people to the reality of their exploitation because religion as a whole wants to tell people that their lot as a whole is God-given, as opposed to being man-conditioned. So if you see that you are poor because God has willed it, you are more than likely to continue to pray to God to right your condition. But if you know that your poverty is not God-conditioned, but it is socially conditioned, then you are likely to do something about those social conditions that are assuring that you be poor.

Why do you include in the novel songs in languages other than the English language?

In the course of writing the novel, I became more and more attracted, as I said, to the national songs, songs like those of the Mau Mau which are national songs. Songs which were sung in the 1930s against the British were also national songs. Of course, they form a very important part of Kenya's national literature.

The language issue is a slightly different one, although it is related to the novel in the sense that it was in the course of writing the novel that I came to be more and more disillusioned with the use of foreign languages to express Kenya's soul or to express the social conditions in Kenya. I think a people should express their national aspirations and their national history in the various national languages of Kenya, including the main national language which is Swahili. But all the other national languages, like Gikuyu, Luo, Giryama, Kamba, Maasai, are part and parcel of our national culture and we should express ourselves fully in those national languages instead of expressing ourselves in foreign languages like English.

Most people think of English and French, and German and Russian as international languages. How do you feel your understanding of the expression of a nation's aspirations can then be communicated to an international community, or whether that has any relevance to the whole issue of language?

The question of what is international itself needs to be questioned very seriously because there is a tendency of imperialists, capitalists, thinking of their own culture as being international, and this includes their languages. Often, what they mean by this is that they want their language and culture to hold sway in all those areas under their exploitation. What this means is that if you learn a people's language, and you adopt their culture, you are more likely to see yourself in terms of their world outlook, their aspirations. And you are likely to see their system not really as an enemy system, but as a friendly system with one or two possible anomalies. So, the term international depends upon the base from which you look at it. So, why don't we look at internationality from the point of view of the needs of the peasants and the workers of Kenya? Our national languages are international and national to the extent that they are able to stress the aspirations of the vast majority of not only the Kenyan people but also of peoples the world over. It is the content of internationality whether a language is or is not expressing the needs that affect the mass of the people the world over. In Kenya, to the extent that national languages are the ones which are used by the vast majority of people, of the various nationalities that go to make up the Kenyan nation, then those languages should be used, utilized, and developed, and a literature ought to develop in those languages so that there will be a vital relationship between the writer and the mass of Kenyan people.

14 Ngugi wa Thiong'o Still Bitter over His Detention

Margaretta wa Gacheru / 1979

The following is an excerpt of an interview given to Margaretta wa Gacheru of The Weekly Review *by Kenyan novelist and associate professor at the University of Nairobi, Ngugi wa Thiong'o, who was released from one year's detention on December12, 1978.*

Could you describe some of your experiences of detention, where you were, and what the conditions were inside?

When I was arrested, I was taken to Kamiti Maximum Security Prison, in Kiambu, where I was kept behind stone walls and iron bars for a whole year. I would like to say this, arising from my detention: Detention without trial is really a denial of the democratic rights of a Kenyan national. I believe that every Kenyan has a right to a fair trial in an open court of law. I was not tried in an open court of law. I have never, even now, been told any specific reasons for my detention. I was therefore stripped arbitrarily of my democratic rights as a Kenyan.

The treatment of a detainee in Kenya reduces human beings to the level of animals. The treatment strips every detainee of every human right. For instance, as I said, I was put into Kamiti Maximum Security Prison like a convicted criminal. I had no access to radio or newspapers. I was for a period confined to a cell for twenty-one hours a day under the full glare of an electric bulb. This is mental torture. I found that other detainees had been under similar conditions of being confined for twenty-one hours a day for the previous two years. I had no privacy whatsoever. I was also told that I had to be chained as a condition for seeing my family or for medical treatment. Disease is thus used as a form of physical and mental torture. And the occasion of a family visit is used to humiliate a political detainee because of being asked to be chained as a condition for seeing them. So that though I personally had no direct experience of physical beating in detention, I was always under extreme mental and psychological torture. One is constantly being harassed mentally. I think that the purpose of detention in Kenya has been to break up a person physically and mentally. In other words, to produce a human wreck, a vegetable.

As for the so-called Detainees Review Tribunal, which meets with detainees every six months, it is nothing more than a screening team. It has only powers for advice. This tribunal never tells you why you have been arrested or detained. They plead ignorance about any background on your case. And as I said, their recommendations whatever they are (since they are never communicated to detainees) are never mandatory on the part of the authority that detained you.

While in detention were you in solitary confinement or were you living with other men?

I was lucky in that I was put where there were nineteen other detainees. And I was very impressed by the way in which these detainees had been able to withstand prison pressures for the last three, four, ten years. The detainees also struck me, on the whole, as people who were extremely patriotic, people who loved Kenya and people who had been put in [prison] because they had spoken about the poverty of the masses, or rather people who had spoken for the rights of the poor. So, I should say I was very impressed with them, and I shall never forget my one year of interaction with them in prison. I learnt a lot.

Do you feel any bitterness about your detention?

Well, frankly, I'm very bitter. Detention without trial is nothing not to be bitter about. In fact, I have become even more bitter when peasants and workers come and ask me: "Why did they come and detain you? Why did they treat you so cruelly? Is it because of the play that we did at Kamiriithu? What wrong things did we do in the play?" I find myself at a loss to know what to tell them. Secondly, by not being told why I was arrested and detained for one year, it gave rise to all sorts of rumors and speculations. I know some write-ups about my detention, including I'm afraid, write-ups in the Stellascope publications, tried to implicate me with all sorts of dreamt-up things: like being in possession of banned literature, or being connected with student uprisings, and strange things like that. And I'm bitter because I know, deep in my heart, that the peasant and worker initiative is the correct thing for Kenyan culture. Detention is a horrible institution. It should be abolished.

So you were not in possession of banned literature?

First of all, I believe it is very wrong to ban any literature. I think Kenyans have a right to the literature published nationally, and also to literature published internationally. But once there is a law about possessing certain literatures, I am very careful not to be in possession of such banned material. The books they took from my house were mostly those by Marx, Lenin, and Engels. And books by them are not banned in Kenya. If they are banned in Kenya, I should be told that they are banned in Kenya. The other books they took were twenty-six copies of *Ngaahika Ndeenda.*

Banning of literature also relates to freedom and democracy. Could you discuss the idea of democracy?

Democracy is really a complex phenomenon. It involves the right of a people to criticize freely without being detained in prison. It involves a people being aware of all their rights. It involves the rights of a people to know how the wealth is produced in the country, who controls that wealth, and for whose benefit that wealth is being utilized. Democracy involves therefore people being aware of the forces shaping their lives. I would say, more immediately, it involves people having all their rights. I would even go so far as to say it involves the rights of a people to decent housing, decent clothing, and decent food. It involves a people's right to all the benefits of modern science. It involves a people's right to be able to write freely in the languages of their own choice.

For instance, I believe I was detained because of my creative writing. And also, for the position I have consistently held in the struggles of our national languages and national cultures to free themselves from the stranglehold of foreign languages and cultures. I still hold those views, even more strongly. I still hold that our Kenyan culture must be totally free from foreign domination in at least the following areas: Our national languages, e.g. Kiswahili, Kikuyu, Dholuo, Kikalenjin, Kigiriama, Kimaasai, Kikamba, Kiluhya, and the languages of all the other nationalities have a right to develop. At present, these national languages have been relegated to the dustbins. Instead, English, French, German are given the pride of place in our schools. By being so encouraged to hate their national languages, the children are being encouraged to hate, or at least, to despise the begetters of these languages, i.e. their peasant parents. And they are thus encouraged to admire the begetters of English, French, German, i.e. foreigners.

The children also come to hate or look down upon the cultures carried by their national languages, i.e. the peasant-based national cultures. By the same token, they come to admire the cultures carried by foreign languages, in this case, foreign cultures. Look at our theater for instance. Our theater is dominated by foreigners. The so-called Kenya National Theatre is controlled by foreigners and by foreign-based groups, like City Players. This is reflected in the administration of the Kenya Cultural Centre. The British Council have their offices there. The chairman of the governing council is a British national. Ninety-nine percent of the plays at the Kenya National Theatre and in other theaters in Kenya are all foreign. Look at the plays currently in fashion at the National Theatre. *Oklahoma*, for instance. Other titles are equally interesting: *Gulliver*, *Carmen*, *The King and I*; this is the kind of cultural fare which is being ladled to us Kenyan people. If you look at the record, you'll see that foreign theater in foreign languages has been allowed to flourish freely with governmental encouragement. The Kenya National Theatre is, for example, under the Ministry of Social Services.

National theater in national languages, on the other hand, has not been encouraged. There has been governmental suppression of theater in national languages. And the best example is Kamiriithu Community Education and Cultural Centre at Limuru which produced a play which was seen by thousands of peasants and workers from all over the area. Then the license to perform this was withdrawn, and one of the authors was detained in a maximum security prison.

It is these kinds of things tnat make me feel that national theater, national literature, in national languages have tended to be suppressed, and in their stead, national theater and literature in foreign languages have been allowed to flourish. To go further, I believe that our national theater, our national literature, can only be truly so if they are based in our national languages, and if they correctly reflect our society and the class forces that are at work in that society. For instance, I believe that the play, *Ngaahika Ndeenda*, was very popular because it talked about the extreme poverty of the people. I believe the play was popular because it talked about landlessness in our country. I believe the play was popular because it talked about the betrayal of the peasants and workers by the political "big-wigs." I believe the play was popular because it talked about the arrogance and the greed of the powerful and the wealthy. Again, I believe the play was popular because it depicted the true conditions of the rural people in the rural villages. And so on.

It reminds me in a sense of the image in *Petals of Blood* where a huge tree, a ruthless huge tree, is seen as suffocating little plants and preventing them from reaching out to the light. So I come back to that belief that we must be able to develop our national languages and develop literatures in those national languages, and that that literature must be able to freely and correctly mirror our society in all its strengths and weaknesses. It is only through this kind of mirroring of the truth, or mirroring what is actually happening in our society, that we can build unity and democracy in Kenya.

You have recently described yourself as a "student" of the peasants of Kenya. Could you explain what that means to you?

To answer that question fully, I'd like to see the play *Ngaahika Ndeenda* being restaged in order for everybody to see what peasants and workers can do, when given a chance. This play was not a one-man's act. It was the result of cooperation among many people. For instance, the whole of the Gitiiro opera sequence in the play was written word for word at the dictation of an illiterate peasant woman at Kamiriithu. And anyone who saw the play could tell you that the Gitiiro opera sequence in the play was one of the most beautiful, the most wonderful aesthetic experiences on the Kenyan stage.

Again, if you see the high level of acting and presentation by the peasants and workers at Kamiriithu in that play, you will realize that we have much more to learn from the peasants and workers than we can give them. If you see how they utilize language, how they have collectively designed and constructed their open air theater, then you will realize what potential there is in Kenyan people when allowed to rely on their resources. So I would say that if you want to see your question properly answered, ask the authorities to let the play be restaged so that everybody can be in no doubt as to what kind of play it was, the kind of performance it was, and everything the whole presentation pictured.

You have been the chairman of the Literature Department at the University of Nairobi. Could you tell us what your status is vis-à-vis *the University. And what are your plans for the future?*

At present, I have no plans. I have been waiting to hear a word from the University. But the University has been silent about my position. I have had, in the same period, offers of jobs abroad at fantastic salaries. But at the same time, I know that I cannot accept any job abroad, no matter how high the salary. I am much happier working in a small village, trying to build our culture together with other people. At present I am simply trying to rest and think about one or two things. You see, I have been away for a whole year.

Could you discuss any literary plans you may have for the future?

At present I am not involved in the writing of anything. Nevertheless, *Ngaahika Ndeenda* showed me the road along which I should have been traveling all these past seventeen years of my writing career.

You have been away for a year. Could you discuss the changes you have observed—politically, socially, economically, culturally—since you have been back?

I am trying to read up old newspapers and trying to learn from people what has been happening in our country for the last one year. Nevertheless, I don't think there have been fundamental changes in our society. For instance, I went to Nairobi the other day, and it seemed to me that in one year there are fewer Africans and more foreigners in Nairobi. And I doubt whether anything has been done about the exploitation of Kenya's wealth by foreign merchants. So that foreign economic and cultural interests, in alliance with some locals, are still ravaging our country and nation. But I think that no country can truly develop while the speed of the outflow of wealth from the country is higher than the inflow of wealth into the country. In other words, I don't believe we can really develop while our wealth still goes to feed merchants in foreign countries.

15 Ngugi on Ngugi

Amooti wa Irumba / 1979 (1990)

This selection derives from an 85-page interview conducted in Limuru by Katebaliirwe Amooti wa Irumba on January 6 and 11, 1979, shortly after Ngugi's release from detention; the complete interview forms Appendix 2 of Amooti's University of Sussex Ph.D. dissertation. The complete interview is an important source of information about Ngugi's life and ideas; these extracts, which have been edited, add to what Ngugi has said in autobiographical remarks scattered through his non-fiction and in other interviews. The title given the interview by Amooti—"He Who Produces Should Be Able to Control That Which He Produces"—is taken from a passage that clearly prefigures a central theme of Matigari.

My parents lived partly on land, cultivating little stretches of land here and there, eking a living, and also working on other people's land for wages. My father and mother separated in 1946 or 1947, and thereafter my mother was the one who took care of us; that is, us three brothers and three sisters. She virtually shouldered *every* responsibility of our struggle for food, shelter, clothing, and education. It was my mother who initially suggested that I go to school. I remember those nights when I would come back home from school, and not knowing that she could not read or write, I would tell her everything that I had learnt in school or read to her something, and she would listen very keenly and give me a word of advice here and there.

My parents were not Christians. But at the same time they did not practice much of the Gikuyu forms of worship. My father was skeptical of religious and magical practices that went with rites of passages and rhythms of the seasons. He believed in land and hard work. The landlord on whose land we lived was an elder in the P.C.E.A. [Presbyterian Church of East Africa], then called the Church of Scotland Mission.

I remember one Christmas the wife of the landlord invited the children of the peasants to her house for a cup of tea and bread. The mountain of the slices of bread looked very alluring to us children, and we were eager to get on with the job of demolishing the mountain. But then she told us to pray. My brother and I opened our eyes and looked at one another, and we read the thoughts expressed in each other's face. We laughed in the midst of prayer, and we were heavily reprimanded by the lady of the house. She pointed out the differences between the religious Christian upbringing of her children, which made them possess good manners in God's presence, and that of peasants, which made us possess terrible manners even in Godly presence.

••••

When I grew up I was very much aware of the physical confrontation between foreigners and Kenyans at Limuru. On one side of Limuru was the land controlled by the foreign settlers, and on the other side was the land controlled by peasants and Kenyan landlords. These two sides were divided by the famous railway line from Mombasa to Kampala. Now, the effects of European settlement were basically two. First was the forced removal of peasants from their land, which meant that now they were congested in very tiny dry areas, what the colonial government called the African reserves. Secondly, this same act of forced removal of peasants from their land, and hence their divorce from ownership and control of the means of production, created the beginning of a proletariat in Kenya. The buyers and hirers of this labor power of the people of Limuru were, of course, the settlers, to work their coffee, tea, and pyrethrum plantations. But around 1940, there was built a shoe-manufacturing factory at Limuru owned by the foreign-owned East African Bata Shoe Company, and later a pig processing plant at Uplands, Uplands Bacon Factory. And so from around this time you began to get an industrial proletariat in Limuru employed by foreign capitalists. This pattern, I think, has continued to the present: a peasantry, a rural proletariat (many now working on farms of African settlers who replaced European settlers), and a growing industrial proletariat....

In all my novels I have produced the foreign settlers and their class relationships in Kenya, from this historical experience of Kenya. Again in all my novels I have produced the 1948 general strike of Kenyan workers which at Limuru was carried out by workers at the Bata Shoe factory. So, right from the beginning I was groping towards some kind of class appreciation of our society in Limuru.... I grew up under the influence of Gikuyu peasant culture—songs, stories, proverbs, riddles around the fireside in the evenings—as well as those values that govern human relationships in a peasant community....

••••

It was said that in the foreign missionary schools some things were deliberately held back from students to keep them ignorant about certain facts and aspects of life under colonists. But in the national [Gikuyu Karing'a] schools everything was deliberately given to the students to prepare them to face up to the harsh social conditions under colonialism....In those national schools one was made aware of colonialism as an oppressive force, whereas in the foreign mission schools colonialism was seen as a good thing. National songs, poems, and dances played a very important role in national schools while in the foreign schools Christian hymns played the central role. In other words, in the national schools peasant cultures were at the center; they were glorified or upheld, developed and perpetuated. But in the missionary schools foreign culture and foreign cultural forms of expression were glorified and used to destroy all peasant cultures.

Alliance High School was, of course, very different from all my previous experiences of schools. For one thing, most of the teachers were foreigners; in fact, most of them were British. The emphasis in the education offered to us at Alliance was on production of Africans who would later become efficient machines for running a colonial system. Therefore in Alliance High School politics was frowned upon; Kenyan nationalists were castigated: They were seen as irresponsible agitators, hooligans, and undesirable specimens of human beings. So we were presented with two diametrically opposed images: the image of the Kenyan patriot as a negative human being and the image of the oppressor and his collaborator as positive human beings. Obviously the aim was to make us identify with the image of the collaborator, and to make us grow to admire and acquire all the values that go hand in hand with collaboration with imperialism.

One of my earliest experiences at that school, in 1955, was taking part in a debate on a motion that Western education had done more harm than good. Although I was new in the school, I remember quite vividly standing up and trembling with anger, and saying that Western education could not be equated with the land taken from the peasants by the British. And I remember holding up a fountain pen and giving the example of someone who comes and takes away food from your mouth and then gives you a fountain pen instead. I asked the audience: Can you eat a fountain pen? Can you clothe yourself with a fountain pen or shelter yourself with it? It was, in fact, my bold participation in that debate that made other students in later years elect me secretary of the Debating Society....I remember the headmaster once calling me into his office and warning me never to become a political agitator, that all political agitators were scoundrels.... There was, though, a period when I became rather too serious a Christian, waking up for prayers at five o'clock in the mornings. This may have cut the wings off my social concerns.

My interest in writing really goes back as far as my primary school days. That's when I read Stevenson, Dickens, and many other abridged versions of works by many European writers which were introduced to us by our then teacher of English, Samuel Kibicho. I remember in primary school arguing with a fellow student, Kenneth Bugwa. He told me that one could write a book and I told him, no, you cannot write a book; you might be arrested and imprisoned because you would not be qualified to do so. He was very adamant and argued quite correctly that one did not need to be highly educated, or to be licensed, in order to write a book. This argument had a strange consequence. When I went to high school, my friend went to a teacher training school. In his first year he started to write a book to prove to me that one could do so without being arrested. I can't remember now the fate of his novel, but he sent me excerpts in 1955 when I was in Form One at Alliance High School. I used to say to myself that when I grew up I would like to write the kind of stories people like Stevenson and Dickens had written.

At Alliance High School I was lucky, in that the library was quite adequate for a school like that. There were many novels, and I used to read them. I read Dickens, but also a lot of racist writing like Rider Haggard's *King Solomon's Mines* and the Biggles series by Captain W. E. Johns.* Also, I read liberal writers like Alan Paton. I also remember reading many thrillers, and my first literary attempt was an imitation of the American thriller writer Edgar Wallace. I sent this story to *Baraza* [a government-sponsored magazine], which used to run a kind of literary page in Kenya—that was in 1956—but it was rejected. I remember once stumbling upon Tolstoy's *Childhood, Boyhood, Youth*, and one of my only two published efforts at Alliance was a short remembrance of my childhood influenced by my reading of Tolstoy. There were, of course, the texts used in our literature classes, like Shakespeare's *Macbeth* and *Julius Caesar*; Bernard Shaw's *Man and Superman*; Scott's *Ivanhoe*; and poems by Wordsworth, Longfellow, and Tennyson. Our headmaster was particularly fond of the arch-imperialist poet Rudyard Kipling, and he always made us copy and recite his poems, in particular "If."

At Makerere University the course was based on the syllabus for English studies at the University of London. Thus it was a degree in the history of English literature, from the Celtic times to T. S. Eliot, as well as in the history of the English language. But the real importance of my studying at Makerere lay in this: that for the first time, I came into contact with African and West Indian writers. I remember three authors and books as being particularly important to me: Chinua Achebe's *Things Fall Apart*, George Lamming's *In the Castle of My Skin*, and Peter Abrahams's *Tell Freedom*. At Alliance I had seen *Tell Freedom* held by one of the teachers, and I can remember literally trembling when I saw the title. When I found the book in the library at Makerere, I was overjoyed. I read it avidly and later I read virtually all the books by Peter Abrahams—that was the beginning of my interest in South African literature. Achebe's *Things Fall Apart* started me on West African writers; from then on I followed closely the growth of West African literature. I used to go to the library and look up every item of fiction in West African journals and magazines, especially work by Cyprian Ekwensi (who, I came to learn, was also an admirer of Peter Abrahams). As for George Lamming, his work introduced me to West Indian writers, and this was the beginning of my interest in the literature of the African people in the Third World. Makerere was also important because of the central role of *Penpoint*, which had become the forum for writers in East and Central Africa.

So I would say that Makerere was very important for me because, side by side with the formal literary education, I had through the library access to the kind of literature that told me of another world, a world which was in many instances my own. But African literature and all Third World literature was *nowhere* in the syllabus. African writers were never mentioned in tutorials or in seminars. I discovered them for myself in the library. It was, in fact, a big surprise when I learnt through my own efforts that African and Third World people had, in fact, been writing for a long time—people like Aimé Césaire from the West Indies or other Negritude writers of Senghor's generation. There had been a lot of writing going on in Africa by Africans, and in the rest of the Third World, for centuries. So just as at Alliance High School, I was once again confronted with two diametrically opposed images—the official or Eurocentric image as it emerged through the kind of curriculum I was exposed to in the English Department, and the image of a struggling world as it emerged through the kind of literature that I discovered for myself in the library.

••••

At Leeds University there was at that time a radical intellectual tradition which had grown side by side with a conservative, formal tradition. And as was the case at Makerere, I once again identified with the unofficial, radical tradition. Leeds exposed me to a wider literary world; it made me aware of the radical literature that embraced the Third World as well as the socialist world.

I can remember very well the person who first introduced Frantz Fanon to Leeds. It was Grant Kamenju. He went to Paris, and in an obscure little bookshop he found Fanon's book *The Damned*, which was later published outside France under the title *The Wretched of the Earth.* And of course this book was a very important eye-opener for me and for other African students at Leeds. I think this was the only Fanon book I read at that time, but I read quite a lot of Caribbean literature, at the same time writing *A Grain of Wheat*, and arguing a lot about the problems of colonialism, neo-colonialism, and imperialism, as well as traveling widely in Europe.

The political literature of Karl Marx and Friedrich Engels was important and soon overshadowed Fanon. Or rather, Marx and Engels began to reveal the serious weaknesses and limitations of Fanon, especially his own petit bourgeois idealism that led him into a mechanical overemphasis on psychology and violence, and his inability to see the significance of the rising and growing African proletariat. I avidly read Engels's *Socialism: Utopian and Scientific*; Marx's Preface to Engels's *A Contribution to the Critique of Political Economy*; some sections of *The German Ideology*; Engels's *Anti-Dühring*; and the first volume of Marx's *Capital* as well as his two studies on class struggles, *The Class Struggles in France* and *The Eighteenth Brumaire of Louis Bonaparte*. I was excited when I read in Engels's *Anti-Dühring* the notion that movement and hence change was fundamental in nature, human society, and thought, and that this motion was the result of the unity and struggle of opposites. I tried to use this notion in *A Grain of Wheat*, especially through the image of a grain which has to die in order to bear life. I would single out Lenin's work *Imperialism, the Highest Stage of Capitalism* as an eye-opener on the nature of imperialism in its colonial and neo-colonial stages. Even today I still think that this work ought to be compulsory reading for all students of African and Third World literatures. My first exposure to Marxist literature at Leeds University was also through many of the public lectures organized by the students outside the formal academic mainstream. Writers of progressive imaginative literature—people like Brecht and Gorky—were also important to me. Gorky's novel *Mother* should be read by all African patriots.

Those who produce should control the wealth; *he who produces should be able to control that which he produces*. We have a Gikuyu saying that *Muumbi arugagana icere*, literally meaning that "the

Creator or producer of pottery often cooks in broken pieces or in cracked pots." This describes aptly the nature of any class society, and more so, a class society under capitalism. Labor produces. Capital disposes. The maker or producer of pottery produces pots but he has no pot for his own use; the shoemaker makes shoes, but he walks barefoot; the builder builds magnificent houses, but he himself does not live in them—instead he continues to live in shacks; the mason builds wonderful cities but he himself has nowhere to live; the tailor makes super clothes, but he goes naked, or at best in tattered dress; the miner digs gold, coal, and other minerals and precious stones or extracts oil, but he himself has no decent clothes or shelter or food or cows; the soldier does the risky business of fighting, but glory and honor and salary increases go to the generals; peasants produce food, but they and their own go naked or badly dressed and hungry; the so-called underdeveloped world feeds and clothes and shelters the imperialist world, financing its luxury and arts and sciences and technology, but this underdeveloped world remains impoverished and an object of charity, like the hunting dog that ends up feeding on bones after the master has finished all the meat. The palace walls of a handful of capitalists are painted with the blood and sweat of a million hands. This handful has an army of intellectuals and artists, journalists, parliamentarians, etc., who rationalize and justify this exploitative relationship. But it is also true that all over the world the million hands are in revolt against that exploitative status quo.

••••

I think that if the novel is to be meaningful it must reflect the totality of the forces affecting the lives of the people. And all the great novels, even in the bourgeois critical and literary tradition, have reflected this totality of forces at a particular moment of history. Take a novel like Tolstoy's *War and Peace* or his *Anna Karenina*—surely you will find that not much is left out of these novels. Most of the economic, political, cultural, and spiritual forces at work in Russian society of the nineteenth century are reflected there....On the other side I find very disturbing the tendency by bourgeois and petits bourgeois critics to equate negative aspects of human beings with the true human condition; that is, if you show people as stupid, cowardly, vacillating, always terrified of death or life, sometimes wanting to commit suicide out of sheer despair, then you are said by those same critics to be depicting the true human condition. Why should we equate weakness with the true human condition? On the contrary, I would have thought that resistance to oppression and exploitation, the strong desire in human beings to overcome the negative aspects of nature and all the things that inhibit the free development of their lives—this is the most important of human qualities....We know that the transformations of the twentieth century have been the results of the struggles of peasants and workers. So how can we say that these two classes, whose labor has changed nature, are weak, naive, stupid, and cowardly?

••••

Previously there was a tendency to have peasant and worker characters but give them the vacillating mentality and world outlook of the petite bourgeoisie. This is evident especially in my portrayal of peasant characters in *A Grain of Wheat*. What I have tried to do in *Petals of Blood* is to depict peasant and worker characters in their world outlook and also in their own view of classes and their relationships within their struggle, and especially as a people capable of freeing themselves from the clutches of their enemies, because this is historically true.

••••

The African people must primarily rely on their own resources. To me this seems to be very, very crucial. We've got a saying in Gikuyu that *Ngemi Ciumaga na Mucii*, that is, "the strength of a people must come from themselves, or from the homestead." Only after this can others find the basis for aiding them. You cannot go to war with your eyes on the strength of your friends. That way lies slavery and domination.

---

* Captain W. E. Johns (1893-1968), a former British Air Force officer, wrote 102 adventure stories featuring Biggles, a pilot who later becomes an Interpol detective—all intended, he said, to teach

boys "the spirit of teamwork, loyalty to the Crown, the Empire, and to rightful authority." Despite the jingoism, racism, and stereotypical slang that characterizes the later as well as the earlier books (published in the early 1930s), they remained popular.

16 *BBC Arts and Africa* Interview with Ngugi wa Thiong'o about Literary and Theatrical Activities in Kenya

Greg Wilesmith / 1980

Hello, this is [...] another edition of Arts and Africa. *In a recent program we heard about the current cultural scene in Kenya and, of course, much that we heard revolved around the doings of the controversial novelist and playwright Ngugi wa Thiong'o. Ngugi was, of course, imprisoned by the Kenyan authorities after the production of a play in Kikuyu but was released, following a world-wide outcry, in the general amnesty that followed President Kenyatta's death. However, the full reasons for Ngugi's imprisonment have never been officially stated and he has not been allowed to take up his university post again. So we on* Arts and Africa *were very keen to find out Ngugi's current thinking and were happy to receive an interview from Greg Wilesmith in Nairobi. They began by talking about the recent seminar organized by the Writers Association of Kenya whose subject was the Freedom of the Artist in Kenya—a subject of obvious interest to Ngugi himself.*

The seminar was really held to discuss the status of the artist in Kenya because currently UNESCO will be discussing the same issue at their next conference, so this was part of the contribution by the Writers Association of Kenya toward a discussion and evolution of the status of the artist in Africa. But in Kenya there has been what we consider a very bad or wrong tendency toward restricting the freedom of the artist, and there have been certain instances in Kenya since Independence when writers have been put in prison or harassed in one form or another by the State.

The most important case was Abdilatif Abdalla, the well-known Swahili poet who was for three years put in a maximum security prison for writing a pamphlet saying "Kenya Twendapi?"—"Kenya, where are we heading to?" Then in 1977 there was a case of them stopping the public performances of a play presented by the peasants and workers at the Kamiriithu Education and Cultural Centre in Limuru and subsequent detention of one of the authors of the play, that is, myself, for a year. In the same year another writer and critic, Dr. Micere Mugo, was tortured in police cells. Much more recently in 1979, there was a case of some girls at a secondary school who wrote a play called "What a World—My People!" which was officially entered for a national drama competition. The play was performed in English to enthusiastic audiences but the moment they translated the play into Kikuyu and performed it for their peasant parents, the police moved in and stopped the performance of the play. Subsequently, all the girls involved in writing the play or in acting in the play were expelled from the school. Let me put it this way, the girls were expelled from the school under one pretext or another, but it was very noticeable that all the girls expelled had been involved in the play. I am talking about a general tendency, since Independence, for increasing repressive measures against writers and artists.

Does that take the form of action against people who, like yourself, tend to try and express their thoughts in their tribal languages rather than in the national language of Swahili?

It is very difficult to tell. First of all, of course, we don't call them tribal languages; they are national languages. [...] If you want to communicate with peasants and workers, whoever you are, no matter what part of Kenya you come from, then you have to choose a language understood by those peasants and workers. The fact that it will not be understood by *all* peasants and workers in Kenya is really beside the issue because if you write in the English language, not a single worker or peasant will understand you, whereas if you write in Kikuyu or in Luo or Kiswahili or in Luyia or Giryama, or Maasai, or Kalenjin, at least a section of the peasantry and workers will understand you so you will be communicating with a section of a national audience. Then, of course, there is the time-honored part of translations. For instance, I have now published a play, *Ngaahika Ndeenda*, and the play is in the Kikuyu language. I have also published a novel called *Caitaani Mutharaba-ini* which is in the Kikuyu language but the novel and the play are in the process of translation into Kiswahili and into English and into other national languages from Kenya, certainly in Luo. So it means that if you write in one of the many national languages in Kenya, there is no reason why that work should not be available through translations to all the other communities in Kenya. It is just a matter of time, say two weeks, in between one production and another, or a month or a year. Whereas when you write in each language, you automatically exclude about three-quarters of the population from participation in the literary dialogue.

You're in the process now, I understand, of translating your book Devil on the Cross *from Kikuyu to English. Can you tell me of some of the frustrations of doing that? Do you find that you can't communicate your thoughts as effectively in English as you did in Kikuyu?*

I have never been involved in any translation before, so I am finding it a very challenging task. It is extremely difficult, you know, because the two languages have their own logic and they've been molded by two different cultural experiences; because their syntax is different, Kikuyu grammar is very different from English grammar, and so on. Some expressions are really very difficult to put into each language because they assume a certain knowledge of the culture of the people. When I am writing in Kikuyu, there are many things that I assume my reading public will know so I need only to write to them. Now, to try and put these across in English means a certain amount of difficulties because you cannot, as it were, translate the national cultural heritage into the same book. This is really the main problem.

Can I come back to something, a controversy I suppose you would call it, in Kenya earlier this year. You refused to attend a writers' conference organized by the Goethe Institute. Can you tell me the real reason why you didn't attend that?

There are two reasons. One was, I think, professional ethics. What happened was that my name was put on the program as one of the main speakers. This program was widely circulated but they, the organizers, had never communicated with me to ask me whether I was going to speak on this specific topic at the particular time and day. So I just got a program from my friend telling me that he was going to attend the conference in order to hear my speech. Now I was very, very surprised so I said, "This is wrong on professional grounds." You don't put a person's name on a program without asking for his permission, and even then you don't circulate the program as a definite thing. So I objected to that. Secondly, I have always objected to foreign embassies organizing or trying to organize culture for Kenyans. I believe that it is only Kenyans who can really organize culture for Kenyans.

On that subject though, turning to the National Theatre in Kenya, do you think there is foreign interference in the running of that theater?

Definitely, because for a long time, even today, the Kenya National Theatre is dominated by foreign theater groups, groups like "The City Players," groups like "Theatre Limited" and even recently people like Annabelle Maule who sold her own theater to a private company to come and use facilities at the Kenya National Theatre. You find that there are very few Kenyan-based plays or plays written by Kenyans or Africans, you know, in the National Theatre. For Kenyan theater groups to get access to the theater, it is really an uphill task. So you get a really ridiculous situation in the Kenyan cultural scene, for you find foreign groups performing the history of King Edward, performing plays about Queen Mary and her troubles with Queen Elizabeth in the sixteenth century, having such musicals as *Oklahoma*, or *Boeing, Boeing*, *The King and I* and French ballet and things like that.

Any ideas on how to change this present situation at the National Theatre?

Oh, this is entirely a matter for the Government. The Kenya National Theatre is owned by the Kenyan Government; it's under the Ministry of Culture and Social Services so I think it is for *them* to do something about it. I believe that possibly with the creation of the Minister of Culture and Social Services, something may be done about it. I also believe that recently the Government has set up the Kenya Cultural Council and hopefully this may change things, but only hopefully, I can only wait and see.

One final subject. Do you anticipate you will ever regain your position at the University of Nairobi?

I doubt it.

For what reasons?

Well, I made an application as the University advertised the vacant posts in November 1979. So far, eight months after, no appointment committee has been called, but only for those particular posts. So I am very skeptical about such possibilities.

You had a lot of support at the University?

Yes, the University staff and students, virtually all the staff and all the students would want me to go back to the University. But some people somewhere are hell-bent on preventing me from resuming my teaching duties at the University, although the termination of my duties at the University was entirely illegal.

The University Staff Union has given the University Council an August deadline to reinstate you.

Well, it has been banned.

The University Staff Union has been banned?

Yes.

So you don't think anything will come of that?

Well, I mean I have no idea really but it has been banned and so is no longer operative.

Ngugi wa Thiong'o, thank you very much.

17 Ngugi wa Thiong'o: Interview

Jürgen Martini, Anna Rutherford, Kirsten Holst Petersen, Vibeke Stenderup, Bent Thomsen / 1980 (1981)

Ngugi wa Thiong'o was invited to Denmark by the Danish Library Association to take part in their 75th anniversary celebrations. Whilst in Denmark he visited Aarhus University and was interviewed by the following persons: Jürgen Martini, Anna Rutherford, Kirsten Holst Petersen, Vibeke Stenderup, and Bent Thomsen. The interview took place on 9 December 1980.

KHP: *Ever since you have been here you have been involved in a discussion about Karen Blixen. Would you like to say something about this?*

I must say she is one of my pet subjects. This is partly because she illustrates some attitudes by a certain type of European or Western mind towards Africa, and so when I'm illustrating these attitudes towards Africa by certain racist writers I try to use examples from her. Her name cropped up when I was talking to the Danish Library Association and I mentioned the two or the three types of Africa to be found in the Western bourgeois mind. There is the Africa of the hunter for profit, that is, the Africa of the direct economic exploiter. Then we have the Africa of the hunter for pleasure, that is, the tourist's Africa. I also mentioned that the Africa of the tourist was essentially the Africa of the hunter after profit. The third Africa which I spoke of is the Africa found in the fiction of a certain type of European writer which sets out to interpret the African scene. It was in this context that I quoted Karen Blixen. I find her sinister in the sense that her racism is passed off as an act of love. My main argument is that her declared *love* for the African is really the same kind of love which you exhibit towards an animal. She made definite distinctions between human beings who were Europeans, and animals who were Africans. Within that basic understanding she could love Africans of all sexes, as she says, but very much as part and parcel of the animal landscape. Just to illustrate this point: She creates a character who is her cook and as she is a very gifted writer with words, phrases and details, she is able to create characters we can see visually. But in the end she compares Kamante (her cook) to a civilized dog that has long lived among human beings. In her book *Shadows in the Grass* which was published by Michael Joseph in 1960 she repeats the same racist mythology about Africa. In this book she said quite categorically that African grown-up people had all the mentality of European children of nine. According to her there were some who were a bit more advanced, e.g. the Somali, and they had all the mentality of the European child of seventeen. Now Karen Blixen of course is only one among many who held these racist attitudes towards Africa. They include writers like Elspeth Huxley, Robert Ruark, Rider Haggard, philosophers like Hegel, historians like Trevor Roper, plus many others. In other words she belongs to a certain category of writers about Africa.

KHP: *Do you find that she differs from that other set of writers that you mentioned?*

No, she is basically the same except that she goes beyond them in the sense that at least the others do in a certain strange sense recognize the humanity of the African even when they hate it. But Karen Blixen doesn't say "I hate Africans," she says "I love them," but she loves them as she loves children or animals. In her book *Out of Africa* she says that when she first came to Kenya she studied the game and then she says, "What I learnt from the game of Africa was very useful to me when I later came to deal with the natives"; in other words, in extending this one might say that her study or knowledge of the wild animals gave her a clue to the mentality of the African. So I would argue that she is more dangerous than all of them because she does not concede any humanity to the African. Her love of the African is only when he is understood as an animal or a child. Now when this is understood and accepted she can even be very passionate about him, she can weep, treat him, miss him, she can evoke all the emotions that human beings often have towards a wild creature, and this I'm afraid has been mistaken to mean that she has recognized the humanity of the African when in fact her love is based on a rejection of that humanity.

VS: *Since you have been in Denmark you have met a number of Danish writers and people interested in African literature and in cooperation between rich and poor countries. Do you feel that later generations of Karen Blixen's fellow-countrymen are to be trusted so that there is some sense in continuing the cooperation, or do you feel that the country is better left to itself?*

You put a number of things together. The question of people meeting and having a healthy dialogue is very important. People like Karen Blixen are in fact a barrier to this kind of a dialogue, so by trying to focus attention on a writer like Karen Blixen I would like to see Danish people face up to the content in her work and not just see the beauty of the prose. In that way people can begin to have a real dialogue, even if it is a dialogue about aid. When people like Karen Blixen were developing the racial myths and ideology, in essence it was not really personal. They did it on behalf of certain class and historical forces at work in the world then and even today, and the reason why she is being revived is because the same mythology is having a certain ideological purpose as far as exploitation of Africa today is concerned. Karen Blixen was more than a Danish person, she was the spokesman for the imperialist bourgeoisie or imperialist forces of the exploiting classes all over the world. That is why she is very acceptable in America, in Germany and in England because she articulates an ideology which makes the exploitation of Africa more acceptable. What such writers want to prevent you from seeing is that the wealth of Europe is based on the poverty of Africa. As I told the Danish Library Association, they do a tremendous service to the Danish people in this dialogue we have been talking about, if they bring home to the Danish people that Europe's unbounded wealth is based on the exploitation of Africa. As Brecht reminded us: The food eaten by the wealthy classes in Europe is "snatched from the mouths of the hungry" in the developing world, and the water that they drink is taken from the mouths of the thirsty. We have a saying which is a practice amongst the farmers of my country that when they want to milk a cow they give it some grass so that they can milk it better. Aid is the grass, given to a cow whilst it is being milked.

KHP: *You have said that Karen Blixen serves this ideological purpose. Why do you think there is a need to revive this ideology* *now?*

Because the exploitation of Africa still continues, and this exploitation in the neo-colonialist period of imperialism still needs an appropriate ideology. Karen Blixen, whose racism is projected as love, is more appropriate to exploitation in the neo-colonialist phase than the crude, obvious racism of people like Elspeth Huxley or Robert Ruark. These will not do, but Karen Blixen will do very well.

JM: *During the Frankfurt Book Fair there was a long discussion about what language an African writer should use. There have been some who say you are no longer a Kenyan writer. Perhaps you can say something about this.*

I certainly make a distinction between literature written by Africans in European languages and the literature written by Africans in African languages. A literature written by Africans in European languages is what I now call Afro-European literature: in other words those of us who have been writing in English, French or Portuguese have not been writing African literature at all; we have been writing a branch of literature that can only meaningfully go under the title of Afro-European literature. This is to be distinguished very firmly from that literature written by Africans in African languages, treating African themes. The question of language is obviously fundamental here; as Fanon said, "to choose a language is to choose a world." In the same way when you choose a language, objectively you are choosing an audience, and more particularly a class. You cannot possibly write in English and assume that you are writing for the African peasantry, or even a section of that peasantry. There is no way, because the moment you write in English you assume a readership who can speak and read English, and in this case it can only mean the educated African élite or the foreigners who speak the language. This means that you are precluding in terms of class the peasantry of Africa, or the workers in Africa who do not read or understand these foreign languages.

There are other aspects to language which can only be understood in the colonial context. The colonizing people or nations or classes looked down upon African languages; indeed, in some cases African children at school were given corporal punishment for speaking their own languages. Others have been made to carry humiliating signs for speaking African languages, signs saying "I am stupid!" What happens to the mentality of a child when you humiliate him or her in relationship to a particular language? Obviously he comes to associate that language with inferiority or with humiliation and punishment, so he must somehow develop antagonistic attitudes to that language which is the basis of his humiliation. By extension he becomes uncomfortable about the people who created that language and the culture that was carried by it, and by implication he comes to develop positive attitudes to the foreign language for which he is praised and told that he is intelligent once he speaks it well. He also comes to respect and have a positive attitude to the culture carried by the foreign language, and of course comes to have a positive attitude to the people who created the language which was the basis for the high marks he was getting in school. What does this mean in practical terms? It means that he comes to feel uncomfortable about the peasant masses or working masses who are using that language. So while we African writers continue to write in European languages we are in fact perpetuating a neo-colonial cultural tradition. No matter the subject matter of our novels and plays and poems, and no matter the attitude towards the classes in those novels, poems and plays. If I say that these things can only be articulated within borrowed tongues it means that even at our progressive or our radical best we are in fact continuing the neo-colonial tradition which we are setting out to oppose. In that way we are involved in an immediate kind of contradiction.

So what happens when you write in an African language? First, you create a positive attitude to that language. The reader, when he feels that this language can carry a novel with philosophical weight or a novel which totally reflects his environment, will develop a positive attitude to that language, to the people who created that language, and to the culture and traditions carried by it. And if he begins to have respect for his immediate language, by extension he will also have a respect for all the other languages that are related to his language and to the history and culture related to that language. So to answer your question: The choice of the Kikuyu language was a very deliberate choice; it was a conscious decision, although I was forced into it by the peculiar historical circumstances in which I found myself.

A further point I would like to add to this: For a long time African languages and cultures have not been communicating with one another, but have been communicating via English; in other words, I have a sense of Igboness in Achebe's novels through his use of English. The moment African writers start writing in African languages some of the novels will be translated into other African languages as well as into English. The moment you get an Igbo novel translated into Kikuyu or a Yoruba novel translated into Hausa you are getting these languages and cultures talking and communicating directly and mutually enriching one another. So far from these languages being a divisive force, they become an integrative force, because they will be enhancing a respect for each other's languages and cultures as well as showing the similarities between the various cultures and their concerns.

JM: *You said that you got an impression of Igboness or Yorubaness through the English language. In what way do you think that we can get an impression of Kikuyu sensibility in your novels through the English language?*

I said maybe one can, but I don't think it is very effective through the English language. I have come to realize this after I have written a novel in Kikuyu and collaborated on a play in Kikuyu. What I want to see is the reader's reaction to my own translation of my Kikuyu novel into English. It will be very interesting to see, assuming that the quality of the novel is about the same as the other novels, whether a different type of sensibility will emerge. There is no way in which one can effectively represent one sensibility in another language because all the nuances in one language cannot be passed on to or carried by another language. In writing the novel in Kikuyu I found myself playing around with sequences of sound patterns for the sheer kick of it and also to suggest a certain kind of meaning. Obviously when I translate this into English it will be lost on the English reader, and there is no way I can help this. This is because the sound patterns and nuances depend on certain cultural assumptions in a community.

AR: *You can reach a large audience with drama. I wonder what size audience you can reach with a novel, even when it is written in Kikuyu?*

Obviously the novel is limited in that sense, but both forms are limited to a certain extent, because a play needs actors, so as long as a play is not being performed it is not reaching anybody. And sometimes you get long periods between performances of a play, whereas the novel is there all the time. But I agree with you that with one performance of a play you are reaching many more people than you can reach in the novel form, and even more important, it is a more collective form, but here—and I want to put quite a big "but"—with the publication of the Kikuyu novel I have had experiences which have made me start to question my own assumptions about the real tradition of the novel. When I was teaching in Nairobi, for instance, I would argue that the bourgeois novel in its reader tradition assumed an individual reader, reading silently. But when the Kikuyu novel came out it was bought by families who would get somebody who reads very well to read for everybody. In other words the novel was appropriated by the peasantry, it became a collective form and part of the oral tradition. Even the people who could read Kikuyu preferred to read it in groups, and I have been told that workers in factories during lunch hour would gather together and get one person to read the novel for them. This has made me start questioning the relationship between the novel and the reader. It could well be that the novel has remained this kind of individual thing between the individual and the reader because it has been appropriated by certain classes, but when it is appropriated by the peasantry and the working classes it may very well be transformed into a collective experience.

KHP: *Can I ask you a few questions about your own work? You are concerned with failures rather than successes. All your main characters set out to do something and they fail in varying degrees.*

I don't think I present them as failures. What I try to do is to present human beings as capable of altering their environment. In other words, I do not see human beings as being slaves to their environment. I try to evoke or create human beings who are capable of altering their natural and social environment, but at the same time I am aware of the historical limitations under which they are working. In other words, I have not meant to present a utopia in which all solutions have not only been found but have actually been practiced.

JM: *You are very successful with your male characters, but when you come to female characters, they either tend to belong to a very traditional society or to an atypical group like prostitutes. One doesn't find the modern emancipated women that you find in Western literature and in some African literature nowadays, too. Is this something you find difficult to write about or is it a conscious choice on your part?*

I like to believe that I am as successful in portraying female characters as I am in portraying male characters. This is what I set out to do. But obviously, whether I have succeeded or not is for the reader to say. But generally in fiction one tries to portray those people who *seem* to be exceptions to the norm, though in another sense they illustrate the norm.

Let me put it this way. What I try to do in my novels is to show the dialectical relationships between various aspects of society and reality. When I take a prostitute I want to show that she is a product of all the forces impinging on that society. She is not really an exception to that society; she is a direct product of the economic and political forces in it. And in the same way when I treat certain forces like love, etc., I want to show that they are affected by all the social forces working on society. To put it more directly, I want to show that things like love, hatred, etc. are by-products of the class forces at work in Africa today. I was asked the other day if when traveling through the Western world I had met with any personal animosity, and I explained to the students that it was not really a question of personal animosity. One needed to understand the class basis of all those attitudes. We must have a scientific understanding of the processes that create them.

KHP: *You started by saying that people are not slaves to the environment, they were capable of changing it. And then you went on to make remarks that I would expect you to make—namely that Wanja, the prostitute in* Petals of Blood, *was a product of the economic forces or class forces. Those two statements are contradictory. There is obviously an area in between where you move.*

Yes. Maybe. I think I did correct myself and instead of saying slaves to, I said they were capable of acting upon their natural and social environment or of changing it. I try to show human beings as capable of changing their natural and social environment. With that basis of optimism I do try to look at those forces which prevent human beings from being able to change their natural and social environment. But I should have said that it is not that human beings are not slaves to the natural and social environment but that they need not be so. It is possible to enhance the quality of human life and the quality of human relationships.

BT: *I'd like to focus on the difference between* A Grain of Wheat *and* Petals of Blood. A Grain of Wheat *is more or less concentrated on a single locality whereas* Petals of Blood *has a lot of locations and you use the journey metaphor. At the same time there is a shift from Mugo to Karega, and the focus changes from the teacher to the worker. Are these things connected? Does the shift in focus from a single locality mean you are attempting a more international way of looking at social problems?*

I would probably not use the word international. I don't feel that the writer is static, I believe that he is developing all the time; at least I would like to believe that in my case I am developing all the time. My own increasing understanding and appreciation of the forces at work in human society has made me look at themes which I treated earlier in a slightly different way. That is why I think there is this shift in *Petals of Blood* from a concentration on the vacillating psychology of the petite bourgeoisie to the position of the worker and the peasant, the one alliance of classes which has changed the history of Africa. It is something I am finding out now to be probably one of the faults, not only of my earlier works, but in the works of most of the African writers. Because we come from a petit bourgeois class position we have tended in the past to create peasant and worker characters with all the mentality of the petit bourgeois. You create a peasant or worker character but inject into him or invest him with the particular mentality and outlook of the petit bourgeois class. When we get worker characters who have a firm outlook with a deep philosophy and knowledge of the area around them, then some petit bourgeois critics say "these are not true workers" or "these are not really peasants," purely because they have been used to a worker/peasant character in African fiction who has been given another class consciousness, in this case [that of] the petit bourgeois class in Africa. I think that my shift, my change of attitude to my characters from *A Grain of Wheat* to *Petals of Blood* may be related to this.

BT: *There is a formal change from a concentration on a central character, which is the bourgeois novel, to a collective center. Does this reflect the same change in your ideas?*

Yes, it does, although that aspect had started earlier in *A Grain of Wheat*, but it becomes more dominant in *Petals of Blood*. By the time I came to write *Petals of Blood* and, more recently, when I came to write my novel in Kikuyu, I had become more and more aware of the classes at work in African society, and I tried as far as I could to get characters representing these different classes. I tried to show them as they act on one another, the dialectical relationship and links between all the characters and of course their relationship with the international and imperialist bourgeoisie.

KHP: *I would like to know to what extent Mau Mau is still a social force or a thing talked about in Kenya today. Is it discussed among the younger generation, or is it confined to your generation?*

I think there is a thing which we might call a collective memory. This collective memory is in a sense what we might call history, and I would say that Mau Mau is still part of the collective memory of the Kenyan people. It is not something which people can forget; it is basic and integral to the history of their experience, just as the Danish people's struggle in the past against feudalism is integral to their collective memory.

KHP: *There are several ways of remembering. You can glorify, you can try to find the forces behind certain movements, you can tend to focus on certain aspects. I once read that there was a tendency to ignore the Mau Mau movement because it presented difficulties for those in power. Is the glorifying aspect the one people tend to focus on?*

Obviously different classes interpret their history in different ways; in other words, a historical event will later be interpreted by different classes to meet their different class needs. Let me give you a good example. The other day I was talking about Karen Blixen. Somebody said that she was even given the Hans Christian Andersen prize. So I said to myself, "Oh, yes, this is a way in which a ruling class tries to appropriate the past healthy traditions of a people by giving Karen Blixen an Andersen prize, when the two ideologies are totally in conflict. It is an attempt to make Karen Blixen look as if she is the inheritor of the Andersen tradition in Danish culture and to make it look as if she is part of the linear development of that tradition." So two totally different writers assume two totally different world outlooks. So in the same way, different classes in Africa will interpret history differently according to their different class needs. I am quite sure there are some people in Africa who are totally opposed to the whole notion of Mau Mau and the remembrance of it, but on the other hand the masses of the people want to be reminded. I will give you an example. The other day I saw a Swahili version of a play called *The Trial of Dedan Kimathi*, written by myself and Micere Mugo. It was performed for the first time, and the house was almost completely packed. Even when we went to some rural areas people would flock from miles around to see the play, and you could tell that they were identifying with the issues in the play. One of the most moving commentaries was by a politician who during the Mau Mau had been sentenced to death. It was probably his age which helped him to escape the rope. When he saw the play, he burst out weeping. I would say that there are some people who are proud of that heroic tradition, and there are others who obviously feel uncomfortable about it, and in Kenya this has found its way into literature. There are in fact in Kenya two literary versions of Kimathi. There is *The Trial of Dedan Kimathi*, written by Mugo and myself, and there is another play called *Dedan Kimathi*[1] written by a Kenyan who shows a different Kimathi. Kimathi has been interpreted in literature in very different ways, and I am sure there are some people who like the Kimathi in my version and some who like the Kimathi in the other version.

KHP: *If you look at the Mau Mau movement from the very beginning, it looks as if it was more or less a cry of a suppressed people who at the beginning had no program except to fight the colonists. Do you think that this sort of thing could happen in Kenya today?*

I don't really know that. In terms of the Mau Mau not having a clear program, I think that this is slightly erroneous in the sense that it has been based on inadequate research. Now a number of things are coming to light, and I would like to recommend to you a book of Mau Mau songs called *Thunder from the Mountain.*[2] It is a collection of Mau Mau songs, pre-Mau Mau and songs developed during the actual guerrilla warfare. I think that the book gives a clear picture of the ideological development in the Mau Mau movement which runs counter to the previous interpretation of Mau Mau. The book is even more important because the ideology arises from the songs themselves and not from what the writer says. One must remember that Mau Mau was the first modern anti-colonial guerrilla movement in Africa. The Algerian war came after Mau Mau, as did all the other liberation movements. It was even more important because the Mau Mau guerrillas were completely surrounded by enemies. Unlike Mozambique, which had Tanzania as a base, or Vietnam, which had North Vietnam or China, Mau Mau had to depend entirely on its own resources, on the ammunition which they could snatch from the British enemy forces.

KHP: *You said that workers and peasants could change history. Why then did Mau Mau not change history?*

They did change history. History does not move in a straight line. People take three steps forward, then maybe a step backwards. Mau Mau has changed the history of Kenya, possibly the history of

Africa.

KHP: *Is it perhaps not a problem that the movement was a one-purpose movement whose aim was to throw out the English?*

If you say that the most important aspect in twentieth-century history is, broadly speaking, the struggle between imperialism and anti-imperialist forces, then Mau Mau becomes a very important aspect of this struggle. Imperialism has two stages: the colonial and the neo-colonial. The colonial stage has to be fought before the neo-colonial stage can be fought.

KHP: *I have always thought that the Mau Mau movement must have been the touchstone of Fanon's theory.*

Fanon, of course, had his own experiences in the Algerian war against the French, but no doubt other movements like Mau Mau were behind his theories. All we can say is that in Africa the struggle continues, and therefore the dreams of the likes of Fanon, Kimathi or Nkrumah, Cabral and all the others have not really died, because they are ideals to be achieved.

---

[1] Here Ngugi is referring to the play by Kenneth Watene published in Nairobi by Transafrica Publishers in 1974.

[2] *Thunder from the Mountains: Mau Mau Patriotic Songs*, ed. Maina wa Kinyatti (London: Zed; Nairobi: Midi-Teki, 1980).

18 Ngugi wa Thiong'o Speaks! "I Am Not above the Contradictions Which Bedevil Our Society"

Emman Omari / 1981

Kenya's foremost novelist and writer, Professor Ngugi wa Thiong'o, needs little introduction to the world—or controversy. His latest book, Detained *(which, as the title suggests, is on his recent experience of political detention), has had literary scholars—and his critics—breaking out in a fresh round of pro- and anti-Ngugi debates. Yet, what are the man's own views?*

Prof. Ngugi, I want to start this interview by observing that your attitude to society in your writing has changed. The Ngugi of Weep Not, Child *is not the Ngugi of* Detained. *Can you elaborate on the trend of your thinking to date?*

Everybody changes with time and I wrote *Weep Not, Child* as a student at Makerere University College. My perspective was then shaped by my own experiences, and this has obviously changed over the years because Kenyan history has also been changing. In the sixties many countries in Africa were emerging from colonialism to some form of independence. But, nevertheless, Makerere's education then must be seen in a colonial context. It was basically a colonial university producing an elitist class to merge it between the African peoples and their colonial masters. A student in such circumstances would obviously bear inevitable influences. Over the years I have become more and more involved with Kenyan peoples in search of a liberative culture free from colonial influences. These have changed my perspective and outlook to life and this is reflected in my later works from *Petals of Blood* down to *Detained.*

Let me take you back to historical biases in your writing. You have melodiously clapped hands for active resisters like the Kimathis; and, on the extreme end, you have snapped at the Mumias. I am of the opinion that in our extremity the objectivity is buried and we are bound to miseducate. What do you say to that?

On the contrary, we need to make Kenyans view their history correctly. How a people look at their past is as important to the interpretation of that past, as to how they look at their future. In colonial literature and historiography, Kenyans who were held back for praise were those who collaborated with colonialism in the exploitation of Kenyan people. If you go to schools like Lenana School in Nairobi, houses are named after traitors like Kinyanjui and Mumia. Nowhere do you find such houses named after heroes like Waiyaki, Koitalel, Me Kitilili or Mary Muthoni Nyanjiru. The question we must address ourselves to is: When writing history for our children, which things do we want them to admire? Should they emulate traitors or heroes? We must draw a line between those who held out consistently and those who collaborated.

Some historians would like to look at African resistances as only passive and active. Those who took to armed struggle and those who watched apprehensively all did it for the sovereignty of their state.

An intellectual is not a neutral figure in society. In fact, intellectuals have their different class biases and inclinations. In a class-structured society intellectuals also reflect different class positions and outlook in that society. They are often spokesmen of this or that class position. They articulate a world outlook which is in harmony with this or that class. There are some Kenyan intellectuals who do not see anything wrong with imperialism. To such, therefore, collaboration with imperialism was not necessarily evil. There are also intellectuals who would see imperialism as evil, and they articulate a world outlook which is opposed to imperialism. Those who say everybody collaborated and everybody resisted are confusing the masses not to see the evil in imperialism. They articulate a world outlook in harmony with foreign domination of Kenya.

You have articulated loudly against foreign imperialism, yet you publish with a foreign firm. Isn't this going back to eat your spit?

I have never said that I am above the contradictions which bedevil our society. I have never even said that I have found solutions to those contradictions which are basically social and political in character. I would obviously want to see the publishing industry fully owned and operated by Kenyans. Just as I would like to see a newspaper industry fully owned and operated by Kenyans.

Do you hope to take your manuscript to a Kenyan publisher in the near future?

I have incidentally published my three one-act plays, *This Time Tomorrow,* with the Kenya Literature Bureau. But I want to say that I had nasty experiences in dealing with Kenya-based publishing houses. I remember that, for reasons, Ngugi wa Mirii and I tried to place the manuscript of the play *Ngaahika Ndeenda* with at least two local publishers. One publisher asked us to pay him Kshs. 60,000 in order that he may publish the play on our behalf. He did not believe that a book published in an African language could possibly sell. Another publisher accepted it, but once I was detained, the publisher refused the play. In the end we had to turn to Heinemann Educational Books E.A. Ltd.

Prof. Ngugi, what is your definition of culture?

I have no individual definition; it is simply a way of life.

Do you advocate for aesthetic assimilation or separatism among nationalities?

One thing we must accept is that Kenya is a multi-national state composed of many nationalities. What makes Kenya is in fact a combination of these nationalities. In the same way, what makes *for* Kenyan culture is in concrete terms a combination of the cultures and languages of all these nationalities. Every language and culture has a right to develop. What I would like to see is a situation in which different cultures and languages begin to talk to one another. I would like to see a book originally written in Luyia made available in Gikuyu, Luo, etc. Now we have a situation where our languages and cultures do not talk to each other, they meet only via a foreign language—English. If our cultures, languages, literatures begin to talk to one another, we shall really see a truly Kenyan national literature and culture.

Before and after your detention, Prof. Ngugi, your relationship with a number of Kenyan scholars has been strained. Do you have any reason for this?

It is not a bad thing for people to have differences. It is in fact very important for all Kenyan people to see that different intellectuals stand for different ideological camps, and have their own world outlook. It is for the Kenya people to choose which world outlook reflects correctly their social, economic and political aspirations.

I want to ask you a question, perhaps one you have never been asked before. What is your view regarding life and the future of man in this world of impending atomic bombs?

Well, I look forward to man in a world in which those who produce also dispose what they produce. A world in which everybody is a producer, a world in which there are no parasites living on the labor of other people.

Perhaps I should remind you of James Burnham who wrote in the 1940s. In his two books, Managerial Revolution *and* The Machiavellians, *he argues several ways that Capitalism is doomed, and Socialism is a dream, and a "classless" society such as this one is all utopia. What is your view regarding this writer?*

Well, I am not familiar with this particular writer.

But is such a world possible anyway?

I have said I look forward to that world where producers control their produce. This is what people have been struggling for all over the world, and they will continue to struggle to control the fruits of their labor.

How do you view yourself in national politics?

I have written quite a lot about that in my book *Writers in Politics* and also in *Detained*. My position has not drastically changed. I see myself as continuing to reflect as truthfully, and as correctly, about the historical experiences of Kenya people and especially their long history of struggle against foreign and internal exploitation and oppression.

You have written yourself that in Petals of Blood *you tried to show "that imperialism can never develop our country or develop us, Kenyans." Although I had the honor to review your* Detained *I am tempted to ask, what was your message?*

Basically *Detained* is looking at the phenomenon of detention involved in theoretical and historical perspectives. It is arguing for a world without detention camps and prisons. *Detained* is in fact saying that the Public Security Act should be abolished *now*. And that particular Act is completely inconsistent with human rights and the democratic rights of Kenyan peoples of whatever political situation.

People might have expected to read Detained *in Gikuyu. What made you write your latest two books in English, defeating your linguistic stand?*

First, *Writers in Politics* is a collection of essays, which have appeared in different journals and were given at different conferences, compiled in book form. As for *Detained*, I had a slightly different audience in mind. I wanted to reach that section of Kenyans that might bring pressure on policy makers to change their attitude towards political detentions without trial. If *Detained* will make even a few Kenyans get the whole issue of detention, and the whole issue of democratic rights of Kenyans, it will have achieved its purpose.

One issue discussed in Detained *is the role of the press. What role do you think journalism should play?*

As you know, I have been a journalist myself. I regard journalists as writers. I would like to see a press that allows the widest possible latitude of expression. Different opinions in Kenya should be given equal place in the press.

Your works could be put into two rungs with A Grain of Wheat *as the division point. The upper works reflect an obviously Leftist turn. I wonder whether there is a special reason for this?*

There are two remarkable experiences in my life. One was my involvement with the Literature Department at the University of Nairobi. I had the good fortune of working with a very brilliant group of lecturers in the Department with whom we tried to work out a relevant literature for both the Department and Kenyan schools. Basic questions arose on the relevance of literature to life in a place such as Kenya. This made us move into other directions, and the question of a relevant Kenyan theater was basic. This involved the Department in the annual event of a Free Traveling Theatre which took drama to the people in the country. I would like to emphasize that this was all collective work which has left a profound mark on my thinking. The struggle for a relevant Kenya National Theatre of course put us into immediate opposition to foreign theater and cultural interests that had for a long time dominated Kenyan life.

The other experience was my involvement with the workers and peasants of Kamiriithu in Limuru who too were in search of a relevant theater which would truly and correctly reflect their own lives. I was no longer a teacher at the village: On the contrary, I became a student at the feet of Kamiriithu and Limuru peasants. They obviously knew more about the workings of African languages and history than I did. Therefore the question which arose was the kind of literature that I was going to write which would be consumed by peasants and workers. So the change is merely a reflection of my changing attitude towards my audience. In my later works I started moving towards a position where I was not only writing *about* peasants and workers, but I was writing *for* peasants and workers, and especially in a language they could understand. When I write a novel in Gikuyu or Kiswahili, I can directly have dialogue with peasants and workers.

What has come out of your latest writing is that the artist holds the mirror to society in order to reflect the realities of life. Don't you think this is tantamount to standing on the fence?

It really depends on where one is standing in relationship to both the mirror and the object being reflected in the mirror. In other words, a writer must turn in a social position that allows him to see as much of the society as possible. In my book, *Detained*, I have gone into a lot of detail to explain this image of the mirror relative to writing.

In this connection what role have you chosen as an artist?

In my previous books, and to some extent in *Petals of Blood*, I was writing about peasants of Kenya and their experience of history. But the language I used (English) excluded them as a target audience. This meant I was writing for an elitist readership conversant with that language. I was part and parcel of those African writers who were producing what I have come to call Afro-Saxon, or more broadly, Afro-European literature. This is the writing by Africans, but in foreign languages. I would like to continue to be able to write for the consumption of ordinary people in a language they can understand. As for content, I would like to continue to articulate their aspirations for a better quality of life.

19 "We Are All Learning from History": Interview with Ngugi wa Thiong'o

Onuora Ossie Enekwe / 1982? (1996)

Ngugi wa Thiong'o of course requires little, if any, introduction. His interview with Enekwe was originally recorded more than fifteen years ago when he last visited Nigeria. The fortunes of the exiled novelist have however not changed much over the years, neither his politics, nor those of his beloved land, Kenya, which provides the setting for all of Ngugi's creations.

Ngugi and Enekwe were to meet yet again, this time on the staff of New York University where until last year they both taught Performing Arts in the Department of Comparative Literature. It afforded Ngugi the opportunity to revise the transcript—whose ideas are not significantly amended—and which we have the privilege of printing for the first time.

Anybody who is familiar with your work will not fail to notice that you have been consistently concerned about the condition of people in Kenya: one, the impact of colonialism, the advent or coming of the white man; two, the economic exploitation of Africans by Europeans; three, the economic exploitation of Africans by Africans. What is your attitude to your work before A Grain of Wheat *and* Petals of Blood*?*

I have been concerned with imperialism in Kenya in its two stages: the colonial and the neo-colonial. Imperialism is a total phenomenon—an economic, a political and a cultural phenomenon. So, its impact on the people tends to be all-embracing. So, we can say that the struggle against imperialism is also total: it's economic, it's political and it is also cultural. Writing by Africans then needs to be seen in that context. I would say that my earlier work like *The River Between* tended to be a bit more concerned with the cultural aspect of imperialism but to the near exclusion of economic aspects. And in *A Grain of Wheat*, *Petals of Blood* and in my latest work, I try to see imperialism in all its aspects—economic, political and cultural—and see all the aspects of the struggle against the same.

What do you think you achieved in your first novels, The River Between *and* Weep Not, Child*?*

Well, the struggles against cultural imperialism are very important, since they tend to deal with the liberation of the mind, liberation of the soul, if you like. So, any novel that contributes, even a bit, towards that cultural struggle is important. *The River Between* and *Weep Not, Child* did contribute their bit towards an appreciation of this struggle against cultural imperialism. However, *The River Between* tends to exclude economic and political factors. This contributes to its weakness. The world-view in the novel is idealistic. It does not see sufficiently that values are rooted in political and economic realities.

Could you, then, say that A Grain of Wheat *and* Petals of Blood *are reflecting a new ideological perspective?*

There is a definite shift in the two novels, particularly in *Petals of Blood*. I consider *A Grain of Wheat* to be a transitional novel in the ideological sense. It stands between my two novels (*The River Between* and *Weep Not, Child*) and my later works, like *Petals of Blood* and *The Trial of Dedan Kimathi*. I feel that there is a shift of emphasis in the sense that I tried to look at the different aspects of the African journey of emancipation from slavery, colonialism to neo-colonialism. There is, for instance, in *Petals of Blood*, an examination of the class structure in African societies and the class struggles that are inherent in that kind of structure. Now, my previous works rarely show the class character of African societies.

How did you get to this stage?

My involvement with the conditions in Kenya, particularly in the

Department of Literature at the University of Nairobi. I was lucky to be in a department which had brilliant scholars who were continually asking themselves about the relevance of literature to life and particularly to the Kenyan situation. In the course of my stay in that department, we collectively tried to work out how the study of literature could be made more relevant to the Kenyan situation. We tried to devise a new syllabus of literature for the University and for the schools in Kenya. Again, in asking ourselves questions about the relevance of literature to life, we held public lectures at the University of Nairobi, and these lectures were very useful because of the types of debates and discussions generated. Again, still in the pursuit of that objective of "Making Literature Relevant to Life," we established the University of Nairobi Free Public Theatre, which traveled all over the country during the long vacation. So, I would say that my involvement in the Department of Literature at the University of Nairobi was very important in my own ideological development.

In Petals of Blood, *we come across a young lawyer, a man of ideas, who seems to be an ideologue of the group. He articulates the ideas of the revolution. Considering what happened in Kenya at the time (or before) you wrote* Petals of Blood, *are the activities of the lawyer and the young people in the book similar to what you have in Kenya? Do they reflect the situation in Kenya?*

Yes, the lawyer's views do reflect the ideological position of a certain class. Kenya is a class-structured society with different classes standing in different positions *vis-à-vis* the forces of production and *vis-à-vis* the forces of imperialism. There is the comprador bourgeoisie that actively collaborates with foreign economic interests. There is also a national bourgeoisie, which is very tiny, very rudimentary. By this I mean that class of Kenyans that try to operate a national capitalism. I don't think that foreign capital will ever allow for a liberated national capitalism. Then there is a petty-bourgeois class in Kenya, comprising small traders, farmers, teachers, etc. And finally, peasants and workers. These classes are basically economic, but they do have their ideological reflections. They, that is, these classes, have their ideological spokesmen. In other words, there is an ideological position that corresponds to the economic position of each class. I would say that the lawyer's position represents not necessarily the ideological mind of the working class, but patriotic nationalism of a national bourgeoisie.

We don't know how you came about the character of Wanja. We think she is a very powerful person and we see such a character in God's Bits of Wood *by Ousmane Sembène. They are of the same upbringing and similar experience. Were you trying to create that character (Wanja) deliberately or were you trying to portray what could have happened? Did you want this character to carry some message?*

Well, I have always been interested in the position of women in Africa. I feel that we can never talk of total liberation of Africa unless the woman is also completely liberated, that the success of our liberation should be measured by the extent to which the African woman is liberated. I am interested in the women's struggles and in the position that the Kenyan women occupy in the history of our country. One of our earliest nationalist leaders was in fact a woman—Me Kitilili, a Giryama from the coastal parts of Kenya. She organized coastal nationalities in a struggle against the British occupation of Kenya in the early part of this century. She was old—about sixty years old or more—but she organized the youth, gave them the oath of unity. She armed them and they started fighting against the British. Later, she was arrested and imprisoned many, many miles from her home area. She escaped from prison and walked all the way—about three hundred miles—back to her people to continue the struggle. In 1924, Harry Thuku who was then the leader of the working class in Kenya was detained without trial by the British. It was a woman, Mary Muthoni Nyanjiru, who organized a demonstration demanding his release. It turned out to be one of the biggest demonstrations that had ever been seen in Kenya. Demonstrators marched to the Government House demanding the release of their leader. Nyanjiru was the first to be shot by the British along with a hundred and fifty other workers. In the fifties, again, the Kenyan woman played a very important role in the kitchen, in the forest, feeding the guerrillas and even in fighting. Some of the fiercest guerrilla fighters among the Mau Mau were women. Some were sent to the detention camps, others to ordinary prisons and so on. The Kenyan woman has played a very, very important role in Kenyan history. And a novelist cannot ignore this particular role.

In The Trial of Dedan Kimathi, *what you are trying to do is to create the role of woman as not only the mother, but also a leading figure in the revolution. I think that it is a very important play. Can you please say a few words about the role of that woman in* The Trial of Dedan Kimathi, *especially in relation to the girl and the boy?*

Well, as you know, I wrote this play together with Micere Mugo, a colleague in the Department of Literature at the University of Nairobi, and we tried also to show the need for total liberation. We show the role of the Kenyan woman in Kenyan history. The woman in *The Trial of Dedan Kimathi* is important in the sense that she carries a revolutionary consciousness. She can see much more than the boy and the girl can see. In the forest, she can see a bit more than some of the other guerrillas can see, so she is important in the play as a carrier, if you like, of this revolutionary consciousness.

Can you compare Wanja to this woman in The Trial of Dedan Kimathi*?*

Well, I'd say they are different. The woman in *Dedan Kimathi* is much more conscious of her political role, much more conscious of the need for a revolutionary change in Kenyan society. I'd say that Wanja is not as politically conscious as this particular woman in the play. Wanja has revolutionary energy, without a revolutionary consciousness. I think this is the difference in the two.

So what you are saying is that Wanja has potential for a revolutionary role through experience. How could she develop to become like the woman?

It is a potentiality, of course. In that sense, I am more concerned with the waste of women in a neo-colonial society. Their energy is often imprisoned, if you like, between the bed and the kitchen. Society is the loser for imprisoning or confining women to that position. Take it this way: Since women form half of the population of the country, if you imprison their total abilities, you are in fact imprisoning the abilities of the population as a whole.

It seems that the main achievement of the woman in The Trial of Dedan Kimathi *is inculcating revolutionary awareness in the young people, and also in unifying the people; it appears that you in fact introduced her symbolically as a kind of Mary in the trial of Jesus Christ. Did you want to use the figure of Mary as a kind of symbol here?*

We were not conscious of the parallel. I didn't see that parallel myself, but of course, another reader may well see it. It does not mean that parallel is not there. But we were not conscious of it in writing the play. The play carries our belief that Kenya and Africa would be liberated the time African women become fully politically conscious. The moment they become politically conscious, then things will happen in Africa. And the woman figure is a symbol for these potentialities in the Kenyan and African women.

You seem to be using the Bible in your writing, even in The Trial of Dedan Kimathi. *It appears that you see the trial as a parody of the trial Jesus underwent.*

As I said before, we were not very conscious of these parallels. Now, about the Biblical references in my works, this is not accidental, because for a long time as a child, the Bible was my only literature. The Bible is the one book which is available in nearly all the African languages. It is a common literary heritage, and so it is quite natural that if I want to make references which will be recognized, I will go to the Bible. I make the same kind of use of traditional stories, proverbs, riddles, etc. In other words, the Bible is part and parcel of the literary framework within which I have been writing.

So that explains why in every book you have written there are quotes from the Bible. But one can see a definite shift in your attitude to the Bible as from A Grain of Wheat, *and definitely, in* The Trial of Dedan Kimathi. *In the latter, for example, you consistently undercut certain ideas in the Bible. Does this correspond to the shift in your ideological position?*

Yes, it's definitely part of this shift that we talked about earlier. Obviously my recent works have become more critical, not of the Bible, but of Christianity as a whole. So, you are quite right, Christianity is much more critically examined in *Petals of Blood* than it was, let's say, in *The River Between*. Even in *A Grain of Wheat*, I think, Christianity is not held in an uncritical light.

So what exactly is your response to Christianity right now in relation to the whole struggle?

Well, in all my writings, especially in *Homecoming*, I have been very critical of the role that Christianity has played in the colonization of the African people. I have taken the position that Christianity was part and parcel of cultural imperialism. Even at a very simple level of symbolism, we can see how Christianity weakened African people. If you look at the Christian imagery of God and Satan, the devil is seen in terms of blackness. So in pictures in most churches God was displayed as being white, angels were white, and of course, people who went to heaven eventually wore white robes of purity. The devils and their angels wear black. African people then were seen as sons of Ham who were cut away from God. African Christians were made to sing songs like "Wash Me Redeemer, I Shall Be Whiter Than Snow." Quite apart from that, the Bible was used by the missionaries to preach the doctrine of non-violence, the doctrine of turn the other cheek once one cheek has been hit by your enemy, the doctrine of giving your enemy the inner garment after he has already taken your outer garment, the doctrine, if you like, of your giving Caesar things that are Caesar's, etc. These meant colonial Caesar, etc. You can see that some of these doctrines are designed to weaken African people in the face of imperialist exploitation and oppression. Christianity and the Bible were part and parcel of the doctrine of pacification of the primitive tribes of lower Africa. This doctrine of non-violence is a contrast to the doctrine of struggle, of resistance to foreign aggression, foreign exploitation and foreign occupation of our people's country.

You just mentioned the pacification of the primitive tribes and immediately one remembered Captain Winterbottom in Chinua Achebe's book. I also see Winterbottom in Dedan Kimathi *and Mr. Smith too. Is this part of oral continuation of the joke, as we see Winterbottom, one of the British soldiers, tried in* Dedan Kimathi*?*

Well, yes, it is a continuation of the joke. It is a very appropriate name for this category of people. It is also a kind of intertextual dialogue with Achebe's work.

Also, is the Smith there in a way related to the Smith in Arrow of God*?*

Novels like *Things Fall Apart* and *Arrow of God* have now become part of our common heritage. Borrowing the name consciously or unconsciously is part of the intertextual communication.

We suppose you would place The Black Hermit *in the same group as your early works,* The River Between *and* Weep Not, Child, *in terms of their attitude to revolution?*

Yes, that play belongs to that period, the period of *The River Between* and *Weep Not, Child.* I would say that the play is not as politically clear as, let's say, *The Trial of Dedan Kimathi* or in my plays in the Gikuyu language. The ideological position in *The Black Hermit* is a bit hazy; it is misty; it is not clear and is one of the shortcomings of that particular play.

Apart from the ideological problem in The Black Hermit, *what other problems do you find in the play? For instance, the problem of structure?*

It has got some weaknesses. As you know, it's one of my earliest plays and I was then not as much involved in the theater as I have come to be. There are a lot of weaknesses in structure, in characterization, in the whole dramatic movement of the play. But remember, ideological mistiness and haziness can also ruin the structure of a play or a novel. It is this ideological haziness or mistiness in certain levels that weakens the play.

So what you are saying is that in fact it is not possible to write a play that is structurally correct unless the idea is also correct?

The idea and the tone have to be clear. The clarity of idea, or clarity of content often brings about the clarity of structure. But whenever the central idea is not clear, it leads to the general unclarity of content and structure.

So in The Trial of Dedan Kimathi *this problem has been dealt with as it is essentially a very ideological work. What you achieve there is to deal with the ideological question more conclusively and more effectively. We refer to some of the problems you have been talking about in other works. Even though it's a short script, you have succeeded in bringing the whole problem to life. Would this be an accurate assessment?*

Yes, I would say that the central ideas in *The Trial of Dedan Kimathi* are much more clear than they were in the previous plays. But remember that *The Trial of Dedan Kimathi* was a work of two hands, two minds.

You talked about the theater group that moved round the country in Kenya, the one that traveled from your department in the University. What did you learn from those tours, from the people?

The group was called the *University of Nairobi Free Traveling Theatre.* I was not myself individually part of the traveling troupe. That is, I did not travel with it, but it was part of our departmental program. It was led by teachers like John Ruganda and Waigwa who were involved in theater in the department. This *Free Traveling Theatre* was instrumental in my later interest in having a theater based in villages. In other words, some of us came to the conclusion that while the traveling troupe was important, theater could never take root in Kenya unless it was based in the villages and towns with the people themselves writing their own scripts and performing them themselves. It is this kind of idea that was behind the setting up of Kamiriithu Community Education and Cultural Centre, based in a village called Kamiriithu in Limuru that is twenty miles from Nairobi. Members had been present at some performances of the

University of Nairobi Free Traveling Theatre. And they were the ones who asked for a play to perform. This resulted in my collaboration with Ngugi wa Mirii in the writing of a play in Gikuyu called *Ngaahika Ndeenda.* The play was written in 1977 and performed the same year for these people in the same village. The standard of performance was very high indeed. All the actors were peasants and workers from the area. The impact they made on the people was also very significant indeed. Peasants and workers would travel for miles and miles to come and see the play. Some would hire buses, others public transport to come and see the play which was obviously reflecting their own history, their own lives. You, of course, know that the play was later stopped by Kenyan authorities and I was subsequently detained in prison without trial.

Would you like to tell me what happened in the night or day of performance of Ngaahika Ndeenda. *How did the audience respond?*

As I said, the audience was very enthusiastic. Some of them had followed the production from the initial stages of rehearsal right through the formal presentation. They were part of the play.

You mean the peasants who were not directly involved with the acting.

They were involved in everything. Yes, they added to the script. The production had done a number of things which were a departure from tradition. For instance, the readings were all open to the public. The selection of actors again was done in the open. So, right from the beginning we had audiences. And the audiences grew with the growth of the production. And still, many of them later came in as a part of the fee-paying crowd. The performances reflected an ever-increasing audience. The people who came to see the play were growing day in and day out. And anybody who had seen the play before would still come to see the play a second, third, fourth, or fifth time. I know some who were with the play right through all the rehearsals and right through all the performances. So, these were anticipating lines from actors. They knew the whole play by heart, and they knew what the actor was going to say. If an actor missed his lines, they would correct him. By the way, the rehearsals and the performances were so arranged as to keep in line with the rhythm of life in the village. That is, the rehearsals took into account the working pattern of the peasants and workers. The rehearsals were only done in those periods when these workers were not going to be all that busy in their homes. The formal performances, for instance, were never done at night. They were done in daytime, mostly in the afternoons of Sundays and Saturdays, but towards the end, you could find all the performances on Sundays only. The theater was open, of course, in the heart of the village and incidentally the whole theater with the stage was built by the people themselves.

What type of structure did they construct?

They had a raised stage, but it had no curtains or roof. Behind the stage, there were rooms where the actors could change their dresses, etc. There were no walls separating the actors from the audience. The audience could see the actors coming in or getting out of the stage. They had built the seats for the audience—the type of seats you see in a stadium so that people who sit in front would not obstruct the view of those sitting in the back.

How would you describe the response of the audience during the performance?

Very, very enthusiastic. I can remember a number of times when the rain fell, but instead of going to their homes, people sat back or sheltered themselves in nearby huts to wait for the rain to subside. The actors would rush back to the stage, and the whole audience would return to their seats to see the continuation of the play. So even during the formal performances, when they were paying entrance fees, the audience was still very, very enthusiastic. And as I said, the audiences came from afar and not only the peasants and workers from the village, but people also trekked from distances of well over a hundred miles to come and see the play. They came on foot, in hired buses, etc.

What exactly do you think made them do so?

As I said, the play correctly reflected their history and their lives.

And for the first time, the peasants and the workers could see themselves reflected on the stage, not in a negative light, but in a positive manner. They saw themselves being portrayed as the true makers of history which, of course, they are. So I would say that the content was very important in eliciting this kind of response, as well as the standard of performance. Some people, critics, doubted whether these were really peasants. They thought that these were university students dressed like village people, which of course was ridiculous and showed contempt for the working people. But the standard of performance was extremely high and nothing like it had ever been seen on the Kenyan stage.

Did this response spill over into the community in terms of discussions, reactions, etc.?

Definitely, yes. We started receiving delegations from other villages for advice on how they too could start similar ventures in their own communities. So the play had an impact and effect on people in and beyond the borders of the immediate community.

When you were detained, did these people continue to perform?

Their morale was very depressed by my detention. As I told you, the license to perform the play was stopped by the government so these people could not continue with the play. What they did, however, was to continue with their singing. When I came from detention, a year later, I found that they had brought out two records of the songs they had been composing when I was in detention in the maximum security jail.

The songs were part of the play?

Yes, the play drew very, very heavily on oral tradition, singing and dancing, etc. It was almost like a musical, so the songs they brought out were part and parcel of the play. I remember once taking Chinua Achebe around to see the village theater, and when the peasants learnt that he was Chinua Achebe, they started asking him to tell the world to bring pressure on the Kenyan government so that the license to perform the play could be restored to them.

What happened when the actors danced? Did they dance on the wooden structure?

Yes, they danced on the wooden structure, but it was done in such a way that there was no real wall between the audience and the actors so that the actors could see and be seen by the audience, etc. There was also constant movement between the audience and the stage actors—no real wall dividing the two.

Did some of the members of the audience come out to meet the performers sometimes?

The audience joined in singing some of the songs with which they were familiar.

I would like to return to The Trial of Dedan Kimathi. *You start off with this objective of writing it around Dedan Kimathi but in fact by the time you finish the play, you have not given much attention to his history. What you have done is, in fact, to concentrate on the people, on the woman and the girl and then also on the dialectical confrontation between Dedan Kimathi, the Bankers and the other exploiters. Was this done purposely?*

We saw Kimathi as being much more than an individual. We saw him as symbolizing the people, the masses, who in our view were the key makers of history. So Kimathi is not seen as an individual. He is a symbol of the collective will of the Kenyan people.

So that is why, even though the play is named after him, you spend more time on the people than on Kimathi?

Yes, that is it.

Why did you and Micere introduce the scene where Kimathi has to deal with his brother's betrayal of him? I mean the hesitation, the doubt, the inability to take a firm decision at that time? There is a kind of indecision on the part of Dedan Kimathi once we begin to know about his mother and his brother.

We wanted to show the pitfalls of kinship in a revolutionary struggle. If you put kinship above the need of the revolution, you are bound to fail. But Dedan realizes that and advises his followers never again to put kinship or considerations of kinship above those of the struggle. Dedan Kimathi himself says that his brother and his sister are only those who are with him in the struggle and those who share his ideology and the revolutionary objectives.

We have Dedan Kimathi of history, that is, Dedan Kimathi that we discuss in history and the one that we have read about. But you seem to have created your own Dedan Kimathi. You have made him more like a Marxist fighter. How much of the two Dedan Kimathis do you have in this play?

Well, the Kimathi in the play, as well as the Kimathi in history, are people who were leaders of a revolutionary struggle. Let me recommend to you a book called *Thunder from the Mountains*. The sub-title is *Mau Mau Patriotic Songs*. It is edited by Maina wa Kinyatti and published in London by Zed Publishers. This particular book is very important because it is a record of the songs composed by the Mau Mau guerrillas themselves. So the songs do in fact contain a correct record of the views and objectives of Mau Mau guerrilla fighters. And the songs will prove that the Dedan Kimathi of *The Trial* is closer to the historical Kimathi. Remember that we also did a lot of research on the history of Kimathi. Micere and I even visited the place he was born. And we visited the forest from which he used to operate, and even the place where he was finally captured. We talked to the people who knew him as a child, as a teacher, and as a guerrilla leader. Remember that it was not Marx who created workers and class struggles. Marx learnt from history and not history from Marx.

Yes, in any case it seems to me that because of the fundamental role that economic factors play in Marxist ideology, you can say that in as far as Dedan Kimathi and the other fighters were conscious of this fundamental economic fact, they are, in fact, operating within Marxist ideology.

The workers are the producers of the wealth that they themselves have to purchase. This is true of the workers in Kenya and the workers everywhere. They want to be in control of the wealth which they have produced. And they don't need to read books to have this particular objective. It's part of their lives. It's part of their needs, it's part of their struggle, their very lives that they want to control.

I would like to ask a question about Petals of Blood. *I see that you worked on that book when you were in the Soviet Union. Do you think the novel would have been different if you had written it in Kenya?*

The novel *Petals of Blood* was started when I was in Evanston in the United States, where in 1970/71, I was an Associate Professor of Literature at Northwestern University. But the bulk of the novel was written when I was in Kenya and only the last few chapters were finished when I was in Russia. The novel took about five years to write and four of those years were spent in Kenya and only one month in the Soviet Union. So it was the finishing touches which were worked out when I was in the Soviet Union.

Now, when you were finishing the novel in the Soviet Union, was there anything that happened that could have influenced the work?

Not necessarily. I was all by myself in a place called Yalta, on the Black Sea. I needed that particular month to be all by myself in a place where I did not know the language of the people and where I would not get any disturbance in the course of putting the finishing touches to the novel. The atmosphere at Yalta was very, very peaceful. It was very peaceful, the atmosphere, very conducive to writing. It was named after the great Russian writer Chekhov.

Would you like to talk generally about African writers? You know that many things have been said about African literature. What would you say, in assessment of this literature, especially considering its growth, up to this point?

Let me say something about my latest book of essays called *Writers in Politics*. In this book, you will find my views on the evolution and growth of African literature. There has been an important departure in my position. This has to do with the issue of language. I've come round to the view which was articulated in the sixties by Obi Wali about the necessity for African writers to use our African languages for their creative expressions. And I have come to the view that the literature written by Africans in foreign languages like French, English, Spanish, Danish, etc., falls into a category of its own. It is a misnomer to call it African literature. It can only be called Afro-European literature generally and more particularly Afro-Saxon literature when the literature is written by Africans in the English language, or Afro-French literature which is written by Africans in the French language. But, collectively, I would call them Afro-European literatures. According to the new view, African literature is that literature written by Africans in African languages like the Yoruba, Igbo, Hausa, Swahili, Gikuyu, etc., languages which are indigenous to Africa.

Now, what of writers in terms of the African revolution? How would you assess African writers? Or rather, what do you think that the African writers have achieved in terms of the African revolution?

Well, I cannot talk about the African writers as a whole since they hold different positions *vis-à-vis* the African revolution, etc. But, on the whole, I think they have made an important contribution to all the cultural emancipations of the people. Although often written in a foreign language, it is still a literature that reflects the African environment and personalities, and history. And these are important. After all, our children are now able to read a literature that on the whole shows the Africans in a positive light instead of the way they used to be portrayed in the novels by foreigners. But those African writers who have tried to analyze the Africans in terms of classes obviously are very significant indeed. Here, I am thinking of a writer like Ousmane Sembène whose books, especially *God's Bits of Wood*, have contributed a lot towards our understanding of the struggle for total liberation of the Africans.

20 *BBC Arts and Africa* Interview with Ngugi wa Thiong'o about Okot p'Bitek

Alex Tetteh-Lartey / 1982

This is Alex Tetteh-Lartey welcoming you to a rather special edition of Arts and Africa. *You may remember hearing in the program last week the sad news of Okot p'Bitek's death. Okot p'Bitek was Uganda's best known poet and was celebrated throughout Africa as a commentator on African culture. The work most people will remember him by is* Song of Lawino*—a collection of verse blending modern satirical ironies with a verse form similar to traditional Acholi poetry.*

Now in today's program we pay tribute to Okot p'Bitek and begin with a poem from that collection. It's called "My Husband's Tongue Is Bitter."

Actuality: Poetry Reading

"My Husband's Tongue Is Bitter" read by the Swahili poet Abdilatif Abdalla. p'Bitek was deeply committed to the Acholi language, and maintained throughout his life that the future of African literature lay with the African languages. To talk about his work I have with me in the studio the distinguished Kenyan writer, Ngugi wa Thiong'o, an author equally committed to writing in his own language—Kikuyu.

Ngugi, welcome to Arts and Africa. *Would you say the poem we've just heard is typical of p'Bitek's work?*

I think in so many ways *Song of Lawino* is his best work. It is the work he's best known by, although he did in fact later write more songs. *Song of Lawino* which is about the tendency in the African elite of taking on the ways of foreigners while in fact despising their own. It is later followed by *Song of Ocol* which is the husband's, or Ocol's, apparent reply to Lawino's attack on this aping behavior on the part of educated Africans.

It is often forgotten in a sense that what Lawino is attacking is not necessarily the Western ways. She is saying that Western ways, Western culture is valid to the people who created it. And in the same way African culture and African way of life is valid to the people who created it. Her disillusionment with Ocol is caused by not only his aping Western bourgeois culture but his utter dislike and hatred of his African peasant roots and values. In fact in the later song, the *Song of Ocol*—his reply to Lawino—there is a place where he becomes so tormented with the fact of his being black, that he cries out to God and says something like this, "God, God, why was I born black?"

Now Song of Lawino *was written first in Acholi and then translated in English.*

Yes, again this is another remarkable thing about Okot p'Bitek: that is, his commitment to African languages. In fact his very first work, a novel written in 1953, *Lak Tar* was written in his Acholi—his rural language—and this was in 1953.

When he was barely twenty-one.

Yes. Now when this is seen against the tendency of so many African writers using foreign languages like English, French, Spanish, Italian, Portuguese for the creative exploration of their world, you can see how revolutionary Okot's position in fact was. So I can say that Okot was in fact ahead of his time, because it is only now that so many African writers are beginning to question this tendency of African writers using foreign languages. So we can say that people like Okot p'Bitek with his *Song of Lawino* and his novel *Lak Tar* were the ones who were really laying the basis for a truly African literary tradition.

Would you say anything was lost in the translation from Acholi into English?

He himself says so in the introduction. He says "translated from the Acholi by the Author, who has thus clipped a bit of the eagle's wings and rendered the sharp edges of the warrior's sword rusty and blunt, and has also murdered rhythm and rhyme."

Now you've said that you consider Song of Lawino *his greatest work. Was there anything else he wrote which was quite considerable?*

Well, he was a man of many parts. Let me see now. For instance, *Song of Lawino* was followed by *Song of Ocol, Song of Malaya* and *Song of a Prisoner*. So in fact he has several songs, although none of the later songs really rose up to the quality of the first one. But he was also a scholar and he wrote the very important polemical work *African Religions in Western Scholarship* in which he attacked the tendency of so much African scholarship trying to justify African religions in terms of their proximity to Christianity and so on. He also translated a number of Acholi stories into English, published by Heinemann as *Hare and Hornbill*, as well as a number of poems from the original Acholi into English called *Horn of My Love*. He has also a book of essays called *Africa's Cultural Revolution* published by Macmillan.

Now what sort of man was he? You must have known him a considerable number of years.

I think it's quite true, as the editorial in the Kenyan paper *The Weekly Review* said recently, that he was a man who will long be remembered for his celebration of life. I think he felt life was to be lived and often he tended to shock some people by his directness of expression, or directness of behavior. For him life was to be enjoyed, life was a marvelous thing, so life was like a festival and it should be enjoyed and so on.

Now he has been described here in one of the obituary notices in one of the English papers as a man who could veer from wild conviviality to profound moroseness. Was he that sort of person, very unstable in that sense?

No, I'm not sure about the moroseness (laughter). Certainly he was the kind of person in whose presence...or rather he was the kind of person you could not remain indifferent to. He had this effect on people, I think: He tended to make [people] feel at ease, unless of course they were very, very stiff and very Westernized, in which case he made them feel uncomfortable by his directness, by his spontaneity if you like. But otherwise nobody could be in his presence and not be affected one way or the other by that presence.

Ngugi wa Thiong'o, thank you very much indeed, and on behalf of all our listeners, the best of luck with your writing in the future.

21 An Interview with Ngugi wa Thiong'o

Jacqueline Bardolph and Jean-Pierre Durix / 1982 (1983)

This interview was recorded in Göteborg on 5 September 1982.

J.B.: Mother, Sing for Me, *your last play, was a collective realization. What part did you, the man who had already written plays and novels, play in it?*

First of all, quite correctly, you say it was a collective effort. In fact, it is important to mention that the group which was doing my last play, *Maitu Njugira*, meaning "Mother, Sing for Me," was the same group that did *Ngaahika Ndeenda* (*I Will Marry When I Want*) in 1977: that is, the men and women who came to the Kamiriithu Educational Centre. There is a difference, though, in the situation. Whereas in 1977 the participants in the project came into it without ever knowing the consequences, or rather hoping and in fact thinking that the consequences would never be adverse, on this occasion it was very interesting that they came to the project fully knowing that the consequences of participation might not necessarily be positively beneficial and, on the contrary, might be hazardous to their lives and existence. So we were very impressed by the big turnout of people who came for auditioning.

Now another difference between these occasions, 1981-82 and 1977, is that, in 1977, the group was going to perform *Ngaahika Ndeenda* at the village open-air theater, and the audience who came, came to the village. But, this time, they, from the village, were going to perform at the National Theatre in Nairobi and with some participation from some workers in Nairobi. So that, as the auditioning was done in two places, in the village and also at Nairobi, the turnout of people who wanted to take part was huge: In

Nairobi, over two hundred people turned out. In the village, over two hundred people turned out for auditioning.

There are other differences: The first text, *Ngaahika Ndeenda*, was scripted by Ngugi wa Mirii and myself, and later added on to by the peasants who were the participants. This time, I scripted *Maitu Njugira*. But I'd rather say it was not a question of scripting, more now a question of collecting—collecting old tunes from different people—and in the scripting of these, I worked with different people. So I was really more of an editor of a collective scripting. To show you what I mean, for instance, in a script: There are a number of work songs from different Kenyan nationalities, different cultures—Luyia, Akamba, Luo—and there is no way I could have possibly known these work songs except for the active help from various individuals and this meant not only their collecting the tunes but changing the words here and there to fit into the theme of the musical. As I was saying, it was an active collective effort, not merely a question of just helping me to work in the tune. They actually actively helped in that.

Mother, Sing for Me was directed by a new person as a chief director. Now we can talk of another difference: Whereas *Ngaahika Ndeenda* was more or less contemporary, with a glance at history to explain the roots of the contemporary situation, *Mother, Sing for Me* was set historically in the past—that is, in the period when Kenyan workers were experiencing harsh conditions in the plantations, and especially the harshness of the pass system which they had to carry from one farm to another, or even from their home to their place of employment. Everything was recorded in the pass. The action of the play was deliberately put in the past although, of course, there were contemporary parallels. But definitely the historical setting was in the past.

Another difference was, whereas *I Will Marry When I Want* had a lot of songs in it, it was not structurally a musical. *Mother, Sing for Me* had also a lot of songs—Gikuyu and from other nationalities. It was structurally a musical. Its basis was going to be song, dance and mime, with the minimum of dialogue. We were also going to use slides in it to give historical authenticity to some of the statements.

For instance, all the labor laws quoted in the musical were actual historical labor laws and we wanted to project these on a screen together with the pictures of people who promulgated the laws or those associated with the laws or the historical circumstances surrounding those laws.

J.B.: *I saw you looking at the photographs of the rehearsal. One could see the involvement of the participants. What is your part as Ngugi the creator, the writer?*

There are two stages: First of all, one has to collect songs. Obviously, in collecting songs over a period, there is an organizing principle and it is the writer who provides it, even for a musical. It has to have a loose plot. For instance, you collect songs on the basis of some kind of plot with a broad theme of resistance. So I provided that one. The second stage is collecting the songs and fitting them, and for this you have to work with people. There is no way in which you can do it alone. In particular I worked with two people very actively, very closely. One is a lecturer in University College, another a lecturer from Kenyatta University College who teaches theater. We got the musicians and themes.

That stage is where everybody has gathered together. The direction is taking place. This is where, now, the actors, the workers, come in. Some of the old songs we collected in the projected script are now rejected, new ones are added. The whole choreography means that you change so many things, and this is very collective indeed. So you come to a fourth stage. Because you, as a writer, are arranging all these themes, you also keep a record of them. The fourth stage after the production is to write the script in accordance with all the additions and developments during the rehearsals and the performance. In fact, I have not yet started that stage....

J.-P.D.: *How would you define the writer in this case? Is he in the position of an interpreter of the collective effort?*

I think he is more of an editor. Many people are puzzled when I say that. In *I Will Marry When I Want*, my job was reduced to that of a messenger. Since I had means of transport and others did not have any, it just literally meant that I had to go and collect orders and transport people from here to there. There is no way I could have been present at all the occasions. And, in this one, I was actually playing a similar part, that of a messenger. As we were doing it in Nairobi, I had to keep transporting people for rehearsals. So one is really reduced to that, more of an editor, interpreter, yes, of course.

J.-P.D.: *You are an important coordinating element in this whole effort, and it seems to be the opposite of the isolated work involved in writing a novel. Do you see these two roles as contradictory or complementary?*

I think they are complementary. The problem of the novel is that collective participation is very difficult.

J.B.: *I heard you had a public of listeners for your novels when you had public readings.*

The act of writing can be a problem. I was writing this novel in prison. I had to depend very heavily on other detainees. They also told me different episodes, different proverbs, different aspects of Kenyan history. Each one of them knew different things to do with some aspects of bourgeois life in Nairobi. Some of them had lived there. They knew this life from the inside. So, even that is not as individual as, let us say, when I was writing *Petals of Blood*, or maybe even in writing those novels there was the same process. Only I was not as conscious, maybe, of it as I was in writing *Devil on the Cross*. And even that novel was very collective, though not to the same extent. You do not sit for hours writing a sentence as it is going to be. On the whole, you do keep depending on people quite a lot. Or rather I did. But I do agree with you. It is different, in the sense that, with theater, it is more obviously a collective effort and its success or failure is dependent on that collective involvement. Whereas, with a novel, if you sit down in the presence of the audience, you are fully responsible.

J.B.: *Are you planning a novel at the moment?*

Yes. But I never discuss novels in progress, simply because, sometimes, there is an idea in your head and you do not like it when people ask you: "What are you writing?"

J.B.: *I thought also that, maybe, you were so absorbed by this last play....You said somewhere that teaching and the writing of novels seem detrimental to one another.*

Actually it is a problem when you are teaching and writing novels. I like to have some sense of a stretch. I like to have an expanse of time. I do not work regular hours. When I am in the mood of writing, I like to feel that there is nothing in front of me for that day. I do not even like to feel that I have an appointment with somebody, let us say, at six o' clock. I like to feel there is nothing ahead of me. Now that does not mean that I write the whole day. It might even mean that I do not write anything. I like to feel that there is nothing ahead. But it is a luxury you cannot have when you are teaching. So I think a novel requires a certain amount of leisure. But this is personal. Other novelists might experience this process differently.

J.-P.D.: *How do you see the relationship between being a novelist and being a teacher? Are the two activities in some way related?*

What I used to enjoy mostly at University was, quite frankly, the exchange of ideas. By this I do not mean exchange of ideas in a formal sense, learned men sitting down to discuss. Even during seminars with students, there was that exchange of ideas. I enjoy seminars more than lectures. Some people, even when I was writing, would tell me things which would really set me afire. Nothing to do with how long someone had been at University. It could be the first-year student, someone who was doing literature as a minor course or someone who happened to come to that seminar because he had heard there was something interesting. I found that very stimulating.

J.B.: *At one time you wrote about Caribbean literature. Are you still interested in the subject? What are the books and areas of writing which interest you at the moment?*

I am afraid I have not really been able to follow developments in Caribbean literature. This preoccupation with the development in the Department of Literature from 1969 to 1977 tended increasingly to pull me back from these concerns. And secondly, the involvement in the village tended to make me preoccupied with other things. While I was in Kenya, I was much more involved with just wanting to know more about the Gikuyu language and just the sheer pleasure of mixing with people, of listening to their talk, it did not matter where, in a bar or in a bus, traveling.

In the process of writing *Devil on the Cross*, I had come to acquire another interest in the language, which always enabled one to *see* more, to *hear* more than the people who were talking probably realized. And it was fascinating. But it takes time because you cannot plan it; you cannot say I am going to the bar to listen to people talk. You have to be absorbed in it, naturally.

J.B.: *In* Petals of Blood *there is a lot about the various powers of writing, talking, listening to people, communicating in general. I was struck by the fact that Karega, the one who is very articulate in his political analysis at times, seems to be ineffectual and unable to get through to people, to Wanja especially. Do you think that, more generally speaking, the written text is a form of action, in its way, or is there more possibility of action in the theater?*

Action has various aspects, obviously. Writing about circumstances where action is to operate is as important to action as the practical action itself. Action is a practice and a theory. So, even the act of writing, the way I see it, can sometimes be a form of action. Let me try to illustrate this: There was a time, historically, when people like Equiano were writing, even earlier, or people like Senghor, in the beginning, when, maybe, it was important as part of the whole national assertion for people to say: "We are writing." No matter what they were writing. The sheer act of writing became in itself a form of mission. Later, of course, it was all taken for granted, and it was *what you said* which was important rather than the fact that you said it. O.K., let me come to my writing: Even my beginning—to write in East Africa, for instance—when I wrote *Weep Not, Child*, it was important that a novel was written, irrespective of what it may have said because it generated other forces. But, of course, later, it was what I had to say which became important because the act of having written as an important active factor is later diminished by events. Now we come to my writing *Devil on the Cross* in Gikuyu. It was important as part of the overall assertion, as part of the overall debate—this anti-imperialist struggle in the neo-colonial stage—for me to demonstrate that a modern novel could be written in Gikuyu. It was the only way I could prove the Gikuyu language could be developed in a certain way. The reception of the novel was very interesting because some peasants, but not only peasants, even some petits bourgeois, night-school teachers and so on, could get hold of the novel to look at it and turn it upside down to look it over. And one of them is reported to have said: "So, such a big book can be written in Gikuyu!" So first it was the size of the book which was important. Of course, when more books are written, it will not be the act of writing which will be important but what the novel says which will be important. Writing itself can be a form of action, depending on the social forces it is setting out to counteract or to work with.

J.-P.D.: *In a novel like* Petals of Blood *in which you have space to expand, there is a certain organization of characters which includes contradictory elements. At least several of the characters express very different views and they are all, in their own way, extremely sophisticated. There are many shades of meaning and judgment, and I got the feeling that, perhaps, the novel was a genre in which the writer could best dynamize the contradictions within his own culture and the complexity of the problems he was trying to tackle. Would you say that this is more easily done in a novel or in a play?*

Different forms call for a different kind of approach and what the theater can do, a novel cannot possibly do. There is nothing that can replace the sense of interaction with a live audience; you can never get it in a novel. It is an absolutely marvelous feeling and you can only get it when you are actively involved in the theater. This is the reason why people who get really involved in the theater become really married to the theater, more or less. You do not get a marvelous sense of liberation in a novel, from the point of view of the interaction with a live audience who are reacting and you are counterreacting and reacting in turn. And you can see the same works having entirely different effects on different people. But, at the same time, there is in the novel something you cannot do in the theater. This capacity in a novel to do almost anything it wants to, from describing the smells, all that the five senses can experience, plus what goes on in the heart or in the mental processes. So there is a lot of freedom in a novel, call it integrative freedom, that may not be readily there in other forms. I do not agree with those who say that the novel is dead. It is an expansive medium, capable of so much transformation and altering; it is very elastic.

J.B.: *Novels can also move one: I remember lending* Petals of Blood *to people who knew nothing of the African context and they were extremely moved by it. In some ways it has a universal appeal because of the range of imagination that is found in it.*

For a novel to be successful, obviously, it has to do with how accurately, how faithfully it illuminates human relationships. So what really appeals to people initially is this ability of the novel to treat human lives. So, when a human being comes across this, he is interested also in the circumstances that brought about the pattern of human relationships as revealed in a novel or short story or other forms of art. So the novel is a very important form. I find the same when I read Tolstoy, for instance. I think I get a clearer picture of what it felt like to be in Czarist Russia in the nineteenth century than I get from any amount of historical data. And I get the same thing when I read Balzac in the English translation. And no amount of reading of French history of the period can give one the same amount of clarity of the relationships between the various social forces than you get in Balzac. But the initial reason one goes to Balzac or Zola or Flaubert is not to learn about the social forces. You go because of the human appeal. But obviously you begin to see the other forces that bring about that particular type of relationship between people.

J.B.: *One last question. I suppose you expect it: You were talking today about any language being a language of culture and a language of communication. Is there no place in the future for your using English as a language of communication in your fiction? Are these days over?*

What I meant by this was that, first, a language has two aspects, as a language of communication and as a carrier of culture. If you take the English language, for Japanese people, it is not a carrier of culture. It is just a means of communication. And they could as well have used French, German or Gikuyu or Somali....Japanese is both a means of communication to them and a carrier of the old culture. Each language has that dual character. As for using the English language, there is no reason why it should not remain, in the same way as French or German, a language of communication across peoples. What was wrong was its being used as a carrier of our culture at the same time as our language was suppressed as a carrier of our own culture. For me, I have decided that, for creative writing purposes, like short stories, plays and novels, I shall be using the Gikuyu language for the time being...or in the long run....In the short run, for essays, argumentative pieces, I shall be using English. But I see it as a short-term thing. In the long run, everything will be for me in the Gikuyu language. But there is no reason why it should not be available to people through translations, in the same way as I have just mentioned Zola or Flaubert or Tolstoy or Brecht, and I do not know French, German or Russian. It would not necessarily mean it would be closed to the outside world. It will be available through translations and that way, I think, you are in a better position to appreciate the fullness of African culture, for instance. Now you get it in an edited form. Because, in fact, the novels we get from Africans writing in French or in English are written with a form of mental translation anyway. So, in fact, we are getting an edited form, just the kind of thing you get in a translation, with this difference: In a translation, when there is a defect, you know that this defect could have come from the translation. But, in the other case, the defects become original contributions. The other effect of this is that, whereas a novel like *Things Fall Apart* or *Petals of Blood* is made available to an English-speaking audience or readership, although it is not available to an African-language readership, of course, it could be argued, why could it not be translated anyway into an African language? But why should an African writer write in a foreign language in order for him to be translated back into his own language?

22 Ngugi wa Thiong'o: An Interview

Raoul Granqvist / 1982 (1983)

Raoul Granqvist interviewed Ngugi wa Thiong'o in Umeå 22 September 1982.

---

*You have said: "In writing a novel, I love to hear the voices of the people working on the land, forging metal in a factory, telling anecdotes in crowded matatus and buses, gyrating their hips in a crowded bar before a jukebox or a live band....I need life to write about life."** *Yet* Devil on the Cross *was written in prison. How was that possible? Surely the prison did not provide you with that kind of life.*

The conditions in prison, especially for a writer, are meant to cut away that writer, or intellectual, or political worker, from contact with active life which is the root or the basis of one's inspiration. So I was really pointing out the difficulties of writing in prison, especially for me—and I suppose for most other writers—who need actual involvement in the daily laughter of the people, in their daily cries of sorrow or joy, or in any of their problems, to be able to sustain themselves as writers. In prison it is important to understand the intentions of your jailers. What they mostly want to achieve is some kind of breakdown where the political prisoner denies his previous political stance or denies his previous involvement with people. Once you understand their intentions, you can consciously start working against them. In my case I had been put in political detention in a maximum security prison because of my involvement with peasants and workers in Kenya in the building of a culture that reflected their lives and their political and economic struggles. I thought that I'd fight the jailers by writing a novel in an African language and talking about peasants and workers and their history of struggle against both foreign domination and also internal exploitation and oppression.

How did you look upon your own detention? Did you feel that you were detained as an individual, "in your own right," or as a representative, a scapegoat?

You must understand that what characterizes the neo-colonial ruling minorities in most African countries is their total isolation from the people. They see the people as their enemy, because they, the ruling minority, serve foreign interests which are obviously hostile to the people of the country. So if they could jail the whole population and get away with it, they would. But then to jail the whole population would in fact defeat the very basis of their existence as mediators between foreign economic interests and the material sources of the country. They therefore pick certain individuals whom they see as representatives of certain ways of thinking; not because of that particular individual but because they want his incarceration to be a symbolic act.

You thought of your own detention as an exemplary symbolic ritual, a rite?

Yes, I think that is correct. Our work at Kamiriithu Community and Cultural Centre was collective: It involved factory workers, poor peasants, a few intellectuals from university, petits bourgeois elements like school teachers and secretaries, and so on. I was picked, not because I was the center, but rather because they wanted to set an example and instill a climate of fear in all the others and by implication in every other collective effort in Kenya.

Your fight against the jailers, or the "demons" as you sometimes call them, was then another "symbolic" fight?

Writing *Devil on the Cross* and *Detained* I took up deliberately and very sincerely a defiant position against the social classes that had been responsible for killing democracy in Kenya. The events that have occurred since my detention are proving me right.

You mention in your book Detained *that a psychological warfare was going on all the time in prison. What was your part in this, and how could you collect the strength to wage it?*

You are in prison because you sincerely believe in certain principles and beliefs. In my case, I sincerely searched my own mind to find out whether, in what I had stood for, or in what I had been striving to stand for—that is, in my writings and in my involvement both in my teaching in Nairobi making literature relevant to the Kenyan people and in the kind of theater that we started in my village—there was something wrong. And I could not find in any corner of my whole being anything that was wrong. So the very fact that I was totally convinced that Kenyan people were right in struggling against colonial oppression and exploitation and the neo-colonialism which was aided by a few Kenyans who had imbibed the culture of imperialism, gave me the strength to stand up to the very oppressive psychological conditions in prison. What characterizes such a prison is that your jailers try to use every way possible to break you—like promises, use of a family attachment, and whatever they think you hold dear.

Is a slave-master relationship a condition that easily develops in prison?

An oppressing class or nation or group does not only want to enslave the people, but they want to see those people believing that it was really in their interest to be so enslaved. They want you to think that you are really happy being oppressed; the slave is really happy about his slavery. They even try to suggest that the slave really loves his master.

Your prison became for you an education center. How?

In Kenyan political detention prisons, detainees are not allowed to read books, they have no access to newspapers, to radios, to any type of information, not even censored information. At Kamiti Maximum Security Prison the guards were very careful not to bring in any printed matter, even advertisements or other like matter. Conditions in these prisons are extremely oppressive. So when I say that prison became my teacher, I do not mean that books were allowed and that I made use of the time there to study more, and that newspapers were available, or that I was allowed to correspond with the outside world, or that I was entitled to enter an extra-mural university course abroad. What I mean is that I tried to learn from the very severe conditions in that prison. For instance, I discovered that the warders did not realize that I had been put in because of my involvement with the collective work in my village. They had been given the impression that I was in for something more sinister than that, so if I asked them about the weather outside the prison walls they acted dumb. If I asked anything, even about trees, they would not say anything. But when it came to the question of language they believed this to be harmless, and far from being silent, they suddenly became very outspoken. For me they became very helpful, so I was quite willing not to ask them anything about what was happening on the outside, but learn more and more about their understanding of language. Most of them happened to know Kikuyu very well and were excited about discussing concepts of words and meanings. For me this was like a gift; every day they were giving me a gift, a precious gift. Another source of knowledge were the other detainees who had other experiences that I did not have. For instance, some of the prisoners had been there for eight or ten years. I was a novice in prison, so I was very keen to know how they had coped with being there for such a long time. And I was keen to know about their history.

To what extent would Devil on the Cross *have been a different book if written outside prison, or would it ever have been written?*

In a sense I do not think it could have been written, at least not in its present form. Or let me put it in another way: It would have been a different kind of *Devil.* First, the very strength to embark on a novel in a language that had no previous history of any modern novel written in it could only have come from the grim conditions of prison. In other words, maybe, if I had been outside prison, I might have been tempted to delay this more formidable task, which is to break away from certain traditions and from my own private history of writing in English. To break away from these obviously needed psychological pressure, and I felt this pressure in prison. The grimness of conditions in prison created its own opposite, a fierce determination to achieve something in a Kenyan language. Another aspect of the book is its tone; it is a little more lighthearted in tone, if not in concern. The satiric element is more dominating. If you are living in gruesome conditions, you have to develop a certain sense of humor, sometimes a satiric humor, to be able to look at reality. If you live in grim conditions, this grimness can destroy you. But if you put on a mask through which you are able to apparently laugh, then this can be another psychological prop.

How do you assess the role of Amnesty International and other organizations who worked for your release?

Somehow in prison I did learn about a committee founded in London asking for my release and that of the other political detainees. This was a tremendous source of encouragement. Oppressive regimes like to oppress, but they also like to adopt a mask for the outside. So it is a bit frightening to them when they find that nobody believes in their sort of liberalism, democracy and common sense. This kind of solidarity in support of political prisoners is so vital and necessary. A letter to the oppressive regime or to one's own government to ask them to express concern may seem a small thing, but it may make the oppressive regime uneasy, although it does not appear so on the surface.

What is the current situation in Kenya vis-à-vis *human rights?*

Several people have been detained. They are defense lawyers, journalists and university lecturers. The repression is more organized, more ruthless than at any time in the post-independence history of Kenya. One hopes that international opinion is roused against these arrests.

How do you look upon your own situation?

As a writer from the Third World, I am condemned to continue to voice the cries of protests.

---

* *Detained: A Writer's Prison Notes* (London: Heinemann, 1981), pp. 8-9.

23 Ngugi wa Thiong'o: Interview

Ingrid Björkman / 1982

Ingrid Björkman interviewed Ngugi wa Thiong'o in London in December 1982 when they discussed his play Maitu Njugira, *its background, reception and the reason for its banning by the Kenyan Government. Prior to that she was in Kenya where she interviewed people who had acted in the play as well as people who had seen it.*

Although permission was not granted for it to be performed at the Kenya National Theatre in Nairobi, as was planned, Maitu Njugira *was nevertheless a tremendous success. Whilst waiting for the stage license to arrive, the theater group went on rehearsing at the University. Between twelve and fifteen thousand people managed to see the musical before it was finally stopped. The rehearsals started at 6:30 p.m., but after 3 p.m. it was impossible to get a seat in the hall. Hired buses came from all over the country, even from as far away as Mombasa.*

Why was the musical set in the 1920s and 1930s?

Because that was when British colonialism introduced capitalism into Kenya. Now, to have capitalism you must of course have a wage-earning class. To get a wage-earning class they had to create a landless peasantry and this was done very easily by taking away people's land. The conditions in these plantations were very, very harsh, indeed. The workers could be beaten, even killed.

In order to obtain efficient control of the Kenyan labor force the colonial government passed several labor laws, for example the native registration ordinances, which made it compulsory for adult male African workers in Kenya to wear a chain and a metal container around their necks. Inside the container was an identification paper with information useful to the employer. Together with the paper the container was called the *kipande*. Not carrying a *kipande* was considered a criminal act and carried severe punishment. The emerging African petty bourgeoisie, however, was exempted from the *kipande*, as their labor force was not needed in the plantations. It can be seen that the *kipande* gave the African worker a lower status and thus contributed to the founding of the sharply structured Kenyan class society.

Whilst the capitalist wage-labor system created a Kenyan working class, it also forged the strength and consciousness of that working class against imperialism. Now, in the 1920s and 1930s, the workers of Kenya waged a tremendous struggle against these repressive labor conditions, especially as they were symbolized by the *kipande* system. And there developed songs of the different Kenyan nationalities in Kenya, expressing these anti-imperialist interests and their struggle against the repressive labor systems. So when I was about to script the play, I had to get these songs from different people. In assembling the songs I was helped by many people from different nationalities. There are four types of songs in the play. There are songs which were sung in the 1920s and 1930s, with the appropriate tunes and words. In other cases I have used old tunes and put in new words to fit into the situation of the play. On some occasions there are fresh compositions with new words and new tunes but of course related to the history of the period. And then there are contemporary songs, the tunes of which people are familiar with, but I have moved them back to the earlier period by giving them words that are, broadly speaking, appropriate to those times.

The result of this collective work has been an all-Kenyan musical drama which addresses itself to Kenyans of all nationalities. The spoken text, which is in Gikuyu, is confined to a minimum and the drama relies heavily on mime, song and dance, which are, Ngugi says, "part and parcel of the national cultural traditions of the Kenyan people." Was that the reason why you chose the art form of a musical?

Yes, one of the reasons. The peasants often expressed themselves through song. Their songs were functional. They sang during their work, when they were digging the earth, harvesting, building the railway, and so on. There are songs of fatigue. People sang to get strength and courage. If you look at the struggles of Kenya, you will find that the revolt of the people has often been expressed through their cultural assertions, especially through song.

Another reason for making *Maitu Njugira* a musical was that it was going to be performed at the National Theatre in Nairobi, where of course one anticipated audiences from different nationalities and different linguistic groups, who would not necessarily understand Gikuyu. So I was trying to develop a theater that could speak to people despite the language barriers. In *Maitu Njugira* there was less emphasis on dialogue and more emphasis on action, dance, mime and song.

In Kenya, a few months ago, I interviewed a number of non-Gikuyu-speaking Kenyans who had seen Maitu Njugira, *in order to find out if they had understood the play. Everybody, even quite illiterate informants, had understood it completely and gave me detailed information about the story. And everybody had been profoundly moved. Many had seen the musical several times. I was told that towards the end of the performance the audience had often streamed onto the stage, joined in the dancing, and the whole theater had united in the final song. They had been filled with sadness, with hope, and above all with the feeling that "we are one people, we are all Kenyans." And they had walked home in the warm night singing "A people united can never be defeated." I am told, however, that the ending of the original script was not positive. Is that correct?*

Yes. But the actors rejected the ending, because they found it too pessimistic. They felt that they had to show that despite the tremendous oppression the struggle continues. The fact that one was defeated did not mean that one could not rise up again and continue the struggle.

According to the people who were interviewed, the actors had really succeeded in conveying their spirit of defiance and survival to the audience by emphasizing the symbolic solution shown in different silent scenes: a stick is broken into pieces, one piece after another. Then the broken pieces are tied together into a bundle—and look! It is impossible to break the bundle.

One of the questions I asked was "why had the audience been so fascinated and moved by the play?" Most people interviewed said it was because of the strong commitment and the exceptional creative power of the actors, who were not professionals but workers from Kamiriithu village and Nairobi. How was it possible, people asked, that ordinary uneducated people could perform in such an outstanding way? One of the informants said: "They did not perform. They were themselves."

I think the reason why they participated with such great enthusiasm was that they felt that the play was telling them something about themselves. They felt that the theater they evolved was reflecting the true history of their struggle against the colonial stage of imperialism. And they participated in so many ways, all the time. They taught us how to dance. They rejected songs and added new ones. They really participated in developing the script, which is definitely not the work of one man.

Some of the participants told me how happy they were while working with the two plays. Now they say they have lost their hope. The communal art of traditional society seems to have been revived at Kamiriithu, which must have meant a lot to the villagers?

The important thing is not so much that it is communal but rather what it has to say. It is the nature of reality reflected in that art. In this case the people felt that the theater they evolved was part and parcel of their true history. But of course I think that art, theater, should be communal. Cultural activity is something that is natural for everybody, not just for a few professional artists. Evolving theater is creative. It stimulates, creates discussion.

One reason for my choosing the dramatic art form is that more people get involved. It makes them discuss not only the script but also their social problems. And in the course of the discussion it happened that they changed the script.

Don't you think that they had a feeling that this dramatic action could lead them to another sort of action, that they could help to change their social reality?

I recently read a line from Martin Carter. It goes like this: "I do not sleep to dream, but dream to change the world."* People must not only understand the world but they must understand it in order to change it, to make it meet their needs in a more meaningful way.

The audience felt that the musical was telling them something about themselves, and that was the main reason for their commitment. The play took place on a plantation where the white settler, after having been shot by the workers because of his ruthless oppression, is succeeded by a Kenyan who continues the oppression of the people in the same way as his predecessor. The musical is set in the 1920s and 1930s with a background of projections of slides showing the actual laws regulating the conditions of the workers at that time. However, the audience had felt that the musical reflected not only the social reality of Kenyans fifty years ago but also their own contemporary reality. They had seen the present through the past, and they had realized that Kenyan society had not changed in any essential respect since those days.

To understand this, one has to make it clear how Kenya has developed after flag independence. Have the dreams of freedom been realized? No, they have not. Kenyan raw materials and markets are controlled, and the Kenyan people are ruthlessly exploited by foreign imperialist forces, supported by a corrupt native ruling class which has been educated within the colonial system and has inherited the colonial ideology. The people who fought the struggle of independence have been betrayed. In order to change their conditions they have to unite across the borders of language, nationalities, races.

Now, the economic consequences of neo-colonialism are massive impoverishment of the peasantry and the working population. Politically the ruling regime becomes even more detached from the people and it can only maintain power by detention and murder of democratic dissidents and through military terrorism of the entire population. We have never been allowed to try out democracy in

Kenya and see if it worked. But the oppression was less comprehensive previously, more sporadic than it is now.

But economic and political control can never be complete and efficient without mental control through the control of the people's culture. The native bourgeoisie, through which imperialism in a neo-colonial state like Kenya works, controls the state instruments of coercion, persuasion and propaganda. In their state-controlled cinemas, theaters, TV stations and radio they allow foreign programs. No foreign play or any play by foreign European groups has ever been prevented from staging at the National Theatre. At the same time as *Maitu Njugira* was stopped from being performed at the National Theatre, *Flame Trees of Thika,* a film in seven episodes based on Elspeth Huxley's book of the same title, was bought and screened on Kenya National Television despite a great national outcry. The book pictures the Kenya of the 1920s and 1930s, the same period as *Maitu Njugira,* but from a colonial point of view. Both the book and the film portray Kenyans as dumb creatures, part and parcel of the animal world and natural landscape. A musical, depicting in a Kenyan language and music the heroic struggle of Kenyan workers against the very repressive colonial labor laws, was hounded out of the Kenya National Theatre. But a film showing that Kenyans had no capacity for resistance was given prime time on television for several weeks. Now the Government has increased its control by censoring and even stopping small plays which school pupils perform for each other. The police go through libraries to find out who reads what, and all school text books must be approved by a special commission.

In discussing neo-colonialism one of the inevitable subjects is culture-clash; could you say something about this?

The conflict of cultures is often seen in the simple terms of a conflict between the rural and the urban, or between tradition and modernity, but this is a deliberate mystification of the real conflict. The conflict is class-bound. Out of the struggle for total liberation from imperialism there emerged a new national culture, rooted in the patriotic and heroic traditions of the peasantry. The programmed attempts to destroy people's dances, songs and literature created its opposite. There are today in the colonies and neo-colonial societies two cultures in mortal conflict: a foreign imperialist culture and a national patriotic culture, which is a resistance culture and is both urban and rural. This national culture is in opposition to foreign imperialist exploitation and domination as well as to internal exploitation and oppression by a native ruling class in servile alliance with imperialism.

The period in which *Maitu Njugira* is set was the period when this modern culture of resistance emerged. There was a tremendous cultural assertion. Most of our poets and singers in the 1920s and 1930s as well as in the 1950s were imprisoned by the British for the songs they sang.

Fifty years ago, thirty years ago, the singers of the people were imprisoned by the British. Today they are imprisoned by their fellow countrymen. *Maitu Njugira* is made up of songs from the 1930s which were forbidden then. It pictures the social reality of the 1930s. And it is forbidden today. One can have no clearer illustration of how those in power today have dissociated themselves from their own people and have identified with the former colonial power.

As a writer in what way do you think you can help change our world into a better one?

As a writer I can only help people to understand the forces at work in their society. I can only hope to try as faithfully as I can to reflect all these forces. And I would like people to understand what affects their lives and in the very process of understanding—be they Kenyans, Swedish, British, Americans—help them work out for themselves the options open to them.

---

* This line comes from Martin Carter's poem "Looking at Your Hands" first published in his collection *The Hill of Fire Glows Red* in 1951.

24 "To Choose a Language Is to Choose a Class": Interview with Ngugi wa Thiong'o

G. G. Darah (with the assistance of J.S. Zwingina) / 1983 (1985)

This interview was conducted at 2 Albert Road, London, N1, on 24 March 1983.

The Land Question

We want to talk to you about your literary activities as well as the political situation in Kenya. Let us start with the land question which occupies a central place in your works. What is the peculiarity of the land question in Kenya that makes it such an important theme in your work?

The land question is basic to the history of Kenya, especially the history of colonialism and the anti-colonial struggle. As you know, Kenya was a settler colony, meaning that the British came and settled in Kenya. They did this by taking away land from Kenyans. That is why the land question is so basic to that history. The British colonialists needed labor on the land, so they forced African peoples to work on the land they had taken away from them in the first instance. To get the labor, the British had to institute a very repressive political machinery, because that was the only way they could compel people to work on the land they had stolen. You can therefore see that the land question touches on nearly every aspect of Kenyan history right from 1885 to the present. It is interesting that the Mau Mau freedom fighters called themselves Kenya Land and Freedom Army.

How did the name become known as Mau Mau?

Nobody knows the origin of the word Mau Mau, but the proper name for the organization was Kenya Land and Freedom Army. I think the word Mau Mau may have been a label used for the organization by the British and which stuck with use.

If you consider the participation of the educated elite in most of the anti-colonial struggles, what would you say characterized the Kenyan elite and how it came to be that the land issue was not resolved? In other words, how did the elite link up with the peasant struggle that led to the land question being unresolved after independence? You recall that you refer to this problem in all your novels up to Petals of Blood.

The matter can be approached by looking at the classes generated by colonialism. The colonialism we had in Africa was colonialism of imperialism, that is, colonialism at the stage of expansionism. Which meant of course that the system of production introduced (in Kenya) was a capitalist one. You can now see that the classes generated by this system were the peasantry (which was already there), and for the first time, a working class, because you can't have capital without paid labor. So the process of alienating people from their land also created a working class in Kenya....Initially, this was a small class, but it has been growing since then. The other class generated by the same system was that of clerks and educated elements that were supposed to help in the administration of the colonial system. This is the genesis of that class known as the petty bourgeoisie which also grew in size as the system developed. It is this petty bourgeoisie born out of the womb of colonialism that assumed power in Kenya. Of course, the petty bourgeoisie as I have analyzed in my book *Detained* falls into different categories; there is an imperialist-leaning group, there are the middle elements that see salvation in form of national capitalism, and of course, the lower petty bourgeoisie which believes that some form of socialism is the only system that can bring about change in Kenya.

Unfortunately, it is the group that leans towards imperialism that has managed to control state power and this has meant that they have not brought about any structural changes in Kenyan society. On the contrary, they have continued to strengthen colonial structures.

In Weep Not, Child, *the process of land alienation is depicted; in* A Grain of Wheat, *independence is approaching but there are already doubts about what kind of independence it will be. It is only when we come to* Petals of Blood *that we see an artistic elaboration of the struggles that involve the different classes....*

In writing generally, there are a number of things we take into consideration. Of course there is what the author is concerned about—e.g., the classes in society and the sympathies he has for this or that class, and his own understanding or appreciation of the processes at work, or rather his social vision. I will say that in writing those books, my own perspective was developing all the time, because you can look at the same material from a particular perspective and it will yield a certain insight; and you can look at the same material from another perspective and yet it yields more or fewer insights. I can say the difference between my early works and *Petals of Blood* has to do, I think, with my growing social visions or the shifting base from which I look at Kenyan society.

Would you say that there have been certain events within Kenyan intellectual history that have affected this development? For example, in discussing with John La Rose, who is well-informed on the Kenyan situation, he gave us to understand that the tradition of intellectual radicalism in Kenya is not as pronounced as it is in other parts of Africa. He gave the instance of the role of universities; that whereas in other countries universities have multiplied into campuses and thereby provided opportunities for radical ideas to flourish, there was only one university (Nairobi) until lately, when Kenyatta University College was established. John La Rose seems to imply that your case is a rare one in a generally conservative climate.

No, I wouldn't think so, because the tradition of radicalism in Kenya goes back to the early part of this century. Some of the pronouncements of labor leaders in the 1920s—e.g., Harry Thuku—show that they were in touch with the most radical thought of the time. In 1920, the workers held a big rally in Nairobi to demand the release of Harry Thuku from detention. If you read the early pronouncements of Jomo Kenyatta in the 1940s, their anti-imperialist line is very consistent. If you look at the organization of the Kenya Land and Freedom Army, you will find that it was, in fact, a modern guerilla struggle against a colonial power in Africa. It adopted the method of armed struggle to demand land and freedom.

However, the important point to note is that the colonial power managed to isolate Kenyan radicalism from the tradition of Marxist thinking. Colonialism was very effective in this tactic....If you analyze some of the debates going on in the Literature Department of the University of Nairobi, you will see that some of the publications are first-rate in terms of the social awareness that informs them. The debate over the change of the syllabus to bring in a Third World dimension was very intense when it started as early as 1969....It is in Kenya that there have been the most radical changes in the literature syllabus of all schools. It is unfortunate that it has not been fully implemented, but the perspectives are very deep. But as I have said, the colonial and postcolonial regimes have attempted (but not succeeded) to insulate the people from this kind of thinking.

Now that you mention the international exchange of ideas, would you say that the comparative success of the Algerian anti-colonial struggle and that of Kenya had to do with the role of the elite in each case? For instance, take the issue of betrayal in your works. Would you attribute the menace of tragic betrayal to the character of the elite leadership or the organizational set-up of the anti-colonial movements? Or would you agree with Frantz Fanon that the local bourgeoisie is incapable of effecting an anti-colonial revolution?

Of course the weaknesses of the organization are crucial, but the petty bourgeoisie in Kenya is determined to maintain the colonial structures. For instance, most of the key figures in the present arap Moi regime were collaborators with colonialism. It is these elements that now control state power. There is no doubt that there were weaknesses in the conduct of the anti-colonial struggle. But what is important now is the lesson people learn from that history.

Let us turn to the issue of exploitation in Petals of Blood *as depicted in the image of Sinbad, a character taken from* Arabian Nights. *You refer frequently to this image in the novel, and in your recent talk—*

"Writing for Peace"—to a group in Western Europe you also invoked the image. In a section of Petals of Blood *you say that for as long as Sinbad sits on the back of the Old Man of the Sea the crisis of exploitation will continue.*

The image comes from a particular story which fascinates me in the *Arabian Nights*. You know some of the stories in that book involve the activities or adventures of Sinbad the sailor. In one of his adventures Sinbad meets the Old Man of the Sea, and the old man looks helpless....The situation shows that Sinbad is a parasite. This invokes in me the relationship between the producing class and the parasitic classes in any social system.

Let us consider the appropriateness of the metaphor in the work. Many students these days, who didn't attend the kind of schools our generation went to, will neither recognize the Sinbad personage nor the context from which it is taken....

When one is writing, one does not do so in a vacuum in the sense that one has read certain kinds of literature and has heard stories; and obviously one refers to images arising from what one has read. This happens in all writing. The reader may not have seen any of these references, but it is for him to strive to understand these images.

There is this problem with the compass of the plot of Petals of Blood. *As I told you in an earlier conversation, the novel seems to be straining to encompass a long history of the Kenyan people, going back into the precolonial and precapitalist times....In teaching the book one feels this strain that too much is packed into the life-span of the story. Do you feel the same way yourself?*

As I have told people, the writing of the book took me six or seven years to complete. It is one of my few books which I might call pure exploration in the sense that I had no conception of how the novel was going to develop. So, every single sentence, every single paragraph, every single word, was more or less a wrestling with the new themes. It is a novel which grew with me over a period of seven years. I don't think it contains too much. I think a novel should suggest as much as it is able to. But of course, it is for the reader to assess whether or not the structure is able to carry the burden of the theme....

Take the aspect of Karega's coming into a state of awareness. Towards the end of the book he leaves the village of Ilmorog and comes back a transformed man, having been through the purgatory of exploitation on the eastern coast. But we don't see in action the process by which the workers as a collective *acquire class consciousness. All we hear are hints of the process as we follow the experiences of Karega, Wanja, Abdulla, and Munira. We don't see how the workers gain consciousness as they encounter capital.*

...The structure would not have allowed it. And I was aware of it; you can see how a period of five years is compressed. Karega goes away, and when next we see him, five years have elapsed. I tried to compress his experiences. Maybe this will form the subject of another work....

The Use of Religion

In Devil on the Cross, *we see an interesting use of the symbol of the cross. The cross in the consciousness of most African people who have encountered colonial culture is the burden of a savior. What did you hope to achieve in the reversal of symbolic meaning in the title of the book?*

As I write, I like to use images I think appeal to the people. I know the cross, as you say, would quite easily appeal to a lot of readers because of the influence of Christianity. By changing the image, you compel people to think about it, you force attention on the subject. People are used to associating a cross with a certain outlook; but now, you compel them to look at the image afresh when the Devil instead of Jesus is on the cross.

In A Grain of Wheat, *you focus on the use of Christian religion for the conquest of the Africans' souls. A similar attitude is evident in* I Will Marry When I Want. *But in* Petals of Blood, *especially in relation to the character of Munira, religion is depicted as a revolutionary force....*

There are people who are driven by moral idealism to fight against the ills of society. It has to do with my point of view of religion: that religion often reflects the real ills of society. In terms of reflection, what is often wrong with the religious is that they go on to offer wrong solutions. I think this is one of the reasons religious songs appeal to so many people; it is because of their invocation of real misery. But the same religion is not able to show the roots of this misery and the solution to it.

The example of Munira in *Petals* is used to show the difference between idealism and, if you like, materialism. Munira and Karega represent two opposing world outlooks or philosophical views on the whole work of nature, of society and human thought. There may be a meeting point, but the idealist and materialist world outlooks are poles apart. But to the extent that they are looking at the same subject, there is a meeting point….They differ in how they look at the same material (problem), how they interpret it, and in terms of solutions they offer.

Would you say that this power of Christian religion to tame the mind is absent in African religions? For example, the metaphysical outlook of the Ilmorog peasants does not preclude the alternative of struggling to alter reality. Is it only the Christian religion that invokes justice yet forbids human struggles to attain it…?

A lot of religions, even pre-Christian Judaism, which we see very clearly in the Old Testament of the Bible, tend to be tied up with the social forces at work in the society. You can see how the prophets in the Old Testament were, in fact, social visionaries. All pre-capitalist African religions offered such visionaries. What is special about Christianity, especially when it is appropriated by capitalists, is this insistence on original sin; that whatever may be wrong in the world has to do with the fact that someone has sinned; that it has nothing to do with the social processes at work, but rather with something internal to that person's spiritual make-up. And if what is wrong with society is because of man's original sin, then the solution to the problem cannot be found in society. This is what is really devastating about Christianity.

African Literature: What Language?

Let us consider the issue of the language of African literature which you have commented upon in the past few years. I recall your views in an issue of South *magazine in which you said that a people's imaging of itself cannot be adequately done in a foreign, alien language. You implied that the usefulness of European languages for African literature is limited; that it is better to write in African languages than in the foreign ones....*

I spent some time on this language question in my book *Writers in Politics* because I think it is a very crucial issue. I find it is a peculiarity that African writers as a group do not want to use the very vehicle which is at hand: African languages. It is a historical peculiarity that a whole generation of the interpreters of a society use languages that are not part of that society, although the society has its languages. I see this as part of a neo-colonial tradition in Africa. As long as people persist in interpreting themselves through vehicles (linguistic) that are external to themselves, they are continuing that neo-colonial tradition. Writing in neo-colonial languages is not different from interpreting African history from European perspectives....What we need is to get our perspective correct. An African writer should use his cultural base in Africa to look at the world, just in the same way that a Chinese writer, for example, looks at the world from a Chinese base. It is only African writers who feel compelled to consciously or deliberately refuse to exploit the very resources that are available to them. African writers have gone to great lengths to introduce African rhythms of speech into English, French and Portuguese languages. Why go into all these contortions when the original languages are there to be used...? It is as if we can only be recognized if we excel in writing novels in English or French.

Don't you think the potential audience the writer has in mind determines the language he uses? Take, for example, a plural society like Nigeria where there are hundreds of languages. Many of these languages have no standard orthographies yet. As languages they can carry any thoughts or expressions, but as vehicles for literature, don't you think there will be a problem of readership?

You can see that Christianity and other colonial institutions are, in fact, more advanced than African writers in this respect. Christianity does not see these languages as being too small to put the Bible into. Yet we Africans complain that such and such language is not developed, has no orthography, etc. I have said elsewhere, paraphrasing Fanon, that to choose a language is to choose a class. Fanon says to choose a language is to choose a world. So when we use the English language, willy-nilly, no matter the radicalism in the subject matter, our target audience must remain the audience defined by our ability to use that language. The working class can occasionally cope with that language, but on the whole it precludes the peasantry and a majority of the working class.

The issue to address, it seems to me, is the difference between an oral medium and a written one in the creation of literature. Even when you write in Gikuyu, Yoruba, or Wolof, the peasantry which constitutes the majority of the population at this point in time has no access to the works. The peasantry is not literate in these languages. So how do we tackle this problem?

That is true, and it has to do with larger political issues—the nature of the societies we have, the attitude to the languages, etc. But how has a sizeable proportion of the peasantry and working class in Africa been reached by the Bible?

Mainly through the middle-class interpreters—the catechists and lay readers who read the Bible.

If there are more novels, if more reading material in these languages is available to the peasantry, it will find the ways of overcoming the hurdle of illiteracy. I will give an example. When my novel *Devil on the Cross* came out in Gikuyu in 1980, a startling fact emerged in terms of sales....The fact that another book of a particular size, apart from the Bible, was available in the Gikuyu language, was very amazing to a number of readers. I knew a number of peasants who had the book, and who were amazed that a book could be written in the Gikuyu language. They had always thought that only the Bible could be rendered in Gikuyu. So this was a psychological breakthrough for them. Secondly, in terms of sales, the initial print of five thousand copies was sold out in four months. We had to order a reprint of five thousand. They were also sold out. So within a short period the publishers did two reprints of five thousand each....This was a higher rate of sale than can be achieved by an equivalent book in the English language.

Another interesting point revealed was the nature of the readership....In a way, *Devil on the Cross* was appropriated by the peasantry and integrated into the oral tradition. The book, I know for sure, was read in families. A family would get a copy and ask one of their literate members to read sections to them every evening. And I know a particular family where a literate member was enjoying a certain kind of power playing this role of interpreter. The book was read to groups in buses. Anyone reading a section might decide to read aloud to passengers throughout a journey. A readership also developed in drinking places. There is the story of one particular reader who would go to a bar to read, and would lead the audience to a position where they would want to hear what happens next, and he would stop reading because his glass was empty. And the listeners in the bar would say, "Please have more beer!" Workers in factories read the book in groups during break time.

Another thing which is part of the appropriation of the book by the oral tradition was the amount of publicity this method gave it. Certainly it was not mentioned in the press; there were no criticisms of it in the press or radio. So the publicity must have been by word of mouth. What all this illustrates is that if written literature were available in the African languages people would choose the literature to identify with. There would be the very important interaction between the African writer and the peasantry and the working class. And this would lead to great changes.

The situation I have described above occurred with our play *I Will Marry When I Want* when it was published. It went into three printings within the same year. At the moment over thirty thousand copies in the Gikuyu language have been sold. This was a record sale for Heinemann; in fact, a record for any play written in English or Swahili, or any other language. Even the publishers could hardly understand the phenomenon of a play selling without it being part of the school syllabus. Which means, in fact, that the real audience of our literature is outside of the school system; it is in the peasantry and working class....

The problem to remember, however, is that since we don't have one common African language in any country, it means in effect that any work in any of the languages can reach only a section of the national peasantry. But in class terms it is better to reach a single peasant than not reach any peasant at all. In a place like Nigeria, for instance, a good book in either Hausa or Yoruba could be translated into Igbo or any other indigenous language and it will be speaking to the peasants in these nationalities and they will feel: "Oh, so we are the same; we have the same problems." So the plurality of languages which now looks like a limitation can be turned to advantage.

The Writer Is an Editor

Now that you mentioned I Will Marry When I Want, *let us talk about your dramatic works. It appears that apart from* The Black Hermit, *all your other dramatic works have been done in collaboration with other authors. Is there any special reason why you have chosen to collaborate with colleagues in this area?*

In a sense all works of art are really acts of collaboration—and even the business of novel-writing. When I look at the process of creating a novel, I become convinced that it is not as individual as it appears. If you sit down to relate how this episode or that came from where and from whom, and at what time, etc., you will discover that the writer functions as an editor but using the imaginative sieve as an editorial machine. That is why these days I am not afraid to acknowledge the debt I owe to several people, although I may not mention them by name....I see a work like *Devil on the Cross* as a collective effort with me being the editor, if you like. The same thing applies to the dramatic pieces. It is clear to me that a play like *Ngaahika Ndeenda* was more than a collaboration between two people. Although I'm one of the authors, in terms of contribution of specific material such as songs and other things, we owe these to other people....In a sense the strength of oral narratives and proverbs was due to the fact that the work was a product of collective effort.

The material from the oral lore was added on and on until the work became the essence of our collective kind of wisdom over a period of time.

From the way they appear in print, the speeches of the actors in this play are in verse form. Was there any special reason for this?

I wouldn't call it verse. I find it easier to write the Gikuyu language in such a way that each line contains or carries a complete thought....

You had the Kamiriithu Community Education and Cultural Centre which the Kenyan government attempted to destroy. Is the report true that permission had to be obtained from the government to stage the plays at the Centre?

What happened in Kenya during the colonial period was that a theater group had to be registered before it became a legal organization. And even then, for each play to be produced a license had to be secured from the provincial administration.

Does this law still hold in Kenya?

Yes, every theater group has to be registered. It is a law. In present-day Kenya more than five people constitute a public meeting. And legally they can be arrested and prosecuted if they meet without permission. It has not been easy to enforce the law, but it is there in the books.

How would you estimate the damage to artistic development represented by the Kamiriithu Centre now that it has been destroyed by government?

They have razed it to the ground, but they cannot kill the Kamiriithu idea. It was more than just a center in a little village. It has become a phenomenon.

Is Ngugi wa Mirii, your collaborator, still in Kenya?

No, he is in Zimbabwe where he and others are establishing community centers in different parts of the country.

Similar to the Kamiriithu one?

Yes, they have produced *The Trials of Dedan Kimathi* in the Shona language. This was at a community center far away from Harare, the capital.

Three Continents, One Struggle

Another area we would want to discuss is the tri-continental perspective that has emerged in your critical statements. Since your essays in Homecoming *you seem to be focusing on the literatures of Africa, Latin America, and Asia as a common heritage.*

It is a question of world perspective; it has to do with the idea of base which I mentioned earlier. How do we look at ourselves? How do we look at the international scene? You see, when most people talk of internationalism, often they mean internationalism with Europe as the base. They don't seem to realize that we can look at the international scene with Africa, Asia, or Latin America as a base. My concern is an internationalism with the Third World as the center or starting point; or internationalism that takes the working class, the peasantry, as focus.

Besides the fact of historical and cultural similarity, is there anything, say in the literature of these areas, that appeals to you specially?

It is their literature that fascinates me. It is a product of the same forces that have shaped the life of the Africans. In fact, the literature of Latin American people is of immense value to other peoples. The isolation of African literary experience from that of Latin America and Asia is a weakness in our cultural policy. I wish there were more interchange between the literary traditions of Africa, Latin America, and Asia. For instance, the Korean poet Kim Chi Ha makes (such) a penetrating and accurate analysis of neo-colonialism based on the South Korean experience, and his portrayal has almost a word-for-word application to any part of Africa.

It is clear from your works and statements that you use the weapon of literature in the service of the anti-imperialist struggle. How it is that Heinemann—one of the cultural agencies of imperialism—has continued to publish your works?

We live in a world of contradictions and limitations. The point, however, is how we can turn a limitation into an advantage. Let me give you an example. I wanted *Devil on the Cross* to come out in the Gikuyu language. I wanted the standard of production to be the same as that of an equivalent novel in the English language. I knew the novel could have been produced in some less sophisticated way, but by the terms of the attitudes we have towards the industrialized world's publishing tradition, it was very important that the production of *Devil on the Cross* in Gikuyu be not one iota less in quality than that of an equivalent novel in the English language. This meant that the publishers had to be prepared to invest in the quality of production I demanded....This is what I mean by turning a limitation into an asset....

Do you imply by that that neither the East African Literature Bureau nor the Tanzanian Publishing House can do the job of publishing as well as Heinemann would?

Let me not speculate on the performance capabilities of other firms. But what I would like to say is that even if you get an African indigenous firm that can do the work equally well, it may not be willing to invest in such a project. All I'm saying is that in this case I was turning the contradictions which were there into strength....

As a writer and political activist, how are you able to produce such a number of books and at the same time engage in political activity, teaching, and research, especially given the underdeveloped infrastructures in our society?

Frankly, I always feel guilty that I have not done more. I believe there is always time to do that which ought to be done. My own regret is that I've not been able to do as I feel I ought to be able to do. For instance, I would like to write more novels and plays in the Gikuyu language and produce films in African languages. I would like to do more critical analysis of Third World literatures....I would like to keep up with progressive thinking coming from Nigeria, from Arabic-speaking Africa, etc. It's frustrating to me that I'm not able to do this....Think of these giants of history—Marx, Lenin, Mao—the things they were able to do. If you look at their writings, they are full of the minutest details. I'm always amazed when I read their works; and I feel so small in relation to them. I'm amazed that a human being can do so much in a lifetime. And yet they were able to find time for laughter, for relaxation.

In view of what you've just said, what is your attitude to an African writer who claims to be apolitical?

There is no writer who is apolitical. The point is: Whose politics is a writer espousing in his works? In connection with political activity, the people who are involved in practice seem to produce more works. For example, I found my involvement in the Kamiriithu Community Education and Cultural Centre as very important because it compelled the need for production. The practical demands of the situation made one produce certain works as opposed to when one sits down in a room and begins to ask: "What am I going to write on now?" But in Kamiriithu, the demand of the situation provided one with themes and expressions.

Again, when I came to Britain a few months ago, I had no intention of publishing another book so soon, but the demand of the Kenyan situation compelled me to bring together my essays written recently on the cultural repression in Kenya and the resistance to that repression. These essays are coming out as *Barrel of a Pen.*[1] This is a book which is entirely a product of the campaign for the release of political prisoners in Kenya.

In order to struggle on these various "fronts" simultaneously, how much of your social life do you have to forego?

If you are talking of private pleasure, then a lot. At Kamiriithu, for instance, there was literally no time available to me to go to a bar for a drink….

Finally, what would you say is the impact on the literary scene of the Bookfair[2] event just concluded?

The first remarkable impact of the fair is that it brings together African peoples from Africa, the Caribbean, North America, the Western European continent, and England itself. The coming together has shown that there is a reservoir of tremendous power. I am very excited to see such a sea of black faces surging around books, massing through exhibitions, attending poetry readings, etc. This is evidence of black literary power, a power arising from working class/peasant struggles. The fair is organized around a specific issue as against that of a conference in a scholarly sense. This is a coming together, around, if you like, a practical thing.

Do you think that this kind of crystallization of intellectual resources points to any vision of a more revolutionary practice in the Third World?

I hope it generates such a development; I'm sure it is going to have other effects too. Take, for instance, the discussion we're having now. Although I have always been interested in what is going on in Nigeria, now I will have a keener interest. Also, our discussion on the activities of the Committee for the Release of Political Prisoners in Kenya will compel you to follow more closely than before events in Kenya. We will now be in a better position than before to compare the happenings in Nigeria and Kenya. Those of us in the Committee will now show greater concern about the writings coming from Nigeria, the organizations whose activities advance democratic struggles, etc. This kind of relationship will grow with other people with whom one has had contact during the Bookfair. So, contacts such as these which look very small are really very big in terms of implications.

---

[1] Now published by New Beacon Books, London, 1983.

[2] Second International Fair of Radical Black and Third World Books.

25 Ngugi wa Thiong'o

Jane Wilkinson / 1983, 1984 (1992)

The interview consists of discussions carried out at the Heinemann Educational Books offices in London (July 1983) and at the English Studies Department of Rome University (May 1984). Extracts from the earlier interview have appeared in Italian in Rinascita, *XL, 37 (23 September 1983), pp. 27-8.*

Although you are best known for your novels, your plays have had particular importance in the development of your position as a writer and of course in your life itself. Would you like to talk about this?

Well, my primary interest is obviously the novel, but I have also been interested in theater. Or rather I have been drawn into theater, unwillingly, sometimes, but now it is one of my major preoccupations. I started writing plays in the 1960s and some of my early plays, including *The Black Hermit*, were written when I was a student at Makerere University, but up to 1977 the plays I had written or the plays I had collaborated on with other writers, like the one I wrote with Micere Mugo called *The Trial of Dedan Kimathi*, were all written in the English language. But in 1977 I started working with peasants and workers at Kamiriithu Community Education and Cultural Centre. Initially I was invited by the peasants to work there to help, along with other people, in the development of adult literacy and culture in the village, with theater obviously being at the center of the cultural activities. But I had never before really confronted the issue of language directly until I worked with that community, so the question arose: theater, but theater in what language?

The process of answering that question in theory and practice changed my life. For one thing, when a friend of mine called Ngugi wa Mirii and I drafted the first play in the Gikuyu language called

Ngaahika Ndeenda (I Will Marry When I Want) for that community, we found that they knew the language much better than we did, so it was a kind of revelation to us, this process of having to learn our language anew. Then when we came to write about the history of the people, we realized the people knew their history *much* better than we did for they had been participants in that history, the history of the struggle against British colonialism. Again, working in a collective spirit among the peasants and factory workers was very crucial in my development, really *seeing* the results that can be produced by people putting their resources together so that each person could contribute whatever little or big talent he had in a common pool, which produced fantastic results. The play became very successful, with peasants and workers coming from miles and miles to see this play which was being performed at an open-air theater built by the peasants of the village themselves. But the Kenyan regime stopped the public performance of the play in 1977 and I myself was arrested and detained for a year at a maximum security prison for the whole of 1977-78.

In 1981, we once again tried to revive the theater and the same group from the same village tried to perform *Maitu Njugira* or *Mother, Sing for Me*, scripted by myself. This is a kind of musical drama really, celebrating the struggles of Kenyan workers in the 1930s: Kenyan workers who were struggling against very repressive labor laws. Now this play, this musical drama, was rehearsed in November-December of 1981 and also January and part of February of 1982. But once again the peasants, the theater group from Kamiriithu, were not allowed to perform, even though this time they were going to perform at the Kenya National Theatre in Nairobi. What they did was interesting because they moved to the university premises and continued with their rehearsals, but these rehearsals were public so that about ten thousand people fortunately were able to see them, but these rehearsals too were stopped. Now the regime did something that was even more frightening. On March 11 they came to our village, de-registered Kamiriithu Community Theatre and Cultural Centre, banned *all* theater activities in the village and on the following day, very early in the morning, they brought three truckloads of armed policemen and razed the whole open-air theater to the ground. So the theater which was built with so much effort and love in 1977 is now no more, thanks to the armed policemen of the Kenyan neo-colonial regime.

This was done openly?

Openly, yes. I'm talking about 12 March 1982. But this was the beginning of the current cultural repression in Kenya. Many university lecturers were later detained including many members of the opposition in Kenya. One, for instance, was Ali Amin Mazrui, who had his play *Cry for Justice* performed at the University of Nairobi in May. Two or three weeks later he was arrested and put in detention without trial. Others have been put in prison on trumped-up charges. So you can see that, though my primary interest has been the novel, my interest in the theater has so far been the one that has really changed my life and therefore now I am inevitably more and more committed to theater.

So this is why you chose the theater as a medium of expression?

In a sense I did not choose theater, but theater chose me: I have never sat down to write a play in the same way that I have often sat down to write a novel. I've always written plays as a result of some kind of request, so there's always been some kind of communal demand for me to present a script and this was particularly clear in 1977 when I even thought I had given up on theater. In 1977 there was this demand from the peasants of the village for that kind of script or outline of script in which I collaborated with Ngugi wa Mirii. Theater is very much a communal effort because even if you want to write a script it still needs a director, it still needs actors and, finally, it still needs an audience. Now, in a Kenyan-type situation, theater has another dimension which I think is quite important and this is its capacity for immediate communication. Once you're involved in theater then you see the kind of impact that it can make and, when you see the total group involvement in the whole project, it's like nothing else I know of apart from maybe actual struggle, but in ordinary life theater gives you a special kind of joy and that's why people who go into theater don't want to leave it, although it also has a lot of headaches. I'm sure it's this communal involvement as well as this capacity for theater to make some kind of immediate impact so that you're communicating fairly directly and immediately, that draws me into it. But there's a very big difference between the writing of *The Black Hermit* in the 1960s and the composition of *I Will Marry When I Want* in the 1970s. In the scripting of *I Will Marry When I Want* there was much greater communal involvement: Whereas in 1962 I could write a script and present it to the actors, and the actors would go on stage trying to memorize each line as written in the script, with *I Will Marry When I Want* the people themselves were involved in the development of the script.

When we did the first outline of the play, Ngugi wa Mirii and I, we took it back to the village and, between April, May, and roughly June, people were reading the script and adding to it, commenting here and there and so on, for instance on the use of language. Because of the school system Ngugi wa Mirii and I had been used to conceptualizing thoughts in English, but the people had been using their language all their lives, so they knew it much better than we did and they sometimes found our use of the language was rather defective in places. The old men and women, for instance, would tell us that if you want an old man to speak with dignity, he uses this kind of imagery or this kind of proverb and so on.

When we came to rehearsals of the play, again, this was done in the open and the spectators were as much directors as the formal directors: each person was commenting on whatever was happening on the stage as we were rehearsing. In fact, I remember one actor who was recruited because of the audience. There was one actor who was very thin and tall and he was trying to portray a rich man in Kenya. Now most rich people in Kenya develop what Kenyans call "public opinion": They are very fat, they develop very big tummies, and these tummies are called public opinions because they put their noses or their stomach-noses into other people's affairs. Now, this person was very thin and somehow he was not quite able to portray "public opinion" in the right way, so there was one person in the audience who became very angry and said, "No, look, those people, they walk like *this*...." And he did it so well that the people who were watching him gave him a kind of ovation and so he had to continue playing that role. He was recruited into the play by the spectators.

So there was a lot of communal involvement in *I Will Marry When I Want,* and I can say that the script which has been translated into English was really the result of that cooperative effort, so there is a sense in which you can say Ngugi wa Mirii and I were merely the coordinators or editors. But this was even clearer when I came to script *Mother, Sing for Me. Mother, Sing for Me* was also based on songs and dances from different nationalities in Kenya. Now, I only know two languages in Kenya, so there was no way in which I, as an author, could possibly have been able to incorporate songs and dances from nearly all the nationalities from Kenya unless there was a lot of other people's involvement. So in *Mother, Sing for Me* there was even greater and more obvious involvement of many, many people even before the outline of the script was presented to the actors. Again, in the course of rehearsals they added to the script and, in fact, the script which I now have is a result of all the improvements and additions done during the rehearsal stage of *Mother, Sing for Me.* So in *Mother, Sing for Me*, I was even more of a coordinator than in *I Will Marry When I Want.*

You said during your talk on theater that dramatic form is fairly unimportant to you. Surely your use of song and dance and mime is a choice of form: it's not naturalistic and that's a very important choice of form, isn't it?

What I said was that form by itself, in other words the formal elements, are unimportant *by themselves.* If the play were based merely on formal elements and if it were possible to have that kind of play, it wouldn't really be interesting, but the reason why the people were able to identify with the play was because of the other aspect of form: content. Formal elements are the external manifestation of the real dramatic content which is in the idea—the tension, the dialectical tension in the idea. If this marries with an appropriate form, then it becomes explosive. I'm not saying that formal elements are not important, since these are, in fact, what distinguishes one kind of theater from another, but I'm saying that what gives it its primary importance is in fact the content and that when we're looking at theater and drama, we're looking at that tension in the idea. That's where the real drama is, but the formal elements obviously are very important.

Do you write in verse or in prose, or do you follow a kind of rhythm?

All my plays tend to alternate between verse and prose, but it's not really a planned thing, it just comes out in the process of writing. In the play I collaborated in with Ngugi wa Mirii, *I Will Marry When I Want*, there is a lot of verse form; the dialogue is in verse form. In the play I collaborated in with Micere Mugo, *The Trial of Dedan Kimathi*, written in the English language, you find a mixture of both prose and verse, but *I Will Marry When I Want* is mostly in verse form. *Mother, Sing for Me* is in verse form, but here I was much more conscious of playing around with elements of language. In the course of writing, I arranged the composition in verse form and I played around with internal rhymes. I enjoyed myself a great deal playing around with the language, but the actors were not even aware that what they were saying was actually rhyming all the time.

To turn to Devil on the Cross, *there must be specific linguistic problems when you write a novel in a language that's only beginning to be used for written literature. It can't have been easy for you.... How do you as a writer feel personally about the English language? There must be a certain ambiguity in your relationship towards it....*

Of course it was not easy. Even the conditions in which I came to write *Devil on the Cross* were not easy. Linguistically it was not easy: There are so many unanswered problems in writing in African languages. For one, the orthography is not often very fixed so you find that there may be one or two or even three ways of writing the same word and often you are not quite sure which word to choose or how to write that word in a way that would mean you'd be understood by your readers. The other thing is obviously that we have no actual tradition to fall back on. When you write an English novel or a novel in the English language you tend to assume the whole body of novels and novel writing that has gone before you; you don't have the same kind of tradition when you are writing in an African language. So all these problems are really there. In fact it was when I started writing a novel in the Gikuyu language that I came to realize the importance of certain words I used to read in T.S. Eliot—I think *Four Quartets*, I can't really remember—where he says something about words not being able to stay in one place. You handle this word and you find it'll slip through your fingers: Words slide and crack and do all sorts of funny things.

Writing in the Gikuyu language I came to realize the importance and implications of those words even more, because I could write one sentence or one paragraph in the evening thinking it was saying one thing and in the morning when I came to read it I found it saying the opposite, depending on how one read the paragraph. The challenge for the writer is to write so that when a reader comes to read at least he can move in the direction intended—or probably intended—by the writer.

All these are interesting questions which I think face many writers when they are operating in their own languages and it's part of the excitement and challenge of utilizing these languages that have not much in the way of modern literatures written in them.

Now the English language. I think I used to have complexes about it when I was writing in the language. But now those complexes are really not there because I have found I can now see the English language like any other language. Now I'm fascinated with it as I would be fascinated with French or Italian or with other African languages. It's just one language among several but I don't feel any loyalty to it one way or another. So in fact confronting the issue of my own language has solved my relationship to the English language or any other languages all over the world. For me this language is now a language like any other. It is important because of the culture it has produced, it is important as a means of communication between the English-speaking peoples or those who understand the language, but I don't feel it dominates me now as a writer in the way it used to when I was writing in it.

Looking back at the two versions of Devil on the Cross, *is the English version just a translation or is it an adaptation that differs from the Gikuyu original?*

No, it's a translation. In other words I told myself that I had to do a translation *as* a translation. I had a few problems of course, but I learnt a lot in trying to translate the novel into English. I've insisted with my publishers that any publisher interested in the book has to do it from the Gikuyu original, not, definitely not, from the English translation. So for instance there's a Swedish edition of the book and it was a direct translation from the Gikuyu. In fact the Swedish edition came out at about the same time as the English translation. That means that from now onwards the Gikuyu language will have a direct dialogue with other languages and other cultures without the mediation of the English language. It also means that African languages, through books being translated from one language into another, can begin to have a dialogue. I can visualize a situation where a novel written in a Kenyan language could find translation in Yoruba or Igbo or Hausa in Nigeria and vice versa, so that for the first time the Yoruba language and culture or Hausa language and culture will be having direct dialogue with Kenyan languages and cultures. So I see enormous possibilities for the growth of our cultures through the mutual rendering of each other's work into each other's languages.

What particular problems did you find translating Caitaani Mutharaba-ini *and* Ngaahika Ndeenda *into English?*

I Will Marry When I Want was a joint effort between me and my co-author Ngugi wa Mirii, so that made it easier. I did *Caitaani Mutharaba-ini* on my own, but the problems were the same. The translation made me first of all re-evaluate the whole tendency of African writers using English or French or Portuguese to portray characters who would of course never speak those languages. Now, there has been a tendency in such literature, that elsewhere I've called Afro-European literature, to make those characters talk English or French as if they were really speaking an African language. In other words there has been out of necessity the tendency to want to make a reader feel that what he's hearing is a genuinely African peasant really genuinely speaking an African language with all its rhythms of speech and imagery. But the contradiction is that that peasant or worker is actually speaking English or French or Portuguese in the novel. Sometimes in so doing there's a tendency of creating not necessarily naive characters but characters whose expressions would sometimes sound naive because some of the writers would try to render the syntax of the African speech directly into English or French or Portuguese.

When I translated *Devil on the Cross*, in the first half I was working as if I was writing a novel in English. That is, I tried to see if I was rendering the feel of their speech into English and so on. And then, in the middle, I just realized that this was wrong. Because anybody who really wants to feel the rhythm of speech and syntax and so on can learn the Gikuyu language. I don't need to prove anymore that that character is really speaking an African language, that that character is really indeed an African peasant. If one needs that, he can as I said learn Gikuyu and read the novel in the original. So what I thought was important was to try and get the equivalence in English; it was not necessary to make a reader feel the rhythms of speech of an African language. The novel had to feel natural to an English reader in the same way that when I read a French novel in translation or a Russian novel in translation, it is not the Frenchness of the language or the Russianness of the language that I am looking for. All that counts is the rendering into English the essence of the Russian experience or the French experience in that novel. If I was doing the translation of the novel again I'd probably make a much better job than I did. I know some of my Gikuyu readers who had read the Gikuyu original and now have read the English translation have complained deeply about the loss of certain things in the English translation.

In Detained *you say that a novel is "the work of many hands and many tongues." You have already explained how this applies in your theater, but in the novel the collective aspect is presumably indirect. Would you say your theatrical experience is likely to influence your novel writing?*

Obviously the different art forms interact. That is, what one gains from theater can apply for instance when it comes to dramatic representation of characters, particularly when they're talking to each other. I think drama can help the novelist to avoid long explanatory passages and often help him in dramatizing action in the novel as opposed to explaining, for instance, the emotions. As for the novel being the work of many hands, I felt this very strongly, particularly in prison where in writing *Caitaani Mutharaba-ini* or *Devil on the*

Cross I had obviously to rely on the other detainees and warders. And then I realized that the same collective tendency obviously is there, in the outer society. It's only that one is not so keenly aware of it because there are so many things happening around the writer in ordinary society. It's quite clear to me that there's a way in which the novelist is also a kind of editor: He gets different bits of information from people, different bits of stories about people's lives from different people, and all he does really is give all those stories a form or an outline. But I do agree with you of course that the collective nature of novel writing is a bit more indirect than with a play where people can sit round a table and keep on adding bits and pieces or where people can actually improvise or add to the play as they perform on the stage.

You particularly appreciate the communicative possibilities offered by theater. But I know the original Gikuyu version of Devil on the Cross *also reached people directly, through readings in bars, in....*

Yes, it was fantastic. In a sense you can say that even *Devil on the Cross* was a development of my theatrical involvement, because what happened was that when I was arrested in 1977 and taken to prison at Kamiti Maximum Security Prison, I decided that the only way I could show defiance and have a way of ensuring my own survival was attempting to write in that very language which had been the basis of my current predicament and so I set myself the task of writing a novel in the Gikuyu language. So *Devil on the Cross*, written on toilet paper in prison, was the result of my attempt to connect myself with the very cultural activities I was involved in with the peasants and workers at Kamiriithu and which found their expression in the writing and performance of *I Will Marry When I Want*. Now when I came out of prison in 1978 after Kenyatta died and all political prisoners were given an amnesty—though this proved only to be temporary—I prepared the novel for publication, so both the novel and the play were published in 1980 in the Gikuyu language. The publishers had thought they would publish only a few thousand copies of each, hoping to sell them over a period of two, three, four or five years. But in fact the first editions of each of the works were snapped up within two or three weeks of publication and within the year, that is, between April and December 1980, they had done three printings of the play and of the novel, each printing being five thousand copies, which was a record for them for any novel or play written in any language for sales over the same period of time. Now the reception of the novel and the play was really fantastic because they—particularly the novel—were read in buses, in *matatus*, ordinary taxis; they were read in homes; workers grouped together during the lunch hour or whenever they had their own time to rest and would get one of their literate members to read for them. So in fact the novel was appropriated by the people and made part and parcel of their oral tradition.

The oral tradition is also present—very strongly—in the novel itself, in the proverbs and fables and also in the figure of the narrator. Why is your narrator a gicaandi *player? And why a prophet of justice—what kind of prophet are you referring to?*

Gicaandi is a complex form of poetry among the Gikuyu people. It's very difficult and those who really knew it were very highly cultured. They knew the language *very* well, as well as the culture in which that language developed. Often they used to hold competitions among themselves, weaving words here and there, weaving in riddles and proverbs, and whoever would win by making the other unable to respond to a particular puzzle would win a gourd, the kind of instrument used by the *gicaandi* poets and singers.

The gourds used to have writings on them. These *gicaandi* artists had in fact invented a form of writing like the Egyptian hieroglyphics. It seems they represented some of the important statements with symbols on their gourds, so the whole story sometimes, or maybe the middle part of a story, was already inscribed on their gourd, so they had a hieroglyphic form of writing which circulated only within that circle of society artists. Unfortunately many of these *gicaandi* artists have died; there must be very few still remaining. So by using the *gicaandi* artist as the narrator I was broadly speaking paying homage to that very, very important tradition in Gikuyu literature.

Why prophet of justice? Because the singer and the poet were very highly respected in Gikuyu society and they were seen as prophets, their words were listened to very, very keenly and what they had to say was important. In other words, people took notice of what they had to say about so many problems in the land, about the morality of the different people or about the good life as opposed to the bad life, that kind of thing. So the singer, the poet, the man of words was often seen as a prophet. That's why again this *gicaandi* artist in the novel is both a poet-singer as well as a prophet who would know the truth and narrate the truth.

You have always used a lot of biblical language and symbolism in your works and this is true also of Devil on the Cross. *Could you explain this?*

That is a very important question. The answer to it can only be found within a historical context. Christianity was part and parcel of the impact of imperialism in Africa and for a long time the Bible was the only reading material available to most literate Africans, so quite a number of literate Africans would probably be acquainted with the Bible and stories in the Bible. Even today in many neo-colonial regimes as in Kenya, the church and the bar are the only two venues available for people's entertainment, particularly on Sundays. In our village, for instance, you find a church being erected every other week, in a village which doesn't even have a nursery school or a primary school. In other words, the Bible is part and parcel of that heritage, so to use it or to refer to it you are also referring to a common body of knowledge, a body of knowledge you can assume you are sharing with your audience and that's why I use the Bible quite a lot, or biblical sayings, not because I share in any belief in the Bible, or in the sanctity of the Bible. It's just simply as a common body of knowledge I can share with my audience, and the same is true when I'm writing in the Gikuyu language, I use the Bible quite a lot.

When and how did your writing for children start, how does it fit in with your other work, what sort of stories, characters and themes are dominant?

I've always been interested in writing for children, partly, I must say, influenced by having children, and you find that in most societies in

Africa there is very little reading material for children. Of course there are plenty of stories in the oral tradition, but in a book form, or between two covers, there are very few story books or novels or even books about general information. I also had this need, but I never really came to doing anything about it until I came from prison—prison seems to have been a watershed in my life. So I really started writing for children in 1981 I think—1981 or 1982—and I wrote three books for children, ordinary stories, as part of a projected ten books which deal with the adventures of one character, Njamba Nene, just before and during the armed struggle for independence in Kenya, the armed struggle which was led by the Kenya Land and Freedom Army or Mau Mau. So the hero is engaged in different activities and adventures which will, I hope, give any child different aspects of the struggle for independence, through the eyes of this particular boy, or through the activities of this particular boy. Now I have a problem because when one writes for children, the reactions from the readers are very important, but the fact is that the books were published when I was away, so I have no feel at all of how they have been received. I have no feedback at all.

You didn't try them out on your own children as you were writing them?

Yes, I did try them on my children as I wrote them, but of course it's different when you try them on your own children. When you're reading to them, you'll be adding one or two little explanations or stopping to add this or take out that. So that is really the missing factor in my new venture in writing for children and that is really why I can't tell you very much about them.

Are your books for children on sale in Kenya?

Yes, they are. One came out in September 1982 and the other one came out in December 1983. The first one is called *Njamba Nene na Mbaathi i Mathagu* and it simply means Njamba Nene and the flying bus (or the bus with wings). The second one is called *Bathitoora ya Njamba Nene* or Njamba Nene's pistol (or gun), and the third one is called *Njamba Nene na Cibu King'ang'i* or Njamba Nene and Chief Crocodile. The books are being translated into English by Wangui wa Goro.

What do you feel is your identity as a writer? Do you consider yourself a Gikuyu writer, a Kenyan writer or an African writer?

I can only tell you my practice as a writer. Basically as a writer I am interested in human relationships and the quality of human relationships and indeed the quality of human life. So I am interested in exploring all those social forces that prevent the realization of a more humane quality of human life and human relationship. In our case this is imperialism and its distorting effects, including its distortion of people's capacity to evaluate themselves in relation to their environment, both natural and social. That's the perspective from which I write. As a writer I feel at one first and foremost with Kenyan people who are struggling against neo-colonial oppression and repression; I feel at one with Kenyan people as they struggle against imperialism, in this case an imperialism led by the United States of America. Although there are other Western imperialist interests in Africa, particularly British, West German, French and Italian to a certain extent, the main imperialist interests in Kenya are led by the USA and this is shown by the fact that the USA has military facilities on Kenyan soil. In my view, no president, no party, no leader has the right to commit a people's territory for use by another foreign military power. In other words, I oppose the USA having bases on Kenyan soil, and I support Kenyan people when they oppose that kind of external domination. Now, to the extent that Kenyan people are struggling against imperialist domination aided by the small ruling class, I feel that those Kenyan people are in the same situation as all other African people struggling against imperialism, and in the same way I feel that African people struggling against imperialism and for national independence and democracy are in the same position as all Third World peoples from South America, from Southeast Asia, struggling against the same phenomenon. And I feel that those people in the Third World—whether from Africa, South America, or Asia—struggling against imperialism are in the same battle as, let's say, European peoples struggling against the system of exploitation in their own countries. So in that sense I feel that the struggle of Kenyan people, African people, Third World peoples, is not in contradiction with the democratic forces of peace in Europe today. That is my identity. I belong to Kenyan people, African people, Third World people, all peoples struggling against economic exploitation and social oppression, those in the world struggling for human dignity.

Much of what you have said about language and literature is true also or has been true in the recent past for another literature of African origin, Afro-American literature. Do you see any connection in your own work, in your practical political and literary struggle, with Afro-American writers and their literature?

My own journey towards where I am today has been through all sorts of places. I went to Makerere University College in Uganda where I studied English literature in its traditional form from the times of Shakespeare to just before the Second World War. But I was hungering for a different kind of literature. I started reading African literature which so excited me because I could identify with the assumptions, the background, the characters, the problems. So I started reading Achebe, Abrahams and so on. But I also started reading West Indian writers like George Lamming, so that when later I wanted to do more work in literature I concentrated on Caribbean literature. Again, I could recognize the world of Caribbean literature very well: It's the same world that I knew, the same world dominated by slavery and imperialism in its colonial and neo-colonial stages, and of course the struggles of those people against those different stages of social oppression. I also looked at Afro-American literature and, when later I went to the University of Nairobi in 1967 and in the 1970s, one of the struggles at the University of Nairobi was in fact the struggle to introduce a new kind of syllabus for the study of literature in Kenya, a syllabus which would have oral literature at the center, then written African literature from East Africa, from Africa and from the Caribbean, from Afro-America and so on, and then the literature of Europe, provided it was available in English translation. So the Afro-American literature has been part and parcel of my growing or developing consciousness. But now I'm interested in the whole interaction between the cultures of the Kenyan peoples and the cultures of other African peoples and the cultures of Third World peoples, and then the connection between the democratic struggles and cultures of Third World peoples and the democratic humanist content of the culture of European peoples and so on. Because the democratic content in the humanist tradition of the great literature of Western people is absolutely in harmony with the literature and culture of struggle in Africa, Asia, and South America.

26 *BBC Arts and Africa* Talks with Ngugi about the 1984 Noma Award

Jerusha Castley / 1984

Jerusha Castley: *Hello and welcome. I'm Jerusha Castley and in this week's* Arts and Africa *I'm taking the seat normally occupied by Alex Tetteh-Lartey. In today's program we bring you the results of Africa's most prestigious publishing prize: the Noma Award. For those of you who need reminding, the Award was set up five years ago by Mr. Shoishi Noma, the head of one of the largest Japanese publishing houses, Kodansha. His aim was to encourage the publication in Africa of works by African writers and scholars. Although Mr. Noma himself was unable to attend the announcement ceremony at London's Africa Centre, his secretary Mr. Yasuo Shimada, delivered a personal message on his behalf.*

Yasuo Shimada: *This evening is the public announcement of the winner of the Noma Award for publishing in Africa. It's a very special occasion. As you will be aware, it marks the fifth anniversary of the Award designed to encourage the publishing of books by African authors within Africa. May I express the sentiment of this fifth anniversary event that I am, on my part, more than satisfied with the progress that has been achieved up until now.*

Jerusha Castley: *This year ninety-four titles in eleven languages, from forty publishers all over Africa, were submitted to the judges, and for the first time in the history of the Award, the judges decided the prize should be shared. Joint winner from South Africa is Njabulo Ndebele, for his collection of short stories* Fools and Other Stories. *The judges praised it for its gentle humor and subtle observations, and its detailed evocation of township life and white brutality. Its publisher, Ravan Press, was also commended for its* *persistence in publishing socially committed literature in the face of Government harassment....*

...The other winner of this year's Award comes from Kenya. He is Gakaara wa Wanjau. His book Mwandiki wa Mau Mau Ithaamirio-ini *is written in Gikuyu and tells of the arduous conditions of colonial detention. It's been described as "the single most significant historical document of the entire resistance literature in Kenya." Well, I'm joined in the studio by one of Africa's most distinguished writers, Ngugi wa Thiong'o. Ngugi, would you go along with that description of the book?*

Ngugi wa Thiong'o: Yes, I think that is a very, very correct description of the book. The book takes the form of a diary which Gakaara kept while he was in detention from 1952 to 1959. But it's much more than a diary, it is actually a work of tremendous historical significance. So many people who are important in today's Kenyan history keep on coming in and out of the book, but it is also a work of great literary merit. It is written in very clean, simple prose, but at the same time it is a prose which rises to the level of poetry. So I think it is going to be a very important resource material for political analysts, for historians and for those who are also interested in literature. Thus it combines all those elements into making it a very significant statement and becomes a very important part of the literature of resistance in Kenya.

Jerusha Castley: *You know Gakaara wa Wanjau yourself personally? What kind of a person is he?*

Ngugi wa Thiong'o: Yes, I've met him. He's a very highly dedicated person. You know, he started writing in the Gikuyu language in 1946 and he's been going on, having the faith and so on, and I'm sure it's going to please him a great deal to see the international recognition of what has been a very lonely path for him. But he has stuck to it. He is a man of tremendous courage, very simple, very warm, but very dedicated and very principled.

Jerusha Castley: *But why did he wait for so long before he published a work like this?*

Ngugi wa Thiong'o: You see, one of the problems is that the post-Independence regimes in Kenya, under Kenyatta and Moi, have been very uncomfortable about the whole inheritance of Mau Mau, and you remember only two or three weeks ago, the President, President Moi, reversed a statement in Parliament about the raising of a statue for Kimathi. So you can see that these regimes are very, very unhappy, or uncomfortable about the Mau Mau spirit in Kenya's history. But there may have been a question of probably fearing whether he could get a publisher who was willing to take on this tremendous work although written in the Gikuyu language. Fortunately, Heinemann East Africa took up the manuscript and they never in fact thought twice about it.

Jerusha Castley: Ngugi wa Thiong'o, thank you very much indeed....

27 Ngugi wa Thiong'o Interviewed

Maureen Warner-Lewis / 1984

Ngugi, according to an opinion that has gained currency among intellectuals in the non-socialist part of the world, art is outside politics. What is your attitude to the interconnection of politics and art?

Art cannot be outside that which affects human beings. Art, literature, is about life, about the quality of human lives, about human relationships. Therefore whatever affects the quality of human life, whatsoever affects the changing pattern of human relationships is connected with a legitimate area of art. As such, any art which divorces itself from those social forces that impinge on human lives can only be an art which is denying itself its real life-force. So politics, economics—everything which has to do with the struggle of human beings—is a legitimate concern of art.

What thinkers have most influenced your perceptions of literature and society?

Engels, Marx, Lenin—all the people who have tried to probe issues of human existence, particularly in the twentieth century. There are some books that are crucial to a real understanding of African literature. I've found it almost imperative that people should study Lenin's *Imperialism—The Highest Stage of Capitalism*. Once they do read it, it gives them a clue to so much in African literature. The same for Frantz Fanon's chapter "Pitfalls of National Consciousness" in *The Wretched of the Earth*.[1] It is crucial to an appreciation of what has been happening in so many African countries since independence. Kwame Nkrumah[2] and Amilcar Cabral[3] I admire, but I like particularly C. L. R. James's *The Black Jacobins*.[4] I think it's an absolute must for people, especially African people, to read. Currently I'm reading Aimé Césaire's[5]

Discourse on Colonialism. It's very penetrating, a very important work.

What writers, then, are closest to you spiritually?

I like a variety of writers. For instance, I like Brecht's poems and plays, and when I am depressed these days, I pick up Brecht and read a couple of his poems and feel all right again. But generally, I like nineteenth-century novelists, such as Tolstoy, Dostoyevsky, Turgenev, Balzac and Zola. I also like the works of Gorky, and when I was in prison in Kenya, in political detention, I had the good fortune of having with me a copy of Gorky's plays and short stories, so I used to read him quite often then.

Then, I like many African writers. There is Alex La Guma of South Africa, for instance. I feel very close to Ousmane Sembène of Senegal. And to George Lamming of Barbados in the West Indies. And from Afro-America there is Richard Wright whose novels I like immensely.

What attracts you to these writers in particular?

With Zola and Balzac, it is their comprehensive understanding of the workings of capitalism and the way social forces came to affect the lives of so many. They stood in critical relationship to bourgeois society of the nineteenth century, and so it is their examination of how bourgeois society worked that I really admire. The whole implication of their work, the whole weight of it, is on the side of the oppressed, those who are struggling.

Or take George Lamming. In my view, his novel *In the Castle of My Skin* sums up the whole question of colonialism and neo-colonialism. What is so amazing is that in the 1950s a young person of twenty-four could summarize in one novel the entire experience of Third World peoples' struggles. It is very amazing because each time you go to that novel you can get something applicable to today. I've never asked him, but I'd like to know to what extent he himself was aware of these forces at work, and to what extent he was aware of neo-colonialism as a phenomenon; but it is improbable that he could have known about it because it was not so apparent in the 1950s. But artistically, he was able to see and capture this phenomenon while confining himself to a tiny village in Barbados. I find this absolutely amazing.

As for Richard Wright, his sympathies are obviously on the side of those who are struggling. This point is very important because such a writer's art gets energy from his involvement with the people. With such writers, their very sympathies, the very fact of their close identification with the people's struggles tends to energize their art.

You once mentioned that you liked Sholokhov.

Yes. Sholokhov is very fascinating. What I liked with his novel *And Quiet Flows the Don* was his mastery in depicting human beings being pulled, being torn, if you like, in the context of the Russian Revolution. This reveals his deep understanding of what you may call the dialectics of life. Really, I must have been under the spell of his *And Quiet Flows the Don* when I came to look at Kenyan history. I read his works at the same time I was writing *A Grain of Wheat* and later, before I wrote *Petals of Blood.* So I think his world outlook, his artistic rendering of the struggles of people, had a definite effect on me.

I think all these writers have had a certain amount of influence on me. After all, no artist works in a vacuum. He is affected by all the existing artistic currents of his time.

Now, in 1978 you took a decision to write in your mother tongue, Kikuyu, rather than English. Why?

Imperialism takes on three important aspects—economic, political, and cultural. Now, the objective aim and purpose of imperialism is to get the wealth produced by the people, that is, to control the productive forces of whichever country imperialism dominates. To do that, it instituted deep-seated political control either directly through settlers or by indirect means. But economic and political controls are in a sense incomplete without cultural because when you control people culturally, you are controlling their values, their consciousness. For this reason, all the colonizing nations imposed their languages upon colonial peoples. And even as the language and literature and philosophy of the colonizing countries were imposed on the people, the colonizing powers actively suppressed the languages and literatures of the people.

I can remember, for instance, school students being given corporal punishment when they were caught speaking their mother tongue in the school compound, at play. In other words, mother tongues were associated with images of humiliation, low status, punishment, and so on. On the contrary, when a student did very well in the English language he was always applauded and given prizes. What does this really mean? In effect, they are making a child feel ashamed of his own language, and feel very uncomfortable about the values and culture carried by that language, and also feel a bit embarrassed about the people who created that language which was the cause of his humiliation. By the same token, the child came to associate the English language with positive values, and he came to admire the culture and values carried by the language which was the basis of his praise, his status, his reward....I found it distressing that there was an automatic assumption that African writers could write only in European languages. Mark you, this did not come to me through the process of abstract reasoning. It is simply that in 1977 I started working with peasants and workers at the town of Kamiriithu and it is through this involvement that I started writing in the Kikuyu language. And from that juncture I came to an appreciation that we cannot in fact continue writing in European languages and still claim to be talking to African masses. So the whole question of writing in an African language, in this case a Kenyan language, is very important for me because I think of languages as a key factor in the whole cultural struggle in Africa, which is part of the political and economic struggle.

How would you account for the success of your latest novel, Devil on the Cross*?*

It is very important that one writes in a language that people understand; it is also very important that the language reflect the historical experiences of those people....What happened was that

Devil on the Cross was written in a language that people could relate to directly, especially the Kikuyu-speaking peasantry and working class. And what I find interesting was the way it was read in bars, in public transport. And people would actually get one of their literate members to sit down every night and read for them sections of the novel.

What is your view of the political situation in Kenya today, and what are your thoughts about the country's future?

A fact of Kenyan life today is the suppression of democratic expression. This is a very sad thing. I am particularly saddened by what has happened in the cultural field where progressive cultural expression has all been severely repressed with a view to imposing a conformity of thought which accepts the primacy of Anglo-American interests in Kenya; a conformity of thought to make people not question, for instance, the presence of the United States military bases in Kenya....

The current repression is reflected in the imprisonment without trial of journalists, lawyers, writers, politicians, university lecturers and students, and so on, or in their imprisonment under framed-up charges. All this shows that the Kenyan ruling regime has moved further and further to the right.

As for the future, the important thing is the restoration of democracy. That is the beginning. We must be able to talk. Furthermore, there is no way Kenyan life is going to improve with the continuation of United States naval facilities.

Today humanity is faced with the urgent problem of eliminating the threat of a devastating nuclear war. How could artists contribute to the struggle for peace?

I think artists today, especially those from Africa, Asia, and Latin America, have to realize that there cannot be peace as long as there is imperialism, as long as a minority class dominates the majority of the people, as long as some nations dominate others. Therefore as artists struggle for disarmament and peace, this must go hand in hand with opposition to imperialism and all forms of exploitation and oppression of peoples.

---

[1] Frantz Fanon (1925-1961), psychiatrist and political essayist born in Martinique. He moved to Algeria in 1951 and when the national democratic revolution began he joined the patriots and took part in guerrilla fighting. His books on the Algerian and African revolution exerted appreciable influence on the formation of the ideology of the National Liberation Front of Algeria and on African revolutionary democrats. He wrote his chief and final work, *The Wretched of the Earth,* in 1961.

[2] Kwame Nkrumah (1909-1972), noted leader of the African national liberation movement, ideologue and political thinker, founder and first president of the Republic of Ghana, winner of the International Lenin Peace Prize (1961), played a prominent role in the founding of the Organization of African Unity.

[3] Amilcar Cabral (1924-1973), outstanding leader of the African national liberation movement, founder and General Secretary of the African Party of Independence of Guinea and the Cape Verde Islands (PAIGC), adhered in his theoretical work and everyday activity to the principles of scientific socialism. He was treacherously assassinated by mercenaries of the Portuguese colonialists.

[4] Trinidadian author whose book *The Black Jacobins* is considered a classic on the history of Haiti's struggle for independence (1790-1804).

[5] Martinican poet, analyst and politician (b. 1913). His pamphlet *Discourse on Colonialism* (1950) deals with the liberation missions of the international proletariat. Subsequently he withdrew from the working-class movement.

28 An Interview with Ngugi wa Thiong'o

Raina Whatiri and John Timmins / 1984

Ngugi wa Thiong'o gave the Robb Lectures at the University of Auckland in 1984. While in Auckland he was interviewed for the student newspaper Kia Ora *by Raina Whatiri and John Timmins. The interview was first published in* Kia Ora *on 7 August 1984.*

In your first lecture you said that George Lamming was a big influence on your work. Which book in particular?

It is his work generally, but in particular I was very shaken by his first novel, *In the Castle of My Skin.* It is a work of genius, considering it was written by a young person of twenty-two in the fifties when most countries in the Caribbean and Africa were not independent. But if you look at the book even now, you find it is very, very prophetic in terms of its examination of colonial education and even in its ability to foresee possibilities of a neo-colonial situation.

African writers share similar predicaments. How much communication is there between African writers? What are the current stylistic influences?

African writers know one another through their books, otherwise there are no regular bases for formal meetings and contacts. It is very difficult to tell how much influence any one writer has. What you have to remember is they are all created by a similar situation. If you read a novel from Nigeria and a novel from Kenya or Senegal, the surprising thing is the similarity of the issues they are raising, sometimes even similarities of details of the issues they are raising. This is not because they are copying each other's work but simply because they are responding to situations which are so similar as to produce the same kind of cultural situations.

But the writing does take different forms?

Well, obviously the writers are all individuals with their own individual outlook and their own past literary experience and so on. The attitude and handling of those issues differs, let's say, between the highly politically conscious works of Ousmane Sembène, to those of Wole Soyinka in Nigeria.

In your own writing style you seem to be aiming for greater accessibility even to people who are illiterate. Do you think it is the duty of a writer who is writing from a political standpoint to be accessible to the people?

I believe that question can be split in two. First of all, what has been taking place in literature written in European languages like English, French and Portuguese. I would say that even within that literature one can see a definite movement towards attempting a sense of greater relevance and this is seen often in simpler forms and often a more direct tone as well as a more conscious analytic position *vis-à-vis* the social/political forces at work. For instance, Ayi Kwei Armah's new novel, *The Healers.*

Outside that, you find others who feel that the very languages of Europe as a means of creative writing are themselves the main barrier, and I myself have broken from writing in European languages to writing in Gikuyu, an African language, and there are a number of others who are beginning to question these values. The very use of European languages is a means of their creative activities, but you also find others who, conscious of these means of communication, are going into film, and the example of Ousmane Sembène is clearest and best known. Ousmane Sembène is a very important novelist, who has now become the leading African director in film. For me the language issue is very crucial; the language one has chosen is to choose an audience, irrespective of what the writer may say.

Is there an organized effort to record the Kenyans' oral traditions in the written word?

Oh yes. One of the most important developments in Kenya is, in fact, that of the oral literature and the acceptance that oral literature can be taught in schools and departments of literature at university. The result of this has been more research on oral traditions and also attempts at collecting some of those traditions as well as critical commentaries on those traditions. Quite recently about three books have come out on the different oral literatures of the different nationalities in Kenya. But this is only the beginning. Massive work will have to be done to ensure the preservation of the oral tradition as well as creating the basis for further development of that oral tradition. But the oral tradition is very much alive; it is there all the time because it is the tradition of the people. For as long as the people are there with their languages, so long will there be this oral tradition.

Does a writer see the world from a different perspective from that of "ordinary" people?

No, I don't think a writer is really different from other people; he is simply someone who is seeing the world more vividly, with imagination—that is, somebody through whom various images of that country find expression, but the best writers are, in fact, "ordinary" people. That is why the oral tradition is much more alive than the written tradition. If you go in the bars, or where people are talking, you will find they are creating new words, new expressions, and have a very vivid way of looking at the world. So that, in fact, writers would be better off if they became more and more like "ordinary" people. If they became involved in the struggles of ordinary people, they would become better writers.

Is there a European author who has influenced you?

I admire certain aspects of European literature: Shakespeare, Balzac, Zola, Tolstoy, Dostoyevsky, Brecht; there are many whom I like, who have made important statements on the whole question of human struggles.

What is it like to live in exile? Will you return to Kenya?

As soon as conditions allow, I shall return. But just now Kenya has become very repressive indeed. We have a number of people who have been forced into exile. So, for the first time in Kenya we have exile communities in Zimbabwe, Uganda, Europe, Tanzania and the United States. I got messages in 1982 that I would be arrested on my return so I delayed my return home. I had to go to Europe and to England to help in the launching of my book, *Devil on the Cross,* and it was while I was there that I learnt of the possible consequences of my return. But those warnings had to be seen in the context of what was happening in Kenya in 1982, particularly the arrests and the detentions without trial.

Does a revolutionary situation, comparable to that leading to Mau Mau, exist in Kenya today?

The issue in Kenya today is one of democracy, the right of Kenyans to debate what determines their lives, no matter the differences in their ideas or in their opinions. Because what has happened over the last many years is the continued erosion of those democratic principles, so that all centers of democratic expression have been repressed. An example is the Kamiriithu Community Education and Cultural Centre whose open air theater was razed to the ground in 1982 following the official disbandment of the center by the authorities and the banning of any theater activities by the group near or around the area of its original operations.

Another example is the arrest and detention without trial of a number of university lecturers whose only fault was teaching their subjects and being faithful to their discipline and being conscientious about their work and so on. But the university and its teaching, with all the assumptions that go with a liberal university, were nevertheless seen as a threat by a government that had come to be afraid of any forms of democratic expression.

If that is the case, what does the government want in the university system?

In Kenya there is a philosophy called "Nyayoism"; this is a very dangerous philosophy. It is taken from the Kiswahili word "Nyayo," meaning footsteps. So "Nyayoism" basically means "follow in my footsteps." The assumption behind this is, of course, the necessity of conformity of thought. But in Kenya this becomes even more ridiculous because people are not even allowed to debate what that thought is. So like sheep it means "follow my footsteps."

Is this a deliberate decision on the part of the elite, or has it been instilled by the consciousness created by colonial rule?

I don't think we have quite unearthed the real cultural impact of imperialism on the psyche of those who are ruling in most parts of Africa today. But of course this is worsened by the fact that with independence there was no real break with the economic and political structures of colonialism. So that what you get with independence is more or less the continuation of the same economic and political structures, but of course these have a cultural reflection which in practice means the total identification of the ruling regimes with the values and outlooks of the former colonial masters, and this is seen even in its exercise of power. Their notion of power is often derived from their colonial experiences of power, which meant of course political dictatorships because under colonialism there were no elections, no democratic pretences of any kind; it was Governor's directives and so on. And so, for the new rulers of Africa, their notion of power is derived, in fact, from their colonial experience and often some of the leaders were themselves brought into politics by the colonial institutions.

An example is, for instance, the current president of Kenya, Moi. In 1954 he was just an appointee of the colonial government. He was the appointed member of parliament to the legislative council and was appointed by the settler regime to become the representative. So you can see that unless such a person, quite frankly, undergoes a really radical transformation he is not likely to establish any distance between himself and colonial values. He might even feel grateful to those very institutions for having made him what he is. That is on a personal level, but of course on a collective level the fact that there has been no break with economic and political structures of colonialism means that any political leader, no matter how clever, intelligent, or holy he is, will of course be governed by the logic inherent in those structures.

If that is so, what is the possibility of change? Can the writer show the people how much their consciousness is determined by the social systems they find themselves in?

What a writer can do in neo-colonial societies is really to join people in the struggle for democracy. And with this, I basically mean at a very elementary level of an atmosphere where people can actually debate what is affecting their lives, and to me this is basic to seeking the solutions to the problems of Africa. Democracy cannot be bypassed. The capacity for people to really discuss meaningfully what affects their lives cannot be bypassed. There is no short-cut to any solution. The implication of this, of course, is the break with imperialism because people cannot really debate their lives meaningfully as long as the people who are ruling them are ruling on behalf of external forces that do not feel accountable to the pressures within.

Do you see African languages as the key to participation?

Our languages as a whole have been dominated by foreign colonial languages, so much so that you find situations sometimes where people, or a certain class of people, are not only proud of the fact that they have mastered foreign and colonial languages but also they feel proud that they are incapable of speaking their own languages. So this kind of thing is much more than a need to know other languages; the proper perspective is for people to master their own languages and then others that are useful to them economically, politically, in terms of their national and international relations. That is fair enough. The need to liberate African languages from their present domination by former colonial languages is part of the overall struggle to create proper perspectives with which to view ourselves in relationship to other countries. The aim, basically, will be to have self-reliant economies and political and cultural structures and thereafter relate to other economic structures and political structures and cultural structures on the basis of equality but not on the basis of the dominated and the dominator.

Have the African peoples more or less accepted the boundaries decided on by the Europeans in Berlin, or could there be a move to African unity because of the shared predicaments? Is there an answer for Africa in a common movement?

I do not think that African people as a whole have accepted the boundaries drawn in Berlin, but I think that on the whole the OAU position on this is probably correct for the time being—that is, they feel that it is important that the boundaries inherited at independence should be respected. Personally I think that is correct—with the proviso that when the people of Africa get governments that are really responsive to their needs, then those governments should be in a position to freely examine the question of boundaries, and in their situation there could be any number of ways of solving them, and to me the most positive way would be to go for their progressive union with different African countries.

Hasn't the elite tried to exploit tribal differences to keep a pool of wealth at the top?

Yes, sure. That is one of the problems, the policy of divide and rule originally followed by the colonial powers and now being perpetrated by the ruling minority regimes who see divisions in the various nationalities inhabiting that country as the basis of their own strength as a minority ruling regime. So what they do is to capitalize on regional differences and even the cultural differences between people of the various nationalities, for as long as the peasants and the workers of the different nationalities look at each other suspiciously, then of course they will not be in a position to see who their real enemy is, so that does tend to happen.

If English were to be replaced as the official language of Kenya, which would be the choice?

Obviously in a democratic situation this would be decided democratically through needs. In some countries like Kenya this question has already settled itself since we have the all-Kenya national language Kiswahili which is spoken across the entire Kenya and understood by the different nationalities. Even if it is not understood by everyone, it is by nearly everyone. In addition they have their own mother tongues which should be respected.

So having an all-Kenya national language, Kiswahili, does not necessarily mean the repression of all other languages. All the languages can live in fact in harmony and have a creative relationship to each other. And, of course, in a correct perspective of languages, even other international languages will fall into their perspective, be they English or French, Russian or Chinese or German; it is a question of having the correct perspective of the various languages of nationality, the language of communication across the whole nation state.

What do you think of the current inequalities in global wealth and large numbers of starving people this inequality has created?

In broad terms I share the sentiments of those who call for international economic order. I am very convinced that African countries can feed themselves, can clothe themselves, can house themselves within even ten years of their break with imperialism. I do not believe they are poor because they are poor in themselves, but in fact because their wealth goes to those so-called rich countries. So their poverty is not inherent in their geography; their poverty is explainable in terms of the hemorrhage of their wealth into America and Western Europe generally.

29 A Political Choice

Kwesi Owusu / 1986

Ngugi wa Thiong'o's latest book Decolonising the Mind *summarizes the issues with which he has been passionately involved for the last twenty years. It marks a point of departure as he states: "This book...is my farewell to English as a vehicle for any of my writings. From now on it is Gikuyu and Kiswahili all the way."*

Decolonising the Mind *clearly represents a radical point of departure in your own praxis as a writer and cultural activist. Apart from your call for a return to African languages, you make a powerful critique of what you describe as "Afro-European Literature" since Independence. You were part of this movement which included Achebe, Soyinka, Armah. Why do you now want to break with this tradition?*

The history of my present position is a long one. It goes back many years, possibly from 1962, right through to the early 1970s. The most crucial encounter for me, however, was when I worked at the Kamiriithu Community Education and Cultural Centre. For the first time I was compelled not by theory but by practice to face up to the issues, including the place of indigenous languages in Africa. I was working with peasants and workers, and what language to use was crucial for the whole experiment. Language clearly related to class issues, what audiences we catered for and so on. Kamiriithu was a decisive factor.

In the book you make a flashback to the historic meeting of African writers at Makerere University, Kampala, in 1962. You mention the animated debates about the definition of African literature and draw an acute irony from the fact that even though it was a conference of African writers, those writers like Obi Wali and Chief Fagunwa who wrote in African languages were absent. How did this contradiction sharpen your subsequent consciousness?

There was an assumption that English, French and other colonial languages were the natural linguistic means of creativity for African writers. I was one of the many who took this for granted. Many of the writers I admired—Achebe, La Guma, Abrahams—all wrote in English. This was however a colonial and class assumption. After the conference, something really struck me, and this was an article by Obi Wali responding to the conference. It was called "The Dead End of African Literature," published in *Transition* based in Uganda. The editor sent me a copy beforehand and I found myself unable to respond. I was struck by the forcefulness of his arguments for the use of African languages. Obi Wali's interventions possibly started me on this long journey.

Many African writers make their living from the Afro-European literary tradition. Some would view the return to African languages as a non-starter.

It is obviously a large question with many possible problems. I for one do not think it easy or simple. You cannot just wake up one morning and decide not to work in a language you've been working in. We have been educated in European languages and our attendant conceptualization of ideas, art, politics and economics is articulated in them. There are also other problems. There are few publishers presently willing to invest money in good quality books in African languages and explore market possibilities within and between linguistic communities. The state of translation in African languages is also underdeveloped. But all things said, I see the issue essentially as one of political choice. We as African writers cannot wait till our governments develop the right language policies. Writers have always been pathfinders. I should hasten to add that the tradition of African literature in English, French and Portuguese is a minority tradition. It has no right usurping the term "African literature." It is also a tradition in transition. In years to come it will be in footnotes when people talk about African literature. African literature should refer to literature written in African languages.

At Kamiriithu you explored the whole spectrum of orature, the aesthetic of African creativity, a multi-level, multi-process fusion of the political and cultural, of art forms and language, grounded in the experience, traditions and aspirations of African people. On the general level of Afro-European literature, how do we make the transition from a single medium like writing to the broad range of forms and processes in orature?

I learnt a lot from the women and men in Kamiriithu. African writers have a lot to learn from orature. Literature in African languages also has that whole tradition to draw from. Ironically, the technological developments in the modern world for the first time allow or provide exciting possibilities for the return to the tradition of orature. The peasant world is now made more accessible through media like film and video and radio. In a film you can tell a story visually with music and drama. Once the technology is freed from minority control, artists can interact powerfully with the village. Some of the participants of Kamiriithu later took part in a film called *Oral History* directed by Peter Chapell for British television.

Orature creates a dynamic medium for revolutionary intellectuals and peasants and workers. Kamiriithu highlights the potential of such praxis. What were the highlights of the Kamiriithu Centre?

One of the things I find painful in the African neo-colonial reality is the divorce between progressive and revolutionary intellectuals and the people. In many ways this is necessitated by language choice. These intellectuals assume the world of peasants and workers. I would have thought that their language would also be that of the peasants and workers. At Kamiriithu, we removed the language barrier. What I found interesting was that we were all engaged in the same ideas without the mystifications. We could now exchange ideas. In the course of discussions, different lines emerged, lines not based on linguistic differences but more on visions of life and struggle. The intellectuals experienced a change in their lives and they were never going to be the same people again no matter what they did afterwards. The Kamiriithu experience runs through the book.

You are making statements on culture; how do you see its relationship with the economy?

In dealing with the language issue in Africa, what we are really addressing is neo-colonialism. We can never get away from that. The economics of Africa are still controlled by the West. This economic domination also produces a cultural dependence, a mentality which does not see the possibility of Africa developing from that. The economies of Africa are ourselves. A change in this mentality with adequate steps to remedy the situation will create a new Africa. This change will also reflect a new attitude to our own languages.

Some critics have said the mere adoption of African languages will not resolve neo-colonialism. In a sense, they divorce the language issue from the whole concept of orature which engages that economic and cultural domination in its entirety. How do you prevent the separation of the language issue from orature when the interactions between art forms and media are not highlighted much in the book?

In the forefront of the struggle in Africa are the peasants and workers. They have been using their own languages in this struggle. Any African writer who wants to identify with this struggle has to use their language. It will not be the only solution but it is a *crucial minimum step*. Using African languages per se will not solve all the problems of neo-colonialism. We are talking about meaningful praxis.

A related issue is one of the creative accessibility of the writer and dialogue with other linguistic constituencies. Critics have erred by assuming accessibility mainly in relation to European language audiences. What about pan-African accessibility, bearing in mind the underdeveloped nature of translation?

The question of translation is absolutely crucial. The assumption that you are more accessible if you write in European languages is wrong. In fact, you are not accessible at all to most workers and peasants. On pan-African accessibility I believe that with real language policies we would see more publishing and the development of the art of translation. It should be taught in African schools and universities. This will facilitate new readerships and generate many dynamic possibilities. This process is of course part of the whole solution to neo-colonialism. Translation is crucial. I do read world literatures and I don't have to learn every single language to do so. I don't see why this cannot be true also for African literature in African languages.

When we change the emphasis from the written word to other media in orature, the potential of transmitting ideas from one culture to the other can be great. Ousmane Sembène uses film. Orature opens up new possibilities.

Yes, I agree with that. But obviously as writers we can only talk from the perspective of our medium. Also, we face similar issues in many media as we confront neo-colonialism. In film, we have to deal with issues like minority control of technology and distribution. Media like film and radio, however, open up areas of creativity closer to the people's culture.

I once saw an innovative answer to the shortage of good and relevant films in Africa. The soundtrack of this film had been turned off. Two people with microphones were giving a running commentary, improvising as they went along. This gave a whole new content to the film.

Oh yes, I have seen this also. It can be very dramatic. The realm of popular creativity has many possibilities, rarely explored because of the constraints of neo-colonialism. The second struggle for independence will throw up these possibilities.

How does this cultural revolution relate to the immediate crisis of famine and the politics of debt and aid?

Any part of Africa can feed itself. We are in this ridiculous, vicious cycle of famine and dependence because of the exploitation of our wealth.

What do you think of charitable attempts in the West like Band Aid, Live Aid and Sports Aid?

What Africa needs is freedom, liberation from the economic and political control of imperialism. There is no other solution. We don't need charity; we have the wealth. We have to stop the outflow of this wealth for the benefit of the West.

In conclusion can I ask you what you're doing now? The last major production you were involved in was The Trial of Dedan Kimathi *in London, a couple of years ago.*

Yes, that was with the Wazalendo Players, which involved African Dawn and players from many nationalities around the world. It was very interesting to see the Kamiriithu experiment carry on. I have been studying film and just completed *Blood Grips and Black Diamonds*.

Tell us about it.

This short film engages in the debate about South Africa and sanctions. It exposes the self-interest of those countries refusing to apply sanctions. The film sees the ultimate solution to the crisis in South Africa in the intensification of the armed struggle by the African people.

30 The Role of Culture in the African Revolution: Ngugi wa Thiong'o and Mongane Wally Serote in a Round-Table Discussion

Francis Meli, Essop Pahad, Mandla Langa / 1988

A round-table discussion on the role of culture in the struggle for liberation and independence in Africa took place in London recently between the Kenyan writer Ngugi wa Thiong'o and the South African poet Mongane Wally Serote. Questions were put by a panel of three liberation movement activists—Dr. Francis Meli, Essop Pahad and Mandla Langa. The proceedings took place under the auspices of Inkululeko Publications, with Brian Bunting in the chair. The following is an edited version of the verbatim transcript.

Chairman: *Perhaps the two protagonists could give us a brief outline of what brought them to writing in the first place.*

Ngugi: I am a product of two traditions of education. One is a peasant education. I grew up in a community where storytelling around the fireside in the evenings was a very important art of communication and values. Orature—that is, oral literature—is rich in riddles, proverbs, stories, poetry and drama. The other tradition is one of formal education in colonial schools. It was there that I first became aware of written literature. It was mostly literature by English writers. But when I went to Makerere University College in Uganda, I came across African writers like Peter Abrahams, Chinua Achebe, Cyprian Ekwensi and also Caribbean writers like George Lamming. I had discovered a completely new world. Makerere was also an important center of writing by students. It was a combination of all these factors that inspired me to start writing.

Serote: *It is not one thing that makes a person write, but a* *combination of factors. I began to take writing very seriously when I became aware that writing can become an instrument for liberation, can express what our people are fighting for. I was fascinated by what a poet like Keats was saying about the English people. Then one discovered that there were other writings coming out of Africa. I remember very well reading* A Grain of Wheat *by Ngugi,* Things Fall Apart *by Chinua Achebe, and the biography of Yevgeny Yevtushenko. It was a discovery for me that a writer can become, if you like, a medium through which society expresses itself. It was through Ngugi that I became aware of the issues facing the Kenyan people. It was through Chinua Achebe that I became aware of what was happening to the people of Nigeria. It was through Yevgeny Yevtushenko that I became aware of what war meant to the Soviet people. Because of all this, I began to realize that writing can be used as a weapon for people to fight against oppression and exploitation.*

One other important influence, both politically and in terms of writing, arises out of reading South African literature. This literature was made illegal by the regime, as it banned the ANC and the PAC. Writers like Alex La Guma were banned and also their books. Others like Ezekiel Mphahlele, Lewis Nkosi, Can Themba, Nat Nakasa had been forced to take one-way exit passports by the regime. Writers like Kgositsile and Peter Abrahams had left the country. All of them had written, inspired by the history of our people, the culture of our people, which had its basis in resistance against the apartheid forces and the struggle for freedom. They had all been witnesses to the fighting fathers and mothers in the defiance campaigns, stay-aways, strikes and boycotts and eventually the 1960s when, through their organizations, our people took up arms to fight for freedom.

The novels, short stories, poems and plays of these writers were an exploration of how all of these events influenced relationships between and among people—their aspirations, their courage, fears and frustrations. So, for a young writer like me then, reading that literature and cultivating myself to become a writer, one was faced with a deep and serious conflict. The conflict arises out of a human and natural condition: that one must do one's best to develop. But what is the best: to seek fame and fortune? I did aspire to this and soon learnt through the experience of those before me that that is not for the oppressed and exploited to aspire to. The cost one has to pay for fame and fortune is alienation from the people. Alienation for a cultural worker is shame and death. And there are many kinds of death. The other alternative is to engage in a struggle for the creation of a livable world and future. That, I hope, is what eventually made and makes me write.

Chairman: *You were both educated in schools that concentrated on English literature. Did your school curriculum include instruction about African literature?*

Ngugi: I was educated in colonial Kenya during the fifties and early sixties. The literary education we had was based on English literature. For instance, at Makerere I took a degree in English which meant a study of the history and development of English literature from, say, Shakespeare to, say, T.S. Eliot. Writing by Africans either in African or European languages was not part of the curriculum. In fact, the syllabus at Makerere was entirely that of the University of London. So my own discovery of African writers was outside the framework of formal teaching. I must say that the whole approach to literary education was very colonial, very alienating in that it made African students center themselves in a tradition which was not really rooted in their historical experiences. And that is why my discovery of literature by Africans had such a shattering but positive effect on me—I was literally trembling with excitement.

Serote: *Our schools were very regimented and people had no choice about what they learnt. We had no choice but to learn English. You were made to understand that without English you could not survive in the world. Because of this English meant two things. At one level one became fascinated with English. But at another level, because it was made to appear a matter of life and death, one became very fearful. At primary school you were told that if you failed English, you would fail a class, and in key classes like standard 2 or standard 6 this might mean you would have to leave school. So one had this understanding of English—that it was a fascinating language but at the same time it was a language that threatened your life.*

However, one must accept that English is a very developed language and if you cultivate yourself to become a writer, you begin to discover that there is no horizon for English. English can make you define, understand and express whatever you want to express in the world.

Coming from an oppressed society, coming from Alexandra Township, when you eventually come to accept and understand that you are a writer, you have no choice—you must explore the language so that you can tell the world about the conditions of your life, and the lives of the people you come from. At a certain point it is no longer important whether one speaks English as the English would want it to be spoken so long as one tells the truth about the lives of the people in a ghetto like Alexandra.

Chairman: *Which came first—your interest in literature or your involvement in liberation? Or is it like the chicken and the egg?*

Serote: *In a place like Alexandra one had no choice except to become politically committed. Alexandra is a very closely-knit community. If you talk about a yard in Alexandra, you are talking about a space where on the average thirteen families live next door to one another. Like all the townships in South Africa, Alexandra was not created for free people with a progressive culture in a developed world. Alexandra was created to herd laborers. This is a very unnatural condition for human beings, and it was as a result of this that we developed the aspiration to be free. It is not surprising that Alexandra is one of the areas where the ANC had a very strong base. I recall many times when there were demonstrations, rallies, meetings, generally of the ANC. At a certain point in our lives, weekends were times when we were going to No. 3 Square to listen to what the ANC leadership were saying—Chief Albert Lutuli and many other leaders of the ANC.*

You begin to search in a certain direction in terms of literature, to express the desire to create a better world. Coming out of Alexandra I was aspiring to become part and parcel of the energy that will create a livable world. I thought that one of the ways of doing this was to give expression to the condition of my people through writing and as one does this, one begins to understand the size and depth of oppression. One also becomes aware that one has to become part and parcel of the force that is going to do away with oppression.

So which comes first? I don't think it would be proper to say this came first or that. I think throughout they were a complement to each other. Participation in the struggle became an inspiration. Because one wanted to express the condition of one's people, one also had to further understand what it was that made us become an oppressed and exploited people, what it was that was going to liberate us.

Ngugi: Your talk about Alexandra reminds me of my own growing up in Limuru, Kenya. Modern Kenya is a product of two dialectically opposed processes: that of imperialism or imperialist domination, and of resistance to domination or the national liberation struggle. As you know, Kenya was integrated into the British imperialist system from about 1888, first as a company property and later as a settler colony. This meant that land was forcibly taken away from the people and given to a white settler minority. Kenyan people's labor worked the very land taken away from them. People were also taxed, and this went to build infrastructures for effective economic occupation.

Thus our labor, our capital, our land all helped develop the settler economy. This was effected through military conquest and the subsequent political domination and repression. But cultural domination and oppression were necessary for effective economic and political control. People's songs, poetry, dances, languages, education were attacked and often ruthlessly suppressed. British imperialism for us took the concrete form of economic, political and cultural settler occupation. Racism became the dominant ruling ideology.

But the other process—the more important process in the making of the modern Kenya—was that of national resistance. Thus the British occupation of Kenya at the end of the 19th century was resisted by the Kenyan people of all the various nationalities. This resistance continued in the twenties, thirties, forties and fifties, taking different forms but whose character as a national liberation struggle was being influenced by the intervention of the growing working class. The highest peak of this anti-colonial resistance was the Mau Mau or Kenya Land and Freedom Army which, led by Dedan Kimathi, waged armed struggle against the colonial settler occupation from 1952 to 1962.

I went to school during that period of intense struggle. Some of my own relatives were fighting on the side of the Kenya Land and Freedom Army but others were fighting as loyalist collaborators with British colonialism. In a period of heightened political struggle, traditional ties of blood and region are torn asunder as people take sides in the liberation struggle and this was true of the Limuru and Kenya of my growing up. And there was no way this could not have left an impression in my life. So what's the connection between literature and that experience, at least in my own case?

It is obvious that English literature, the formal literature that I read in schools and colleges, was not talking about the experience we were undergoing in Kenya. In studying English literature I was living in a world of make-believe as far as it concerned my immediate environment. Not that English literature was entirely useless. You see, English literature has two traditions. One tradition expresses the culture of struggle, the culture of the working class, the democratic aspiration for change and for a better life in a better society. The other expresses reactionary anti-people sentiments with stagnation and decay rather than social struggle being seen as more in tune with the human condition. Some of this literature, particularly when depicting people of the colonies, becomes downright racist and anti-human. But for me even that literature which reflected democratic sentiments for change was using as its frame of reference the British and the European experience of history.

The discovery of African and Caribbean literature for me was a rediscovery of the world around me, a world of active struggle, a world ringing aloud with demands for change. Betrayal, treachery, but also heroism and glory—these themes in the live drama around me were distilled in the literature that I had discovered. I had come from a world where ordinary working people—the peasants and workers of Limuru—had risen to heights of glory in their struggle against the colonial giant and this was being confirmed in the written words and images of the new writers. In short, this African literature was largely anti-imperialist and this was clearly in harmony with the values for liberation that had driven thousands of peasants to the forests and the mountains to drive out the British colonial enemy from their soil.

Pahad: *Not all artists and writers in Kenya and South Africa have seen culture as their contribution to liberation. How do you see culture as a weapon in the struggle against oppression?*

Serote: *Maybe basically the question to ask is this: Why does a writer write? When a writer writes, the most important thing is communication. This is the way we started, and this is how people gain political consciousness at a certain level at home. Blacks want to tell whites, everybody, about their conditions of life, and they want to talk to each other about them and what they are going to do. You have to take sides and you begin to say, "I am on the side of the blacks against the whites" or "I am on the side of the people who are fighting against apartheid." I was brought up in a community which had chosen to fight against oppression and exploitation; to have taken an opposite position would have been to sell out. I had made a choice to use writing as a means of communication among people, and as a writer who was part and parcel of the struggle my writing became a weapon.*

Ngugi: Literature is part of culture. And culture is a product of the twin struggles with nature and with other humans to procure the means of our survival. But if culture is a product of our history—that is, it evolves historically—it also reflects that history and the entire value system born of that history. Now in a situation where one nation or class is dominating another economically and politically, it means that the culture and the value system born of that situation is itself class-conditioned and will carry the marks of domination and oppression. But it will also bear the marks of resistance. In other words, in a world of oppressor nations and classes on one hand, and oppressed nations and classes, the literature and culture emergent will reflect the intense struggle between nations and classes.

Inherent in that situation are two types of values or outlooks: that which is on the side of domination and repression and that which is on the side of resistance. Now any literature emerging from that situation will be expressing and reflecting an outlook which is closer either to the oppressing nation and class, or to the struggling nation and class. So in that sense, no literature and no writer can escape from taking a position in the social struggles of our times. A writer can of course claim that he or she is not taking sides, but it has surely to do with what leaves his pen, no matter his own conscious knowledge of his intentions.

Secondly, a writer himself, as a human being, is living in a class society and whether he likes it or not, he is himself conditioned by the position he or she occupies in that society. His own outlook is already affected by his class upbringing and his conscious or unconscious class sympathies and habits. Once again the literature he or she produces will be affected by his class-conditioned habits of thought and practice and therefore takes one or the other side in the social struggle between classes and nations or, in our world today, in the world-wide struggle against imperialism. Literature becomes an even better weapon of struggle when a writer is aware or conscious of the struggling ideologies in the world.

Literature is indeed a powerful weapon. I believe that we in Africa or anywhere else for that matter have to use literature deliberately and consciously as a weapon of struggle in two ways: a) first, by trying as much as possible to correctly reflect the world of struggle in all its stark reality, and b) secondly, by weighting our sympathies on the side of those forces struggling against national and class oppression and exploitation, say, against the entire system of imperialism in the world today. I believe that the more conscious a writer is about the social forces at work in his society and in the world, the more effective he or she is likely to be as a writer. We writers must reject the bourgeois image of a writer as a mindless genius.

Meli: *We are discussing the question of the social responsibility of* *the writer. Comrade Ngugi, do you see a change in the social responsibility of a Kenyan writer from the colonial period to the period after independence? You were arrested in the period after independence. What is the new element in the post-independence period? Also what makes a writer famous? Is it the way he uses the language or the way he expresses the feelings of the people? What is social or international recognition?*

Ngugi: The nature of struggle against imperialism is changing all the time even as imperialism changes its form and particularities in time and place. The writer must be aware of the changing circumstances and act accordingly. In the fifties and earlier, Kenyan people were struggling against the colonial phase of imperialism. During that period, the writer on the whole was in harmony with the anti-imperialist thrust of the people's struggle. It was clear who was the enemy. The racism of the settler colonizer ensured this clarity. The color of the skin marked the boundary between the colonizer and the colonized. Even the collaborating loyalist Africans—the Buthelezis of colonial Kenya—felt the racism. The oral artist was at the forefront in articulating the anti-colonial sentiments of the Kenyan people. When adapted to the needs of the struggle, the songs and poetry of the oral tradition of the peasantry became a very powerful means of rallying the people together against colonialism.

With independence in 1963, imperialism in Kenya merely changed its clothes. It now took the form of a neo-colonial arrangement. Today in Kenya the major banking and financial institutions are owned by the Western monopolies. Most of the industries and big commerce are owned by U.S. and Western-based transnationals. So you find that Kenya's economy—finance, industry, commerce, agriculture—is an extension of Western imperialism. But the visible ruling class is not the international bourgeoisie. It is Kenyan. It is visibly African. But it is a comprador native bourgeoisie controlling the machinery of the state on behalf of imperialism. And like its colonial settler counterpart, this overseer class has become very repressive.

There is nothing uniform about the writer in neo-colonial Kenya. There are now writers and artists who are on the side of the state machinery of neo-colonial repression. But there are others—and fortunately the majority—who are trying to articulate the cry of the people. The responsibility of the progressive writer in a neo-colonial state is made difficult by the fact that the clarity of who is foe and who friend is blurred by the uniformity of color between the ruler and the ruled. But for such a writer to be effective, he/she has to be even more conscious of the balance of class forces in the national and international scene.

As for the question of fame...I believe absolutely and unashamedly so in the capacity of the alliance of the Kenyan peasantry and working class to struggle for and actually create a new Kenya. They took on British colonialism and forced it to retreat. As a writer I have always tried to articulate the position of that alliance as effectively as I could within my limits as an artist. Progressive writers must pay special attention to form. If I believe in something I want to put it across as persuasively as I can. I believe that power and beauty and courage and heroism and real humanity are on the side of those who struggle to change all the social forces that deform humanity. Part of the responsibility of a progressive artist is to find the appropriate language with which to express the feelings of the people. A writer should not write with a view to fame or to international recognition.

Langa: *My question deals with some problems writers encounter when dealing with concepts like anti-colonialism, anti-imperialism, even anti-apartheid, where you find a person sometimes does not know when to stop when it comes to polemics. A poem can be full of slogans against imperialism, against apartheid, but completely devoid of any literary merit. How do you avoid this? The other thing is that writing and maybe most fields of cultural activity, as Yuri Babash said, are very heavily into the realm of ideas, and the world right now is divided along the lines of progressive and reactionary ideas. How do you marry these two extremely important tensions?*

Serote: *I will try to share some experiences with you. I have lived in three countries so far and wherever I was, I tried to interact with the cultural workers of those countries. The first was South Africa.*

When I left South Africa in 1974, a movement was developing that was dominated by black consciousness. We were together with Mandla Langa at that time in this movement. The political commitment that informed our writing at that point is frozen in the slogan "Black man, you are on your own." We were writing for black people, and we were saying it is very important that black people talk among themselves about how they are going to liberate themselves.

You must bear in mind that the ANC at that time was operating purely underground; there was no mass movement as we know it now. It was very important for the oppressed in South Africa to have a way of expressing their aspirations to become a free people. Black consciousness at that time was saying to the black people that they must find a way, although undefined, of doing this. In that sense I think black consciousness was positive and the cultural workers who participated in black consciousness were also positive.

The most serious and dangerous weakness was that we were ignoring history and the struggle of our people in the past. If we had known more about our history, we in the black consciousness movement would have understood that we were not the pioneers we thought we were. Nevertheless, the black consciousness movement contributed to the political consciousness of the oppressed people and indicated to them that they must find a way out of being oppressed.

I left South Africa at a point when the black consciousness movement had already, it was obvious, reached its height and in fact was beginning to retrogress. The leadership of the black consciousness movement were either banned or in prison or in exile. The years after 1976 made the rank and file as well as the leadership better acquainted with the history of struggle in South Africa, and the result was that the majority of the people who had been active in the black consciousness movement began to move towards the African National Congress.

Then I moved to the United States, where I lived for three years. My leaving South Africa coincided with a series of events reflecting the direction of politics internationally and at home. In South Africa the regime, through its security police, had decided to finish off the black consciousness movement, and by the time I reached London in October 1974 en route to the United States, most of the leaders, some of whom were my close friends, had been detained, to appear a year later as the SASO 13. The victory of Frelimo through armed struggle over Portuguese colonialism was, to the South African masses, a great promise for the future. Then there were Guinea Bissau and Angola and the defeat of American imperialism in Vietnam. So my mind, on entering the United States, was a tapestry of dreams and nightmares.

I had followed the Afro-American struggle through the Black Panther books and publications and through literature, films, photographs and paintings, so I had no illusions about the American dream. At the same time I do differentiate between the American people who have and do uphold the true ideals of democracy which some founding fathers enshrined on the wall for the brave to fight for. Participating in some creativity with both black and white American cultural workers was, I expected, the moment when I would fathom the true American dream. It was after I had been up and down the United States, reading poetry, participating in cultural conferences, rallies and demonstrations, that I heard Angela Davis speak at a book launch by a young black writer who was killed by the police by mistake in Harlem.

There had been few, very few moments when I heard confidence expressed about the wish of the people to be free. Many times I had heard guilt, cynicism, despair and doom expressed. Many times blacks told me I was mad to come to the United States. And I saw and heard that their hopes were pinned on being one day united spiritually and physically with the motherland, Africa. I myself knew very little about Africa. In retrospect I realize I may have shared the same fantasy about Africa. I wrote Behold Mama, Flowers *out of my US experiences, dreams and battle.*

Then I met Africa. The 1976 New York demonstration against the killing of students and young people in South Africa on June 16 that year told me something. I had worked hard to mobilize, organizing for a maximum participation in this demonstration. It became obvious that many people were outraged by these apartheid killings, and hundreds and hundreds of people turned out, poured into the Harlem streets and the Manhattan streets, marching to the South African Consulate. There was no doubt that human beings had been outraged.

I listened before the march as the stewards reported how the police, on granting permission for the march, gave strict orders about how the march was to be conducted and which route it must follow. To me it did not make sense. To other people it did. That told me I could not fight the American police. I was then already packing my bags. By 1977 I was in Gaborone, Botswana.

I met many young Batswana writers and playwrights, like Barry Seboni, Cedric Thobega, Andrew Sesinyi, Sebotso Molefe. Also Bessie Head and Beauty were there. All of us watched with one eye the Zimbabwean struggle unfold, as Bessie would say, "at great human cost." We discussed whether there was anything to write about in Botswana and also whether South Africa would ever be a free country for blacks. These discussions were endless, and I suspect they still continue.

Eventually we emerged with a cultural group called Medu Art Ensemble. The group consisted of Batswana, South Africans, and European and American expatriates living in that country. The high point of the group was when it spearheaded a festival and conference of South African Arts under the theme "Culture and Resistance." On the one hand it is a great pity that, for whatever reason, extremely few Batswana participated in the creativity and in the discussions. On the other hand, hundreds of South Africans—Africans, Coloureds, Indians and Whites—came and for seven days we went through the concept of "culture being part and parcel of the struggle for a united democratic and non-racial South Africa." We went through each art form, searching its meaning, understanding how other people have used it and plotting how we intended to use it. "Culture and Resistance" was a turning point in the history of the South African cultural movement. On the one hand it was a confirmation of the creation of this movement. On the other hand it was a beginning of an era for the arts which would seek to become a weapon for freedom in the hands of the oppressed.

Chairman: *What do you say about the writer who identifies with the revolutionary process, expresses all the right ideas, but does not produce good literature?*

Ngugi: That's why I said earlier that, if I believe in something, I want to put it across as persuasively and as effectively as I can. And so for me the question of form and artistic effectiveness is part of that correct political tendency. Now, what would be ruinous artistically would be for a writer to take rhetoric and not the concrete experience as his starting point. Rhetoric abstracted from the concrete experience is the surest way to bad art. Of course, not all the writers are gifted in the same way. By that I mean there are some people who are obviously more effective with words than others in the same way that some people can sing more effectively than others irrespective of the content of their songs. I believe, though, that the more one is really involved in the struggle, the more effective one can be even in the artistic expression. After all, where do ideas come from? In production and all the struggles engendered by that are the springs of new ideas and words. Struggles in industry, in commerce, in the fields, the cry of the factory worker as the police bullet hits him, the sense of triumph as the people overcome—all these are part of that concrete world of struggle and change. I strive to capture the movement of life, the motion of things, the ebb and the flow. I believe writers and artists can guard against abstractionism by actually relating the concrete experiences of their people.

Chairman: *Is it possible to be a good writer and a reactionary?*

Ngugi: Not quite. One can be good at handling words but express a world outlook which strengthens the forces of reaction. In literature there are many examples of this. But they are not necessarily good writers or, say, great artists. Yes, they can use words, they can tell a story with a surprise ending or one that keeps the reader, as it were, hanging from the writer's pen. But in the end the untruth they are trying to express comes to undermine their effectiveness as artists of the drama of the human soul. The writers who impress most as creative artists exhibit a strength even where there are contradictions in their work because they do not gloss over the real contradictions at the heart of our social being. Some tendencies within their work might be backward, but in the main the weight of their sympathies as writers is on the side of human freedom and progress....

Pahad: *What do you say about Kipling?*

Ngugi: Well, I don't know much about Kipling, but I would say that some of his poetry and stories come alive only when, despite his sympathies for imperialism, they capture contradictions in imperialism....

Take a writer like Tolstoy. Some tendencies in his outlook are backward-looking but the weight of human sympathy in his novels is on the side of the peasantry. Or a writer with an apparently reactionary outlook like Dostoyevsky—the weight of sympathy is on the side of human suffering, the tremendous need to end human suffering.

Serote: *Generally speaking, we all agree that a good writer is one who contributes to the ideas of doing away with oppression, exploitation, disease, helping to create a livable world. But that does not mean that a racist, for example, cannot be a good writer for racists, if one measures the ability to spin out words and express ideas, even about racism. But good writing should be writing that makes the world a livable place.*

Ngugi: An artist has the capacity to reflect the world in which he lives, like a mirror. One can talk of a writer as being good or bad to the extent he or she is able to effectively reflect that world with all its contradictions, irrespective of his conscious ideologies—to reflect a certain reality, say, of struggle, with all its contradictions. But the other side of the coin is that in reflecting the world a writer also expresses an attitude towards the world. In the situation of, say, imperialism and anti-imperialist struggle, he is taking an attitude towards one or other of those two forces and his sympathies are on one side or the other. Sometimes there can be contradictions between the social realism of the reflected image on the one hand and the weight and sympathies or the conscious attitudes to what is reflected. There can be apparent discrepancy.

Langa: *What are the criteria we ourselves use in judging whether literature is good or bad? Many of the criteria we use have been thrust upon us by our socialization and education. Is there any experimentation to produce what one might call a new aesthetic outlook?*

Ngugi: There has always been a new aesthetic in the sense that the springs of life are there all the time, but in some situations there is a struggle between the new aesthetic and the old aesthetic. The apartheid system, for example, embodies in it the aesthetic of a dying world, a dead world of smell, a putrefied social system, so that you can only feel disgust at it. As for those who are struggling in South Africa, their struggle contains the germs of the new aesthetic. The new aesthetic and the old aesthetic are actually in struggle and what one really wants to see in works of art is the beauty of resistance, because there is tremendous beauty in resistance.

One sometimes sees in films people completely identifying with a character who is down and who then rises. That moment of rising, from being down, never fails to capture people's imagination when expressed in sculpture, in music, in poetry, in a novel. There has been a tendency sometimes to equate what is human with whatever is negative. All the weaknesses of our situation are universalized as being the human condition. But why should we regard what is a weakness in our present situation as the universal condition of our being? What about the other way around, stressing what is strong in us, what is beautiful, what is positive? Why can't that also be seen as an expression of the universal truth of our being, of our existence? Why should we view the acceptance of defeat as somehow more human than the refusal to accept defeat? For me it is more human to refuse to be oppressed, to refuse to be downtrodden, to rise even when you are down. Brecht once said, I think in one of his poems, that when you are down, when you think you are defeated, that's the moment to fight.

Chairman: *We haven't defined what we mean by a new aesthetic. It* *seems to me that what we are trying to do is reassert an old aesthetic. We should establish criteria based on human values and not on money. The difference between reactionary art and progressive art is fundamentally the question whether the artist is trying to satisfy the needs of the widest section of people. A reactionary artist is one who looks to ruling class interests or the interests of a restricted group. He may be very gifted but he expresses the aspirations only of a certain limited section. Artistic values should be based on the need for an artist to associate himself with the deepest aspirations of the widest section of the people. This means that we have to make a class analysis, or an analysis based on the struggle for national liberation, as part of the process of evaluating.*

Ngugi: In a colonial situation the struggle for national liberation is the basis of the development of a new ethic or aesthetic. The concept that people are creating the new man and woman in ourselves, as it were, contains the new ethic or aesthetic. It is not divorced from the old completely. The new society is being created out of the old, is rising from the struggle against the old. The new ethic is constructed from the historical process. The people are creating in struggle, they are raising the progressive aesthetic and ethic to an even higher level, even as they themselves as human beings are rising to new levels of awareness as human beings.

Serote: *It is very important for us to note that at present in South Africa the Congress of South African Trade Unions (COSATU) has decided that culture is going to become part and parcel of resistance and is creating structures within COSATU which are going to deal specifically with culture. This is a very positive development in the unfolding cultural movement in South Africa because the workers are going to become active participants in the various cultural manifestations. The aspirations for defeating exploitation and oppression will be expressed by the majority of the people as represented by the workers, who experience the rawest oppression and exploitation on a daily basis. The workers are going to use culture not only as a means of resistance but also as a means of defining the new South Africa.*

Chairman: *One of the remaining subjects on our agenda is the question of language.*

Ngugi: The question of language in African literature must be seen in a historical context. We must take the languages of the peasantry and the working class in Africa as a starting point. African languages are used by the majority of the nationalities on the continent and the languages of the people should be our starting point.

I see it as a limitation that we do not engage the people in the very languages they speak and use. That's why for me, after working with peasant workers in Kamiriithu, in Limuru, in 1977, in languages they could understand and therefore developing a new type of theater with a new type of resonance, which was reflecting their condition as workers, I think I could not go back. Once my eyes were open, there was no way I could go back to the old situation where I had become a prisoner of the English language. I feel liberated because I can write in my languages; my novels can be read by workers who understand that language. That work can be translated into any other African language if necessary, into English, Russian, German, Japanese and be made available to any other people in the world.

So I feel free, liberated and for the first time I feel that as a writer I have got my audience, that my relationship to my class audience is somehow complete. Of course there are consequences for this. I had two examples recently. As you know in 1977/78 I was put into political detention, precisely because of engaging in progressive democratic theater in a language the people could understand and therefore engaging in debate about issues of liberation and developing concepts by which people could understand a situation and fight it out. After my release I stayed in Kenya for some time but was banned from getting jobs anywhere in Kenya and eventually was forced into exile. I have been living in exile here in Britain for the last five years.

Ironically, living in exile in Britain has made me even more deeply sensitive to the issue of language and that's why very recently I wrote a book called *Decolonising the Mind* which discusses the whole issue of language in African literature. The problem of being in exile is that one is away from the material basis of one's imagination. You need to be in that bus, to hear that phrase being used by a people quarrelling or laughing or whatever. You need to be near a factory to hear those little things which set the imagination flying. Those images that one encounters when one is walking about, those gestures, that laughter—you miss all that when you live in exile. Using a certain language, you miss a situation in which you are interacting with new development in that language, and so on.

Anyway, when I was in exile here I wrote another novel in the Kikuyu language called *Matigari ma Njiruungi*. It is difficult to translate the title into English. It means something like "those who survived the bullets," it means "the patriots who survived the liberation struggle," but in a sense also "those who are continuing that struggle"; it combines all those things. I wrote it in 1983 but it was published in October 1986 in the Kikuyu language. In February 1987 there was a government-initiated operation against Matigari! On that day in February the special branch, that is the political police in Kenya, went to all the bookshops and seized all the copies. They also went to the publisher with a lorry and collected all the books which were in the warehouse.

So the novel written in the Kikuyu language in exile in Britain cannot now sell in Kenya. Yet my novels in the English language are selling; they are on display there. So I feel the question of language has become very important for me.

I also learn a lesson from our adversaries, who are sensitive to the importance of polemicising in the language the people speak. The Bible will be available translated even in the tiniest African language. You find that people, in searching for concepts by which to understand or explain their world, often go to the Bible as the only literature that's available to them in those languages. We are really being deprived of the weapon of ideology with which to fight out the neo-colonial situation. We are continually being dominated by French, English and Portuguese.

Serote: *As comrade Ngugi says, the question of language is* *important because, as with the objectives of liberation, the question of language is finally how we express our condition. The day our people are able to express our objective of being alive, which is to be happy, the day all of us can express that, you will also see that our laughter will have a different ring from the time when we cannot express the condition of happiness.*

It is very important to promote languages because in so doing we are promoting the energy of the people. Promoting language within the context of the unfolding liberation struggle is also promotion of the energy which must change the world.

Ngugi says the security police in Kenya were sent out to search for his book. I am just thinking, what is going to happen in South Africa the day Afrikaans and English are molded into a toi-toi, * *when whites who speak Afrikaans and English move into toi-toi and express the condition of their lives, their aspiration to become totally part of the struggle? Because this is what toi-toi is about. When in those universities, in those suburbs we suddenly hear toi-toi in English, toi-toi in Afrikaans, in the mielie fields, in the platteland, then South Africa will be a very different place.*

The question of language is a very emotive issue which relates to the consciousness of the people. It's very important for people to be able to say what they want, not feel that what they want is dictated to them or imposed on them. Yet while it is important for us to promote the different languages, we should also understand that the question of language has been used to divide people. In South Africa, people who come from the Northern Transvaal, the Vendas, when they come into Johannesburg, they hide the fact that they are Vendas, they don't speak in Venda. People who come from the same area, the Tsonga, when they come into areas like Johannesburg, hide this fact. We should find a way of promoting Venda and Tsonga so that people in those areas can speak in their languages and express their condition of life. But I am suggesting that we also have to find a language that is international to everybody.

Meli: *A word on the cultural boycott.*

Serote: *We must support the cultural boycott because this is a weapon of the oppressed which they have acquired to state their condition of oppression to the world and ensure that the world isolates apartheid culture. Yet we do have a problem which we must deal with. Ngugi's books* A Grain of Wheat *and* Petals of Blood *have been widely read at home. It would be a very serious contradiction if we were to apply the cultural boycott to those two books because they have contributed to our understanding of and participation in the struggle, especially the young people.*

Ngugi: Yes, as a Kenyan who actively supports the South African struggle and who believes and has written that the liberation of South Africa is the key to the liberation of the continent, I would like to support and be guided by whatever policies are defined by those who are in the struggle in South Africa. But I do see the possible contradictions that Wally is talking about. We must find a way to isolate apartheid culture and all the cultural forces that strengthen the apartheid system, while at the same time we strengthen the culture of those who are in the struggle.

I can see this contradiction, the need on the one hand to isolate all the cultural forces that strengthen apartheid, and at the same time have international solidarity with the culture of those who are struggling. It is important in another way also, for us, because the literature of the South African people has meant a lot to those out of South Africa.

---

* According to the *South African Concise Oxford Dictionary*, toi-toi (toyi-toyi) is "a dance step characterized by high-stepping movements, typically performed at protest gatherings or marches."

31 Ngugi wa Thiong'o: *Matigari* as Myth and History: An Interview

Maya Jaggi / 1989

Ngugi wa Thiong'o's latest novel, Matigari ma Njiruungi, *was written from exile in London in 1983 and published in Kenya in the original Gikuyu in October 1986. Based partly on an oral story about a man searching for a cure for an illness, it is addressed to a "reader/listener," thus emphasising its oral qualities, and is said to be set in no particular country and at no fixed time. In the novel, the character, Matigari ma Njiruungi (literally "the patriots who survived the bullets"), returns from the forest after the armed struggle for independence, having defeated the colonial Settler Williams and his African accomplice, John Boy. Burying his arms, Matigari seeks his home and family, only to find a land in the grip of fear, and extremes of wealth and poverty, owned by multinationals and governed by a corrupt, Western-oriented elite led by "His Excellency Ole Excellence" and the ruling KKK party, whose emblem is a parrot. The house Matigari comes to reclaim has been usurped by the sons of Settler Williams and John Boy. Aided by an orphan, Muriuki, a prostitute, Guthera, and a striking worker, Ngaruro wa Kiriro, Matigari goes in search of Truth and Justice, acquiring legendary status throughout the country following altruistic deeds and "miraculous" escapes from prison and mental hospital—escapes which are ironically revealed to have been effected by human sacrifices rather than divine intervention. After an unsuccessful search, during which Ngaruro is killed by police, Matigari realizes that "Justice for the oppressed comes from a sharpened spear," that the enemy can be defeated only by words of truth and justice backed by the power of armed force. Unable to retrieve his buried arms, after setting fire to his house Matigari is chased and wounded by police and, together with Guthera, flees into the river, and probable death. It is left to the orphan, Muriuki, to retrieve Matigari's arms and continue the struggle.*

As Ngugi writes in his preface to the English translation, after publication of the novel in Kenya, intelligence reports suggested that a man named Matigari was roaming the country making subversive demands, and there were orders for his immediate arrest. Subsequently realizing its mistake, the government banned Matigari ma Njiruungi *in February 1987.*

Maya Jaggi asked Ngugi wa Thiong'o to speak about aspects of Matigari, *in London, on publication of the English translation in May 1989.*

Historical Allusions in *Matigari*: Their Significance for the Present

The character of Matigari can be seen first in a general sense as representing the collective worker in history. That is why the novel is in fact not set in any particular country, though it is clearly set in Africa. In the sequence of the novel, Matigari lays down his arms and returns to claim his collective inheritance, only to find that it has been taken by those who were part of the same set of social forces he had struggled against. Yet he does not seek out and challenge the new occupants of his house immediately. Instead he travels around the country posing questions about Truth and Justice. Again and again he returns, in a song, to the central paradox of history, in which the producer is reduced to begging while the parasite is elevated to a position of power over the producer. Why, he wonders, are the producers seldom the ones who control their own wares? In posing such questions, Matigari is, in my view, addressing a fundamental issue of the twentieth-century world. He is asking what is the truth of history, since history as we know it does not contain the fact of this inherent injustice. This question is important everywhere in the world today where the paradox has not been resolved—whether in Africa or elsewhere—and its relevance goes beyond the history of a particular country or a particular period.

Even in terms of African—or specifically Kenyan—history, the collective nature of Matigari is important. There is a scene, for instance, where Matigari confronts those who have occupied his house. When they ask him who he is, he replies that he has always been there, that he was there at the time of the Portuguese, back in the fifteenth century, and at the time of the Arabs and of the British, though their response is that they were not asking for history lessons! Again, when Matigari says that he worked all the industries and all the farms, that he made all the clothes and built all the houses, this is not to be taken literally! This is an important dimension of the novel, and so far, of the critics I have read, few have seen this aspect. They have been treating Matigari as though he were a highly individualized character inhabiting a specific historical period—perhaps because they have been conditioned by the realism of the previous novels to expect realistic characters—instead of seeing his character as more the representative type you might find in myth.

There is, of course, another side to the novel, what you might call the "particular" side, which obviously has allusions to the armed struggle for independence in Africa. This took place essentially in the 1950s in Algeria and Kenya and the novel specifically calls to mind the Mau Mau struggle of the Kenya Land and Freedom Army. An article I wrote in 1983, just before I wrote *Matigari*, was entitled "Mau Mau Is Coming Back" (in *Barrel of a Pen*), but what I really meant in the novel is that the spirit of Mau Mau is still very much alive in Kenyan society. I think many more people are now looking back to that period of the 1950s, not with a view to returning to it, but just in order to learn the lessons arising from that period, lessons about the achievement as well as the failures of the Mau Mau intervention in the history of Kenya.

There are, in fact, two sides on this issue. On one side there are members of those forces opposed to the neo-colonial structures and arrangements in Kenya, who have begun to look into Kenyan history, and derive inspiration from the whole tradition of resistance. The resistance theme is becoming very important in intellectual discussions on the fate of Kenya—its present and future. And while Mau Mau is one of the highest aspirations of that theme of resistance, its roots go back at least to the fifteenth century, with the struggle against the Portuguese. So Mau Mau is a central theme of present-day Kenyan political debate.

On the other side, there are those who are part of the social forces represented by the present Kenyan regime, who also symbolize historically those forces that sided with the colonial regime. In Kenya more than in other countries, the continuity between the colonial period and the neo-colonial period is very stark. Sometimes this continuity is marked by identity of the actors whose role has been in supporting the external forces dominating Kenya in both colonial and neo-colonial periods. A good example is President Moi himself, who in 1954 at the height of the Mau Mau struggle, was appointed into the colonial settler legislature. You can see the dichotomy: on the one hand there were those who were engaged in armed struggle to overthrow colonialism, and on the other was Moi literally helping in the drafting and formulation of policies designed to defeat Mau Mau. There are other continuities in Kenyan history. For example, the Kenyan army is a virtual continuation of what used to be called the King's African Rifles, which were used in the struggle against the Mau Mau armed forces. So the Kenyan army has been brought up in traditional anti-people practices inherited from colonialism, and which continue to the present.

Now, those forces do not want to hear about Mau Mau. When the debate about Mau Mau became very heated, and almost engulfed the whole of Kenyan society in 1984, President Moi himself banned public debate and discussion on the issue. Another example of this anti-Mau Mauism in the rhetoric and practices of the present regime is the imprisonment of the historian Maina wa Kinyatti for six-and-a-half years. He has now been released, but is in exile, and his imprisonment symbolizes that particular anti-Mau Mau trend in the present regime. Superficially, the regime may fear the possibility of armed struggle being waged against it. But in a deeper sense, it sees the threat in the implications of the social and political goals of Mau Mau. Since the Mau Mau struggle and the Kenyan people's struggle was for complete independence and complete freedom—meaning the capacity of people to control their wealth, their values and so on—this goal of course goes against present trends in the Kenyan regime's policies. So what they fear from Mau Mau more than the possibility of an armed struggle is the political, economic and cultural implications of that debate.

The Novel's Theme of Resistance and Re-Arming

What *Matigari* is doing—at least in intention—is posing a challenge. About three-quarters of the novel is concerned with a quest for Truth and Justice. Matigari asks: "Is there a solution to our problems, without violence? There must be another way." I see this as a question of democracy, with democratic participation clearly being an important theme in the novel.

In relation not just to Kenya, but to Africa as a whole, *Matigari* is saying that neo-colonialism must end because Africa cannot possibly develop or find its true liberation while neo-colonialism holds sway; and a very important aspect of neo-colonialism is, of course, democratic repression. This is so because, without a real commitment to social change—economically, politically and socially—people will inevitably become increasingly alienated from whichever social group is in power. That group in power then has no alternative but to resort to force: either you bring social change, or you use force to prevent it. And if you use force, the question is, what options are you giving the population? If you constantly repress the people (and in the case of Kenya, the level of repression is very high), what are you telling the people to do? So, although in mythic form, the novel is still very analytic, it is asking what options are available. And it is saying that if you follow a certain course, then you must accept the consequences of that course, because you cannot have your cake and eat it: you cannot close all avenues of debate and stifle democracy, yet not expect that people will find ways—whatever those ways—of fighting against that oppression.

In another sense, the most fundamental question being posed in the novel is that of resistance and mass intervention in history. *Matigari* is saying that people have to intervene in their own history one way or another, but the question is how to do so when the structures are so undemocratic. The form intervention takes in such circumstances will always depend on a number of factors, such as the level and intensity of repression, and the capacity of the people to organize themselves. It could take the form of, say, mass demonstrations or mass uprisings. But whatever the form, it would have the character of what has been described as the forcible entry of the masses into history. It is not a question of making revolutions for the people, but of people themselves making their own revolutions, not only to change the present economic and political arrangements, but also to bring about a sense that they can be masters of their own environment; to make them confident that they can control the world in which they live.

In terms of the ideas of disarming and re-arming in the novel, once again, the important conception is the collective nature of Matigari. National independence was a very important stage in people's struggle, but it also often took the form—in most countries—of a disarming of the people in every way: mentally, spiritually, economically and politically. To try to depoliticize people is a form of disarming them, making them less alert; at independence, people were told that politics were now over, and that it was possible to achieve development without politics. To tell people that neo-colonialism and subservience to the West—being exploited and oppressed—are the answer, or to tell them to follow blindly in the footsteps of a person who is leading them to the grave*—these are attempts to disarm the people. So it is important to see the question of arms and re-arming in terms of its total economic, political, cultural and social implications.

The Continuing Role of Literature in Exposing Neo-Colonialism

I address a particular theme in all my works: the liberation of the people, economically, politically, culturally and psychologically. In other words, if there is any one theme in my works it is one of the liberation of the collective human spirit. For as long as this has not happened, and for as long as there are forces conspiring towards the continuing domination of the human spirit, so long shall I continue to address that subject. For I do not go outside history for my themes; they are derived from history and current social practice.

The fundamental question posed by *Matigari*—of the paradox of history—is not only relevant to the current phase of neo-colonialism. Even without neo-colonial structures, if it were another phase of our history where this paradox has not been resolved, *Matigari* would still have relevance. However, this is not to diminish the importance of neo-colonialism: It is a very important theme and one which, in my view, has not been sufficiently examined by writers. What is needed is for us in Africa and the Third World to become as conscious of neo-colonial arrangements and their economic, political and cultural implications, and to be horrified by them with the same force, determination and sincerity, as we were *vis-à-vis* colonialism.

The tremendous struggle going on in the world today is the struggle for the mind. People can be made to view history in a way which is sometimes against their very interests. You find this tendency in newspapers, radio, television. People are bombarded with words, images, scholarship of different kinds, all having more or less one aim, to rationalize the present-day inequalities between nations and races, and within nations, and to rationalize the differences or contradictions between the majority who produce and the minority who control. All this activity is not purely because newspaper editors, television owners and those who control academic establishments crave mental exercise. The object of the struggle is the mind of the people. In such a situation, the role of literature—progressive literature—is vital in continuing to draw pictures that correspond to the reality—particularly if they are drawn from the standpoint of the majority of the people. It is very important that people in the democratic and progressive academic and literary worlds continue to create images from the people's standpoint.

Matigari as Oral Narrative

There are various symbolic levels in *Matigari*, and I was trying, using a very simple narrative technique, to go beyond all that had been attempted in my previous novels, in terms of this symbolic treatment. I found, in this context, that the conventions of the oral narrative solve a number of problems—problems, for instance, of time and space.

On one level, *Matigari* is a simple narrative, a sequence where events follow one another in an apparently linear way. But it has a lineality which, in fact, negates the linear sequence of events. In an oral narrative, characters can travel from spot "A" to spot "B" in a matter of seconds, or they can travel to and fro in time. For example, at the beginning, Matigari is seen as travelling across many hills and valleys, but it is only 10 o'clock by the time he reaches his destination. Or, later, he says that he has travelled through the country, using trains, buses, *matatus,* but you do not actually see him riding a bus or train. He also goes into the wilderness. Yet, in terms of a specific time-scale, this probably only takes place within a period of about three days.

I had achieved this break with linear time in *A Grain of Wheat* and *Petals of Blood* through using multiple narrative voices, and flashbacks which were really seen as continuous in the present, where past, present and future were all contained in the same moment. The present is heavy with the past and also pregnant with the future; that is the notion I was trying to capture in these two earlier novels. But even those techniques become restrictive because of the realism which is being assumed. Only by dispensing with time and space in the manner of an oral narrative, could I explore the possibilities of breaking with linear time without recourse to these devices. I also realized that the assumptions of the oral narrative, and dispensing with time and space, are not as arbitrary as they might at first seem, given how the mind works. It is the oral narrative that follows the structure of the mind: at one moment, when I mention, for example, the word "home" to you, even as we are talking, your mind can travel to any other location and be back here. You can travel home, recover images of your mother and father, and return, while never having left! We can even quickly return to images of our childhood. As people talk, there are multiple references—to their childhood, to the spaces they have occupied, to their experiences, and so on. So this is not an arbitrary narrative device.

The oral narrative has an obvious and intended symbolic dimension. It is very simple, and there are certain motifs that are repeated, some contained in the chorus or the songs. Say, the hero is going in search of a lost person in the next country or town, or even in the next world, and he travels around asking for the way; he may ask in the form of a song, so that the song may contain the repeated motif. *Matigari* employs motifs in this way, using different words, but the same motif.

The novel is really a symbolic poem with multiple references, but I have seen reviewers trying to fit it into the restrictive jacket of a realist portrait—even though the novel does not pretend to be that at all. Matigari, for example, says at one point that he has been looking for truth among the nests of birds in the trees. I have been very fascinated by various critical readings of the novel, where people have not been able to respond to these symbolic levels, despite their being so obvious.

The Reception of the Novel in Kenya, and Its Subsequent Banning

I was greatly saddened by the banning of the novel in Kenya because, whatever the social implications of the novel, I was very much looking forward to discovering people's reactions to its literary qualities. As a writer, I was much more fascinated by this aspect of the novel than by any other. I wondered if people would respond differently to it as compared with, say, *Devil on the Cross*.

Unfortunately, I could not be there to see the reaction, but the pattern that was beginning to emerge was very interesting. Two or three weeks before *Matigari* was due to be published formally in October 1986, it was already selling in the road-side bookshops in Nairobi, so some people must have smuggled copies from the printers long before the publication date. A publisher's rep was sent to verify this situation, and the publishers then bought up all the street copies, so we do not know how many copies had already been sold before the publishers intervened. And, of course, little did the publishers know that the government itself would interfere with the formal bookshops, when the novel was banned in February 1987. As to sales, about 4,000 copies of the novel were printed, and about 700-1,000 remaining copies were seized by the government from the publisher's warehouse. So around 3,000 had at least travelled to the bookshops. What is difficult to estimate is how many copies had been sold before the police raided the bookshops. From what I could gather, though, sales had been brisk and, of course, every copy would have a multiple readership.

Though the period was too short for a detailed assessment of people's reactions, in terms of dissemination and reception there is no doubt that *Matigari* was received very well. Like the previous novel, *Devil on the Cross*, it was read on public transport and at social gatherings, such as eating places, people's homes, and so on. It is also quite clear that people started talking about Matigari as though he were a living person, and perhaps the banning of the novel was prompted by the extent to which people were talking about this individual, Matigari—some of them even calling him "Mzee" as a term of respect. He has actually become quite a character: Someone rang me, trying, I think, to find out about the English translation of the novel. Speaking in the clandestine language that Kenyans are used to, he asked: "How is the old man?" For a time, I did not understand, but then he continued: "We hear that the old man has learnt English, and that he might be going for an examination on the thirty-first of May." Then it clicked, since that was the date of the UK publication, and we started having a conversation about *Matigari*!

Language and Translation: The Future for African Languages

Had there not been an intervention by the government, the same pattern of translation would have been followed as occurred with *Devil on the Cross*. *Matigari*, originally in Gikuyu, would have been translated immediately into Kiswahili and then into English, or any other language in the world. Instead, only the English translation is available now, although someone has just finished translating it into Japanese. (It is a translator who has learnt Gikuyu, and has translated directly; she wanted to complete the Japanese version before the English translation came out, so that she would not be influenced by what she read in English.)

We have now, in fact, in the contract of the originating publisher, closed the option for people to translate from the English, by insisting that *Matigari* must be translated directly from the Gikuyu. Obviously, translators may check additionally with the English, but we have been very firm on this because there were loopholes in the case of *Devil on the Cross*: Though the Swedish edition was translated from the Gikuyu, the German and Russian translators used the English edition. The tendency has been to take the easy way out—through the English translation—which means that the work will become further and further removed from the original in terms of its spirit and meaning; a translation is also in a sense an interpretation, in its choice of words.

Now it has become even more imperative to translate directly from the original, because this translation is not mine, but Wangui wa Goro's. One cannot assume, as in the case of *Devil on the Cross* (which was the author's translation), that the English version is equally the author's work—even his work as a translator. I do not want to put myself into a position where I feel that every book I write must also be translated by me; no author can commit himself or herself to that. The translations into English should be treated in the same way as those into German, French or Japanese, where I have no direct say. Of course, with the English version I have a vested interest, because it is a language I understand. But nevertheless, once one has good translators, they should be able to do the work. If they look hard enough, people will find ways around the problems of translating direct from the Gikuyu. There is no reason, for example, why people cannot collaborate on translations, with one person who knows the original language, and another who can use creatively the language into which it is being translated.

What becomes important is that authors, writers and academics must start responding to African languages. For example, in the United States, and all over the world, there are experts on Africa—historians, philosophers and so on—who do not know a single African language. It is only with regard to Africa where, once again, the continent is taken so much for granted that people assume they can become experts on the region without having to concern themselves with African languages. It is inconceivable the other way round, that there could be a scholar on, say, French history or French philosophy, who could not be bothered to learn the French language. Yet, it is taken for granted that you can know Africa through French or English or Portuguese—through the languages of the colonizing powers—which carries yet more insults and injuries.

Ultimately, it is for the people of a particular language culture to open out their language in a literary way, because, if you look at the history of languages, it is not possible for anyone outside a particular language culture to initiate a way forward for that language. Admittedly, in some cases, missionaries have done more for African languages, by having people read the Bible in, say, Gikuyu or Igbo or Kiswahili, than African writers themselves—though the missionaries were not, of course, doing this for the sake of African languages or cultures. Nevertheless, it is for African writers to enhance their languages, literature and philosophy, just as writers have done for other cultures throughout the world.

The object is for colonial languages to occupy their proportionate position in society. English and French may remain minority languages, but they will at least not be the dominant languages for expressing African culture, and this will also affect the literature produced in those languages. There will be a more natural balance. It is important for us to remember that there have always been literary works in African languages. It is simply that the discussion of African literature since World War II has been dominated by literatures written in colonial languages. My concern is that this literature has even taken on the title of "African Literature," completely obscuring the fact that there has been a history of literature written in African languages which, correctly speaking, is African literature. This other, hybrid tradition should have another, more appropriate name.

What I think will happen is that the younger generation will probably experiment with African languages. As African writers find that they can communicate and be published, and derive status as writers, even if they write in African languages, this will definitely increase their tendency to resort to African languages as the means of their creative expression. That is why I insisted on this direct translation clause, although my position now seems to be a minority position among practicing African writers. Nevertheless, I still hold onto it very firmly. I see a situation where an increased focus on African languages in schools, universities and other institutes of learning will also mean increased attention to the art of translation. Because now, whereas many African people can handle at least two or three languages (in the case of Kenya, that means English, Kiswahili and whatever is their mother tongue), what has not been developed is their capacity in those three languages to a level where they would feel free to translate from one to another. So a combination of various forces should make for a breakthrough in literature written in African languages: a combination of publishers willing to invest, a government with pro-African language policies, writers willing to experiment in African languages, and translators who take pride in African languages—whether their own or not. But the primary responsibility is for the writers themselves.

---

* A reference to the philosophy of President Moi of Kenya, embodied in the slogan of "Nyayoism": "follow in my footsteps."

32 Ngugi wa Thiong'o

Jane Wilkinson / 1989 (1992)

London, 20 September 1989

At the beginning of Decolonising the Mind, *you say this is going to be your "farewell" to the use of English even in explanatory prose, not only in literature. Is this still your position?*

Yes, it's still my position. It just means that I shall be using Gikuyu mainly, like some people operate in English, in French, in Chinese.

In the chapter on fiction in Decolonising the Mind *you talk about your research for an appropriate form and an appropriate content for what was to become* Devil on the Cross, *emphasizing particularly the importance of orature in this process. Reading* Matigari *one feels there has been a similar kind of development. Is this so?*

Yes. *Matigari* is based very much on orature, particularly the narrative techniques and certain assumptions about time and space, or perhaps not so much assumptions as attitudes to time and space in oral narratives where often time and space are fairly flexible. I like this idea of being able to move freely in time and space.

Reading Matigari *I kept thinking back to some of your previous works. It seemed almost as if you were voluntarily recalling characters, incidents and themes that had appeared before. Was this a conscious strategy?*

No, I was not aware of that. I suppose you're right in the sense that there's an attempt at summing up experiences arising from the previous attempts. But then in every writer's work there are echoes of previous literary texts.

I was wondering if you were trying to sum them up and bring them forward in a new development.

Not necessarily. I was much more aware of the need to exploit the oral forms of narrative. In *Matigari* even the narrative tone is supposed to be very much like an oral tale. I wanted to write a tale that could do the work of *Devil on the Cross* or *Petals of Blood* in terms of multiple references, without necessarily having the same kind of narrative voices. I wanted to make it refer to different moments in time and space while having a very clear narrative continuity.

Something that struck me particularly was that, in comparison with the characters of your previous works, Matigari seems to be much more openly and much more explicitly a kind of Christ figure, a Messiah figure. You actually state this, whereas previously similar analogies are left more implicit.

I think it arises from this attempt at multiple references within a simple narrative, these multiple echoes of different experiences. The biblical myth is there: the notion of birth, death and resurrection. There are allusions to the Last Supper, Christ and his disciples. But there are also references to many other things: for instance, to the natural cycles of birth and death and germination. Also seasons.

Another echo is that of Dedan Kimathi and the legends surrounding him....

Yes, the making of a legend, myth-making. I'm interested in how myths grow, how the human imagination captures the essence of things in terms of myths, of heroes and hero-worship and all that.

To take up on some of the characters in the book, the female figure seems considerably less important than in most of your previous works.

Yes, Matigari is all-consuming. In a sense both the woman and the boy are really different aspects of Matigari, and Matigari is different aspects of the woman and the boy. They are all part of one another.

You could say Guthera is Matigari, and Matigari is Guthera, and Guthera is Ngaruro wa Kiriro or Muriuki, any way you like. I just got three figures who could be father and daughter or man and wife and child, or brothers and sisters. They're just different suggestions; there's no attempt at having romantic idealizations or anything. They are echoes. I know many of my readers have been looking for Wanja in Matigari, but Matigari is not like that at all. Matigari is a collective figure, his particularities are echoes of different facets of our history. There is one scene where he meets John Boy outside the house and John Boy asks who he is. And, in order to explain who he is, Matigari has to go into history and say he has been there even before the times of the Portuguese in the sixteenth century. John Boy says he doesn't want history, but Matigari *is* also history, of course.

One of the most intriguing symbols in the novel is the "riderless horse"; could you say something about it? Or do you want to leave it to the reader's imagination (at the beginning you invite the reader to use his imagination and apply the novel to his own situation)?

It keeps cropping up. The novel opens with memories of the hunt and it ends with Matigari being hunted in the same way. No, I've no idea what it means. Do you know what it means? It could be anything!

33 An Interview with Ngugi

Dianne Schwerdt / 1990

This interview took place at the Flinders University of South Australia in September 1990.

It has become increasingly evident in both your fictional and non-fictional writing that you consider the role of the African writer to be an essential part in the struggle against neo-colonialism. So in Writers in Politics, *for example, you talk about the fact that "a writer has no choice...that every writer is a writer in politics." Can you comment on your own writing as part of the communal resistance movement?*

Generally speaking, my writing falls into three periods. There is first the two novels which I wrote during or just before Independence—that is, *The River Between* and *Weep Not, Child.* Then there is the novel I wrote soon after Independence, *A Grain of Wheat,* actually written in 1965-66 and published in 1967. Whereas *The River Between* looked at the coming of colonialism, *Weep Not, Child* is set during the armed struggle led by Mau Mau against the British colonial presence. What the two books miss, obviously, is a broader, if you like, historical consciousness or political consciousness.

The resistance fighters and their political awareness are not as central to the two novels as they should have been. *A Grain of Wheat* tried to rectify that. It is set just a few days before Independence and a few days after Independence, but it goes to and fro in time, examining, if you like, through different eyes, the same period covered by *The River Between* and *Weep Not, Child.* It glances at the past, it glances at the present and it glances at the possibilities of the future.

But in *A Grain of Wheat,* there is a far greater historical consciousness, a greater political awareness and, as you are aware, the resistance is central to the novel. The novel also signals certain divisions in postcolonial Kenyan society. It also signals a certain ideological shift in my approach to that society. In the preface, I do actually make a statement which later becomes important in my work as part of the resistance culture of the neo-colonial era. You know the preface—I can't quote it in full, but it says that whereas many of the characters are fictitious except historical figures like Kenyatta or Waiyaki, who are unavoidably mentioned because of their role in the history of Kenya, the situation was real, too real for the peasants who fought the British, yet who saw all of what they were fighting for being put to one side. This is 1966, three years after Independence. The new consciousness was already beginning to affect my work. For instance, in *Petals of Blood,* the historical context is broader, the resistance culture is central to the novel. There is now a definite ideological shift in the sense that the consciousness becomes rooted squarely in the peasantry and the working class.

The same can be seen in my other works, in, for instance, the play *The Trial of Dedan Kimathi,* which I collaborated with Micere Mugo in writing. The question of the centrality of literature in anti-neo-colonial resistance is best articulated in the preface to the play where it says fairly strongly that literature and history should be on the side of those who are struggling. So *A Grain of Wheat* and *Petals of Blood* belong to the same period in my literary development.

Then we come to 1977 where now I abandon the English language as the medium of my creative writing and I become very active, strongly affected and influenced by my work at Kamiriithu, and everything that follows from that: the writing of the novel *Devil on the Cross,* the attempt to produce a play, *I Will Marry When I Want,* and eventually the writing of *Matigari.* But I see my works, particularly the ones starting with *A Grain of Wheat,* over all, as part of the resistance culture in the postcolonial era of Kenya's history.

In that you seem to be reinterpreting history, rewriting history in an unofficial way, how central to that task is the reinterpretation of Mau Mau and reinterpreting the activities of heroes like Dedan Kimathi?

In a way I feel that in Kenya there are two histories. There is the official history which cancels or underplays the role and centrality of Mau Mau, and the whole anti-colonial tradition from Waiyaki, Me Kitilili and Koitalel to Independence, and even after.

But there is the other history which I believe is the real history, the history of how the Kenyan people have not only acted on their environment and changed it, but in particular how their resistance to colonial domination and now to the neo-colonial distortions of our society is changing their society, has changed their society, and is continuing to change their society. So in that sense, I feel that what I have written since, say, *Petals of Blood,* and particularly what I have written in *Devil on the Cross* and in *Matigari,* are more consistent with that real history of the Kenyan people's history of political struggle, of attempting to change things for the enhancement of the rights of the Kenyan people.

So much so that in fact in Matigari *you talk about the unfinished war, referring back to the business of the 1950s, and in fact in* Devil on the Cross, *in* Petals of Blood *and in* Matigari, *you seem to be suggesting that the people have to look at this reinterpretation of history and to make choices whether to accept the* status quo *and be passive or to reject the* status quo *and become active, become resistance fighters...?*

Yes. In the case of, say, *Matigari,* one is saying that the colonial structures have not been destroyed, and in some ways the post-colonial society is really a neo-colonial society which continues the basic structures of the colony—colonial politics, colonial culture and values basically, and at the base of course are the repressive traditions of the colonial order which are reproduced after Independence and being made the only basis on which stability can be established. So in *Matigari,* the idea is really that the anti-imperialist resistance can only be successful with the destruction of the neo-colonial structures. I take very seriously the dictum by Kwame Nkrumah—what is implied in his statement that neo-colonialism is the last stage of imperialism.

You seem also to be implying in Matigari *and* Devil on the Cross *that there is a certain emphasis on individuals having to make choices, moral choices about what they need to do, but in terms of taking action, action rests with the collective. How do you see the individual* vis-à-vis *the community?*

Yes. Individuals make society. Society makes individuals. There has never been a true Robinson Crusoe in history. Individuals have to make moral choices between conflicting demands and alternatives. But real social change is born of collective action. In *Matigari,* Matigari himself is not seen as an individual, although there are features of an individualist character, but he is seen more as a collective, he is more of a collective than an individual. You remember when he meets John Boy and Robert Williams at the house when they are on horses and they ask him, "How and why do you claim ownership of this house? Tell us the reasons." And you remember Matigari goes back four hundred years before the present and says he was there at the time of the Portuguese. He has always been there. So he could not be meaning just himself as an individual.

So he claims collective ownership.

Yes. Collective ownership. For when he says he used to work in all the factories, and he worked all land, there is no chance that he could have been in all these places simultaneously.

And in contrast to that you have John Boy make a speech about individualism stating "our country has remained in darkness because of the ignorance of our people. They don't know the importance of the word 'individual' as opposed to the word 'masses'...You walk about fettered to your families, clans, nationalities, people, masses. If the individual decides to move ahead, he is pulled back by the others...My father knew this; that is why he sent me to school and ignored the idiots who were mumbling nonsense about sharing the last bean." So that John Boy acts as the extreme opposite of collective ownership, and you set up this dichotomy between two notions of ownership.

Yes. What John Boy is really talking about is what has been described as Social Darwinism, the survival of the fittest, even if he has to wade through the blood of a thousand others. Survival of the fittest, which is obviously opposed to Matigari's notion that everybody is each other's keeper.

I had a question, too, about the way in which you portray women. You start with a very strong character, Mumbi, in A Grain of Wheat, *and then Wanja who changes sides halfway through* Petals of Blood, *then Wariinga in* Devil on the Cross *who takes action on behalf of the collective but in fact acts alone and so presumably will be hunted down and punished, and then Guthera in* Matigari. *Can you comment on the position of women and the role women have played in the resistance movement in Kenya?*

Well, they have been an integral part of the resistance movement. It is not a movement by men with women joining in to help. They have all been part of that movement, playing different roles. I would like to cite the example of Kitilili, who was an old woman from the Coast who in 1912 or thereabouts organized the youth in the area and in fact mounted an armed struggle against the British. She made the people take the oath of unity and she organized the youth to fight—she really is a remarkable woman. But of course there are others, like Nyanjiru from the workers' strike in the 1920s; there is also Field Marshal Muthoni of the Mau Mau era in the fifties, and while we are mentioning it, there were of course thousands of others. If you look at the colonial era, for instance, you know that the urban labor force was mainly men. When you are looking at the peasantry as a political, historical-cum-social force, you are thinking about women mostly. When you talk about the centrality of the peasantry to the movement, then we have to remember that the majority of the peasantry is clearly women.

The way you portray Wariinga in Devil on the Cross *is interesting. It seems to be the case that personal liberty and national liberty are in some way linked. Wariinga has to gain personal liberty, review the way in which she perceives herself in her customary role, before she can be of use as part of the collective struggle.*

Yes. One is thinking here of the whole question of a colonized consciousness which can limit someone's capacity for effective organizational work. It may even prevent that person from even seeing the necessity of organized resistance. In fact where colonized consciousness is dominant, the individual can't actually see the importance of organized resistance, organized communal response, even passive resistance. In that sense personal and national awareness are interlinked. They have impact on one another.

You've shown increasingly a distrust of the educated elite, the intellectuals, for reasons which I think are quite obvious. When you look at, say, Armah's novels, his intellectuals seem to play little part in the resistance struggle; they in fact withdraw from society, as a general rule. Given your views on the role of writers in society, would you say writers like Armah, Soyinka, Achebe and others have in fact abdicated from the role that they perhaps might responsibly fill?

All the works of those writers are very important in their different ways. They have all, in my view, made very important contributions to the democratic process in Africa.

I was thinking in particular about the Teacher in The Beautyful Ones Are Not Yet Born*—his position of withdrawal is, I suppose, critically treated by Armah, but Baako in* Fragments, *his withdrawal from society is treated with some sympathy—he goes mad at the end.*

I look at the works of African writers as a whole as a comment on the postcolonial society and without singling any particular writers out, they do give very valuable insights into the nature of postcolonial society, dissecting it really, and in the process, by implication, showing the possibilities of renewal.

In Matigari *and elsewhere you describe a regime that silences intellectuals and writers, and your own writing in fact led to your detention in 1977. What role can the writer play in Kenya now at this present time? What are the risks?*

Well, the risks are there obviously in postcolonial Kenya, as you know very well. The imprisonment of writers is just one example. There is the case of Abdulatif Abdulla who in 1969 was imprisoned for three years.

There is my own case in 1977-78. There are cases of other writers like Al Amin Mazrui, who in 1982 was imprisoned for two and a half years, after he wrote his play *Cry for Justice*.

Then there's the whole question of other writers being forced into exile. There are many Kenyan writers who are currently in exile. There is a question of Kenyan writers being forced into censorship, or into silence, whatever suits the regime of the country. But of course, there is the case of writers who are collaborating with the regime at the highest level of the law-making machinery of that regime—some of them have taken a very dubious position *vis-à-vis* the whole question of silencing critical writers.

In Decolonising the Mind *you state that choice of language and the use to which language is put are central to people's definition of themselves. You talk about the Kamiriithu project being the turning point. You began to write in Gikuyu. You talk about the slave mentality, colonization nurturing self-hatred, and so on. How central is choice of language to the process of decolonizing the Kenyan people?*

Yes. If you look at the whole postcolonial scene, almost all knowledge which is gained by African intellectuals at the universities, places of higher learning, institutes of science and technology, schools of literature and the arts or whatever, all this knowledge becomes encased in English or French or Portuguese. Now, how many are there in each of the African nationalities who have access to knowledge encased in English or French or Portuguese? The most knowledge is encased in languages which have nothing to do with the people. In that sense, you can say that the liberation of African languages is central to the liberation of the general society.

A question that you raise in discussing the language of African fiction, again in Decolonising the Mind, *is "how do you satirise [the] utterances and claims [of the Mobutus and Mois] when their own words beat all fictional exaggerations?" You seem to have answered that in the narrative style that you have adopted in* Devil on the Cross *and* Matigari. *How much is that related to oral literature, and is this a style that you will stay with in any further fiction writing in Gikuyu?*

There is a big challenge for satirists in Africa. In a neo-colonial society, so many things are so completely distorted by the ruling regimes that it becomes almost impossible for satire to capture the distortions of reality, but nevertheless writers do try to find various ways in which they can capture these absurdities that are more fictional than fiction itself. I have tried to explore and utilize oral forms in my work. My novels more and more reflect the oral form. They explore the oral form in a novelistic tradition, yes. That is what I have done so far in *Devil on the Cross* and in *Matigari*. I would like to try to see what more I can do differently with themes, images, styles, tones, forms of the oral tradition. But that is not to say that I want to repeat the *Matigari* act. I just want to see what more I can do in that tradition.

It is not a tradition or style of writing that Western audiences are used to, but then again your audience is not primarily Western now, but Kenyan.

Yes. But oral literature (orature) is party to all societies. The great national literatures have rooted themselves in the culture of the peasantry. I think African literature will be even more firm—that is, the written part of the literature—by exploring all the possibilities found in the culture of the peasantry, and this culture as a whole has been expressed through the oral tradition.

In Matigari *the protagonist comes to the conclusion that liberation is only possible through armed struggle. "Justice for the oppressed comes from a sharpened spear." So, in the novel a violent revolution seems inevitable. Do you think this is true for the Kenyan situation?*

One is trying to warn all the time. One is writing warning signals all the time. One is saying that given A and B and C and D and all of that, that the consequences are this and that. The novel is saying that if you shut off all the means of self-expression, what alternatives are you leaving? What are you really forcing people to do? If a regime becomes itself a terrorist state against its own people, what is it really asking people to do? The novel as a whole is really pointing at what the terrorism of the neo-colonial era, particularly under the leadership of Moi, is doing. It's forcing people to look for the same kind of solutions, or similar kind of solutions, as those which compelled the British to retreat. It's really a warning, through a general analysis of neo-colonial society, that neo-colonial repression is inevitably driving the people to seek for solutions in all ways.

Like being pushed against the wall.

Kind of, because when you kill a population—I mean, many governments do at least make pretences of protecting the population! But when a government itself actually uses terrorism against the people, it loses all moral authority, all legal legitimacy, all moral legitimacy. In such a case, people are not duty-bound to obey such an anti-people terrorist government.

I'm just wondering, would it be appropriate, since you have been the official spokesperson since July 1990 for the MwaKenya Movement, would it be appropriate to comment on what that movement is currently seeking for the Kenyan people?

Yes. First of all, what the movement is looking for is contained in the Draft Minimum Programme published in 1987. Among other things, it is really asking for democracy as a basis of organizing society. You can't really have democracy and neo-colonial structures at the same time, because the two are in basic contradiction. So the questions of democracy and social change are linked to questions of neo-colonial structures, neo-colonial culture and values.

Ngugi, you are committed to reversing the degenerative effects of colonialism on Kenyans through your writing and through your involvement in community theater. Now as an expatriate writer, how can you sustain this commitment?

Being in exile is always a terrible thing because, as a writer, one is cut away from the rhythms of life, which are carried by the language. One is cut away from those images that trigger the imagination. On the other hand, if a writer takes it as a challenge, it can stimulate somebody to try even harder to find the connection with the real struggles going on. He may miss one or two things but on the other hand, he so strives that the challenge itself may produce, you know, a work which more realistically reflects the struggles of the people. *Matigari* is a good example of this. Written in 1983-84, published in 1986, it was actually banned from the bookshops in Nairobi in 1987 by the regime. So the novel obviously must say something about what was going on. Yes. Exile is my challenge.

Ngugi, thank you.

34 The Third World Mainstream: Ngugi wa Thiong'o

Simon During and Jenny Lee / 1990 (1991)

Ngugi wa Thiong'o is a Kenyan novelist, playwright and critic, and an outspoken critic of the Kenyan government. In 1978 he was detained by the Kenyan authorities after the banning of one of his plays, Ngaahika Ndeenda. *He has been living in exile since 1982, and most of his novels, critical essays and plays in the Gikuyu language have been suppressed in Kenya. His works in English include the novels* Weep Not, Child, The River Between, A Grain of Wheat, Petals of Blood *and* Matigari, *and several books of* essays *on culture and neo-colonialism* (Homecoming, The Writer in Politics, Barrel of a Pen *and* Decolonising the Mind). *Simon During and Jenny Lee interviewed him in Melbourne in September 1990.*

Simon During: *One of the problems we have in Australia is that there isn't much information about Kenya. What's happening there seems almost unbelievable, given the promise of the decolonization moment. Can you describe how that has happened?*

Ngugi: It is very difficult to separate what is happening there today from its origins in the colonial setup, which, as you know, was very repressive. The structure of our society was very much a pyramid: White settlers occupied the top of the pyramid, and African people occupied the broad base at the bottom of the pyramid. Economically, politically and culturally, this structure did not change very much with independence. Very few barriers to social mobility were removed. So there was not adequate economic restructuring after independence. The result was political alienation from the postcolonial governments of Kenyatta and then Moi, and the result of this alienation was that the regime resorted to the same colonial measures to maintain stability—the police boots, the military violence and so on. This was true under Kenyatta, and it is also true under Moi. In effect, this has meant the suppression of political opposition; for instance, between 1963 and 1966 there was a measure of democratic debate within the nationalist camp who took over power from the British, but after 1970, with the banning of the only opposition party that was ever legally registered and recognized in Kenya, the Kenya People's Union, Kenya became a *de facto* one-party state. In 1982, it was made a *de jure* one-party state. But all along, any political and cultural organizations which were not controlled by the government were suppressed.

Jenny Lee: *Was that partly a matter of conflict between ethnicities within Kenya?*

Ngugi: I don't think so. I think too much emphasis has been put on ethnicity in African politics, and that has been very misleading. Interpreting the politics of any country in terms of the regional origins of the actors tends to downplay the economic, political and social factors, the historical forces that have created the situation. For instance, by the early 1970s, when Kenya was being described in the West as an island of stability and democracy, the opposition in Kenya was saying quite clearly: "Look, there's no democracy in this country. Kenya is a neo-colonial setup. The situation is going to lead to some sort of social explosion one day." Meanwhile, the Western press described Kenya as a modern Western state where everything was fine, more or less, except for a few corrupt practices here and there. Yet now, when what we were saying would happen has happened, they turn around and say, "Aha, it's because Moi comes from this tribe and the opposition comes from another tribe." Repression is repression, no matter who does it, and it's got certain consequences, irrespective of the ethnic origins of those who are practicing undemocratic measures.

During: *What is the possibility of a successful struggle against the regime?*

Ngugi: I think what is important in Kenya today, and in many neo-colonial countries, is political democracy. The democratic state is the most vital and necessary stage in our long struggle, because we must put accountability to the people at the heart of any economic, political and social solutions to our problems. This is what has been wrong in Kenya, where the regime does not feel accountable to the people. People don't matter, really. The regime may feel accountable to Western capital, but not to the people. We regard accountability to the people as a measure of any political or economic system.

Lee: *Your position there would mark quite a shift from the one-party state ideas of some other African socialists, wouldn't it?*

Ngugi: Put it this way: Wherever there are many interests in society, those interests have a right to express themselves and organize themselves. Even if you suppress those interests by force, they will still find ways of organizing themselves, so it is better for them to express themselves and then negotiate a solution that draws its legitimacy from the people.

During: *Why are the authorities so frightened of your work being performed in Gikuyu?*

Ngugi: Again, it is to do with the question of the people. The percentage of people speaking and understanding English in our country is very small. It is true that English is the language of education, of administration; it is the official language, it is the language of state coercive power, of justice. Every Kenyan who has gone to school will understand English. But the English-speaking population is still a minority socially *vis-à-vis* the working people, who would understand Swahili, for instance, as well as speaking their different nationality languages—Gikuyu, Somali and so on. When you write in an African language, particularly if what you write also expresses critical views, what you write reaches the masses—in class terms, it reaches the working people. Of course there are contradictions; there are many nationality languages in Kenya, meaning that if you write in one of the nationality languages, you do not necessarily reach all the peasants and all the workers of Kenya simultaneously. But at the very least, when you write in an African language you are reaching that social class, whereas when you write in English you do not reach those social strata at all. I think that what Kenya needs at the moment is a population that is able to think for itself, that is able to conceptualize things for itself and find solutions for itself.

Lee: *Is your work available in Kenya?*

Ngugi: Yes. There are a few contradictions in our society. A lot of my work is available in English in bookshops in Kenya, even today. Books like *Weep Not, Child, The River Between, A Grain of Wheat, Petals of Blood*—even, I think, *Devil on the* Cross—sell in Kenyan bookshops. They are now not used very much in schools; the government has played down literature as a subject of study in schools, because they think of literature as a subversive enemy. But my last novel, *Matigari,* is not available. That is the novel that came out in 1986, and it was seized from Kenyan bookshops and from the publishers' warehouse by the police in February 1987. My plays are available in book form, but they are not allowed to be performed.

During: *To what extent are the plays repressed because they are helping to politicize an unpoliticized peasantry, and to what degree do the plays express a politicization of the peasantry that's already in place?*

Ngugi: It's a mixture of both. The plays themselves, like *Ngaahika Ndeenda (I Will Marry When I Want),* reflect very well the anti-colonial systems as well as the anti-neo-colonial systems, because they depict quite accurately the contemporary social conditions in Kenya, and in particular the struggle of the peasantry and workers in factories and so on. So in one sense the plays reflect real-life struggles. But at the same time, when people actually see those struggles they know so well put in a framework they can understand, it is as if the plays are expressing what the people already know, but it helps when what they already know is given, if you like, shape and form.

During: *That's reflected in the process of authorship, isn't it? To some degree they are collective productions?*

Ngugi: Yes. My other plays were authored individually, but my later plays evolved communally, particularly the ones which were community-based, like *Ngaahika Ndeenda,* and another one that is not published yet, called *Mother, Sing for Me.* These evolved through communal involvement in discussions, and through alterations in the course of those discussions and the performances.

I lost the chance of making those sorts of plays when I left Kenya. That is one of the disadvantages of being in exile. *Ngaahika Ndeenda* evolved in 1977, when I was working at Kamiriithu Cultural and Community Centre, and *Mother, Sing for Me* was developed with the same community in 1982. Needless to say, both were stopped by the Kenyan government, the first one by the Kenyatta regime and the second by the Moi regime.

During: *In your work, you have a pretty scathing attitude towards Christianity. Is that changing with the impact of liberation theology in Kenya?*

Ngugi: I'm scathing about the role of Christianity in colonial contexts, in Africa and elsewhere. But remember that in the same works I have shown individual Christians who work against oppression. What is happening in Kenya today is really very encouraging and in some ways very moving, to see the clerics as well as some Islamic leaders coming out and speaking out for democracy and social change.

I remember in 1984 or 1985 I wrote an article in which I felt—not despair, but I was feeling upset that there had been so much silence about the Kenyan situation. I had said the same thing in my book *Barrel of a Pen,* that silence was one of the greatest enemies. I said a time has come when silence before the crimes of the neo-colonial regime in Kenya is collusion in social evil. And I went on to say that we Kenyans were really helping that social evil by our silence. Now what is really encouraging is to see that what I have called "the psychology of silence and fear" has been broken in Kenya, and the clerics are leading.

Lee: *Would that be mainly in the urban areas, or in the countryside as well?*

Ngugi: In the urban areas, but also in the countryside. Obviously, it isn't all the clerics who are speaking out, but it is a significant minority. I hope very much that the values of speaking out, the values of criticizing, will become entrenched in the Kenyan population from now on, so that no regime of terror will be free from the critical gaze of an outspoken population.

During: *There seem to be two strands in your thinking, one of which draws a lot from Western socialism, the other of which is interested in preserving, and moving out from, local traditions, local knowledge, local struggles. To what degree do you see a tension between those two strands?*

Ngugi: I don't think there is really a contradiction. I believe that people must act with the reality around them, but that reality around us is not isolated from other realities. I take the position of John Donne, who said that "no man is an island," and I believe that, whatever our starting point is, we are part of a wider reality. But the question of the starting point is crucial, the question of the base from which we are looking at reality. There is the tendency for the colonized to be made to look at themselves through a Eurocentric gaze, instead of eyeing Europe from their own base in Africa. Not only do they view themselves through a Eurocentric gaze, but also from a gaze defined by the ruling social forces in Europe. I want us to change our perspective, to look at ourselves from an Afrocentric base, but also to look at ourselves from a social base in the people.

Lee: *What part would reflection on what's happened in other African countries play? I was thinking that from the point of view of an African socialist, especially in East Africa, the Tanzanian experience is fairly crucial. How would you see the forces in Kenya situating themselves in relation to, say, Nyerere's model?*

Ngugi: I believe that the biggest problem for Africa is to break from the neo-colonial hegemony of Western Europe. You look at the economies of most African countries: They're so closely tied, they are really an extension of those of Europe. One is not advocating isolation, but I am thinking of the problems of African countries creating national economies that can relate to other world economies on a basis of a greater degree of equality. An African country—be it Kenya, Tanzania, Uganda even—is independent to the extent that it has been able to minimize the neo-colonial relationship to Europe, economically, politically and culturally.

During: *In your essay "National Identity and Imperialist Domination: the Crisis of Culture Today" you write: "Far from destroying tradition, modern technology, e.g. video, cinema, television and radio, should make it possible to reclaim the positive aspects of traditional peasant cultures which are withering away under the pressures of economic exploitation." Are you involved in that kind of work yourself?*

Ngugi: Yes, I have tried. And, by the way, when I said that, I also wrote about the issue of the ownership and control of those technologies. The cinema, say, could really be a people's technology or a people's art form, but look at the control. The revolutions in modern information technology could democratize many things, including access to culture. Where before it was not possible for many people apart from the imperialists to attend, say, symphonies in performance, now it is possible to get the same high-quality performances through cassettes and so on. Again, take cinema: Where before it was only accessible to those who were able to go to the cinema house in the city, videos now can make good cinema available to quite a large section of the population. But who controls all of that industry, the information technologies? Again, in our own case in Africa, it is controlled from the West, and within the country by a small group of people. I would like to do more in cinema, but I have not been able to do as much as I would like to.

Lee: *It would be very hard to do from exile, wouldn't it?*

Ngugi: Yes. Working on a film project, for instance, there is always the problem of raising money. A lot of these modern technologies require a lot of money, which is a very big problem.

During: *And they do bring with them a kind of international mass culture. In a lot of Third World countries, Hollywood and American mass-cultural products have had a huge impact. What is your* *position on that?*

Ngugi: It's true; it's a kind of package deal, so to speak. Again, the problem is one of control, because when you talk about international mass culture you are actually talking about international mass culture as defined by a very tiny group in the West. You are not talking about an international mass culture of the democratic traditions in Western Europe, say, which would be a very positive thing for the world; you're talking about an internationalized version of the culture of a tiny group in the West, of how they view the world. If they were talking about the internationalization of the values of the democratic struggles in Europe and the world, this would be of benefit to the world; it would not be a negative thing.

During: *That would involve some sort of hybridization, wouldn't it? I'm thinking, for instance, of the music of Zimbabwe, which was important in the struggle, and is now available and widely played in the West, but it's neither local nor international; it's something else.*

Ngugi: One of the advantages that this modern technology can have is that, say, music from Kenya could be immediately available in Japan, and music from Japan could be immediately available in Kenya. It is again an exchange of what is positive in the music, making it freely available to people in Australia, in America and the other way round. But so far internationally the exchange at the level of culture has been unequal.

Lee: *One of the interesting things is that, as a result of the quest for novelty—music and publishing are the two instances that immediately come to mind—although the control remains consolidated, culturally there has been a process of diversification. One of the great ironies is that the cultural diversification, for example the much wider availability of Third World literature and music in the West, has actually gone side-by-side with the consolidation of control, even in this country.*

Ngugi: Everything carries its opposite in a sense. The fact that this technology is available does mean there are possibilities of using it for a diversification of culture. It does mean art, literatures, music being more available than ever before to the people in the West, and the other way around. When the control of these technologies is really democratized, so that the positive values in the different cultures are brought through and become dominant, we shall be moving towards the basis of a genuinely democratic world culture with a common set of values.

During: *I guess in some senses that is easier to imagine in a country like Kenya, where there is an obviously oppressive regime, than in the kind of tolerant repression of a place like Australia or America, where it is hard to see any possibility for a liberation struggle, or any possible connections between culture and liberation.*

Ngugi: I can see that might be a problem, but the way I look at it, whether in Australia or in Kenya or wherever, is that culture is closely tied up with issues of economics and politics, because they are parts of the same process. Culture in general is dealing with the area of consciousness, of values, of feeling about the universe; that whole area of our being affects the kind of political choices we go for, and also often affects our economic relationships. So culture is such an integral part of our economic and political being that it can never really be divorced from those processes. And while there are inequalities or distortions in economics and politics, the same distortions are reflected in the area of culture. The struggle for economic and political readjustments or restructuring within any one society will also necessarily involve cultural restructuring and rethinking. So we can say that cultural liberation is an integral part of the economic and political liberation of the universe.

Lee: *In publishing your own work over the years, have you yourself encountered cultural barriers?*

Ngugi: So far there has been no problem in terms of content, or in terms of any pressure towards one kind of orientation or another. Culturally, Heinemann have been quite broad-minded; they were also the ones who published my novels in the Gikuyu language. This does not mean that the contradiction between African-based publishing and foreign-based publishing does not exist; it is a structural problem.

Lee: *How do writers who are still in Kenya gain access to publishers these days? Are there any local publishing houses?*

Ngugi: I think there are; I don't really know how many there are. I know there was a time when publishing in Kenya was thriving. I don't know how much it has been affected by the current repression in the country. I would guess that local publishers cannot afford to be too adventurous in publishing dissenting views, because they are more amenable to state pressure than, say, an international publishing house. There is an irony here, that publishing with an internationally based publishing house may be more of a protection in a neo-colonial setup than publishing locally.

During: *If I can ask you the classic question, I imagine that the situation in which you became a writer and the situation in which you now find yourself as a famous international writer are rather different, but why did you become a writer?*

Ngugi: Well, I am really a product of a storytelling society. I was always interested in stories at home, and then I started reading stories when later I came to school and learnt how to read and write. I suppose it was a combination of my upbringing at home and also my exposure to literature at school and university.

During: *Was there a lot of cultural value attached to writing?*

Ngugi: When I was beginning, writing was a kind of minority practice, but remember that when I started writing, there were quite a number of writers who had already started writing and were being published in Africa as a whole—people like Chinua Achebe, Wole Soyinka, Ezekiel Mphahlele, people like Peter Abrahams—and black writers writing from the Caribbean, like George Lamming. That was part of what inspired me to want to write.

During: *To what extent was that a break with traditional communal life?*

Ngugi: I grew up in a peasant community, where storytelling in the evening was an important part of our entertainment. I grew up at a time when, although many of our traditions had been interfered with by colonial authorities, still quite a number had remained fairly intact, and they were a very important part of one's education in a peasant community.

During: *Your early works do appear more Eurocentric than your later works. Am I right in thinking that they are more involved in the psychology of the characters, that there is a more traditional privileging of character over the political force of the text?*

Ngugi: Maybe there was a time when the exploration of the psychology of the characters was a bit too dominant in my work, but it is a question of where you place the balance, really, because psychology is important. But I think what was wrong was that there is a danger of trying to explain social and economic phenomena in psychological terms. There is a tendency in psychological writers to say that social problems could be resolved psychologically rather than the other way around.

Lee: *Yet, from the point of view of a Western reader, I remember encountering the early books and finding them quite a revelation, because in the African writing I'd read up till then the characters were mostly fairly archetypal. Coming from a different culture, in a way I felt at the time that I was getting more understanding. So I suppose both approaches serve their purpose in different ways.*

Ngugi: Let me put it this way: If you're writing about a human being, we eat, we wear cloches, we attract, we struggle with nature, we struggle, we struggle for power; but the human being is also made of a heart, of a mind, and all those things are going on at the same time. So the challenge for a writer, for me anyway, is how to express all those things—the socio-political being as well as the psychic being. Because the inner life of a human being is important. Some of the writers I really admire are writers like Tolstoy, say, who are able to express all the aspects of human life—the social aspects as well as the psychic aspects of human personality. I would like to be able to do that, quite frankly; my own struggle is how to create a novel that will express the total human personality.

During: *In your later work the current situation in Kenya is experienced as a kind of emptiness by some of the characters, especially the male characters, that they feel a kind of lack that is not just a personal thing; but that is not so true of the women characters.*

Ngugi: One of the features of a neo-colonial society is that it does not make people feel that they are the makers of their own lives. People *are* the makers of their own lives, in Kenya, in Australia or wherever, and the struggle for liberation is to make people feel that. If you look at Kenya, you can see this constant attempt by the ruling authorities to deny people the capacity to make their lives meaningful. More than five people cannot meet. There are six of us here now; in Kenya, this would constitute an illegal assembly, and technically we could be arrested. How do you come together to make cultural life, to make political life in a spontaneous way, to be creative? How do you arrange your funerals? How can communal rituals be arranged in a way that is authentic and comes from within if you are always conscious of having to go and seek permission before you can really express yourself?

During: *This question is from my feminist students, who say that for them, coming from a Western feminist position, there is a sense that the women in your novels tend to be drawn very much from a male point of view, particularly in their sexual characters. Is this a comment that you've encountered elsewhere?*

Ngugi: Well, I don't like to respond to comments on my work; I like to know what social and ideological basis comments are coming from, because depending on their ideological base, people obviously see very different things in different works and characters. However, I'm very interested in what women critics have to say about the women characters in my work, and I always learn from that as much as I can. However, if it is a question of attractiveness, their physical being, their inner life and so on, I think it is very important that people appreciate beauty, form, whatever. I cannot pretend that, as a man looking at a woman, I don't see beauty. Sincerity in fiction is terribly important for me, and I try to see women characters as well as male characters in terms of the totality of their experiences, their struggle with nature and their struggle with one another, and not just take one aspect of their experiences and make it an explanation of the entire phenomenon.

During: *Why are women so often the strongest characters in a political sense?*

Ngugi: In colonial society, where men often do the work in factories and so on, when you talk about the peasantry in Africa as a social class you are also basically talking about women, and about their labor, struggling with the land, struggling with a whole sector of the economy that is often not recognized or appreciated. It is not that women are not occupied in other sectors, but by the very nature of colonial distortions, colonial control, mobility and so on, it has worked out that way. And in liberation struggles, again, the peasantry has been the mainstay, and, the majority of the peasantry being women, they have been part and parcel of the liberation process.

Lee: *Where do you find the inspiration for your writing while you are in exile?*

Ngugi: I think that my struggle over the language issue is quite important in this respect. I do feel so strongly now about writing in African languages that I will keep it going no matter where I am. There are the obvious disadvantages of being in exile: I am cut away from the sources of my inspiration, the phrases, the market places, and so on. I can't pretend that I don't feel that loss. But it becomes a challenge to overcome that. *Matigari,* for instance, was written while I was in exile, and it has become one of the more important books that has exploited the traditions of oral literature and so on. Now I am a visiting professor at Yale in the English department, and when I am there, what I do is develop a critical vocabulary in the Gikuyu language. I write critical articles and papers in the Gikuyu language. When I am invited somewhere, I would do a version in English to deliver it from, but it would originally have been written in Gikuyu. So I am collecting quite a body of critical literature in the Gikuyu language. What I am interested in there is that there is as yet no critical tradition, in a literal sense, in the Gikuyu language. I will find out as I go along whether it changes how I perceive some of the critical terms and critical theories. I don't know what the result will be.

During: *Would you invent words, for example?*

Ngugi: Not necessarily, but the challenge is to see how one can go into the roots of the African languages, see what you can develop from there, see what you can borrow from other related languages, see what you can borrow from European languages.

During: *Do you have an audience for your critical writings in Gikuyu?*

Ngugi: It now passes around as unpublished manuscripts among a small group. We have a group of us at Yale just now, working in this area, and the *Yale Journal of Criticism* is currently publishing one of my articles in Gikuyu with an English translation, and I'm quite pleased with that.

During: *When I teach your work here, I often find it difficult because of the distance and the privilege that one has as an heir of the colonizers. What do you think that a white academic in Australia should be doing with your work in terms of teaching?*

Ngugi: Just what they would do with any other work. It depends on the ideological starting point, the critical approaches, the world-view. I find that some Western critics feel more at home in African literature than others. The text is there, and that is what we have in common as critics. How we interpret that work very much depends on our political attitudes, our value systems, our critical approaches and our attitudes to society.

During: *So you don't believe that there is an African theory of literature or criticism that is most appropriate to writing from and about Africa?*

Ngugi: An African critic, say, who does not see that imperialism is a problem is in the same category as a Western critic who doesn't see that imperialism is a problem. The important question is the values that a given critic identifies with. Is a given critic, whether African or European, approaching criticism from an idealist standpoint, from a metaphysical outlook, or does the critic see the connections between economics, politics and psychology, the connections between what is happening in Australia or Kenya and what is happening in the world?

There is a tendency to see Third World literature and culture as secondary, to see Western literature as the mainstream and other literatures as being peripheral. My argument is that Third World literatures are in fact the mainstream, and therefore Third World literatures and cultures are integral to our analysis and understanding of the twentieth century. In that sense, Third World literatures should be an integral part of the syllabus in education systems all over the world.

35 Ngugi wa Thiong'o

Feroza Jussawalla and Reed Dasenbrock / 1991

The Kenyan novelist Ngugi wa Thiong'o, born in 1938, is the chief proponent of African literature in African languages. After a remarkably successful career of writing such English novels as Weep Not, Child *(1964),* The River Between *(1965),* A Grain of Wheat *(1967),* Petals of Blood *(1977), and of creating and translating such politically powerful plays as* The Trial of Dedan Kimathi *(1976) and* I Will Marry When I Want *(1982 translation of* Ngaahika Ndeenda *produced in 1977 in Gikuyu), Ngugi has abandoned the English language in favor of Gikuyu, his mother tongue, as the medium of his creative expression.*

In London, in June 1988, at the launching of Storms of the Heart: An Anthology of Black Arts and Culture*, *Ngugi made a firm restatement of his personal and literary conviction that African literatures must be written in African languages. This is a position that Ngugi has held since 1977 and continues to restate, despite the fact of his exile in England and now in the United States and the criticism that his reading public is primarily in English. In his* Decolonising the Mind *(1986) he traces the processes through which he came to this conclusion, notably his reaction to the 1962 "Conference of African Writers of African Expression." This conference had accepted what Achebe had called "the fatalistic logic of the unassailable position of English in our literature." Ngugi began to rethink this acceptance of English across the years, first by calling for the use of Kenyan languages as the medium of education. With* Caitaani Mutharaba-ini *written during his 1978 detention, Ngugi abandoned writing in English as the medium of his creative expression and began to use Gikuyu. However, he did translate* Caitaani *as* Devil on the Cross *(1980) himself. With his latest novel,* Matigari ma Njiruungi *(1987), Ngugi has stopped translating his own work and says, "I have lost interest in the use of the English language."*

Ngugi's position has attracted much attention. He summarizes the debate over his position as follows:

"A debate has been raging around my book Decolonising the Mind, *which deals with the politics of African language literatures. Some participants in the debate are clearly in support of the challenge in the book, that African writers should stop serving foreign/colonial and neo-colonial languages such as French, English and Portuguese, and turn to the development of African languages by writing in them. Other participants in the debate form a group which feels embarrassed at even the slightest mention of African languages."*

In the following interview, Ngugi articulates his conception of the future of African literatures in African languages despite the banning of some of his works in Kenya, the only area where a Gikuyu-speaking audience is likely to be. Yet he also maintains that his position is that of one *writer committed to* one *position and is by no means an ideology that he wishes to impose on all African writers or, for that matter, all writers from recently independent nations. In this interview Ngugi lays out his position apropos the political and literary questions that have risen as a result of the stand he has taken. And the way the interview moves from the abstract taking of positions to a discussion of Ngugi's own work is true to the spirit of Ngugi's recent work. He is a good deal more interested in discussing political and cultural questions than he is in discussing the nuances of his own works, thinking perhaps that they can speak for themselves. What follows is actually a composite of several interviews over the years, initially with Feroza Jussawalla at Duke University in North Carolina and then later with both editors in London.*

Feroza Jussawalla: *I want to ask you first about the choice of language. Should English be the medium of expression for African writers or, as you have been advocating since 1977, should African writers only write in African languages?*

Ngugi wa Thiong'o: I believe that it is very important for African writers to use African languages for their creative expression. The situation in Africa is a little absurd when you take into account that the majority of the African people speak African languages and that only a tiny minority speak French or English or Portuguese. This means that when Africans write in these languages, they are basically addressing themselves only to that very tiny minority.

Reed Dasenbrock: *I don't know if you're aware what an impact you've had with that position. Almost everyone we have interviewed for this book has had a definite, strong response to your position. In some cases, they have brought up your name saying, "Ngugi says we should do this." The West Indian writer Roy Heath was saying that your work was a real inspiration to him, in choosing to write more in Creole or nation language in the West Indian situation.*

Perhaps we could start with some questions about the implications of that position. You've made it clear that you're going to be doing your own writing in Gikuyu. But what about a black writer in Britain, like some of the other writers in the anthology Storms of the Heart, *who may be trying to reach people in Britain. What's the language option there?*

Ngugi: Individual writers must use whatever language best suits their particular situation. I was thinking more of a collective position. I see what is typically necessary for Africa. Obviously the position of writers will be determined by the audience they want to reach and by the language at their individual and collective disposal. Every situation will vary. I don't expect to see a writer brought up in Britain and who has learned the English language all his life to start learning another language at age forty or fifty and start writing in it. But just as Caribbean writers or Afro-Americans are going more and more to the roots of their own language, the young black writers in Britain will go to the roots of the language as spoken by, say, the black community in Britain. But for African writers, I'm very clear about the necessity of the use of African languages. After all, nearly all African writers have a choice. I can only think of a handful of African writers who could not use an African language and write as well as, if not better than, their contributions in the English language.

This is also true all over the world. Writers write in their own languages for their own communities and nations. I'm not saying anything Dante didn't say. I am embarrassed when I get a very strong, and at times hostile, response to what is so obvious.

R.D.: *What do you think of Achebe's new novel,* Anthills of the Savannah*? Were you disappointed that he didn't write it in Igbo?*

Ngugi: No, no, no. Mine is a general argument, not a moral judgment on the practice of any individual. As I said, writers will respond to situations according to their own circumstances, but whatever the path taken, it does not alter the general argument that I've been trying to advocate in my book, *Decolonising the Mind*. Ninety percent of the population in Africa today speak only African languages, and we need to reach that ninety percent.

F.J.: *Does the banning of your work in Gikuyu change your attitude even a little bit?*

Ngugi: The basic argument remains whether my book was banned or not. If anything, it strengthens the case for writing in African languages. If there are such strong reactions from the government, then writing in Gikuyu must be doing something which writing in English does not do. Writing in an African language enables me to reach a certain social stratum that was always bypassed by my works in English. Rather than being discouraged by that kind of government reception, I should become more encouraged by the reception of my work in African languages by the people.

F.J.: *But isn't there a danger that this will cause greater language fragmentation in Africa? Will the Gikuyu be able to communicate with the Igbo, and the Igbo be able to communicate with the Zulu?*

Ngugi: Why not? It is the actual practice in the world today. Gorbachev and Reagan met in summit meetings, deciding the fate of the world, talking and smiling and trading jokes, even though one used American English and the other Russian. They did not have to abandon either English or Russian; they just had to accept that one spoke Russian and the other English. They were able to find a means of communicating with that fact as the starting point. The truth of the matter is that the vast majority of African people speak different languages today. And therefore the starting point for any writer is that reality, the language spoken by the people. If I am writing for this audience, I have to use the language they use. I persuade them into my vision of Kenya, Africa and the world in the only language that they can understand. We must not forget that many languages in the world communicate through translations.

F.J.: *This is essentially the statement you made at the book launch of* Storms of the Heart, *when you said that to achieve decolonization of the mind you need to work in the African context.*

Ngugi: Yes. The real language that one is looking for is the language of struggle, the language of transformation of our various societies. Eventually, this language can only be found in the actions and feelings and thoughts and experiences of the working people. Therefore to discover that real language of struggle is to find an identity, to identify oneself with the struggles of the working people. When one discovers that real language of struggle, whichever formal language one may be using, whether English or Gikuyu or Swahili or Igbo or Hausa or American or Chinese or Russian, then it will be reflected in one's work.

F.J.: *I understand that in South Africa, the government is trying to promote local languages and cultures, the Zulu versus the Xhosa, to break down communication in English among the various groups. Isn't there a kind of reversal there, where if the people start speaking in their own languages, they stop communicating with the revolutionary cultures? That seems to suit the government just fine.*

Ngugi: It doesn't, because speaking one's language does not stop people from communicating with each other. People putting their language first doesn't mean that they don't know or must not know other languages. When the English learn English, it does not stop them from learning French and German and Chinese on top of their national tongue. So in the same way, making African languages primary doesn't prevent Africans from learning other languages of the world. The South African people will learn English, they will learn German, French, and they will speak their national languages, using them according to their circumstances and their needs. I am sure that if the South African people use South Africa's languages to call for the unity of the people against apartheid, the South African government would be the first to ban these books. Already, in terms of cultural resistance, when I've seen South African people singing songs of revolution, they sing them in the different African languages. One of the most famous songs is *Nkosi Sikelel' i Africa,* an anthem composed in Zulu. It is a song which any person who comes from the continent, whether north, south, central, east, west, responds to. The South African regime does not like that song and does not encourage it being sung in Soweto or in Johannesburg.

F.J.: *What are the politics of language specifically in Kenya?*

Ngugi: English was always a colonial language in the sense that English came with the colonization of Kenya. It was the language used in the schools, it was the language of education and of administration. This is still the case. In Kenya, even today, English is the language of education, of administration, of trade, of commerce, of everything. But Kiswahili is the all-Kenya national language, understood by a large section of each of the nationalities in Kenya. And traditionally each of the nationalities has its own national language, like Gikuyu and so on. Most of us were educated in English. The books we read, the literature we were exposed to was mostly in English. So when it came to writing, it was almost inevitable that we would write in English, unless we were very conscious of the opposite, or unless we were very conscious of the implications of what we were doing. It was easy for people to write in the language of their colonization because it was the language of their conceptualization, the language of education, the language in which they attempted intellectually to grasp the world around them.

I believe that the language issue is a very important key to the decolonization process. What is really happening now is that African thought is imprisoned in foreign languages. African literature and African thought, even at their most radical, even at their most revolutionary, are alienated from the majority. In English, this thought is not available to the majority, it is not vitalized through its communication with the majority, the people.

If you take the Gikuyu-speaking nationalities alone, we have about five million people, but only five percent of that five million people can effectively read, understand, and use the English language. Ninety-five percent have the Gikuyu language as their only means of communication. I know that when I'm writing in Gikuyu, I'm reaching many more people within that nationality than if I wrote in English. But in addition to that, I believe that it is important that such works as I may write in Gikuyu be made available in other *African* languages. Translation among African languages is important; that means that the African languages will be communicating with one another. And if a literature develops from that communication, that literature will be reaching many more readers overall than if we're using only English, French, or Portuguese, as is the case for most African writers today.

F.J.: *How about the urban majority, though? Would the urban majority in Africa, in major cities like Nairobi and maybe in various West African cities such as Lagos, be speaking English and the various pidgins? Do you think that would be a relevant medium of communication?*

Ngugi: Every language spoken by a people, even when it's borrowed, has its own validity. But in this case, I ask myself why should an African writer go out of his way to be using other people's languages when he or she has his own language? For everyone who speaks pidgin, there are thousands who speak their own languages, and even those who speak pidgin English or other sorts of English nevertheless have their own fully fledged national language to which they have access.

F.J.: *I wonder if we could talk about how this complex linguistic situation in Kenya has shaped your own work. Your first few books are all in straight Standard English. Then, while you have narrative in Standard English in* Petals of Blood, *you begin to incorporate some words and phrases in African languages, in Gikuyu or in Kiswahili. It seems to me that in* Petals of Blood *you were already in transition towards writing in Gikuyu.*

Ngugi: *Petals of Blood* was a transitional novel, my last novel in English; but language experimentation was only a small part of this novel. I was writing about peasants and workers and their struggle against colonialism and other forms of foreign domination. This was true not just of *Petals of Blood* but of all my novels. And yet none of the people who formed the subject matter of my novels could possibly read them because the novels were encased in a language to which they had no access. My change from English and towards African languages as a means of my creative writing came in 1976-77 when I worked at the Kamiriithu Community Education and Cultural Centre. Kamiriithu is a small rural village, about thirty kilometers from Nairobi. There I was trying to develop a community center to develop resources, skills, and also culture with theater at the center. I have told the story of that experience in my book, *Detained: A Writer's Diary* and in *Decolonising the Mind.* As we confronted the struggles of the people, we found that we no longer could avoid the issue of language. When you work in a village, you know what language you've got to communicate with. The only way to do theatrical performances in a village, for instance, is to use the language of the people. In this case it was the Gikuyu language. When the play was successful, it was banned by the government, and I myself was put in political detention for a year. That was 1977-78.

F.J.: *Why were you sent to jail? Was it because of* I Will Marry When I Want*?*

Ngugi: They didn't explain anything, but I'm sure it had something to do with the play, *I Will Marry When I Want,* which was scripted together with the peasants from Kamiriithu. The play talked about the history of struggle against colonialism, particularly the peasants' history of struggle as led by Dedan Kimathi, the leader of the Kenya Land and Freedom Army, Mau Mau. But the play also reflected the social conditions under which they worked after independence. All these factors probably made a neo-colonialist state like Kenya feel uncomfortable about a play by the people, which seemed to be critical of what had been happening since independence.

F.J.: *Sometimes in your early work, too, there's a sense of "our own people betray us." Did you have the feeling that the people who* *should have been making the changes you dreamed about let you down?*

Ngugi: Oh, yes, of course they let the *people* down. The people expected real economic, political and cultural changes after independence. They didn't expect to continue being producers who produced but did not control that which they produced. They did not want to continue being the people who fed and clothed every other person but themselves. They did not really expect the kind of political repression which, I'm afraid, has come to Kenya, particularly since 1982, with the detention without trial of university lecturers and students, and other people who are deemed to be holding views which are contrary to that of the neo-colonial regime of Moi. And then there have been so many killings by the government! So, for all those reasons, I would say that the people felt let down, but nevertheless, I think the struggle has to continue, and the struggle continues, even up to today.

F.J.: *Do you see a parallel between the Kenyan and the South African situations? Do you think that despite a change in the apartheid regime, there will still come another period of transition where the people of South Africa will still have to suffer?*

Ngugi: Well, obviously the two situations are dissimilar, and also similar, in the sense that the real powers behind South Africa are the Western financial interests from New York, Bonn, Paris, Tokyo, and so on. Those financial powers are still also the powers behind most of the repressive neo-colonial regimes in not only Africa but in the Third World as a whole, in places like South Korea, Marcos's Philippines, El Salvador, Pinochet's Chile, and so on. But despite the fear of a possible neo-colonial outcome, it is *absolutely* the right of the South African people to make their own history, just as it is the right of the Kenyan people to make their own history. And whatever errors, whatever shortcomings, it's still their right to make their history and no foreigners, however generous, however brilliant, or however stupid even, have the right to control the affairs of another people.

F.J.: *Now that you're a writer living in exile, does your sense of audience change? Are you still trying to reach people in Kenya?*

Ngugi: I am continuing to attempt to reach the people in Africa. Even my children's stories, the *Njamba Nene* stories, are meant to raise the consciousness of children in Kenya.

F.J.: *How effectively do you think you can continue inspiring the struggle from overseas?*

Ngugi: These are the hazards of being in exile. A writer needs his own home and the society around him. To be able to function effectively, a writer needs the inspiration of his own community. I should, for instance, be where the language I use is being spoken. Being away from Kenya has its limitations. But it is also a challenge. One can see some problems much more clearly. In that sense, one can get strength and stamina from the continuous struggle to meet the challenges of exile.

F.J.: *How does it feel to be writing Gikuyu where there are not many Gikuyu-speaking people around you?*

Ngugi: As I said, there are always limitations in writing in exile, but the attempt to keep up with the language while being away is a challenge for me as a writer.

F.J.: *Because Gikuyu itself is changing in its own context, and you're not catching the current idioms?*

Ngugi: Yes, it is changing, you know, all the time. A writer needs to catch that phrase which is being used in a bar, that phrase which is being used in a restaurant, in a taxi, in the market place, in the shopping center. He needs all that and more. He needs to be in touch with the *feel* of the language, the rhythm, the music and all that. A writer misses all that when he is far away from where the language is located.

F.J.: *Was writing* Matigari ma Njiruungi *very different from writing in English when you used to?*

Ngugi: Well, it was much more enjoyable. My novels in Gikuyu have a strange irony. The first one, *Caitaani Mutharaba-ini,* was written in prison and the second in England, so in a way both were written in exile.

R.D.: *You translated* Devil on the Cross *yourself, but Wangui wa Goro is translating* Matigari. *What differences are there between translating your own work and having it translated by someone else?*

Ngugi: For me, translating my own work was very difficult.

F.J.: *Why? Did you find yourself rewriting parts of it?*

Ngugi: No, when I was translating it, I tended to become impatient, because I had gone over the same material before during the original creation process. And now I was going over the same novel, but just doing the translation. There was no real excitement. But I have also lost interest in the use of the English language. By this I mean that there was a time when I was very fascinated with what I could do with the English language. Make it sing, for instance. The nuances. But not now, in that way. Another frustration is the inability to render the satiric dimensions of the novel in English. Gikuyu readers of *Caitaani* feel that the original was better than the translation was.

R.D.: *At a number of points you indicated through italics that the words were in English in the original. These are things you can't get in English.*

Ngugi: Yes, the play on words is difficult to convey in translation. This is because of the three-language situation in Kenya. English is the official language, Swahili is the national lingua franca, as it were, and then there are the nationality languages like Gikuyu, Luo, and so on. By playing with this language situation, you can get another level of meaning through the interaction of all three languages.

R.D.: *It seemed to me that you did more of that in* Petals of Blood, *where there's a fair amount of Gikuyu and Swahili, than in* Devil on the Cross, *at least in the English translation, where more of it gets translated.*

Ngugi: The difference is that, in *Petals of Blood,* the characters are speaking English and occasionally using Gikuyu. In *Devil on the Cross,* you get the correct perspective, where the character is actually speaking Gikuyu or another African language, with occasional phrases or words in Kiswahili or in English or French or German or any other language. That's how it would be in the real life of such characters. So you lose that in translation. You would lose that also in my play, which has not been published, *Maitu Njugira (Mother, Sing for Me*), in which I deliberately made use of the three-language situation in Kenya in which different classes use different languages.

R.D.: *So you have some characters speaking in English and some characters speaking in Kiswahili.*

Ngugi: Yes. A worker on a settler plantation is in the perfect situation for the use of three languages. The settler would be using the English language. The overseer would be using Swahili. And the different workers from different language groups would use their own languages. So the mediating language would be Kiswahili. That kind of situation is reproduced in *Devil on the Cross,* I think, and also on a small scale in *Matigari ma Njiruungi.* Most readers of *only* Gikuyu or *only* English would lose the satiric dimensions of the other languages. Of course it's possible to code-switch, but that loses some readers as well as the resulting irony.

F.J.: *Is* Matigari *available in Gikuyu in Kenya?*

Ngugi: The book has not been formally banned, but it was seized by the police. The story goes that the president, Moi, heard people talking about a man called Matigari who was going around the country preaching revolution. He asked for the arrest of that man. The police were going around the country asking for Matigari, but then they came back and told him, "No, he's not a real man, he's only a character in a book." The book came out in October 1986. For four months Moi let "Matigari" roam around the country, preaching revolution. Then he was stopped in February of 1987. The book was seized from all the bookshops in the country.

F.J.: *But can the book still circulate?*

Ngugi: It is difficult to tell. Three to four thousand copies had been sold by the time it was seized. Whether those three thousand copies are circulating or not is difficult to tell. But there is much borrowing and even copying of books in Kenya, so people probably still borrow and pass along copies.

R.D.: *When they banned the book, did they destroy all the copies that were for sale?*

Ngugi: They didn't make a formal announcement when it was banned. They just seized the book in all the bookshops. And they went to the warehouse of the publisher and took all the copies in the warehouse. So they won't dare publish the book again. The regime must of course have actually burned the books seized.

R.D.: *That didn't happen to* Devil on the Cross, *did it?*

Ngugi: No, *Devil on the Cross* went scot-free.

R.D.: *What's the difference, do you think?* Devil on the Cross *is just as radical, just as political.*

Ngugi: I don't really know, I can only guess. I think what happened is this. *Devil on the Cross* is a very satiric and metaphorical novel. Some of the characters have such outrageous names and behaviors and characteristics, in scenes like when the robbers in the cave are competing for the honor of being the greatest robber, that if they had banned it, then people might be thinking that the regime identified with the characters who were being satirized, that they were accepting that they were the robbers being depicted in the book. So I think they were probably embarrassed and silenced by the nature of the book.

R.D.: *Your novels in English were never banned, were they? Was* Petals of Blood *ever in trouble?*

Ngugi: No, but it is discouraged in the schools. In Kenya, they allow *Weep Not, Child, The River Between,* and *A Grain of Wheat* to be taught in the schools, but they discourage the teaching of *Petals of*

Blood, Devil on the Cross and subsequent writings. They make a distinction between my first three novels, which are supposed to be "artistic," and my other novels, which are supposed to have "abandoned art for politics." That's how some of the intellectual henchmen of the regime explain it.

F.J.: *What do they mean by "abandoned art for politics?" Because they provoke revolt?*

Ngugi: They're saying the first three books are artistic, but the later books are no longer artistic, just politics.

R.D.: *Do you think that if you were still writing in English that your books wouldn't be banned? Do you think it is because you're writing in Gikuyu?*

Ngugi: It's a combination of factors. It's a question of audience, but it's a question of the content of the books, obviously, because if the book or books were praising the regime in power, I'm sure they wouldn't mind it being written in Gikuyu or Swahili or some of the other African languages. But if the book is written in the language of the people and is critical of the existing order and is addressed to and is being received by the peasantry, by the working people of Kenya, then the government fears that this might give the people "wrong ideas."

R.D.: *Is there a greater tolerance for publication in English because it is less likely to reach working-class people? Certainly,* Petals of Blood *was as revolutionary as your later books, yet it has had no difficulty.*

Ngugi: Yes, this is true. That's why the language factor is important. When you're talking of the English language, you're talking about five percent of the population. And of that five percent, probably only one percent read books. So anything in English is reaching only one percent of the population. Essentially, this is why the government can tolerate what is written in English, whereas for them writing in Gikuyu is a bit more dangerous. If I sell a thousand copies of a book in Gikuyu, I know the readership would not be just a thousand. It might be ten thousand, because normally the books would be read by many people. A lot of people line up and say, "I'm next" and "I'm next." It is also read in families and in groups. This is why they are much more fearful of works written in African languages.

R.D.: *What about* A Grain of Wheat? *That book seems to be an attack on Kenyatta and on the people who took over in Kenya after independence. It's set on Independence Day, and the man who is going to be celebrated, Mugo, turns out to be the traitor. I have always read that as a kind of allegory about the bourgeoisie in Kenya, that they got the credit for independence but didn't really do the work. It seems to me that Mugo is the figure for Kenyatta there: He took the credit for the struggle, but didn't really engage in it.*

Ngugi: It may not have been conscious, but obviously there is an element of Kenyatta in Mugo. By the time I was writing *A Grain of Wheat,* I was already very critical of what was happening in Kenya and saw the seeds of what has now become common knowledge. But in 1966 or 1967, when I wrote the novel, what I was saying was heretical.

R.D.: *Is that why you created the character Mugo in the way you did? At least by the end of the novel, I think most readers—at least today—would see a certain kind of equation between Mugo and Kenyatta.*

Ngugi: That's correct; there's a parallel.

R.D.: *But you have to read the whole book to see that. Did you do that indirectly because you knew that to attack Kenyatta directly at that point would put people off.*

Ngugi: No, it wasn't as conscious a criticism of Kenyatta as that, but there were those implications. In the original draft, I ended with a chapter, a simple radio announcement, that the people, the freedom fighters, who had come down from the forest and mountains, had returned to the mountains to continue their fight. Then, in another draft, I changed this to the beginning. I had this statement at the very beginning of the novel, as a radio announcement, so that the whole novel was going to be a kind of an explanation as to why they were returning to the mountains.

R.D.: *So you backed away from that a little bit.*

Ngugi: Yes, I cut out the radio announcement. I would have had to write many more chapters of the novel to show the connection between their return to the forest and what was happening in Kenya.

R.D.: *Is that why you did it indirectly?*

Ngugi: The main body of the novel remained. It was only the radio announcement that I had removed. But nevertheless I did write a small preface which said quite categorically that what the peasantry had fought for had been betrayed. It's still there in the novel. I don't think by 1966-67, when I wrote that, many people were thinking of the betrayal of the peasantry in Kenya. And for that reason, I suppose it was so outrageous, it didn't seem to make an impact, it didn't seem real. It *was* fiction.

R.D.: *So they just brushed it aside, you think?*

Ngugi: The novel was just slightly ahead of its time in its critical perceptions of the postcolonial regime in Kenya. Too ahead for the regime to have noticed the implications.

R.D.: *But if there is this criticism of the status quo already in* A Grain of Wheat, *then how can it be seen with the first two novels as nonpolitical?*

Ngugi: There are real differences between the early and the later novels. The first novels, although they are political, are not as clear about the class dimensions of the struggle. The connection between the national and the class oppression is clear in *Petals of Blood, Devil on the Cross,* and in *Matigari.*

R.D.: *Both* Petals of Blood *and* Devil on the Cross *also differ from the first three novels because they feature a group, who functions as* *a protagonist, more so than individual protagonists.*

Ngugi: Yes, they are based on the collective struggle.

R.D.: *Here, too,* A Grain of Wheat *seems transitional. I see a critique of leadership working in* A Grain of Wheat. *The novel seems to say, "Don't trust leaders entirely, people need to struggle on their own." Hence the move in the latter novels towards a more collective sense of narrative, a group of characters rather than just one protagonist. So why, in your most recent novel,* Matigari, *has there been this return to a hero or single protagonist?*

Ngugi: The protagonist in this case is a kind of collective protagonist; he's a collective leader, as it were. The novel opens with an address to the reader, "You see, this, too, is fictitious, the action is pure fiction and the country of the setting is pure fiction. So readers should create their own country and place those actions in the country of their choice." And then he says, "So one is supposed to choose one's own time. If you want to place it yesterday or last year or many years ago, you are free to do so." In other words, the reader is invited to choose a time, a place. So there is a collective protagonist who is not really bound by time or space.

R.D.: *And then the reader is invited to relate that back to his or her experience.*

Ngugi: To whatever is relevant to what you know. In this case, of course, the Kenyan reader identifies with Matigari. Matigari is asking awkward questions about truth and justice in his country, the kinds of questions which must be on the minds of many Kenyans.

R.D.: *So the Kenyan government in banning it did something similar to what you were saying they wouldn't want to do with* Devil on the Cross: *They pointed a finger at themselves. They said, "Yes, we recognize this portrait." In banning the book, aren't they recognizing the relevance?*

Ngugi: Oh, yes, definitely, they supply their own country, time, character, setting, and so on.

R.D.: *You said, "Do what you want," and they said, "This is about us."*

Ngugi: Yes. In a sense, the regime's seizure of the book was the first critical reception of the book—no, not the first, the second critical reception. The first one was by the people because they were reading it and talking about it, and they were appropriating it into the oral tradition just like they had earlier done with *Devil on the Cross*. They were reading it in buses once again, were reading in their own homes, in groups, and so on. There was a wide reception of the novel, of the character Matigari. The second reception was that of the government in banning it.

R.D.: *Do you think they'll ban it when it's published in English?*

Ngugi: I don't think Heinemann will publish it in Kenya. I think they're publishing only an international edition in English.

F.J.: *There's been a good deal of attention paid recently to the colonial period in Kenya, through the film* Out of Africa. The River Between *is a direct parallel to* Out of Africa, *in a sense a rewriting of it. What do you think is the cause of the new nostalgia for things colonial that is pervading all our media?*

Ngugi: I don't see it really as nostalgia. I see this playing a very important role as part and parcel of the ideology of neo-colonialism. Every political and economic system has its own ideology, and I believe the economic system of neo-colonialism also has its ideology. And this ideology is being passed on through works like *Out of Africa.* Karen Blixen was not very different from other settlers. She didn't say, "I hate the African people!" She said, "I love African people." But she loved them the same way that people love their animals, their house, and goods and so on. And the sentiment that's expressed in her work as part of the relationship between, let's say, the settler and the Kenyan people, was one of charity, aid, benevolence, which are in fact some of the sentiments which now tend to govern the neo-colonial relationship between the Third World and Western countries. That's why she becomes much more acceptable, and in some ways, much more relevant today, because she makes this form of neo-colonialism acceptable. For example, Reagan vetoed Congress's call for comprehensive sanctions against South Africa and proclaimed before the entire world that he was doing this to prevent the African people from suffering more. This was despite the fact that these African people themselves were calling for the very same sanctions. A work like *Out of Africa* expresses the ideology that went with Reaganism and Thatcherism.

F.J.: *The tradition of imperialist or neo-colonialist writing is something you've set yourself very firmly against. What literary tradition do you see yourself a part of? What kind of literary tradition did you grow up in as a writer, and what kind of literary tradition do you want to be identified with?*

Ngugi: Obviously, I'm part of several traditions. One, of course, is the peasants, the tradition of storytelling around the fireside and so on.

F.J.: *An oral tradition.*

Ngugi: Yes, oral tradition, or orature as we call it. Then of course, there's a Western literary tradition—that is, a written tradition: Dickens, Balzac, Tolstoy, Dostoyevsky, and Faulkner, and others. Of course, one can talk now about a literary tradition that includes Third World writers, like George Lamming, Narayan, and others. So I'm part of that also, but in my recent work, particularly *Matigari ma Njiruungi*, I found myself leaning more and more heavily on traditions of orature.

F.J.: *I suppose we have all read some Dostoyevsky and Tolstoy in translation, and now you want us to read you in translation. Will we lose something there?*

Ngugi: Yes, of course, translations always lose something. But I think what is gained is much more than what is lost. In a sense, I could not wait to learn French, and Russian, and German for me to be acquainted with Balzac, to be acquainted with Tolstoy, with Brecht, and with other people who are important to me.

F.J.: *Do you feel a relationship to Afro-American traditions? Do you draw on the works of Afro-American writers? Do you think they're drawing on yours?*

Ngugi: Yes, I think they are. But so are we. There's a very vibrant connection between Afro-American traditions in literature and those from many parts of the Third World. I know that African literature as a whole has borrowed quite heavily from the Afro-American literary tradition, and I hope vice-versa. Writers like Langston Hughes, Richard Wright, Amiri Baraka and Alice Walker are quite popular in Africa.

F.J.: *Just to conclude now, can you say what the role of criticism is in the development of Third World literature? What should the critics be doing?*

Ngugi: The critical and the creative traditions feed on each other. First of all, criticism is an integral component of literature. But the critic who contributes to the writers' evaluations, to the assessment of gains and losses, who asks questions—all this contributes to the overall development of literature in any community.

F.J.: *Now, you're living here in Britain. What do you see as the future of the multicultural British-born generation, West Indian, African, Asian, that we are faced with?*

Ngugi: I'm sure that they are having, and they're going to have, a very big impact on this society. They've already had a big impact. Their struggles and economic assertion, cultural assertion, political assertion, is definitely part of the overall democratic struggle in this country. The democratic struggle in this country, the struggle of the working people in this country, will never be the same again. So the black presence here can only accelerate, I think, the movement of social revolution.

---

* This anthology was edited by Kwesi Owusu and published by Camden Press in London.

36 Ngugi: In His Own Words

Nonqaba Msimang / 1991

Kenyan writer Ngugi wa Thiong'o was thrown behind bars for writing in his own language. He talks to Nonqaba Msimang about the vital role African literature can play in enabling people to hear and tell their own stories.

"I'm really decrying the situation in which we have to debase our languages in order to immerse ourselves in other people's languages. By the way, it is not true that if you debase your own language, you become better in other people's languages. On the contrary, if you take a child who is equipped with the language of his own culture, he is more and better equipped to absorb other languages because he has learnt how languages work in a cultural context."

That is the gospel of literature according to Ngugi wa Thiong'o, one of Kenya's most famous writers. But the Kenyan government prefers the adjective "notorious." In 1977 Ngugi incurred the government's wrath when he started writing in Gikuyu. He repatriated his language, thus enabling the majority of Gikuyu to hear and tell their own story about the struggle for independence.

Ngugi is a passionate advocate of writing in African languages, believing that it is the writer's duty to throw his or her lot in with the oppressed. His views on neo-colonialism and its effect on African literature have cost him his motherland, Kenya, forcing him to live in exile in England for the past eight years.

Ngugi's head-on collision with the Kenyan government was caused by a Gikuyu play, Ngaahika Ndeenda *(*I Will Marry When I Want*),* *which he wrote with Ngugi wa Mirii and which was produced and performed by rural people from Kamiriithu Community Education and Cultural Centre.*

On November 16, 1977, the government stopped public performances of the play and the following year he was detained. He says he had been toying with the idea of saying goodbye to English for quite some time. Detention made up his mind.

He felt that if he was thrown behind bars for writing in his own language, then Gikuyu was going to be his medium of communication.

What is literature?

Literature is imagination in words. Literature looks at reality through images, but those images reflect certain realities. They reflect what is happening on the land, what goes on in the factories; they reflect social, economic, political relationships, struggles and cultural values. Literature reflects the life of the people.

What do you consider as African literature?

I tried to deal with this problem in *Decolonising the Mind.* African literature is literature by African people. Now I would even add further and say it is written by African people in African languages, but having said that there are other problems with that situation. For instance, because of colonization there are African writers who write in English and French. But in the main I would say African literature is literature written by African people in African languages. Now I would put even more primacy on African languages.

Why?

Because, as I said in my book *Decolonising the Mind,* I cannot perceive of French literature in Zulu, Russian literature in Xhosa, or Chinese literature in Swahili. I see a problem in conceiving books written in English as African literature.

African writers writing in English or in French say that if they wrote in African languages, they would be limiting their market.

would say that even if a language is spoken by five people it has a ight to a literature, to a culture. I look at it as a language being used y real living communities in Africa. The question is: What are the ctual languages being used by people currently in Africa? A market s a changing phenomenon. It depends on who is publishing.

But if by market those writers mean there is no readership for African languages, it is clearly not true. If I write in the Gikuyu anguage for as long as there are people who speak Gikuyu, then that ommunity is a potential market. Whether they buy the books or not vill depend on their economic capacity, the level of interest, whether he books are available, the supply and demand, etc., and we should ut these in perspective. There have always been books written in African languages. It's only that they are not known internationally nless the books are translated. But there are writers in Zimbabwe, n Kenya, in South Africa who are writing in their own languages.

How did your books written in Gikuyu sell?

Very well. In the case of *Caitaani Mutharaba-ini*, which was later ranslated as *Devil on the Cross*, it sold very well. The publisher had riginally printed 5,000 copies. He was hoping to sell them within wo years and that, he considered, was doing quite well. But the 5,000 were sold within three months so he had to do a reprint.

Heinemann Publishers?

Yes. So within the same year he had three reprints of the book. From what he tells me the book has now settled to about five undred copies a year. He says it is comparable to how he sells the ooks in English, especially those not supported by the school ystem.

Why is the school system so crucial?

The school system is a ready market. There's a ready reading public: rimary schools, secondary schools, universities and colleges. But ther books depend on the general reading public and my books are supported by a general reading public because they are not part of the school system.

What about your books in English?

Some are, like *Weep Not, Child* and *The River Between.* But the Kenyan government has been frowning on my books, especially the ones that follow *A Grain of Wheat*, like *Petals of Blood* and of course those in Gikuyu.

Why have they frowned on them?

I suppose it has to do with the nature of the Kenyan regime. It is a neo-colonial regime where economically we are literally an appendage of the West. This is also reflected in our cultural practices. For instance, on the level of culture, our inspiration comes from the West. Virtually ninety percent of Kenyans are foreigners in their own country.

What do you mean?

Take a peasant who has been, say, accused of murder. He goes to a court of law. The judge will be English-speaking as will the prosecutor, arresting policeman, the defense, the interpreter, so when he is in that courtroom he is the only person who is not in a position to participate fully in the whole discourse. That is why I say most Africans are made foreigners in their own countries at the level of cultural practices. If you write in English, your books are accessible to an English-speaking community, which is a tiny minority. That minority is part of the ruling elite so you can see the implications of writing in African languages in a neo-colonial situation.

When did you decide to write in Gikuyu? In Decolonising the Mind *you said it was your last book in English.*

It's a long process. The internal debate about languages is shared by most African writers, even when they opt for English, French, or whatever. In my case, after writing *A Grain of Wheat*, I felt that, okay, I'm writing about the Kenyan people's struggle for liberation but the same people would never be in a position to read what I'm saying about their own participation. I said no, there's something wrong about the situation where I'm writing about Kenyan people in a language that is not Kenyan.

You once said, "We African writers are bound by our calling to do for our languages what Spenser, Milton, Shakespeare did for English, what Pushkin and Tolstoy did for Russian, indeed what all writers in world history have done for their languages."

Yes. I cannot blame the English for not writing in the Gikuyu language. It's me who knows the Gikuyu language, who can sit down and write in that language. Swahili is the same, Igbo, Yoruba, Luo, Amharic; it is writers from those communities who can develop those languages.

Why do you strongly believe that every writer is a writer in politics?

All writers live in a world where what they can or cannot do is determined by power. Who wields power in a society? To what ends is that power being put? Even if I'm writing about peasants or about love, how can I escape the effect of the operation of organizational power on those values? If a person is hungry or without clothes, shelter, surely the whole relationship to love, sorrow, happiness will be affected by the facts of hunger, lack of clothes, and so on. I cannot write about love in isolation of all these factors.

In her book The Black Interpreters, *Nadine Gordimer said because most African writers are what you call writers in politics, their books are not literature as such. They are merely a testimony of social change. She went on to say that "it is unlikely that anything they write will last."*

I haven't read the book, but on the contrary, literature—all literature at its best—is a testimony of change. When literature captures the sense of movement, the sense of change, it is capturing the very essence, the very principle of life. So a literature that is a testimony of change is one of the highest literatures possible. However, the question of content and form is obviously important because if I write a political essay, it is different from a story which takes some of the issues as part of the world of my characters. If a writer feels deeply about those issues, he should put them across as effectively, as intensely, as beautifully as possible. The reader should see the highest expression of hunger, love, emotion, anger. When the character feels very strongly about something, that involves the economy of words. Silence becomes more potent than words. It can be reduced to a look, a gesture. Literature is life.

Parents in South Africa are taking their children to white schools for a number of reasons. One of them is Bantu Education which was designed to prepare Africans as hewers of wood and drawers of water. Such schools don't have books written in African languages. Parents are aware of that but what comes first is their children's future in the South African economy. Consequently, some even use English at home.

Being rooted in, say, Vilakazi or Dhlomo does not make a person less able to cope with any other literary traditions of the world. Quite frankly, those multiracial schools need to be liberated. They need to be integrated, not the other way around. There's nothing wrong with multiracial schools as such but there's no reason why they should not be using African literature, African philosophy, as the basis, including the struggles of the peasants, taking the majority of African people as the basis of the whole educational system.

Talking about liberation, how about people who are "educated," who feel that because they have MAs and PhDs they are expected to quote Charles Dickens, D.H. Lawrence or Simone de Beauvoir?

Once again, I find it ridiculous that I can be very proud of my knowledge of French, and I'm totally ignorant about my mother tongue. It's very shameful, very embarrassing. To me it is higher for somebody to be rooted or to be grounded in, say, Achebe, Sembène, Dhlomo, Nyembezi and, at the same time, to be able to quote Simone de Beauvoir, Sartre, Brecht, Tolstoy, etc. It is a richer experience for me.

What is the damage to the African child?

We need to use the word alienation here really. We look at the world through certain images. All people have images of themselves. We have mental images of ourselves, of what is around us. Literature is those images in written form.

When you make a child not learn literature which has images which reflect his own world, you are destroying that child, because you are making that child look at the world through images that often distort that world, or that make that world absent. In other words, his world does not exist. He will identify with the world that seems to exist, and it is a world that is often in conflict with the actual, real images he himself had formed about his own world and the world around him. It is a process of alienation. You make children uncomfortable with what is around them. About themselves.

37 Ngugi wa Thiong'o: Moving the Center

Charles Cantalupo / 1993

The following interview in English took place on the afternoon of January 23, 1993, in the living room of Ngugi's home near Newark, New Jersey. Larry Sykes and I arrived there slightly early, and Ngugi was not yet back from NYU, where he taught and where he enrolled himself in an intensive language course in French. While we waited for him to return, Ngugi's wife, Njeeri wa Ndung'u, welcomed us with friendly conversation, a bowl of the new crop of clementines, which she refilled often, and glasses of a tropical fruit juice which I did not think was available in this part of the world, although I was born and raised here. We were joined by four of Ngugi's children: Lashambi, the proud recipient of a letter from Nelson Mandela, responding to her homemade greeting card on his release from prison; Nduucu, who was just about to return to Oberlin College for the spring semester; Wanjiku, a student at NYU, who was helping her mother in the kitchen; and Njooki, a student at Chad School, who was also helping her mother. When Ngugi arrived, he invited Larry and me into the living room, where we spoke until we could no longer resist the aroma of roast goat, which Njeeri had prepared for us for dinner.

Congratulations on the publication of Moving the Centre. *Was it a coincidence that its publication date coincided with the holiday celebration of Martin Luther King's birthday?*

It was pure coincidence. It was supposed to come out in November 1992, but I kept on doing corrections, and this delayed its appearance. But it was a good coincidence. Particularly just before his death, Martin Luther King was talking about moving the democratic center from its prison in the establishment to creative locations among the people.

Does Moving the Centre *develop and extend any of the ideas of your last book of essays,* Decolonising the Mind*? Since its publication in 1986, it has achieved the status of a popular, required text for non-Euro-American and multicultural literary study. Does* Moving the Centre *pick up where* Decolonising the Mind *left off?*

Some of the essays in *Moving the Centre* were written after *Decolonising the Mind,* so obviously they do extend some of the ideas already contained in *Decolonising the Mind.* Some of the items were papers given at conferences, and often these conferences were responding to some of the issues in *Decolonising the Mind.*

Decolonising the Mind as a text has become so talked about, that wherever I go, in conferences and in countries in Africa and outside Africa, I'm obliged to answer questions about *Decolonising the Mind.* These questions are reflected in some of the papers in *Moving the Centre*.

At the same time, *Moving the Centre* is a book that developed almost accidentally. The initial suggestion had come from my publishers, who said that since I would no longer be writing in the English language, and that I would be using Gikuyu as my primary language in writing, they wanted to put together all of the articles and papers I had already given and which were not yet published. It started as a project to bring together anything which I had and which had not yet been published. Yet in the process of putting the various items together, we came to realize that a certain pattern was forming, and that certain essays and papers, whether given in 1982 or in 1991, could be grouped around certain themes. In other words, we found that actually running through all the papers and items were certain motifs which held the essays together...

...and this explains the book's being organized into four sections: "Freeing Culture from Eurocentrism," "Freeing Culture from Colonial Legacies," "Freeing Culture from Racism" and "Matigari, Dreams and Nightmares."

Moving the Centre *contains an emotional essay, "Many Years Walk to Freedom: Welcome Home Mandela!" on his historic release from a South African prison, after he had served twenty-seven years of a lifetime sentence. In the book's preface, however, you note that, although the essay appeared first in English in the New York based African-American news magazine,* Emerge, *"the Gikuyu original of the Mandela piece is still in...[your] drawer...among a good many others." You also say that "In their different destinies, the two pieces illustrate the difficulties in the way of those writing theoretical, philosophical, political and journalistic prose in an African language, moreover in conditions of exile."*

What happened was this. In March—I was then at Yale—there was an announcement that Mandela was to be released. Planning a special issue on this historic event, *Emerge* asked me to write an article for it. I said to myself, I can't write about Mandela's release in English. I have to do it in the Gikuyu language, I have to do it in an African language. What does his release mean to me as an African? As a Kenyan? As a human being for whom Mandela and the South African struggle has meant so much? So I wrote the entire piece in the Gikuyu language. And it became very interesting. The flow in the article arises precisely from that. There's a sense of engagement with the Gikuyu language.

In the preface, I was just trying to point out some of the difficulties that people writing in African languages currently have or can face. For instance, there are very few journals in African languages, there are very few forums, that wholly utilize African languages. Write an article in the Gikuyu language, as I do, and often it does not have an outlet, unless it is published either in translation, as in the case of the article on Mandela in *Emerge*, or with an English translation published side by side with the original Gikuyu text, as happened in the case of the article on language in *Moving the Centre*, "Imperialism of Language: English a Language for the World?" It was also originally given for the BBC, but later published in both languages by the *Yale Journal of Criticism*. In fact, the Mandela article, in the Gikuyu language, has not yet been published.

To be asked to write suddenly on Mandela was a kind of supreme moment of theory in practice in terms of your decision to write in Gikuyu, a theme which is...

...very close to home, so to speak, yes.

In your new book's title essay, "Moving the Centre: Toward a Pluralism of Cultures," you evoke your days as a student at Makerere University College in Uganda. Writing "I can still recall the excitement of reading the world from a centre other than Europe," you remember in particular "one of the characters in George Lamming's novel, In the Castle of My Skin, *[who] talks of his suddenly discovering his people, and therefore his world, after hearing Paul Robeson sing 'Let My People Go.'" You go on to say, "He was speaking of me and my encounter with the voices coming out of centres outside Europe." Do you still experience this "excitement of reading the world from a centre other than Europe," when you read contemporary literature?*

Of course, not the same way. Obviously there are more voices coming from Kenya, from Africa, the Third World. The literature from Africa, from Asia, from South America, is increasingly becoming a part, an integral part, of the teaching of literature in different places. For me that "excitement" really came at a particular moment in history: at a particular moment in my growing up, discovering this new literature. It's a moment which is obviously difficult to repeat, for me. But it will be a moment that many other people from Africa, Asia, and South America may experience, especially if they have not been exposed to literature from a world which has molded them.

Let's discuss America. In Moving the Centre, *you cite DuBois's observation that racism is "the problem of the twentieth century." Have the riots in Los Angeles in 1992, and/or Bill Clinton's election as President of the United States altered any of your views on racism?*

I believe that what I say about racism as an ideology in the third section of *Moving the Centre* is still pertinent today. Racism has been so much a part of the Western world, so much a part, an integral part, of the twentieth century, that it's something which has to be continually fought against consciously and deliberately. Obviously, there is a difference in a sense. Racism is recognized more and more as a social evil that has to be addressed, and that's very important. But, as I said, it's been so much part of structures of domination and subjugation that it cannot be really eliminated until those structures of economic, political, and cultural domination have been altered sufficiently to be the real base for group and social equality.

American universities and academics have been attacked for advocating what has become known pejoratively as "pc" and "political correctness." Yet their efforts, at least in theory, and occasional excesses of puritan zeal notwithstanding, are primarily to become more sensitive to and, more importantly, inclusive of the many different kinds of people who attend universities today. Nevertheless, they are attacked precisely for being engaged in "moving the centre," to use the phrase with which you title your new book of essays, within our nation and between nations to "the real creative centre among...people" of equal status, regardless of any conditions of gender, economics, race, religion, sexuality, and physical ability. Repeatedly and eloquently in Moving the Centre *you advocate "opening out the mainstream to take in other streams," "moving towards a pluralism of cultures, literatures and languages," "understanding all the voices coming from what is essentially a plurality of centres all over the world." Your political agenda is international, yet it is distinctly applicable to American universities and the nation itself, too.*

Yes, obviously it's a healthy trend, a trend that redresses imbalances—obviously, it's important and it should be encouraged. But it has to go beyond just the universities. It has to be at the very structure of economic and political power, where the problem is. In eliminating racism, as well as sexism, we're talking about empowerment: a people's lack of empowerment. The basic question is a question of economic, political, and cultural empowerment of peoples: of creating conditions that allow for that kind of empowerment. With that corrected, there's a question of people's attitudes, individual as well as group, which will ultimately change. But the fact that a trend consciously addresses the problem is a very, very positive thing. It's the real correct thing to do.

In Moving the Centre, *I find many of your political tenets more gently expressed than in* Decolonising the Mind. *For example, in the introduction to the latter you identify the United States as the leader of international imperialism, simply presenting "the struggling peoples of the earth and all those calling for peace, democracy and socialism with the ultimatum: accept theft or death." Strong words. Do they fully and accurately describe the situation in the 1990s? How can the situation change for the better? How would you advise a new administration in Washington to begin constructive change of US policy in Africa?*

To come back to an earlier comment: both in *Decolonising the Mind* and *Moving the Centre*, one is writing about moving the center in essentially two ways. In the twentieth century, what you see between nations is definitely structured on inequality. There's no doubt in my mind that if you look at the world as it is today, the West, as a whole, still bleeds the Third World, the countries of Africa, Asia, and South America. This is clear even if you take it at the level of the burden of debt, the financial burden. Many economists now say that the Third World countries are net exporters of the capital that they so badly need—through debt servicing, through their repayment of debt. Third World countries need capital but, in fact, they end up exporting capital to the West. Because they borrow money from the IMF or World Bank, or from the West generally, many of these countries are now completely burdened by the interest they have to pay on the loans. So, they end up giving more to the West: the very capital the Third World countries actually need for their own development. There is still a structural imbalance between the West and the rest of us, so to speak. This imbalance is basically economic, but it is also political, and it has cultural implications. So, moving the center, in an international situation, is really a movement toward correcting this structural imbalance.

Within nations themselves, within Africa, or in America, or in the West, there is also social structural imbalance between the few in all these countries who control the resources and the majority of the people in each of these areas. I talk about moving the center *within* nations, yes, and *between* nations: This thesis runs throughout *Decolonising the Mind.* It's also there in *Moving the Centre.* In the past, whenever countries in Africa have tried to opt for a different path of social development and to break with the colonizing or neo-colonizing structures of relationships, as in the era of the Cold War, there was hostility from the West. So, we see some of the worst dictatorships being supported by the West. I'm talking about countries like, say, Zaire with Mobutu, Kenya with Moi, Malawi with Banda, the Central African Republic in the days of Bokassa, say, and countries like Cameroon with Biya, or Barre in Somalia. This support of dictatorships, which repress their people internally, prevents the only possibility these countries have of getting out of this vicious encirclement. The ability to get out relies entirely on the energies of the people. But the energies of the people cannot be relied upon if they are repressed. So, my own feeling is that it's really in the interest of everybody in the world to encourage and support democratic trends in Africa, even when those democratic trends result in social and economic programs that do not necessarily meet the approval down to the details and fit the capital market economies of the West. I think if political change emerges democratically in these countries, this should be allowed to develop. Obviously the state in many African countries has to play a more active role in economic and social development, whether people like it or not. There's really no other way. The question is, what kind of state, controlled by whom? Are they just states under dictatorships, or are they democratic states that will respond to the people?

Without government repression and its insistence on doing things only in its own way, the energy of a people on their own will emerge—no matter what form it takes.

Yes, exactly. You need to release the energies of the people. You must create what one African thinker, Babu, has called enthusiasm for production! But with the dictatorships in Africa, often supported by the West, there has developed a kind of cynicism: a collective disbelief, and this is very dangerous for development. We need new people-based democratic movements that will generate incentive for change and renewal.

Have you just described what has happened in Somalia? Has such cynicism and collective disbelief destroyed Somalia from within? And allowed the traditional colonial powers, in lieu of any established local government, to return for the allegedly humanitarian reason of solely assuring the distribution of food?

Look at postcolonial Africa, whether Somalia or Kenya or Zaire—concrete examples. Moi of Kenya, during the colonial days, was working with British colonial settlers to prevent independence for Kenya. In other words, at the height of the Mau Mau armed struggle against the British in Kenya, he was a British appointee in the colonial legislature. Yet now, in post-independence Kenya, he is the one who is wielding power, and until recently with the full support of the West, the British in particular. Mobutu of Zaire, during the colonial days, was part of the Belgian colonial army, suppressing the Zairian people. Yet post-independence, he becomes a leader. Take Uganda. Before Museveni, there was Idi Amin. Idi Amin used to be, again, part of the colonial army, fighting against African nationalism. Yet in fact when he came to power, through a military *coup d'étât,* he was immediately received by the then French president Pompidou. He was received by the queen of England. He was given a state, red-carpet welcome in the West. Bokassa of Central Africa—he's no longer there now—used to be a friend of the French president. Barre of Somalia was part of the Italian colonial army. All of these leaders had power supported by the West. They were a part of the Cold War era because they said, "Okay, we are anti-communist," or "we are anti-Marxist," and, of course, it was supported. Look at these leaders very, very carefully: They never see their inspiration as coming from the people, because they know very well that their being in power is not dependent on Somalian people, on Kenyan people, on Zairian people. They don't owe a single loyalty to those people, because such leaders don't feel—and essentially it's true—their power is derived from the people. So, they don't fear that they will lose their power to rule, as long as they have the monopoly of the gun and of support of Western governments. They don't feel accountable to the people. If democracy is not allowed to flourish freely in Africa, we shall continue to have a proliferation of the same problems.

Let's shift from government and democracy to writers. In "The Writer in the Neo-Colonial State," you state a writer's alternatives: "silence or self-censorship....Or he can become a state functionary....Or he may risk jail or exile, in which case he is driven from the very sources of inspiration. Write and risk damnation, avoid damnation and cease to be a writer. That is the lot of the writer in a neo-colonial state." Do you yourself feel these restraints? Do you know writers who feel these restraints? In some ways, you have overcome them, or you've been forced to overcome them. Is democracy going to affect that? If democracy is allowed to flourish, surely the role of the writer will get better, too.

Obviously, I hope for more democratic space to give writers more room to articulate their visions, to be themselves as writers. In Africa, particularly the Africa of the Cold War, the political climate was very hostile to writers. Indeed, it resulted in horrible actions: Writers have been killed in Africa, writers have been forced into exile, and other writers who remain at home have been forced to side either with the government, as has happened to some writers in Kenya, or else to practice self-censorship. Others, of course, continue writing and articulating their visions, but they risk all of those other things: death, exile, or jail.

What about women writers in particular? They too must challenge and break through social conventions, yet there is the imposition of sexual stereotypes and the politics of gender. For a man to challenge social conventions and break free of hopeless alternatives is sometimes easier than for a woman.

Yes, it's true. But remember, there are prominent African women writers, and politically they face the same problems: speak out and face jail, exile, death, censorship and all that. There is also, of course, the habit, the problem of gender discrimination, or of structural discrimination, and women writers have to articulate all of these burdens of gender, race, and class.

What happens if the democracy movement in African nations is suppressed and suppressed—to a point of extinction? Is this possible? You write in the introduction to Moving the Centre,

"Cultures under total domination from others can be crippled, deformed, or else die....Hence the insistence in these essays on the suffocating and ultimately destructive character of both colonial and neo-colonial structures. A new world order that is no more than global dominance and neo-colonial relations policed by a handful of Western nations, whether through the United Nations Security Council or not, is a disaster for the peoples of the world and their cultures."

This sounds elegiac, although this feeling is mitigated at the end of your book. Do you think you have seen a culture deformed, dying and finally left for dead?

I was giving two alternatives. Cultures that are completely dominated can die. Equally well, countries which are in complete isolation from others can fade. In fact, cultures in the past have developed through a healthy balance of give and take. For instance, African cultures during the colonial era suffered structural damage because of colonial domination. In the era of slavery, there was even greater damage, because this meant the removal of human beings who are the basis of the development of culture. There was structural damage to a people's capacity to evolve their own languages and their culture. There is a necessity of cultural give and take on the basis of economic and political equality between groups. Otherwise, as in the case of colonial or neo-colonial imbalances, the cultures of those who are the victims of imbalance are likely to be deformed. In a situation of economic and political equality between groups, cultures can develop on the basis of give and take. Countries will borrow from each other naturally those elements that are healthy to each country.

You make a similar point about African languages and their

borrowings. In Moving the Centre, *you confidently assert,*

"African languages will borrow from one another; they will borrow from their classical heritages; they will borrow from the world—from the Caribbean, from Afroamerica, from Latin America, from the Asian—and from the European worlds. In this, the new writing in African languages will do the opposite of the Europhone practice: instead of being appropriated by the world, it will appropriate the world and one hopes on terms of equal exchange, at the very least, borrow on its own terms and needs."

Your theory sounds as if it has an enormous, healthy appetite. In the same passage, you also cite Bakhtin's observation that "Latin literary language in all its generic diversity was created in the light of Greek literary language," and you go on to ask "the rhetorical question: ...is it possible to conceive of the development of Greek literature and culture without Egyptian and other Mediterranean cultures?" In your view, African languages play as rich a role in the future as they have in the ancient past.

Look at the United Nations, in terms of imbalance. In my mind, it is an organization which should be strengthened. It should be the hope of the world. New and rising nations can be politically and economically strengthened by the empowerment of a United Nations. But it has to be democratized itself! The Security Council, the executive body of the United Nations, is dominated by basically Western, white, imperial nations. In other words, they can veto anything, even against the will of a majority from Africa, Asia. Look at the languages of the United Nations organization. They're nearly all Western, European languages. We want a strong United Nations organization, but we want it also to reflect genuinely the multiplicity of world cultures and peoples, and not for this organization to become an instrument of U.S. foreign policy, or an instrument of the foreign policy of Western powers.

I was talking with the poet Michael Harper, and he recalled that James Joyce once said that a writer's language is his homeland. Do you feel that way? Do you feel that way about English and/or

Gikuyu, or just Gikuyu?

That language is one's homeland? Well...

Is that enough emotionally, or just intellectually?

To have a language is to have a world, in more senses than one at the personal level—obviously a writer carries language in him, and he has his connection with whatever is the language of his choice. When he's writing a novel or a poem, he'll have dialogue with the voices or the characters in the language of his choice. But languages simply are not a matter of personal acquisition. They are also a matter of social communities. When languages of a group are suppressed—through whatever means, economic, military, or whatever—the language of the individual is affected. If I had a language as a writer, but that language had no community of speakers anywhere in the world, then I do not think that that language would really be my world. In other words, I am able to possess language as my world precisely because it is the language of the community.

Maybe Joyce worked towards a language of no one's world. Maybe it was a solace yet a lonely world in the end, a world like Finnegan's Wake, *that few could understand?*

James Joyce comes from Ireland. Ireland has the longest colonial history *vis-à-vis* England, vis-*à*-vis the West, and I think he may have been avoiding the implications of that: not facing up to that reality, that Irish reality. If there was no community of English speakers anywhere in the world, then that language for Joyce would not have been meaningful and enough. Language becomes meaningful at a personal level precisely because that language is part of a wider community.

Do you ever feel alone or frustrated in your own strong advocacy for the cultural imperative of writing in Gikuyu and African languages in general?

No, I don't worry. Throughout history languages have had to struggle, to fight. There is now a need for more literature in African languages, and eventually they will emerge out of their marginalization. In Africa, and in the West, there are now increasingly more and more debates about this very issue of languages. It really is important. I don't feel that I am very lonely, and of course, I'm not the only person who's advocating or who has ever articulated this. I'm only one of a whole series of people who have been saying, "Look. This is important. It is crucial that people's languages are recognized. It is important that there is literature and philosophy, and so on, in these languages." The problem is that there are often not enough financial resources given for the development of those languages.

You have some remarkable stories, recalled in both Decolonising the Mind *and* Moving the Centre,

"of instances of children being punished if they were caught speaking their African languages. We were often caned or made to carry plaques inscribed with the words 'I am stupid' or 'I am an ass.' In some cases, our mouths were stuffed with pieces of paper picked from the wastepaper basket, which were then passed from mouth to mouth to that of the latest offender. Humiliation in relation to our languages was the key."

In another autobiographical passage from Moving the Centre, *you also recall your youthful, "whole hearted affection" for Robert Louis Stevenson's* Treasure Island, *Charles Dickens's* Oliver Twist *and the popular series of adventure stories based on a fictional twentieth-century hero of the British empire, James Bigglesworth, nicknamed "Biggles."*

Was the English language a kind of "first love" who betrayed you?

There's nothing wrong with the English language. There's nothing wrong with French, There's nothing wrong with any language in the world. It's very important that what has been produced in these languages—in Chinese, in Japanese, in Finnish, in Swedish, in whatever—is a part of human heritage. They're all very important. Equally well, what's produced in African languages—in Swahili, in Gikuyu, in Yoruba—is also a part of human heritage. Suppressing the languages of three-fourths of humankind, we are suppressing three-fourths of human heritage. For persons growing up in Africa, fully in the world of their languages, in the literature of their languages, there's nothing wrong with them acquiring other languages as well, and enjoying fully whatever has been produced in those other languages. There's even nothing wrong in African languages appropriating whatever is best that has been produced in and through other people's languages. There would be nothing wrong with ancient languages appropriating the best that has been developed in African languages in a healthy give and take. When economic structural imbalance is corrected, these borrowings from each other would be a natural, organic, healthy development without competition, if you like. Acceptance or rejection would be a part of a healthy dialogue...

...which is a point you make repeatedly in Moving the Centre.

I'd like to turn from the issue of what language to choose to a specific word. "Struggle" is a word that recurs often in your essays. In the preface to Moving the Centre, *you cite Hegel's principle, "Without struggle there is no progression," and you go on to state that "Culture develops within the process of a people wrestling with their natural and social environment. They struggle with nature. They struggle with one another....What is...often officially paraded as authentic African culture today is virtually a repeat of the colonial tradition: tourist art, dances, acrobatic contortions emptied of the content of struggle." When did you discover that "struggle," "the content of struggle," is a major theme in your writing? In your youth? At Makerere?*

It was gradual. "Struggle" is a part of nature and part of our history and cultures. As a central concept in my aesthetic or cultural vision, "struggle" has been developing, I think, starting from my essays on writers and politics. One can see this theme become more and more dominant in my cultural theory and aesthetic theory. "Struggle" is central to nature, to human art and to my history.

In Moving the Centre, *you say that* Devil on the Cross *was "an attempt to reconnect myself to the community from which I had been brutally cut by the neo-colonial regime in Kenya." You observe the same about yourself, though more generally, in another passage: "Writing has always been my way of reconnecting myself to the landscape of my birth and upbringing." Described in this way, writing sounds like a kind of religious act, if we consider that the word "religion" is derived from the Latin "re," meaning "back" or "again," and "ligare," meaning "to bind" or "connect." For writing to be an act of reconnecting—to a kind of happiness, solace, truth—yet also to be primarily about struggle, seems paradoxical.*

There is a connection between the organic development of a language and the organic development of a culture. Each form of development is not one-sided and both are developed through struggle. As biological creatures who are human beings, we live in two conditions. We develop under conditions of internal development within our own biological structures. But we also live in conditions of an external environment, say, the air we breathe, and so on. Our external life is an integral part of ourselves. None of us can live without breathing in air, for instance. Yet at the same time, air is out there, external to us. It's give and take or die. By emphasizing the ideal of organic development, I mean that whatever comes from outside, say, the air we breathe, must not deform internal development. Taking in air supports our internal organs, yet if there is too much, like a blast of air, it can hurt one as much as a lack of air. This is a kind of healthy struggle and a system which must not be deformed by either external circumstances or by such internal imbalance so as to completely deform the possibilities of development.

This almost sounds mystical.

Not quite. If you examine nature, that's how people develop; that's how even trees develop. When there are floods, for instance, or hurricanes, there is a kind of overdose from the external environment, so that trees break, and so on. But the same air, under normal circumstances—the air that trees and human beings breathe—helps their own development.

Let's discuss Moving the Centre's *last essay, "Matigari, and the Dreams of One East Africa." It derives from a trip you made to Tanzania in 1987. Could your return to Kenya be on the horizon?*

Not as long as Moi is in power. Anything can change, obviously, although it's been very disappointing that the Moi dictatorship continues in Kenya. There have been, of course, some healthy advances, and we hope that this will continue to develop. But I still would find it very difficult at present to go back under the Moi regime because what is really happening is that, although there have been some advances, some very important advances—I don't want to deny that—I do not think that the cultural, political climate has really changed. As long as Moi and his regime are there, the same distortions that created a community of Kenyan exiles will continue.

Another "structure of domination and subjugation," to use your words from before.

This is a clear-cut dictatorship, and it continues. The Moi regime is one of the problems, and as long as Moi is there, we shall continue to have those problems. What we want in Kenya, in Africa, is not simply democratization in terms of having political parties. We're talking about a democratic culture. We're talking about the right to organize: not just political organizations, but cultural organizations, social organizations. We're talking about the right of people to move freely within their own countries. We're talking about whether they be workers, or peasants, their being able to organize freely. This is what some of us mean by a democratic culture in the country, which is not like life in a country like Kenya where, for instance, even now people cannot meet without a legal license. The right to move freely, the right to organize freely, the right to assemble freely, are the basis of creativity. The moment that that is affected, obviously, it also affects individual creativity.

In the preface to Moving the Centre, *irrespective of any particular economic or political power, you evoke as the greatest power "the real creative centre among the working people in conditions of gender, racial and religious equality..."*

...of the people, wherever they are. And that we can actually do, to get real, genuine national and international creativity.

If that was the case, would East Africa—East Africa in its entirety—become one country?

My own hope, quite frankly, is that. When I travel, say, from Kenya to Tanzania, or Uganda, or Somalia, or Sudan, I see their problems as so similar that I feel that these countries would be better off uniting. I don't have any mystical notions about nations. Nations definitely do grow, do change. There's nothing that says that nations cannot change and that they cannot combine. So my belief, my hope, is that African nations will come together, and that people will come together under one form of umbrella unity.

"Matigari, and the Dreams of One East Africa" offers an embodiment in East Africa itself—its "kaleidoscope of colours, cultures, and contours of history"—of the book's recurring theme: the "plurality of centres" and the "pluralism of cultures, literatures and languages."

A united East Africa would of course have its own individual characteristics: again, all those particularities are very, very important. But there really is no reason why Tanzania, Kenya, Uganda, Somalia, Ethiopia, Sudan cannot be one political region.

Does this last essay signal a new stage of development in your work? When you say that there's no reason why these countries can't be one, and, in the same essay, that an "awareness of the land as the central actor in our lives distinguishes East African literature," you sound less ideological than you sometimes do in your more recent work.

You mean the last essay wasn't as polemical?

It was very beautiful, emotionally and visually.

More reflective.

The political theory is perfectly embodied in vignettes of eating, fishing at night, or dress, and this is a style which is different from, though not necessarily unconnected to, most of the writing in Decolonising the Mind.

I occasionally use that style. Come to think of it, it's also partly there in *Decolonising the Mind. Decolonising the Mind* has a lot of personal recollection: childhood days, capturing this type of moment, but it is put in a wider polemical, intellectual context. My essay on East Africa is a development of that. *Detained* uses it an awful lot—this personal life.

Yes, but with not simply as much natural beauty, an "awareness of the land," as you say, and its domestic scenes.

It's in my novels a lot. Certainly in *A Grain of Wheat,* the landscape is beautiful; I am very conscious of the landscape. Some of the more interesting pieces in *Petals of Blood,* especially at the end, are actually pure description: of changing seasons, the season of harvest, the season of planting, the season of things growing. There's quite a lot of that. In my last two novels, *Devil on the Cross* and *Matigari,* the actual landscape is not so dominant. But even that's not true in *Matigari:* When Matigari is moving across the land, the hills and valleys, and when he dies—or rather, when he meets his fate, whatever it is—in the river, and when he's being hunted. In visual terms, you can see him as part of the landscape. Many times you don't see him as a figure but as almost part of the landscape.

Do you have any new books that you're working on, any new novels?

Not at the present, you know, but there's always something, obviously.

Would you ever think of putting on some of your plays again, in connection with the Performative Studies position you now have at NYU? Including students, the great wealth of musicians in New York, its large and diverse artistic community?

I've only been at NYU since June of last year. I'll have to see how things work out. I'll see how I fit in New York, before I know exactly what to do.

It was just an idea. I think it would be great.

38 Ngugi by Telephone

Tami Alpert / 1993

We were reading Ngugi's play, I Will Marry When I Want, *in English class. My teacher, Mr. Gern, proposed a number of questions to help us explore the play and its author's intentions. I thought what better way to know what Ngugi was thinking than to ask him directly. I would telephone him.*

It took me a week to find his telephone number. First I called Kenya and spoke to an operator who said he had moved to England. Then I called England. The operator there looked for him all over England, in all the different cities, but couldn't find him. Then I called a friend from Kenya. She told me that he was now in America. I got hold of his son's number and he gave me Ngugi's number. Finally I tracked him down.

"Hello. This is Tami Alpert and I am a student at Stuyvesant High School in New York City. Your play, I Will Marry When I Want, *is very interesting and I was wondering if you could just answer a few questions about it for me."*

"O.K. Yes. You know the play? You do many books by African writers?"

"We are studying Africa right now. We read your book and Achebe's Things Fall Apart.*"*

"What do you want to ask?"

*I looked at my sheet of questions, which Mr. Gern had helped me with. "I was wondering what the significance of the title is—*I Will Marry When I Want*—and if it has a different meaning in Gikuyu."*

Ngugi replied, "As you can see from the play, it is taken from the song sung by the drunk character at the beginning and also by Kiguunda at the end when he loses his land and he is out of work like the other one. Obviously it is meant to remind people of the similarities in the situations of the two characters. When you hear the song at the beginning and then at the end sung by somebody else, you think about the two situations. But it is also an idea of rebellion. In many countries people are expected to marry. This idea that I will not necessarily do as I'm expected to do—there is an element of rebellion there. The song itself was very popular in Kenya some time ago among young people when they were slightly rebellious against tradition and authority. But not in a criminal way. Just in sentiment. So the title was taken also as a reference to that very popular song. Remember in the play that the idea of marriage is one of the central themes. Kiguunda and his wife marry according to their national ways. They also have to marry according to the church. The play is about marriage, but is also about the idea of cultural differences. The Christian marriage connotes one kind of value system. The national wedding ceremony connotes another type of value system. The title has a number of suggestions and the reader can look for them. Even the author may not be in the position to tell everything about his work."

What was my next question? He seemed so willing and happy to talk with me. I remembered that he had written a book about why he stopped writing in English. What was it called?

Ngugi answered, "*Decolonising the Mind.* In addition to explaining why I stopped writing in English, the book also discussed the politics of language in Africa. The idea is important for African writers and African literature to develop in African languages. This is so the majority of the people in each of the language groups can have access to and can read the works of those writers. The idea is for African writers to help in the development of their own languages. I thought that since I am a writer telling others what they should do, I must put that into practice myself."

I was amazed when Mr. Gern told us that Ngugi went to jail as a result of his writing. I couldn't understand this, so I asked, "What happened to you? Why did you leave Kenya?" I wondered if he would want to talk about it. He did.

"I went to jail in 1978. I have also written a book about this called *Detained.* It is by the same publisher as *I Will Marry When* I *Want.* The play was part of a community activity in a place described on the cover of the book. What happened is that the Kenyan government did not like very much the people speaking about their own problems in a play."

"Why?" I asked again.

"Because the Kenyan government at that time and still now is repressive. It is sort of not democratic. They like to speak on behalf of the people instead of letting the people speak for themselves. When a play makes people speak for themselves, they feel uneasy. They punished me by stopping the play, arresting me and putting me in jail. It was not only to punish me but also as a warning to others not to follow in my footsteps. I was in jail for a year."

When I asked Ngugi if the play was still done today in Africa, he told me, "Yes. In some places, but not in Kenya, although the book is still on the bookshelves." *I remembered that we weren't able to buy the books in New York, and my teacher had to get them sent from England. When I told Ngugi this, I was surprised to hear him say that the distribution of African books in the United States was very poor. He said that he was sad because this denies a whole generation of Americans access to a crucial literary tradition in the understanding of the twentieth century!*

He asked me if I had any more questions I wanted to ask. Remembering the classes in which we argued about the politics of the play, I said, "Yes. I Will Marry When I Want *seems to be very Marxist. With the collapse of the Soviet Union and the other countries that were Marxist, have your politics changed at all?"*

Ngugi answered, "When one looks at a word like *Marxist*,

particularly in relation to literature, it can be very misleading. It is just a label. When it comes to art, theater and novels, one must experience the works themselves. What I tell people is this. Do you know Marx? Karl Marx? History did not learn from him. It is he who learned from history. Do you get the idea? Meaning that people live. They work; they struggle; they eat; they marry; they quarrel; they fight. That is the reality. Marx and others observed this and they drew lessons or conclusions from this daily struggle that we all face. We are all dealing with the same issues, the same history. If some ideas look like some others, it is all very fine, but the main idea is to look at the reality itself. This is very important, especially when it comes to art and literature. You should look at the plays and try to understand what the people do. How they live and how power is expressed in that society. How is power organized in that society? How are wealth and power distributed in that society? How does that affect people in the areas of culture, in their psychology, in their values and how they relate to one another?"

Ngugi's answer reminded me of another discussion we had in class. My teacher and some students were wondering if the play wasn't a little too polemical against foreigners, so I asked Ngugi what he thought about this interpretation.

He replied, "Of course, when it comes to art, different people interpret things differently. My play is not anti-foreigner as such. But it is very important for people wherever they are, whether it is in Africa or here, to see how their particular situation is affected, not only by conditions in their own country but also by relationships between their own country and other countries. Those relationships can be ones of domination or dominating. Those internal relationships, as well as external relationships, affect people's lives, even when they don't see them directly. It is quite important for art and literature to examine all those relationships because they affect us wherever we live."

I listened to Ngugi and he seemed to understand his country and *to love his country so well. I was curious if he had been back to Kenya recently, and when I asked him if he had, I was stunned by his reply.*

His voice remained gentle as he told me that he was still in exile. He had left Kenya for England in 1982 after his other play, Mother, Sing for Me, *was also stopped by the Kenyan government. When he came from prison in 1978, he went to continue working in the community in Gikuyu at Kamiriithu. But after the second play was stopped, the theater itself at Kamiriithu, where the original* I Will Marry When I Want *was performed, was razed to the ground by the police. For ten years he had been away from his country. He was now a professor of comparative literature at NYU.*

I had one more question. "If you ever have any free time, would you come visit us at our school?"

"Yes," *he replied*, "and if you ever have any more questions, just give me a call."

39 "The Strength of Our People Is My Inspiration"

Trayo A. Ali / 1995

Kenyan-born Ngugi wa Thiong'o, a professor of Performance Studies and Comparative Literature at New York University, is one of the foremost of African writers.

Professor Ngugi, one would like to find out why there has not been any substantial change in the major themes—or if you like, the capital theme—of African literature in terms of issues tackled by African writers. The focus was, and still remains, within the dichotomy of traditionalism and colonialism. What is the real problem? Is it lack of imagination? Why are very topical issues such as poverty, corruption, dictatorship, ethnicity (or tribalism) in African communities not handled sufficiently?

First of all, I do not actually agree with the assumption behind the question. In spite of the limitation that a lot of this literature is available only in English, French or Portuguese, within that limitation, African literature has as a matter of fact achieved a lot. You know that African writers have tackled issues of colonialism, issues of military coups, they have tackled issues of contradictions between ethnic communities in Africa, and even in terms of the form of the novel for instance, within the linguistic limitations they have also been experimenting with the novel, with the theme as well as with the form. For instance, if you look at the work of Ben Okri, who is already an important figure in African literature, you can see what he is doing with oral and traditional work. Sometimes you call it "magical realism": What is being done is tremendous. In fact, my only problem is that I wish all these problems, so well tackled by many African writers of genius and ability, were actually available in African languages. I wish what was contained in African literature in Portuguese, French and English was actually available in African languages. Otherwise, again with that limitation, African literature and African writers and their products are quite frankly the nearest thing we have to a pan-African property. You can test this: Take any major African writer, say, Ama Ata Aidoo or the Nobel Prize winner Wole Soyinka. If you travel anywhere in Africa, be it Zimbabwe, South Africa, Kenya or wherever, people see them and recognize them as their own writers. They do not say, "This is a Ghanaian writer" or "that is a Nigerian writer." They rather see them as African writers wherever they go. So I object to the assumption behind the question, and emphasize the achievements of African writers.

When you call on African intellectuals and writers to decolonize their minds, what does that mean?

What I mean by this is that it's only African people—the African artists, intellectuals and thinkers—who can, and have a duty to, develop African languages. As you know, the whole independent era of Africa has seen a lot of writing and research work by Africans, and a lot of intellectual output by Africans in *all* fields of learning, but very little—if any—of that output finds its way back into African languages. And this is a very anomalous situation, and I think it's this situation that is contributing to underdevelopment in Africa, in a way. Or in other words, if you look at it the other way around, if as much of this knowledge as possible was also available in African languages, I think we could have moved further than we are now.

Who are the audience of Professor Ngugi the writer?

Well, as for the question of audience, again it has been raised a number of times, and once again, this question is related to the question of language. And I cannot say whether I consciously thought of my audience or not when I was writing in the English language, say, my novels *Weep Not, Child* and *Petals of Blood.* Of course, when I wrote them in English, automatically I assumed an English-reading audience. I do not mean English people, but say, English-knowledgeable, or that audience knowledgeable in the English language. But when I am writing in Gikuyu, of course I am assuming a readership that knows the Gikuyu language first and foremost. This has social implications, because those who know an African language and use it are, in social terms, the majority of ordinary working people. So in terms of reaching the bigger audience socially, or in class terms, I am reaching, I think, a more important audience, as far as I am concerned. But what I have written in the Gikuyu language, say *Devil on the Cross*, has also been translated into Kiswahili, so they are available to Swahili-speaking people in Kenya. The novel has been translated into English, so it's also available for the English-reading audience. It also has been translated into German, Norwegian and Swedish, so it's also available for the readers in those languages. But my primary audience is still African people.

Some commentators criticize you as being a tribalist, writing in the Gikuyu language and promoting the Gikuyu culture.

It's not true. People can quarrel with the ideas in my writings. What is in *Devil on the Cross*, what is in *Matigari*, what is in *Petals of Blood*, what is in *The Trial of Dedan Kimathi*? They can disagree with them, but those ideas are what they are. Can anybody with any honest assumptions really say that any of those works promote, in any way, ethnicity? Or is it not a fact that I have always called for the unity of all the working people in Kenya and in Africa? Is it not a fact that, for instance, in my book *Homecoming* I said there are only two tribes in Africa? The "tribe of haves" and the "tribe of have-nots." And it's the tribe of the haves, who are the minority, who exploit the have-nots within the nation or within the African continent, and do not unite to refuse or to alter the convictions that have produced the two "tribes."

Back to your name. When you decided to change it from James Ngugi to Ngugi wa Thiong'o, did this bring any sort of change spiritually for your literary work?

I think it's very important to realize that when I changed my name I was not *really* changing it but reclaiming my own name. In other words, in the process of growing up I changed from my own name (James) but I was only returning to my real reality. But a question of naming has a wider implication. When we make any achievements as an African people, to whom do we give that credit? We give that credit to aliens. To English names or any other names, but not to African names. African names lost completely. Even when we achieved anything, that achievement is associated with those names. And I think this has, in spiritual terms, been a very negative thing for African people wherever they are. Take for instance the African people in the diaspora, it is not their own fault, but they were denied their own naming system in their own languages. If you research what African people in the diaspora have done, they have contributed a great deal in the areas of science, sports, etc., but we do not really know them because these achievements are signed or carry the signature of English or Western names. Even here in Africa where our men and women have achieved so much, sometimes by our naming factor we give credit to, say, the English naming system. Now, so I said to myself, I do not want to be in a position where a child who looks up to me for whatever reasons thinks that is who I am, because I carry a non-African name. Let him know me as Ngugi wa Thiong'o, so they know that African names can also carry achievement and there is nothing to apologize for.

Back to the African literary scene. North African writers' work is not sufficiently incorporated into African literature. What do you say?

First, I do not quite accept the assumption behind the question. I believe that we have been in danger of accepting the Western notion that there is an Africa which is north of the Sahara, and an Africa south of the Sahara. This thinking goes back to the work of some of the European thinkers of the nineteenth century. In order to prove that Africa was primitive, they did not know what to do with Egypt. For instance, how did they account for the rise of Egyptian civilization? By saying it was not really an African civilization and that there were really two Africas, the Africa south of the Sahara and the one which was part of the Mediterranean, and that one, by implication, was European culture, so that Africa north of the Sahara is not really *true* Africa, and we carry those beliefs (which are dangerous assumptions) among ourselves. The fact is, in reality, African writers from North Africa will use French, use Arabic, and sometimes they use their languages, but not very much, and some of the works are available in translation, whether in English or French. Nevertheless, there could be—and there should be—more work done in researching African literature from all parts of Africa. I personally, for example, like the works of Nawal el Saadawi—from Egypt—and when I teach a course in African literature, I always include her works as part of what I am teaching, and I do not consider her as belonging to an Africa north of the Sahara and myself belonging to the "real" Africa. We belong to the *same* Africa.

You are both a writer of extraordinary depth and beauty and a political activist. How does that political activism affect your objectivity and emotional balance when you write?

My approach to art is that I do not see the arts as separable or separate from life. I mean if art is a reflection of life, if it's produced by life and if art is about life, then it has to take into account that it has been produced by life which has economic, social and political aspects, and many other aspects. That is what life is about. Even emotions like love, hate or whatever are products of this complex aspect of community. So when I write I do not say to myself, "Now I must bring politics in, I must bring economics in." On the contrary I see that the very process of forming a human, his relationships, are shaped by economic, political and other aspects of the society. So when I wrote my book, *Weep Not, Child*, or *The River Between* or *Petals of Blood* or the many novels in the Gikuyu language like *Devil on the Cross* and *Matigari*, I was basically looking at human relationships. But what had shaped those relationships were the historical factors and historical realities of Africa—Africa in Africa, and Africa in the world.

Do you think the concept of democracy is working or workable in Africa?

Democracy is absolutely necessary, it is not even a matter of privilege. It's necessary for the development of Africa. Because in order to develop African people, we need a whole range of ideas quite freely expressed and soon. We need all those creative ideas and initiatives. Initiatives will not occur freely in an atmosphere where there is political repression, or in an atmosphere where people fear for their own lives. Or where they feel that if they say what they want to say, their families would be in danger. Even in a family, people have different opinions, and they have to debate on what is going on; then what about a nation or a huge family, a continental family or a national family? We must be able to express ourselves. Nobody should ever be penalized in Africa for having a different idea from another person.

What gives you strength or inspires you to write?

I would say not so much that strength is driven, but the other way round. Writing is part of art, art is an expression of human beings. So we are expressing ourselves all the time in different terms whether we are writing or not. Writing is only one particular form of human self-expression. My own inspiration, quite frankly, has been and I hope will still be, what I think is the most important thing about African people. The fact that historically there is a struggle, particularly in the last four hundred years, I imagine the debt which we carry with it through slavery, the slave trade, the devastation of our continent, colonialism. We overcame that. Of course you have other problems now in the colonial relations and all that. I am sure we have to overcome those. But look at where we have come from and where we are. The strength of our people is really the most inspiring phenomenon for me.

What is the chief problem that the African writer faces?

It varies from country to country, depending on the socio-economic climate of one's own country. But if we take—say, just in terms of credit and symbol—Wole Soyinka, being a Nobel Prize winner from Africa, and he had to flee from Nigeria for his own life, what does that tell us about the situation of the African writer? Does Soyinka really have to flee for his own life, or should not at least the Nigerian government protect his life by every means possible? So that is an indication of some of the conditions that African intellectuals are facing.

So what is the future of African literature in your opinion?

It has a future, but that future, quite frankly, is a future which is rooted in African languages. African languages for the entire continent. Of course, I would like to see a policy on African languages emerging (I mean all African languages should be developed), but I am also talking about the importance of the continental languages of communication like Kiswahili. I do not like the idea of monolingualism, I believe in a multi-lingual society, but if one language emerges as a language of intracommunity or inter-nation or international or, in our case, continental and pan-African communication, that is also an advantage. When I was in Ghana I met guys who spoke Swahili very fluently, as though they had lived in East Africa all their lives, even though they learnt Swahili in Ghana, and I was very impressed. So we must use a language which enables us to communicate amongst ourselves; but at the same time we must develop all African languages, insofar as those languages belong to their people, if you really believe in an African personality.

Do you think it's realistic to call on African governments to actually implement indigenous African languages policies? Is it something that is likely to happen, even in the long term?

In a sense we have no choice in this matter. Because either we hand over to our children an African people with our own personality, or we hand over an Africa which is no more than, say, a cultural and linguistic extension of Europe. Also, if in fact we are going to develop, and become an equal member of all the nations of the earth in the twentieth-first century, then the knowledge which we acquire should somehow—or by every means necessary—be available to African people. And the only way it can be available to the African people is through their languages, because these languages are the reality. They are spoken by the majority, and if you believe that the majority is the agent for development and transformation, we really have no choice in the matter.

You are a corresponding member of the Board of Directors of the DuBois Centre. Could we hear a few words from you about the Centre?

The DuBois Centre is a symbol of the reunion of Africa with its diaspora, because it brings together symbolic leading figures of pan-Africanism. W.E.B. DuBois himself, who devoted his life to the betterment of black people wherever they are; George Padmore, who is a kind of an organizer for the pan-African movement; and Dr. Kwame Nkrumah, who opened Ghana—and Africa, for that matter—to embrace these great figures.

40 A Conversation with Ngugi wa Thiong'o

D. Venkat Rao / 1996 (1999)

Ngugi wa Thiong'o is a much admired writer in India. More significantly, and quite appropriately, his admirers exceed the "reformed Indians" (to adopt Ngugi's phrase) of the Englit academy. Grassroots activists, civil rights defenders, journalists, and writers in various languages are in communication with his work. Several of his works have been translated into the South Indian language of Telugu.[1] Not surprisingly, some of these translations were done by the well-known activist poet in Telugu, Varavara Rao—when he was himself in prison.

Ngugi's visit to India was occasioned by an international conference on the Nationality Question. The conference, organized by the All India People's Resistance Forum (an activist front), was held in Delhi in February 1996. In his two-week visit Ngugi made two presentations at the conference and traveled to other Indian linguistic regions to give talks and meet people.[2] As a small testimony to his reception in India it could be pointed out that during his visit every day several newspapers published articles on him, translations from his work (in Indian languages), and interviews with him.

From being a trenchant and persistent critic of colonial and neo-colonial regimes, Ngugi's concerns today seem to be with the work of culture in the shadow of global, financial capital (or "capitalist fundamentalism," as he calls it). The culture of his concern now ranges from the most elemental to the highly rarefied, from the language of voice and song to that of music and film. The term he uses to map this range is "technology" in the widest sense. In our efforts to decolonize our minds from the devastating effects of colonial and neo-colonial control, Ngugi argues, we must begin to gather and grasp our resources and means of imagination: "Technology is certainly one of the means of production of images. But once one has acquired the technology, what stories does one tell with one's pen, what pictures does one draw with one's camera, and what song does one sing with one's microphone? This depends to a certain extent on the degree to which we have decolonized the languages of image making, the film language and the languages of sound."

Ngugi describes the activity of "decolonizing the means of imagination" as an ongoing struggle to "move the center" of culture not only from its assumed location in the West, but also from the privileged groups in various societies to other domains "that are other linguisitic centers through which we all can look at the globe." The task of the critical intellectual today, Ngugi argues, is to make possible communication or dialogue between languages that have been marginalized by the assumed centrality of the West. In order to move the work of culture in this direction, Ngugi and his wife Njeeri have started the journal Mutiiri, *a journal devoted entirely to publishing in the Gikuyu language. The journal encourages translations from any language in the world into Gikuyu: "This is only a tiny step in a long journey." He said that the conference on the Nationality Question itself exemplified a move toward such a dialogue and hoped that "this will be followed by more steps so that we can intensify the dialogue."*

The conversation was recorded on 22 February 1996 in Hyderabad.

Interestingly, there appears to be an unbroken continuity of themes you deal with in your writings—concerning modern institutions such as education, religion, political system, etc., but the forms in which these are explored vary from novel to novel (detective thriller oral/folk narratives, political fables, realistic narratives, etc.) In other words, documentary themes prevail but formal experimentation continues. Given your position that content must eventually determine form, how would one explain this discontinuity of form and content, on the one hand, and continuity of documentary themes, on the other?

The themes are created by [the] historical situation in Africa—colonialism and resistance against colonialism are persistent themes; in the present, neo-colonialism—they are constant themes, part of the history against which I am writing. A writer changes also in terms of how he or she approaches the same historical moment. One becomes more and more aware because one is evaluating the themes. In *Weep Not, Child* and *The River Between,* the form is linear, the narrative unfolds from point A to point B to point Z. When we come to *A Grain of Wheat,* we get multiple narratives and time frames shift...It's like I wanted to see how the same events looked at different times—looked at by different characters located in different times, from multiple centers. I continue the same technique in *Petals of Blood*...When I came to *Devil on the Cross,* two things happened. I change[d] language. I had to shift the language to Gikuyu...When you use a language, you are also choosing an audience...When I used English, I was choosing [an] English-speaking audience...Now I can use a story, a myth, and not always explain because I can assume that the [Gikuyu] readers are familiar with this...I can play with word sounds and images, I can rely more and more on songs, proverbs, riddles, anecdotes...I maintain multiple centers, in a sense, simplify structures...For instance, *Devil on the Cross* is based on a series of journeys.

You believe that "every writer is a writer in politics. The only question is what and whose politics." Do you think that there is a necessary continuity between thematized (consciously held views) sentiments or convictions of "political" intent or broad generalities such as the oppressed must unite, the writer should be on the side of the exploited, etc. (a large part of middle-class Telugu writing today is sloppily sentimental and unreadably didactic), and the possible politics of practice in literary writing itself? That is, is there some kind of politics specific to formal concerns of literary writing?

First of all, let me say [that] writing out of ideological convictions, of course, is very important. One has important ideas that arouse one's anger, passion [and] commitment...But of course when one is actually writing fiction or poetry and so on, it is very important that one lets those ideas emerge from concrete reality...In other words, to try and not necessarily impose those ideas on the situation, but rather examine concretely those ideas [that] emerge from the concrete historical or social situation. So when you are writing a narrative, it must be clear; at least it must appear interesting, and to the reader a character must be alive and interesting. There is no reason why one wants to read a fiction as opposed to a political pamphlet...So you go to a fictional narrative for a different kind of experience [than that for which] you go to an essay on political problems. So the fictional narrative has to be artistically compelling to the reader, and I would say this is a challenge to fiction writers. Because there is no way [you] can simply impose your views, your ideology, no matter how much you are convinced of that ideology, onto a situation. Rather, the situation concretely should be the one that generates those ideas.

Would you agree that it is possible to segregate the "politics in writing" from the thematized political sentiments? As you know, literary histories get written and they in turn canonize texts and movements for their formal avant-gardism. At the other extreme we could have writings which proclaim their political rightness by pouring out motifs, themes, which are already identified as politically correct ones. Consequently, the latter takes recourse to populist narrative recountings (adventure thrillers, event-centered narrative episodes, etc.; once again I am thinking of political writing in Telugu) thus formally remaining [affiliated] to consumerist modes of writing. How do you negotiate this paradox? Would you ask, in the context of writers in radical politics, to consider the question of form itself as a model of thought and practice?

One has to be careful not to write one's own convictions [as if they] are controlling the narrative. Obviously one wants to go to [a] fictional narrative for something different than what makes one go to a piece in a newspaper or in a book about politics.

It boils down to two: (1) the question of language, and (2) how you use words, imagery. How you let the event unfold, and particularly language. Otherwise, in my view there is nothing wrong in the writer experimenting with different forms. I myself use in *Petals of Blood* [a] very popular thriller structure, a mix of thriller and detective structure...or the investigative detective structure and I use that for different reasons...One can use popular forms and subvert [the] ideology those popular forms have been serving in the past...So you can experiment with forms, there is nothing wrong with that. The question for the writer in the Telugu or Gikuyu languages or any [other is that] it is very important [to engage with] the question of language. You can actually learn a lot from how words are used in our oral narratives because when we listen to our oral narratives, we will find some very strong imagery, very strong characters, very interesting situations. And, for instance, when you listen to our proverbs, they are memorable because of the structure of the words, the rhythms that make them stick [in] the mind. So words are very important. In my view, the more political the narrative is, the more it needs to meet certain artistic standards in the usage of words, imagination. One should care very much about the language so that it becomes interesting.

[The question of form] is very important...That's why I say it is like when you are convinced, [when] you have certain convictions, then it is important to express those convictions in [the] best form possible, in the most effective way possible...However, we have to be very careful we do not get [so] obsessed with the form [that] we forget the content.

No, I don't mean formalism in any way...

The key thing is one has a story one feels strongly about, one has passion, one is writing because of passion. Writing is not mental...it comes from passion, something about which the person feels very strongly.

You know the academic institutions are obsessed with classifying, labeling, and neatly packaging literary works for consumption. There is also a lot of dishonesty in this kind of work, as you know. In the context of such an industrious dishonesty, what are the ways available to the politically interested literary critic to listen, to reflect upon genuinely alternative literary efforts coming from the fringes of our worlds? I thought your point about the remarkable phrase "moving the center" (as opposed to Naipaul's "finding the center") has something to tell us in this context.

I use the phrase "moving the center" in the context of moving the center from its assumed centrality in the West to where it should be in a multiplicity of centers all over the world. Because each of our own experiences can be a center from which you look at the world—our language, our social situations become very important as bases [for] looking at the world. I was also thinking about this moving the center from its assumed location within a nation or nationality, from its assumed place among a minority class strata, into what I mean is its creative base among the people. But once having said that, we must be prepared to learn. Quite frankly, one of the most important things is how we must be prepared to self-renew ourselves by interacting even with the thoughts which are hostile to our own situation. Because one can learn more from hostility at times than from friendly advice. So even when conditions are hostile to ours, we can learn from them. It is the same for literature. We must be prepared to learn from different literary inheritances of our [people] and other people...We must be prepared to learn from criticism—sometimes hostile critical evaluations, sometimes friendly, imaginative and sympathetic interpretations of our own work.

You write that the exploitative systems of capitalism and imperialism must be overcome—and countries which were exploited, instead of rejecting the evil of capitalism have simply adopted it. Now the point as a general truth has validity, but how does one translate it into a course of action? What does this mean and what does this involve in the everyday life of individuals who are caught in this system?

The strength of that system is in producing us in the ways we would reproduce ourselves in ways regulated by the system. The strength and reach of the system seems more powerful as it works through and by means of us. Now what does it mean to challenge or break with such system?

How do I approach this? See, [in] my own practice as a writer, I must look at everything from the standpoint of the most oppressed center in society...In other words, I try and judge the progress of any society from that standpoint, [and] so I evaluate capitalism from that standpoint. I even evaluate post-cold war changes that are taking place in terms of that standpoint...What we see is [that] after independence—even after [the] post-cold war situation—is, quite frankly, the continued deprivation of people, more misery. In fact, the gulf between the poorer nations and richer nations of the West is widening and within each of those nations, particularly [in] Africa, the gulf between the poor and rich is becoming really enormous. When I travel from New York to other parts of the world, I see that the whole world is connected—but in the image of the beggar...You see the beggar and the homeless persons in every capital city in the world. I say, in a system that is not able to cope with that reality, there is something amiss...Because development for me is really about development of human beings—not a few human beings but human beings that constitute [every] society. I know that many people have been now educated into saying, "But what can we do, what could be done, this is human nature. There have always been problems. Oh, nothing can be done." THIS IS WRONG. In my view the key thing is continuing [to] struggle all the time and not to be educated into accepting defeat, into accepting that very negative view of human nature that things never change.

Actually, I *wanted to ask a question about your fascination for Conrad, especially your fascination for the defeat or failure as a theme in Conrad's writings. Failure is in fact an important theme in your own work. Take Waiyaki (in* The River Between), *for instance: He is educated, he knows...but he fails...but I want to ask you another...*

No. I can talk briefly about Conrad. It is true there was a time when I was fascinated by Conrad. I am still fascinated by him. He is one of the few writers for whom imperialism was one of the central themes in their works. But there are shortcomings in Conrad; his critique of imperialism becomes impaired by his attachment with British imperialism. He comes to assume that one type of imperialism is better than the other, this imperialism is slightly better than that. I feel that this impairs his vision. He does not actually have faith in those forces which can change imperialism; he is very despondent when he comes to portraying workers' efforts to overthrow it or when he portrays people—racists in Africa in *Heart of Darkness* or Asians in *Lord Jim* and others. There the people are made to look as if they are waiting for their parents or a white hero [who] would come and save them.

There is a danger of misreading your work when you write and speak about imperialism/capitalism as nothing but theft/robbery, and modern institutions as sanctifying these corrupting practices. Would you, then, agree with the view that the culture of imperialism did not have complete success precisely because despite such violence we are still able to talk and continue to think together? That epistemic violence is also a kind of enabling violence?

Well, each phenomenon generates also its opposite, so, for instance, when there is repression, it generates its opposite because of resistance. [This] is not...to say colonialists were allowed to roam through the world freely. Take the instance of colonization of Africa. Even the actual colonization, [and] at times military exploitations, were opposed by Africans; they fought back. Even when you admitted colonization and you had a direct colonial administrator, a new class emerged...We had to organize differently in urban centers, in work-places and so on. So even when there is capitalism and imperialism, you also have the opposite: the resistance and forms of organization that embodied values that in fact were a negation of those of colonialism and imperialism. Hence, for instance, during [the] anti-colonial struggle when colonialism came, we could also see people's dances, people's literature, songs, in areas of culture. What happens during the struggle [is that] people rediscover their songs, they inject old forms with new content of anti-colonial struggle. They create new songs, and new narratives. This is really amazing that something new [emerges] out of very negative circumstances, in times of repression.

I want to ask a couple of questions. Could you talk a little about your current work? Would you suggest some long-term collaborative explorations (institutional) between, say, some Indian academics/writers/activists and their counterparts in other parts of the world?

Let me start with the second question first, about cooperation between writers. I believe in this very strongly, particularly when it comes to [the] struggle to write in non-European languages, in nationality languages. Sometimes people who write in nationality languages feel a sense of despair...because they think that they are not as well-known internationally as their counterparts who write in English or French. By that I mean someone has been writing novels in Telugu for several years, and another person one day writes a novel in English, and he becomes known as the writer, and the one who has been writing in Telugu is not even invited to international conferences. One feels discomfiture about this. That is why it is important to find ways of cooperating in joint efforts and in exchange of experiences. I am sure we should be able to find ways we can create international forums when prison writers writing in different languages can actually sit down and exchange experiences.

I may not be able to read a novel in Telugu [and] you, say, in Gikuyu, but at least I can know the experiences in writing in Telugu or other nationality languages in India. But apart from that, as a [form of] cooperation, it is important that what is originally written in Telugu can be translated into African languages directly and those written in African languages can be translated into Telugu directly. In other words, [we] can find ways [of] making our languages dialogue [with] one another, and that is very important in terms of our creation and so on.

What am I working on just now? I am working on a few books of essays. But the more important [job] that I am doing now is editing a journal in [the] Gikuyu language. What I am doing in this journal with my wife Njeeri is to [create] a forum for those who are writing in Gikuyu directly. We don't have such journals in our languages. But we also want to try and publish translations from other African languages, Asian languages, and from European languages, and see how this goes. This is taking a lot of my time because I do want to succeed, so we put a lot of time to it. We [have] produced three issues so far and we hope to continue with three more this year. I am interested in stories and poems originally written in Telugu. Obviously, I cannot read Telugu just now but we can use English as it facilitates translation.

A quick question. Suppose someone says I don't understand your writings. What is your reaction?

Two things: I myself don't quite understand [what I read sometimes]. But it can also be that they themselves do not take the necessary time sometimes to see the work again. Some people who have read my novels *A Grain of Wheat* and *Petals of Blood* have said, "Oh! I don't understand them, etc.," because they are used to [a] linear narrative structure of storytelling. I tell them actually the linear storytelling structure is not true to reality because in reality people do not tell each other stories in a linear mode. They constantly interrupt each other. OK? You tell an episode and one of the persons says, "That reminds me of something else," and they might even tell their own story before they come back to the main narrative, and so on. Also, our minds are always making multiple references and so on.

---

[1] Telugu is a South Indian language of Dravidian origin, spoken by 68 million people in the State of Andhra Pradesh. Hyderabad is the State capital of Andhra Pradesh. Telugu is the first Indian language into which some of Ngugi's work has been translated. (So far, *Devil on the Cross, Detained,* and *Matigari* have been translated.)

[2] Ngugi's two presentations in India, "Nationality Question in Africa" and "Decolonising the Means of Imagination," are published in the conference proceedings, *Symphony of Freedom: Papers on Nationality Question* (Hyderabad: All India People's Resistance Forum, 1996).

41 *Voice of America* Interview with Ngugi wa Thiong'o

Lee Nichols / 1996

This interview took place 30 March 1996 at Stony Brook.

Ngugi wa Thiong'o is well known to our listeners in Africa. He is one of Africa's foremost writers, originally in English and now almost exclusively, if not exclusively, in Gikuyu. Prof. Ngugi is Professor of Comparative Literature and Performance Studies at New York University, in New York City. Professor Ngugi, can you tell us a little bit about what performance studies is about?

This is really a theoretical study of the phenomena of performance in general. Here theater is seen as one of the many forms that performance can take. Sports and rituals and games are other equally valid forms. Previously the notion of performance used to be confined to the areas of drama and theater. But when you look at human life, it is like a variation of performance. The concept itself opens ways of looking at even other literary genres. I have offered courses ranging from "Orature: The Basis of Contemporary African Theater" and "The Aesthetics of Resistance in the Performance of Black History," to courses on "Performance in Prison Literature."

And Comparative Literature: What field are you working on in comparative literature?

This emphasizes literature, but in different languages. You look at what is common and different in the various language literatures. But you can also look at literature in relationship to history, politics and other disciplines. In some conservative comparative literature departments, they confine themselves to literature across European languages mainly. Such departments become merely centers for the study of European literatures in Italian, Spanish, German, French and

English, for instance. At New York University we try to be more open to comparisons across a wide range of languages and disciplines because for us Europe is just one center of human imagination among others from Africa and Asia and South America. What is important is the comparativity of literature, crossing borders of language and disciplines, without departing from the particularity of literature as literature.

Do you deal particularly with African literature, or with all world literatures?

My base is the African world. I draw on the entire field of African and black literature, but once again comparativity is the emphasis. In a course like, say, "Imperialism and Modern Literature," one can draw on African and European writings. I am very concerned that we do not compartmentalize literatures produced by Africans in different European languages into divisions that de-emphasize the Africanity in favor of the linguistic origins. We also need more comparative work between continental African literature and diasporan African literatures. There is also the need to do comparative work between African literature and literatures from other parts of the world. I also look forward to a time when we can do more comparative work in African languages; and between literatures in African languages and other language literatures. Comparativity is important because it encourages intercultural awareness, and it will be the basis of a genuine study of global literature. Comparativity should begin with a healthy respect for all languages.

At the African Literature Association's 22nd annual meeting, you received the Fonlon-Nichols award for excellence in literature, and in battling for human rights in Africa and your country, Kenya—although you've been in exile since 1982. The Fonlon-Nichols award is based at the University of Alberta, in Canada, and it is named for the late Bernard Fonlon, a noted Cameroonian literary scholar and writer, and for Lee Nichols, myself, for my interviews with African writers, including Ngugi wa Thiong'o, and for my civil rights activities in the United States. What was your reaction to receiving the award?

I am particularly pleased with the aspect of the award which has to do with human rights because I think that literature at its best should serve the cause of human rights. The first and most important of human rights is simply the right to be. Human life in Africa should be seen and treated as sacred. Africa has lost that value which used to be so important an aspect of our cultures. Now African governments can literally wipe out a thousand African lives within days without raising a national or an international uproar. Literature should help us in returning to the notion of the sacred in human life. The second is the right to live in an environment in which human life can be what it should be. The ecological, economic, political and social conditions that prevent human life realizing its humanity should be and must be targets for our pens. The third element of human rights has to do with the quality of human life. This is a primary concern of literature. The right to life means also the right to live fruitfully, to live a life that increasingly makes human lives the meaning of life. Literature should increase the spiritual wealth of a people.

The appalling state of human rights situations in Africa was dramatically illustrated by the execution of the Nigerian writer, Ken Saro-Wiwa, by the Abacha regime despite appeals from all parts of the world. No meaningful international action was taken against the regime. This gives a signal to other regimes: that they can murder writers with impunity, just as they have been murdering hundreds of peasants to ensure social stability for finance capital. Ken Saro-Wiwa's crime was organizing resistance to environmental ruin by Shell and other oil companies. Are other regimes very much different from the Abacha regime? Not the Kenyan one certainly. Only last week newspapers in Kenya reported the brutal execution of a human rights activist. His name was Kariuki Nduthu, the Secretary General of the Nairobi-based Release Political Prisoners Committee. On a Sunday night, the Moi regime sent a murder squad to his place and they clubbed him to death. It is reported that when the police later arrived on the scene, they were more interested in his typewriter and papers and books than in the body. The Abacha regime in Nigeria and the "Dial for M" regime in Kenya are examples of terrorist states. The entire global human community should outlaw such regimes.

Literature and the arts are part and parcel of the struggle for those human rights which are being abused by the terrorist states in Africa. And because this award is associated with that struggle for human rights in Africa and other parts of the globe, it is important in that it underlines the role of literature and the arts in that struggle.

Then you don't believe in "art for art's sake?"

Art is a product of life. It also reflects that life in the two senses of mirroring and contemplation. Literature as I said is involved in the question of the quality of human life. What are the conditions that prevent the realization of a higher quality of human life? Even art for art's sake should expose all the barriers to collective human self-realization because that is the mission of art. If art is struggling to realize its mission in human life, then obviously I believe in that kind of art for art's sake. Human life is art's sake.

What are you writing now?

I am editing a journal in the Gikuyu language. It is called *Mutiiri*. "Mutiiri" is a word with several meanings, but all expressing the idea of the guardianship, the mentor, the prop, the supporter. It is a journal that aims at helping Africa prop itself up. I am trying to create a model to show what is possible in African languages. There are very few outlets for those writing in African languages. I believe it is very important that there be fora for the different African languages. And then what's originally written in Gikuyu or in Yoruba or Hausa or Kiswahili can be translated into other African languages, and that way we pave a way for a dialogue between our languages.

How often does your magazine come out?

Three times a year. Currently, it is based in the Comparative Literature Department of New York University. I believe this is the first time that a journal of modern literature and culture in an African language has the base and the support of a mainstream department in a major university. So we take the task as being very important, a pioneering kind of task.

Do you have much of an audience for that journal? Who would read it?

The journal is aimed at those who can read and write in the Gikuyu language. The idea is to show that if the Gikuyu language, which is not very different from any other African language, can sustain a modern literature and thought, then the same is possible in any other similarly situated languages. Just now we are creating a readership along the way. There is, of course, resistance. Some of those educated in English have come to believe that they cannot read an African language. They get a copy of the journal, read one or two paragraphs, and they shake their heads and proclaim the difficulties they find in reading an African language. Now some of these people have spent years, maybe thirty or more years, reading in English and they are not prepared to spend even a day trying to see if they can read fluently in their own language. It is so absurd. We are trying to expose this absurdity. Fortunately, and this may surprise you, it is some of the younger people who have shown greater interest in the language. They realize that in a world which is rapidly becoming more and more of a global community, the question of identity, the question of their place in such a world, is also becoming more and more important. If we Africans do not take the necessary steps, there will be no Africa in the twenty-first century. If we lose our languages, we shall become linguistic appendages of French and English and Portuguese.

Then your audience would be exclusively in Kenya at the present time?

Yes, mainly in Kenya. This would not be a problem except that the state is very hostile to African languages. It is hostile to any national initiatives and this includes creativity in African languages.

Will they let your journal into the country?

Well, we hope that they do.

Will they stop it?

They can, of course, stop it. They have the power. They control the state and the territory, but there are readers outside the country. So even if the regime were to stop it, the journal can still survive. And it will be there waiting for a time when people will be free to let their languages talk to each other in freedom.

Are there any writers besides yourself who are now writing in Gikuyu and that you can include in your journal?

As I said, we have so far produced only three issues. Each issue is about 160 pages, in all those issues there have been contributions from old and new writers. My contribution to the journal is mainly on the editorial side.

42 Ngugi wa Thiong'o: *Penpoints, Gunpoints, and Dreams*: An Interview

Charles Cantalupo / 1999

No African writer has as many major, lasting creative achievements in such a wide range of genres as Ngugi wa Thiong'o. His books include novels, plays, short stories, essays and scholarship, criticism and children's literature. His fiction, non-fiction and drama, from the early 1960s to the present are frequently reprinted. He is the founder and editor of the groundbreaking Gikuyu-language journal Mutiiri. *A political exile from Kenya, Ngugi—as he is known worldwide—is currently the Erich Remarque Professor of Languages at New York University, with a dual professorship in Comparative Literature and Performance Studies.*

Baudelaire writes, "De la vaporisation et de la concentration du moi. Tout est là." ("The dispersion and the reconstitution of the self. That's the whole story.") It's not. This is a primary message of African literature and art today. Ngugi wa Thiong'o is one of its primary exemplars.

This interview focuses on Ngugi wa Thiong'o's book of essays Penpoints, Gunpoints, and Dreams: Towards a Critical Theory of the Arts and the State in Africa *(Oxford: Clarendon Press, 1998). Based on the four lectures he was invited to give at Oxford University in 1996 as a part of the Clarendon Lectures in English Literature series, and subtitled "Towards a Critical Theory of the Arts and the State in Africa," the book moves freely and universally, from Plato to Okot p'Bitek; pre-ancient Egypt to postmodern New York; the Macaulay colonial minute to Marx to Mau Mau; from the war between art and the state to "the beautyful ones...not yet born." In the book's preface, while Ngugi gratefully recalls a pleasurable and productive stay at Somerville College, he also notes, somewhat tongue-in-cheek perhaps, a feeling of rebuke from "a huge portrait of Queen Elizabeth I...[on] the wall of the dining-room of Jesus*

College for my unfavorable reference...to her edict of 1601 in which she had called for the expulsion of black people from her realm." At Somerville, the college of Margaret Thatcher when she was a student at Oxford, Ngugi feels "another rebuke for [his] claims...that the capitalist fundamentalism of which she and Reagan were the leading apostles was wreaking social havoc in the world and generating other forms of fundamentalism in opposition or alliance." His apartment abuts "Margaret Thatcher Court."

The interview takes place on a mild and gray Veteran's Day afternoon. A landscape of missing ceiling panels, hills and valleys of paper, mail clutter, catalogues, piles of folders that have never been vertically filed, books, empty bags, quite far-back issues of African literary journals, and many half-filled boxes of Mutiiri, *Ngugi's NYU office looks out on a rare, mercifully undeveloped patch of downtown Broadway. Noticing that Ngugi has lost his voice due to a cold, I sympathize. He replies that characters in his new novel lose their voices, too.*

My voice is back.

Good. Many of your first publications appeared in the Makerere University English department's literary magazine, Penpoint. *You call your new book of essays* Penpoints, Gunpoints, and Dreams. *What are some of the connections between the two? Is the repetition deliberate?*

Yes, there is a connection. *Penpoints* is a good name: penpoints—the power of the pen. I was interested in the power of the pen. The echo is there.

The subtitle of your new book is "Towards a Critical Theory of the Arts and the State in Africa." Much of your previous non-fiction— Decolonising the Mind *and* Moving the Centre, *for example—might be described in similar terms. What provoked you to continue in this vein? What new critical and political issues for you in the last five years make these new essays further departures "towards" formulating an aesthetic as well as taking a political stance?*

Two things. Although I'm calling it "Towards a Critical Theory of the Arts and the State in Africa," a better or more appropriate subtitle might have been "A Performance Theory of the Arts and the State in Africa." The question of performance is more pronounced here than in any of my previous works. That is quite important to me. Second, in this text I'm much more interested in the nature of art and the nature of the state, and their relationship: something which I have not explored in my previous works. I've touched on the subject here and there but without a coherent framework. Art's war with the state is basic to the nature of art and the nature of the state, any state. There is always the possibility of conflict between the state and art.

The concept of "performance" has become a uniting theme in your work. You write of it "in the narrow sense of representation of an action as in theater and in the broader sense of any action that assumes an audience during its actualization. The concept of performance is opening out new possibilities in the analysis of human behavior, including literature. The exercise of power, for instance, involves variations on the performance theme." Indeed, you are a professor of Performance Studies. What drew you to this new scholarly discipline? How did your life and writing prepare you, perhaps without your knowing it, for this new field? There is a sense in your writing that you are learning from it at least as much as you are contributing to it with your work.

Of course, I've been in theater all my life. I've worked in community theater in Kenya: in the Kamiriithu Community Education and Cultural Centre. And this, of course, brought me into conflict with the state in Kenya. My work in theater has been a preparation for this. I have also gained from using the term as a conceptual tool. So much in society depends on "performance." It provides new insights into certain behaviors. It is central to so many things. For example, you can't have religion without performance: performance—weekly, daily. Think of all those festivals. Think of performance in a wide sense. Performance enables people to negotiate their way through the various realms of being. Performance is a means for people to realize their unknown, even if it's only in the imagination. Performance is a very important concept. I have learned from it, but also I have been involved in it.

Is an emphasis on "performance" a way of advancing postcolonial critical discourse? As you discuss it, the concept of "performance" would seem to broaden and, perhaps, revitalize postcolonial studies.

Yes, and not only the postcolonial but many disciplines. The concept of performance can also be used to look at some of the older disciplines and to reinterpret some of the older texts. For example, Elizabeth Claire's work on performance and dance in Jane Austen has let us see what we hadn't before in the eighteenth and nineteenth centuries. Performance is a concept that enables many things to be looked at differently. In classical writings, too, like Plato, for instance, the context of the dialogues is a performance in the dramatic sense. If you look at Plato's *Republic*, the dialogues exist within the larger context of their dramatization and, furthermore, the contexts of dramatic and religious festivals. There is a kind of performativity all around. The concept, however, must not become too wide or so broad that "anything goes." I take, for example, two features like representation and the assumption of an audience to be very important. In other words, a farmer planting crops ordinarily for the production of whatever he wants to eat or sell could be called a performance. But if I'm demonstrating as a farmer that I plant crops so that people can come and see how this is done, that would be a performance that is assuming that there is an audience. Even though this is an act I am actually doing, I am representing another action. The audience is very important.

Another large, perhaps parallel theme in this book is orature. You write that "Orature...is not seen as a branch of literature but as a total aesthetic system, with performance and integration of art forms as two of its defining qualities. It is more basic and more primary than the other systems of the literary, the theatrical, and the cinematic because all the other systems take one or more of their main features from orature." You consider orature, "a unifying force," including "the four aesthetic systems of the written, the oral, the theatrical and the cinematic." You argue that "The centrality of orature to all the other systems calls for a reconfiguration and regrouping of disciplines" in which "their hierarchical ordering...is denied" and there is an end of "the historical rifts separating theorists, critics, and practitioners." What are some of the critical historical and geographical factors that have led you to such a conclusion? How has it influenced and changed your own writing and thinking?

If you look at orature in all societies, classical or contemporary, it refuses to draw very firm boundaries between disciplines, genres or forms. If you take a story, an oral narrative for instance, it will contain dance or music. The work might also involve audience participation, a chorus, or even the audience as a chorus. Often there are songs themselves or songs that involve dance variations. In some cases the word for the song and dance is the same. A song, a proverb, whatever: It suggests other forms. As important, performance is central to the study and realization of orature, as well as narratives, proverbs, whatever you do. Performance is central, unifying. There is a performance to space, to architecture, to sculpture. The assumption in classical orature is that the boundary between the natural world and the supernatural is fluid. In terms of aesthetics, the integrative aspect of orature is a very important element. Many disciplines and activities come under the umbrella of orature. The theater is a halfway house in which the realization of the drama is for it to become orature. The realization on stage of a musical composition embraces the concept of orature. While it integrates the many different possibilities of performance, orature also allows for the differences, for example, among narrative, song or drama.

Orature and performance work together. Is performance a means to embracing orature?

Performance is central. They are not synonymous. Performance is what distinguishes orature from literature, even in the most obvious way: When you are reading a novel, you don't need a performance.

You're completing a new novel. Are there ways in which your thinking about orature and performance has affected the novel?

Yes, but we won't go into too much detail about it because writing is a complicated process. Performance is central to the new novel. It is a state of performance. The characters are engaged in the constant performance of their own being for the narrative. You never quite know who they are. Often they reinvent themselves through performance. Even I, as their author, do not know where or how the whole novel is going to end except in the constant performance of their own being.

Is this a reinvention both in public and private?

Yes. The characters in this new novel constantly reinvent themselves. I don't know if they are making progress because I've only done the first two drafts. My wife, Njeeri, is now reading it. She's at the house and maybe you should call there.

For sure—I'll call later. In the meantime, you may recall that William Blake called the Bible "the great code of art." In the introduction to Penpoints, Gunpoints, and Dreams, *you assert that "The goal of human society is the reign of art on earth." Taken out of context, this could almost sound like a kind of* fin-de-siècle *aestheticism for the twentieth century much like what happened at the end of the nineteenth century in the West. The slightest familiarity with your work, however, reveals anything but the aesthete. What do you mean by "the reign of art?"*

I associate my concept of art with creativity, movement, change and renewal. I'm thinking of a much more ethical society than what we have now. This "reign of art" would subsume or transcend the coercive nature of the state: a more ethical, more human society that is constantly renewing itself; art embodies this. I remember, historically speaking, a time when there was no state because I grew up in a society where literally there wasn't a state, at least in its centralized form. Art precedes the formation of the state. The state embodies a static concept of conservation, holding back. Of course, when the state is also controlled by a class, it is an instrument for much more holding back of society. Creativity, art embodies the principle of what our hands do anyway: change. Creativity is really the essence of what is God and what is human. God is changing: We change the environment, we change when we plant, when human beings sow. When human beings plant one seed, this will produce more seeds out of one. We take what we raise and transform it for the better. We see many transformations, like the advance of science and technology, although their benefits these days do not necessarily go to enhancing the lives of the majority of the people.

This brings us back to the war between art and the state. A bomb hits the garden.

The central logic of both art and the state is for each to work itself free—which creates opposition. In reality, however, it is not always absolute. There is sometimes an attempt at mutual corruption. The state will corrupt art. Art will try to influence the state. Some artists try to align themselves with the state.

Yet you describe the "war between art and the state" as "really a struggle between the power of performance in the arts and the performance of power by the state—in short, enactments of power." You assert that "The performance space of the artist stands for openness; that of the state, for confinement. Art breaks down barriers between people; the state erects them." What of an alliance or at least a correspondence between art and the state? Historically, maybe we have seen moments when this has been possible, but has it ever lasted? Are there any benefits when art and the state work together?

The moment you open out democratic space, this is important for art: You also open the space for creativity. Historically, there are moments of great revolutionary change when you can see art and the state anticipating and almost together working out a new world. Art anticipates a new world. Revolutionary forces in society are always anticipating that world. But once a state, even a revolutionary state, comes to power, the very nature of the state is to hold back. A permanently revolutionary state is almost an impossibility. Even a revolutionary state has to pass laws. It has to constitute what it considers to be stability of some kind. It's aim is to repeat itself.

You write that "There is no state that can be in permanent revolution. Art, on the other hand, is revolutionary by its very nature as art"; and "Art has more questions than it has answers....The state, on the other hand, has plenty of answers and hardly any questions. The more absolutist the state, the less it is likely to ask questions of itself or entertain questioning by others."

Even a novelist at his poorest does not want to reproduce his previous work. I think of art in terms of permanent revolution. Permanent, constant revolution is not inherent in the nature of the state and its operations. Constant revolutionizing, reinventing itself is inherent in the nature of art. The artist considers reinventing himself all the time. The state has to conserve. Therefore, the possibility of conflict is always there.

You write, "Where...there is no democracy for the rest of the population, there cannot be democracy for the writer." What is the role of African-language writers in contributing to economic, political, and cultural empowerment, strengthening civil society and current, emerging democratic traditions and governance, and reforming the language of African political discourse?

All over the world art is constantly attempting to return language to the people. Any moment of exceptional literary achievement in a national tradition signals a writer's return of language at its fullest to people in their daily life. In the context of Africa, writers need to return to the languages actually spoken by the people to enlarge the space of people's understanding to include more experiences. A writer makes a language for its speakers to comprehend their universe better than ever before. African languages can play a big role in Africa's democratization, its spiritual awakening and enhancement. But that spirit is repeatedly crushed because English and French continue to dominate a continent where most people speak African languages.

Penpoints, Gunpoints, and Dreams *contains an extensive re-interpretation of the allegory of the cave from Plato's* Republic. *Roughly speaking, you argue that the dominance of European languages in the critical discourse of the majority of African intellectuals sets them, so to speak, forever outside the cave: the space of which they neither re-enter nor open. You also offer Ayi Kwei Armah's novel* The Beautyful Ones Are Not Yet Born *as a kind of alternative to Plato's story. For example, replacing Plato's ideal, incorruptible, true philosophers with Armah's "beautyful ones" who are to lead the African state of the future, you write,*

"Such intellectuals, whenever they are born, will grow their roots in African languages and cultures. They will also learn the best they can from all world languages and cultures. They will view themselves as scouts in foreign linguistic territories and guides in their own linguistic space. In other words, they will take whatever is most advanced in those languages and cultures and translate those ideas into their own languages. They will have no complexes about borrowing from others to enrich their own....They will see their role as that of doing for African languages and cultures what all writers and intellectuals of other cultures and histories have done for theirs."

What led you to Plato?

"The beautyful ones not yet born" is a very beautiful phrase. The image of the cave is very distinct. It's an image with a logic that goes against Plato's philosophy itself. The assumption of the allegory of the cave that philosophers who see the light must come back—that an elite should come back to the people in a cave—goes against Plato's advocacy in the same book of an hierarchical society with categories like philosopher kings, the warriors and guardians of the state as opposed to its more lowly workers. Such an elite in fact does not return to the people. My work in performance has led me to re-examine more and more, or go back to and revisit classical Greece. I've found that it was a very oral society. To think of that society being literate in terms of writing is a twentieth-century projection. In reality, we see a very oral society. Socrates, for instance, is working within theories of orature, conversing in the marketplace. Dialogues take place as he's coming from there or going to a festival. They take place in and around the house, by the fireside. He's not a writer. In a sense, this society exemplifies a kind of orature and Socrates is actually a philosopher within the oral tradition. Plato's dialogues assume a kind of orality. Even bad translations cannot kill or hide this. It is everywhere.

In Decolonising the Mind *(1987), you describe the condition of most African intellectuals being educated only in Europhone languages as "literally...[a] split between the mind and the body of Africa, producing...nations of bodiless heads and headless bodies. The community puts resources in the education of a people who will never bring home their share of knowledge." In your new work, you write*

"[A]n intellectual is a worker in ideas using words as the means of production. It means that for Africa the thinking part of the population, the one with the pool of skills and know-how in economics, agriculture, science, engineering is divorced from the agency of social change: the working majority. At the level of economics, science, and technology Africa will keep on talking about transfer of technology from the West. There are countless resolutions about this in regional, continental, and international conferences. Yet the African intellectual elite...refuse to transfer even the little they have already acquired in the language of the majority below...knowledge researched by sons and daughters of Africa, and actually paid for by the entire working majority who need it most, is stored in European-language granaries. There can be no real economic growth and development where a whole people are denied access to the latest developments in science, technology, health, medicine, business, finance and other skills of survival because all these are stored in foreign languages. Ignorance of progress in ideas is a guarantee against rapid economic growth."

Do you see any signs that the African mind and body need not be split by language in the future? As you yourself write, "If some of the best and most articulate of the interpreters of African total being insist on interpreting in languages not understood by the subject of their interpretation, where lies the hope of African deliverance?"

In Greek mythology, Zeus employs Prometheus to make men out of mud and water but, in pity for their state, he steals fire from Olympus and gives it to them. The image of fire is very strong for me. It is central to knowledge...light, technology, heat. Fire changes things. Fire is almost everything. I'm not surprised that many people used to worship the sun. They were not all that wrong in seeing the sun as

God, the source of everything. The question is whether Prometheus leaves the fire to the gods or gives it to humans. Does he give them the fire or does he say that they can only use this fire when they come up the mountain. The whole idea is that he brings the fire to them. But where is the fire when we African intellectuals refuse to dialogue in African languages, the language of the vast majority of our people?

Citing Marx's observation "that an idea grasped by the masses becomes a material force," you suggest that "language is obviously the best, the cheapest, and the most effective way of disseminating such ideas." Does this imply that the discouragement and outright suppression of education and writing in African languages, even now in a postcolonial era, is a deliberate means of social and political oppression of, perhaps, the worst sort?

If and when African intellectuals are progressive, for example, through an emphasis on democracy, there can still be a fundamental contradiction about their ideas if, as in the biblical parable, their light is hidden under the bushel basket of European languages that the majority of the people do not understand. In this sense, African intellectuals continue, ironically, a tradition of their own enslavement. They are like people who work for a feudal lord. Their happiness, even though they are honest, depends on working in his house. Their sense of being connects to their constant narration of what goes on around the feudal lord, his comings and goings.

American slave plantations also had their house hands and field hands.

We are operating with European languages where there are African languages whose space we could be opening out.

Are you suggesting that writers and scholars make a deliberate choice of language and that there is no "sitting on the fence" concerning this issue amidst the struggle of African people for greater cultural, political and economic empowerment within a democratic space?

Yes. After much wavering, I came to this conclusion in my book *Decolonising the Mind.* But in *Penpoints, Gunpoints, and Dreams* I take a firmer position. I look at language and a whole history of interpretation over five hundred years. I trace the issue of plantation slavery and how language is used as a way within the plantation of keeping practical communication bound exclusively to itself. Not only are various African languages suppressed as a means of communication among the slaves. Colonial plantations themselves enforce their own language as a means of enclosure, be they English, French or Spanish. They never meet unless through conquest or reconquest. The colonizing power in Africa of Europe similarly keeps people bound to its languages. Yet the struggle of African people in the "New World" also takes the form of creating new languages. These people's conditions of life also mean a struggle to construct the world in their own terms. Thus we find Creole languages, patois and much more. Africa should learn from that tremendous struggle to recompose a new world: to create new languages that owe their being to African languages. Colonizing principles are very clear about the role of language. The widespread practice of linguistic engineering would create a vast army of Africans whose interpretations in the languages of their colonizers would reinforce their power over their subjects.

Linguistic engineering: This sounds a little like "ethnic cleansing." To recognize the hyper-conscious and deliberate imposition of colonial languages and not merely their absorption is a horror, indeed.

Ironically, in not working more through African languages we are continuing, even when we are conscious of it, a neo-colonial system that still binds African people. At an economic level, Africa produces raw materials that are processed in Europe and returned to Africa. At the level of culture, we see the same pattern. We draw our own resources in African languages and this is processed in English or French and then brought back as a finished product in French or English for African consumption. And still it does not reach a level of consumption as great as if it had remained in African languages, in the same way that gold that is mined in Africa and brought back from Europe is too expensive and inaccessible to all but the few. In the same way, we draw upon the linguistic resources and life of Africa, even in political struggles, and they are processed in English or French. But when they are brought back in this form, they are lost and inaccessible to the vast majority of the population who only speak African languages.

You call "the ascendance of capitalist fundamentalism and the Darwinian ethical systems which it is generating ... the mother of all fundamentalisms, religious and nationalistic." You insist that "there should be no ambiguity about the necessity to abolish the economic and social conditions which bring about the need for charity and begging within any nation and between nations, and language should sensitize human beings to that necessity." "Art," you claim, "should join all the other social forces in society to extend the performance space for human creativity and self-organization and so strengthen civil society." You even predict that "just as it was the case in some pre-capitalist societies, it is possible that...[in] a post-capitalist society, production will be geared not towards social domination of others but towards meeting human needs, culture and creativity will reign." Is a "reign of art" precisely in African languages a key to democratic empowerment and success in such a struggle?

The empowerment of African languages is clearly part of this process. If we look at the period in our history when questions of privatization and profit become the barometer for progress in society instead of class solidarity, what do we find? Consider Yugoslavia now with its ethnic massacres and when there was more emphasis on class solidarity. The moment we come to a post-Cold War de-emphasis of class begins a new period of ethnic fundamentalism. It corresponds to a puritanism of capitalism. This fundamentalism of finance capital occurs within the same period of all sorts of other fundamentalisms, sometimes even in alliance with it, as in Christian-right fundamentalism; or in opposition to it. How do we fight against this force of fundamentalism, whatever form it takes, which seems to threaten people who often do not understand what is threatening them, as class solidarity has been de-emphasized in recent thinking in favor of national wars, ethnic and religious boundaries or whatever seems to present some kind of assurance and stability more readily known? Art connects. It says that human beings are connected. Art says, "Look. We are connected. It's like ecology. Human beings are connected: trees to animals to other human beings." Art tends to say, "we live in one universe, you know?" Art seems to emphasize spirituality, the spiritual expression of human life.

The role of art is to break through fundamentalisms?

Yes. To break boundaries and borders that separate.

43 Ngugi wa Thiong'o in Conversation

Harish Trivedi with Wangui wa Goro / 2003

Ngugi wa Thiong'o was born in 1938 in Limuru, Kenya and educated in Uganda and the University of Leeds. His early novels Weep Not, Child *(1964),* The River Between *(1965) and* A Grain of Wheat *(1967) explored traditional Kenyan society and the impact of colonialism on it, while with* Petals of Blood *(1977) he began to show a more explicit political concern with neo-colonialism. As a teacher in the Department of English at the University of Nairobi, he called in 1968 for the abolition of that Department as a step towards cultural decolonization, a theme he has developed in essays collected in* Decolonising the Mind *(1986) and* Moving the Centre *(1993). In 1977, he was detained for a year without trial in a maximum security prison, where he began to write his next novel in his native language Gikuyu,* Devil on the Cross *(published in Gikuyu 1980, in English 1982). On a visit to Britain to promote this novel, Ngugi went into exile in 1982. All copies of his next novel,* Matigari *(published in Gikuyu 1987, in English 1989), were seized in Kenya and an attempt was even made to arrest its fictional hero. Ngugi wa Thiong'o has been a professor at Yale University and at New York University and is now Director of the International Center for Writing and Translation at the University of California at Irvine.*

This interview was recorded in London on 21 June 2003. Also present was Ms. Wangui wa Goro, translator from Gikuyu into English of Ngugi's novel Matigari, *who asked a couple of questions (as indicated) and helped with the transcription.*

Harish Trivedi: *You have probably been the most radical of all the Third World, postcolonial writers that we have read in English. You have constantly advocated a trenchant agenda on decolonization,* *conducted a campaign against neo-colonialism and even against what you call "self-colonization," and you've been a tremendous model and influence. I would like you to talk specifically about the role of language, bilingualism and translation, especially in the context of the conference on "Cross-Cultural Translation" at the School of Oriental and African Studies here in London at which you gave a lecture on "Languages in Conversation: The Role of Translation in the Making of a Global Community."*

You have said that you have had a career in two parts: the first, when you were writing as James Ngugi, in English, what you called the "Afro-Saxon novel," and the second, when you began writing as Ngugi wa Thiong'o and wrote in Gikuyu what you call the "African novel." What caused the move from one to the other?

I wrote *Weep Not, Child*, *A River Between* and *A Grain of Wheat* and published the three novels under the name James Ngugi. James is the name which I acquired when I was baptized into Christianity in primary school, but later I came to reject the name because I saw it as part of the colonial naming system when Africans were taken as slaves to America and were given the names of the plantation owners. Say, when a slave was bought by Smith, that slave was renamed Smith. This meant that they were the property of Smith or Brown and the same thing was later transferred to the colony. It meant that if an African was baptized, as evidence of his new self or the new identity he was given an English name. Not just a biblical, but a biblical and *English* name. It was a symbolical replacing of one identity with another. So the person who was once Ngugi is now James Ngugi, the one who was once owned by his people is now owned by the English, the one who was owned by an African naming system is now owned by an English naming system. So when I realized that, I began to reject the name James and to reconnect myself to my African name which was given at birth, and that's Ngugi wa Thiong'o, meaning Ngugi, son of Thiong'o.

HT: *Does the word Ngugi mean anything?*

It means work, hard work.

HT: *Was the move from one identity to another connected at all with the controversy regarding* Petals of Blood *and your imprisonment after that?*

No, I rejected the name in 1977 and whenever my books were reissued I asked the publishers to use the name Ngugi wa Thiong'o. Now you could argue that this was in some ways the beginning of my questioning of the whole naming system—including language—because language after all is a naming system. We use language to name our environment and to name reality and so, from being called James to using English as a way of naming my own world, was really the same thing.

HT: *In the Book of Genesis, at the beginning of Creation, Adam names each object and that's what it becomes.*

Exactly. So I had been questioning this, and after the publication of *Petals of Blood* in July 1977 the question of language came up in a big way, for by that time something important had happened to me. I started working in a village called Kamiriithu, in a center which later was called the Kamiriithu Community Education and Cultural Centre. And because I was working in this community, the question of language became no longer an abstraction—something you just think about mentally—but something which now demanded a practical response. The work we did in the village obviously had to be done in an African language, in this case the Gikuyu language. And then we did a play together in Gikuyu, *Ngaahika Ndeenda*, or *I Will Marry When I Want*. And it was really a turning point when the play was closed down by top government officials—the Moi regime, the Kenyatta/Moi regime—on 16 November 1977 and I was imprisoned from 31 December 1977 to 12 December 1978—for a year. And it was when I was in prison that I made one of the most important decisions in my life, that I would continue writing in the very language which had been the reason for my incarceration. So my connection with what I call the genius of the Gikuyu language was effected and continued in a maximum security prison.

HT: *You have worked with the community and chosen to use the language of the community but you began as a student and then as a teacher of English literature. Did you find that you experienced, initially, some kind of distance, some kind of alienation—because of your colonial education—from your own community when you went back to it?*

There are two things: first of all, let's face it, English literature is a great literature and the English language carries many important critical and intellectual traditions. So to come into contact with English is to come into contact with something both negative and positive, and the positive has as much to offer as any product of any other language. There are many great English writers—Conrad, Jane Austen, Shakespeare, Dickens, George Eliot—and that tradition is very important. But nevertheless, important as it is, it does not really reflect the human condition as expressed in the actualities of my history, of my culture and of my environment. It was really when I came into contact with the novels written by African writers—Peter Abrahams, Chinua Achebe—and most importantly the Caribbean novel—I'm thinking of the work of George Lamming—that I felt that he was reflecting a world which was familiar to me. He was talking about a colonial world and the colonial world was really my world, I was a product of that world, and this recognition was very, very important to me.

HT: *In linguistics there is a theory—as I'm sure you know—by the name of the Sapir-Whorf hypothesis, that any language reflects the world-view of its speakers; that what they can say—what they can even think of—is determined and delimited by the language. Would you say that there are things in Gikuyu that you could never have said in English, or are now saying very differently?*

I'd say it's a case of saying them differently. Each language has its own capacity, its own possibilities. As I said, English is a great language—no doubt about it. But so is the Gikuyu language, so is Hindi, so is Gujarati, so is Yoruba, so is Igbo—they are all great languages. What colonialism did was to make us think of English as somehow *the* language and make us think less of our own languages.

In other words, it was colonialism which gave us this hierarchical arrangement of languages where some languages seemed higher than the others or some languages seemed lower than the others. But every language carries a memory-bank of the experiences, the feelings, the history of a given community and culture. As an African when I'm writing in the English language, I'm actually—ironically—also drawing on that experience of my language equally. And what I'm doing in reality is taking away from the Gikuyu language to enrich English. So when I'm writing in Gikuyu, I'm really exploiting the possibilities of that language and I have found it very, very liberating for me in expressing my environment.

HT: *In that connection—as you're aware—there is a particular strand in postcolonial theory that argues that postcolonial writing by its very nature is translation because when postcolonial writers write in English, they are mentally, subconsciously always translating from their own native language. Do you think that that is properly to be called "translation"?*

It is definitely translation in many respects. When I wrote *The River Between* which is about a Kenyan community's initial encounter with colonialism, that community, in historical reality and time, speaks the Gikuyu language, and what they are thinking about—their land, the effect of colonialism—they are really thinking in the Gikuyu language. So when I write about the impact of colonialism on characters who are the products of their culture and I make them speak in English in order to capture their lives and thoughts, I must be translating—doing a mental translation. It is very true of all writers who are writing about one community, or about characters who are the product of one culture, in another language. I would say that my novels—*The River Between*, *Weep Not, Child*—are mental translations. What happens in that process is that there is an original text which should have been there but which is lost. But when you have a true translation, you do actually have two texts. Now in the case of *Weep Not, Child*, *The River Between* and *A Grain of Wheat*, that original text is not there.

HT: *Have your early novels been translated back into Gikuyu?*

No, not yet. I am involved in the work of the International Center of Writing and Translation [at the University of California at Irvine] where we are talking about restoration concerning the whole of Africa. Some of the best products of the intellectuals and artists from the communities who have been trained in English draw their strength, their stamina, if you like, from their languages. But what's happening is that the original text is now lost to English. English gains, the language from which they draw loses. So we are saying that we are not interfering with those texts as they are, and they are works of genius, but we are asking: Why don't we try to focus on restoration? For example, in the case of Wole Soyinka who writes in English, why shouldn't his texts be available in other languages—in Gikuyu, Zulu, Igbo, in all those other African languages. When I talk about the original I don't mean that the writer, for example Wole Soyinka, should write in Yoruba—he writes in English and that was his choice. But what I'm saying is that through translation we can actually restore languages through a combination of writers, publishers and translators.

HT: *Speaking of this kind of restoration, Vikram Seth in his preface to the Hindi translation of* A Suitable Boy *says two wonderful things: one, that his novel would now be available in the language that he heard resonate in his own ears as he was writing it in English, and two, that now, even some of the characters in the novel would be able to read it.*

Exactly! That actually sums up the whole situation very well! So, it is not just me; all over the world we can focus on promoting this idea and it can become a program, rather than just one writer here and there.

HT: *But can some of the major Third World postcolonial intellectuals also be restored similarly, what with their kind of idiom, orientation, and addressivity, especially with regard to the First World, especially the American academy?*

There new questions and new challenges will arise. But I am thinking more of the kind of writing which draws on a particular language and culture, and perhaps works of imagination will be better suited. In this context I'm putting a bigger accent on the role of translation. And translation is perceived at the International Center for Writing and Translation as conversation, and a conversation assumes equality. It is not necessarily true now in the current climate, but it is important to see it as an idea or a possibility. We hope that translation can be seen as a language through which other languages can—and should—talk.

HT: *I was struck by your formulation in your recent lecture that translation should be seen as a "conversation" rather than as "dictation" by one language to another. But as you have just said, this kind of translation as conversation rests on an assumption of equality between the two languages. Now, given the dire asymmetry in all kinds of relations between the West and the rest, is such an assumption well founded?*

It isn't now, but our assumption expresses this idea and also puts an accent on translation not as dictation, not one-way traffic if you like. We're grouping languages into what we call dominant languages which obviously are mostly located in Europe, English for example, and marginalized languages, which are "marginalized" but not "marginal" (marginalization does not mean that the language is actually marginal), and we envisage focusing on a model where there is conversation among marginal languages. Let me give you the example of Gujarati, Yoruba, Zulu, Igbo. Where is that kind of conversation among them? But also we want conversation between marginalized languages as a whole and the dominant languages, such as English. So it becomes a multitateral or a multi-sided kind of conversation.

But in this case, given that asymmetry you were talking about, and given the fact that for historical reasons there may not be any two people who can simultaneously converse in, say, Yoruba, Igbo and Gujarati, we must pose a different question in order to challenge English, so that the dominant languages enable and do not disable the marginalized languages. If you look at the past, it is true that English enabled intellectuals to express their own genius and culture. But by enabling it also disabled because these intellectuals and artists from the Third World did not have a platform where they could express their languages and their cultures. When we say enabling without disabling, what we mean is that we now can use English to enable a conversation between Yoruba and Zulu for instance—using English as a meeting point between two languages and then translating them into each other.

HT: *But do you think that as English becomes more and more of a global and dominant language, it will enable our own local languages more or actually disable them?*

If you don't ask the right questions you will disable them even more. When we say that we challenge a dominant language to enable without disabling, translation in that multi-sided sense is definitely one of the answers.

HT: *I'm not sure I get this. Yoruba and Gujarati translated into each other will enrich and enable both Yoruba and Gujarati. But if Yoruba translated into English is translated into Gujarati then I think both may be serving the cause of English rather better and becoming subservient all over again.*

We can't wait until we have scholars who know both Gujarati and Yoruba.

HT: *I thought every shop-keeper in Nairobi would know both Gujarati and Gikuyu?*

No, no. The idea is obviously for people to be able to talk to each other directly, and there is no substitute for that. But I'm saying that where that is not currently possible, then you can use English as a meeting point. In that case you are using it to enable rather than disable, because what it is doing is enabling a conversation between Zulu and Yoruba. You might have a combination of a Gikuyu scholar and a Hindi scholar coming together and using English as a medium through which to talk to each other.

Wangui wa Goro: *Can I ask a question please? Could you talk about your experience in Asmara?*

Asmara, in Eritrea, was very important. In the year 2000, there was held there, to my knowledge, the first conference of writers and scholars in African languages—one of the most incredible conferences I've ever been to.* And in the Asmara Declaration, the writers gathered there called on the African languages to take on the challenge, responsibility and duty of speaking as representatives of the continent. For the first time, you actually had papers on African languages and literatures written in the African languages, and the challenge for that conference was how to get them interpreted simultaneously. It was not perfect by any means but we wanted to meet that challenge. So it was very important.

HT: *May I ask you about your own practice as a translator. You are a busy man and are yourself a creative writer, so why did you decide to translate your own work, to write it twice over?*

I have gone through three kinds of experiences here. One was of translating my own work, auto-translation, and another of having them translated by someone else. I translated *Devil on the Cross* into English myself, but *Matigari* was translated by Wangui wa Goro along with two children's stories. And then finally, with my new novel, *Wizard of the Crow*, I've done my own translation. First of all, because of the debate going on about African languages and English, it was very important to me to ensure that there was not only an original text in the case of *Devil on the Cross* but also an English text, to prove and to show that when one writes in an African language, one is not invisible for other communities such as the English-speaking communities. So it was very important for me to have that text available in English even if it meant writing it twice over, first originally and then in translation. I found translating it very interesting and as I said, even when writing *The River Between* and *Weep Not, Child*, there was a kind of mental translation going on anyway. Now writing is a tremendous experience, and having your work translated by someone else is also a tremendous experience. My new novel, *Wizard of the Crow*, is a huge work which I have been writing every single day since May 1997—about two thousand pages in double space. I have attempted among other things many innovations in language in that novel and I was working so closely with a translator that I thought I might as well do it myself! But the ideal for me is to write in Gikuyu and have my works translated by somebody else. My books have been translated into Norwegian, into German, into Kiswahili and it is not *I* that have done all those other translations!

WwG: *Criticism has come that you are afraid of relinquishing the English language. Think of your statement saying that you were no longer going to write in English.*

But I have already relinquished it! I don't actually write in English now, I write in Gikuyu. I am privileged in terms of translation. And let's face it, we're working in an environment where English dominates and is powerful so I can't say that I won't interact with it. All one can do is to make sure that there are texts in the African languages, and in this case I make sure that there is a text in Gikuyu. If the English text does not see the light of day, that is fine as long as there is a text in the Gikuyu language.

HT: *Are there any texts of yours which are only in the Gikuyu language?*

Not just now, but there is a journal which I edit called *Mutiiri* and it is entirely in Gikuyu and we have now had seven issues of it. This means that now we have a platform which has seen the emergence of many Gikuyu-language writers. So my commitment is not only in terms of me writing in the Gikuyu language but I've gone a stage further and helped in creating a forum for other Gikuyu-language writers. I'm hoping that what is being done with the Gikuyu language can be done with other African languages.

HT: *Are there any other Gikuyu writers who are translated into English and have international visibility?*

Not translated, but there are other Gikuyu writers.

HT: *Were there any major Gikuyu novelists before you?*

Not in the Gikuyu language. It was my decision to write in Gikuyu.

HT: *So, you were the founder of the Gikuyu novel!*

(Laughs) What I would seriously say is that my decision was very important in creating that possibility, but even more important has been the journal *Mutiiri* which has functioned in the same way that journals have functioned internationally. We now have more women writers in Gikuyu and we have writers who were previously writing in English but are now writing in Gikuyu. Some of them are brilliant poets. I am thinking of someone like Gitahi Gititi who has really found his voice as a poet in the Gikuyu language and does really incredible things with the language; he is brilliant. I think of writers like Waithera Mbuthia who before *Mutiiri* wrote in English and has now blossomed in the Gikuyu language; she is now doing translations as well. And there was a student who contacted *Mutiiri* and decided to write his thesis in the Gikuyu language. He has now finished and got his Master's last year from Cornell. What he did was to provide a copy of his research also in English, so there is an English version and a Gikuyu version and I think it is an original step that he has taken as an example of what can be done.

HT: *I remember I was quite thrilled when I first read about your intention to stop writing in English and to write instead in Gikuyu—and then I found that your first novel in Gikuyu,* Caitaani Mutharaba-ini *(*Devil on the Cross*) was published in Nairobi by Heinemann! So Heinemann publishes you in English and Heinemann also publishes you in Gikuyu and you seem to be between the devil and the deep blue sea, for your Gikuyu publisher is still a metropolitan Western publisher!*

No, actually in this case, although it was the same publisher, they had a branch in Nairobi, Heinemann Kenya, who published me. It was very important that these metropolitan publishers did publish in African languages.

HT: *But Heinemann in Nairobi publish mostly in English, don't they?*

Yes, they do and they publish very little in Gikuyu, but the venture of publishing in the Gikuyu language has continued, and they have continued to publish in African languages although publishing in English is still the dominant trend. But I think they have shown how a publishing house can publish in the African languages. And Heinemann in Kenya has now become locally owned and has changed its name to the East African Educational Publishers.

HT: *Are there other publishers in Nairobi publishing only or mainly in Gikuyu?*

No, not so far. What is missing is publishers who are willing to publish in Gikuyu and other African languages and this is very important. In Kenya, the chairman of a group of African publishers is about to establish a Centre for the Advancement of African Languages and Literatures (CALL) and the intention is to use the center to publish solely in African languages.

HT: *May I ask you to comment on an aspect of your life and career which in postcolonial theory is also called "translation" though I'm not sure that I myself am entirely happy with that. For example, Rushdie says, "We are translated men," meaning not any translation between languages, but using the etymological sense of "translation," of travelling across from his home country to a Western country—and in that sense he says he is a translated man. This kind of "translation" is often used to mean exile, being forced to live outside one's country. But again, isn't there a difference between a writer like Rushdie who lives abroad by choice and someone like you who had to leave home for reasons of personal* *safety? Do you think of yourself as a "translated" man in exile? How has exile affected your work?*

No, I don't think of myself as a translated man...I think of myself more as a transported man. *(Laughter)* What is the meaning of living in exile? There is of course willing exile and forced exile. But there is another sense in which writers who live in the Third World live in exile—by writing in English or French. And as I have argued in *Moving the Centre*, they have an exiled or alienated relationship with their culture and language, and that is a much deeper exile than a physical one whether chosen or forced. The problem of exile is being forced away from the location of inspiration. A writer feeds on what he encounters—in a marketplace, in public transport, in a religious center; those images are very important. So for me it is very hard that I have been taken away from the Gikuyu language environment. I have been deprived of that and I need that contact. But there are also some positives. I have always tried to reconnect and the result of that continuous attempt at connection is the journal *Mutiiri* which has had an effect on writing within Kenya and on my own writing of *Wizard of the Crow*.

HT: *Does the crow have any special significance here?*

I don't think so. It's a humorous title, and it's funny as there's a kind of contradiction: the wizard is a powerful and feared figure but we don't fear the crow much. Whenever I tell it to people in Gikuyu they always laugh.

HT: *Finally, looking back over your career, you started writing with a strikingly radical agenda some forty years ago, which caused excitement and hope in people who read literature all over the Third World. Now, forced out of your country, reconnected with Gikuyu but deprived of a Gikuyu-speaking community, and generally looking at the way the world is going—globalization, neo-colonization, the emergence of the United States as an even greater super-power than ever before—what do you think is the extent to* *which that agenda or vision you had has been fulfilled or is likely to be fulfilled?*

With globalization, as with every phenomenon in history, there are always negatives and positives. The globalization of technology, the global reach, also brings possibilities for ordinary working people to contact each other across national lines. Now intellectuals from Asia and Africa can communicate about the problems of the South much more easily than ever before. So it is not all negative. These opportunities can be exploited by forces which are working for a more human world.

HT: *Yesterday at your lecture I was struck by the ambition you conveyed, the idealist vision you sketched out, which seems still to be burning bright at least within your own heart.*

Oh yes, I'm always affected by these possibilities. For instance, now I'm heading the International Center for Translation Studies in the University of California at Irvine and I have begun to see the possibilities of enabling communication among marginalized languages, between scholars and writers. I get very excited about my involvement in the idea of this dialogue with writers from Ireland, from Asia, who have come and met with writers and scholars from Africa. It is clear that it won't change the world, but it is an important initiative.

HT: *Is there an element of paradox here that such hope is being nurtured through institutional location and support in what we regarded as the greatest neo-colonial power?*

But everything has its own contradictions and it's just a case of what aspect of the contradiction you want to highlight. It was always there. All the leaders of the anti-colonial movement—where were they educated? Gandhi, for instance, was called to the bar at the Gray's Inn in London. Jomo Kenyatta, Kwame Nkrumah—they were all educated in colleges founded by the colonial authority in Africa and some were also educated in colleges abroad. What is important is the connection between phenomena. Wherever I am I look for connections. I don't say to myself: Now I am in America and there is no connection between America and Kenya; I am at Yale and what connection has Yale to Kenya? And I found that there was a connection behind the founding of *Mutiiri*, because founding it in New York University meant that it was located within a mainstream Department of Comparative Literature, and it was also helping an African-language voice in Kenya.

HT: *Have the political circumstances and other factors improved enough in Kenya for you to think of going back?*

Yes, absolutely. I wish to state this categorically: As from December 2002, I am no longer in exile. We have a new government and the old Moi regime is no longer there, so the conditions that forced me into exile are no longer there.

HT: *Are you contemplating going back to Kenya at any stage?*

Yes, next year; I'm going there next year.

HT: *But not to live there?*

Not permanently. I have a job in the University in California...unless something cropped up in Kenya.

---

* This conference titled "Against All Odds: African Languages and Literatures into the Twenty-First Century" took place 11-17 January 2000.

Bibliography of Interviews with Ngũgĩ wa Thiong'o: 1964-2003

[* indicates that interview is included in this volume].

---

* de Villiers, John. "The Birth of a New East African Author." *Sunday Nation*, 3 May 1964, p. 10.

* Nagenda, John, and Robert Serumaga. "A Discussion between James Ngugi, Author of *The River Between* (Heinemann), Who Is Studying at Leeds University, John Nagenda, a Writer from Uganda Who Has Just Spent Some Time in the United States of America and Is Now on His Way Back to Uganda, and Robert Serumaga from Uganda Who Is Studying at Trinity College, Dublin." *Cultural Events in Africa*, 15 (1966), i-iii supp.

Woolf, Cecil, and John Bagguley, eds. "James Ngugi." *Authors Take Sides on Vietnam*. London: Peter Owen, 1967. P. 57.

* Marcuson, Alan, *et al*. "James Ngugi Interviewed by Fellow Students at Leeds University, Alan Marcuson, Mike González & Dave Williams." *Cultural Events in Africa*, 31 (1967), i-v supp.

* Ndonde, E.C. "Problems Confronting African Writers." *Nationalist*, 6 December 1968, p. 4.

* Friedberger, Heinz. "Kenyan Writer James Ngugi Interviewed by Heinz Friedberger in Nairobi." *Cultural Events in Africa*, 50 (1969), i-ii supp.; longer version in German by Heinz Berger in *Afrika Heute*, 15 October 1970, pp. 309-12.

Darling, Peter. "My Protest Was against the Hypocrisy in the College." *Sunday Nation*, 16 March 1969, pp. 15-16.

Keeble, Elizabeth. "[Interview with James Ngugi about Writers' Workshop Organized at Makerere University College]." *BBC University Report*, 95 (1970), 1-5.

** Duerden, Dennis and Aminu Abdullahi. "Ngugi wa Thiong'o: James Ngugi." *African Writers Talking: A Collection of Radio Interviews*. Ed. Cosmo Pieterse and Duerden. London: Heinemann Educational Books; New York: Africana Publishing Corp, 1972. Pp. 121-31.

* Sander, Reinhard, and Ian Munro. "'Tolstoy in Africa': An Interview with Ngugi wa Thiong'o." *Ba Shiru*, 5, 1 (1973), 21-30; rpt. in *Critical Perspectives on Ngugi wa Thiong'o*. Ed. G. D. Killam. Washington, DC: Three Continents Press, 1984. Pp. 46-57.

Spicer, Laurence. "[Interview with James Ngugi about *The Trial of Dedan Kimathi* and Plans for Performance of It at Festac]." *BBC Arts and Africa*, 153 (1976), 1-5.

* Harrison, Charles. "[Interview with Ngugi wa Thiong'o about *Petals of Blood*]." *BBC Arts and Africa*, 194 (1977), 1-3.

* Shreve, Anita. "*Petals of Blood.*" *Viva*, 3, 6 (1977), 35-36.

* Esibi, John. "'Open Criticism Is Very Healthy in Any Society.'" *Sunday Nation*, 17 July 1977, p. 10.

Egejuru, Phanuel Akubueze. [Excerpts from interviews with Ngugi]. *Black Writers: White Audience: A Critical Approach to African Literature*. Hicksville, NY: Exposition Press, 1978. *Passim.*

Beasnael, Sem Miantoloum, and Maurice Coles. "Interviews with Ngugi wa Thiong'o." Part Four of "The Mau Mau: Symbol of Revolt and Violence in the Works of Ngugi wa Thiong'o." Master's Thesis by Beasnael, University of Chad, 1978. Pp. 131-48.

* Parker, Bettye J. "*BBB* Interviews Ngugi wa Thiong'o." *Black Books Bulletin*, 6, 1 (1978), 46-51; corrections noted in 6,2 (1978), 14; *First World*, 2,2 (1979), 56-59; rpt. as "Interview with Ngugi wa

Thiong'o (James Ngugi)" in *Critical Perspectives on Ngugi wa Thiong'o*. Ed. G. D. Killam. Washington, DC: Three Continents Press, 1984. Pp. 58-66.

* Anon. "An Interview with Ngugi." *Weekly Review*, 9 January 1978, pp. 9-11; Swedish translation by Mikael Dolfe and Nils Aage Larson. "Intervju med Ngugi wa Thiong'o." *Permanent Press*, 13-14 (1980), 74-76.

Magina, Magina. "People Have a Right to Know." *Africa: An International Business, Economic and Political Monthly* (London), 90 (1979), 30-31; *Africa Currents*, 14 (1979), 5-7.

* Gacheru, Margaretta wa. "Ngugi wa Thiong'o Still Bitter over His Detention." *Weekly Review*, 5 January 1979, pp. 30-32; rpt. in *Sunday Nation*, 28 January 1979.

Laudan, Peter. "Revolution mit der Bibel: Ein Gespräch mit dem Schriftsteller aus Kenia Ngugi wa Thiong'o." *Die Zeit*, 11 May 1979, p. 43.

Kreimeier, Klaus. "Kampf um die eigene Kultur: Warten auf Ngugi wa Thiong'o / Besuch bei einem der grossen afrikanischen Schriftsteller." *Frankfurter Rundschau*, 12 May 1979, Zeit und Bild section, p. iii.

Egejuru, Phanuel Akubueze. [Excerpts from interviews with Ngugi]. *Towards African Literary Independence: A Dialogue with Contemporary African Writers*. Contributions in Afro-American and African Studies, 53. Westport, CT: Greenwood Press, 1980. *Passim*.

* Amooti wa Irumba, Katebaliirwe. "He Who Produces Should Be Able to Control That Which He Produces: Those Who Don't Work Shouldn't Eat at All." Appendix 2 in "Ngugi wa Thiong'o's Literary Production: A Materialist Critique." Ph.D. dissertation, University of Sussex, 1980; excerpt as "The Making of a Rebel" in *Index on Censorship*, 9, 3 (1980), 20-24; *Positive Review*, 1, 4 (1981), 28-31; *Staffrider*, 4, 2 (1981), 34-36; *Drum* (Nairobi), April 1982, pp. 47-

48; partially rpt. as "Ngugi on Ngugi" in *Ngugi wa Thiong'o: The Making of a Rebel: A Source Book in Kenyan Literature and Resistance.* Ed. Carol Sicherman. London, Munich, New York: Hans Zell, 1990. Pp. 18-26.

* Wilesmith, Greg. "[Interview with Ngugi wa Thiong'o about Literary and Theatrical Activities in Kenya and His Own Writing in Kikuyu]." *BBC Arts and Africa*, 347 (1980), 1-4.

Bolsover, Anne. "[Interview with Ngugi wa Thiong'o about the Role of the Writer and His Choice of a Language]." *BBC Arts and Africa*, 367 (1981), 4-5.

Lampley, James. "'Resistance Is the Only Choice.'" *Africa: An International Business, Economic and Political Monthly* (London), 114 (1981), 69-70.

* Martini, Jürgen, Anna Rutherford, Kirsten Holst Petersen, Vibeke Stenderup, and Bent Thomsen. "Ngugi wa Thiong'o: Interview." *Kunapipi*, 3,1 (1981), 110-16; 3,2 (1981), 135-40.

Walmsley, Anne. "Ngugi wa Thiong'o: Free Thoughts on Toilet Paper." *Index on Censorship*, 10,3 (1981), 41-42.

Simmons, Michael. "Chronicler of the Winds of Change." *Guardian* (Manchester), 7 January 1981, p. 8.

* Omari, Emman. "Ngugi wa Thiong'o Speaks!: 'I Am Not above the Contradictions Which Bedevil Our Society.'" *Weekend Standard*, 28 August 1981, pp. 11, 15.

Anon. "Kenia no Sakka Ngugi shi ga raisei [Kenyan novelist Ngugi comes to Shizuoka]." *Chūnichi*, 11 November 1981.

Tetsuya, Shibayama. "Kenia no Sakka Ngugi shi ni kiku [Some talks with Kenyan novelist Ngugi]." *Asahi Shinbun*, 11 November 1981.

Anon. "Kenia no Sakka Ngugi wa Thiong'o shi [Kenyan novelist Ngugi wa Thiong'o]." *Mainichi*, 13 November 1981.

Shogo, Shiraishi. "Kenia no Sakka Ngugi shi ni kiku [Some talks with Kenyan novelist Ngugi]." *Yomiuri*, 13 November 1981.

* Björkman, Ingrid. "Ngugi wa Thiong'o: Interview." *Kunapipi*, 4,2 (1982), 126-34.

Githieya, Muthoni. "'A Creative Spirit Cannot Be Silenced.'" *Africa: An International Business, Economic and Political Monthly* (London), 132 (1982), 73-74.

Sandberg, Agneta. "Ngugi wa Thiong'o skriver bara på kikuyu: Vårt eget språk blev ett vapen! [Ngugi wa Thiong'o Only Writes in Kikuyu: Our Own Language Became a Weapon]." *Röster i Radio*, 7 (1982), 50-52.

* Tetteh-Lartey, Alex. "[Interview with Ngugi wa Thiong'o about Okot p'Bitek]." *BBC Arts and Africa*, 449 (1982), 1-4.

Versteeg, Ferry. "Gesprek met de Keniaanse schrijver Ngugi wa Thiong'o [Conversation with the Kenyan writer]." *NRC Handelsblad*, "Cultureel Supplement," 23 April 1982, p. CS 2.

Bryce, Jane. "Ngugi: My Novel of Blood, Sweat and Tears." *New African*, August 1982, p. 36.

Fraser, Robert. "Writer on the Cross." *Africa Now*, August 1982, p. 84.

Granqvist, Raoul. "Ngugi wa Thiong'o: författare och agitator [Ngugi wa Thiong'o: Writer and Agitator]." *Vasabladet*, 16 September 1982; also in *Vertex* (Student Magazine at Umeå University), 28 September 1982.

Bitov, Oleg. "Vosprian', Sindbad! [Take heart, Sinbad!]." *Literaturnaia Gazeta*, 1 December 1982, p. 15.

Jönsson, Ulf. "Möte med Ngugi [A Meeting with Ngugi]." *Arbetarbladet*, 29 December 1982.

* Bardolph, Jacqueline, and Jean-Pierre Durix. "An Interview with Ngugi wa Thiong'o." *Commonwealth: Essays and Studies*, 6,1 (1983), 98-106.

Bini, Obi. "Interview with Ngugi wa Thiong'o." *Africasia*, April 1984, pp. 57-58; French translation in *Afrique-Asie*, 307 (1983), 51-53.

Clason, Flin. "Teatern en symbol som måste förgöras [Theater, a Symbol That Must be Destroyed]." *Ny Dag*, 48 (1983), 10.

* Granqvist, Raoul. "Ngugi wa Thiong'o: Interview." *Kunapipi,* 5,1 (1983), 44-48.

----------. "Ngugi wa Thiong'o: författare i fängelse [Ngugi wa Thiongo'o: A Writer in Prison]." *Amnestybulletinen*, 1 (1983), 14.

Höjeberg, Elle-Kari. "Ngugi." *Fönstret*, 1 (1983), 22-23.

Skjønsberg, Simen, and Helge Rønning. "Kultur, politikk og identitet: Samtale med Ngugi wa Thiong'o [Culture, politics and identity: conversations with Ngugi wa Thiong'o]." *Samtiden*, 92,3 (1983), 18-22.

Swenson, Fredrik. "Vi, afrikanska intellektuella, har mycket att lära av arbetare och bonder [We, African Intellectuals, have Much to Learn from Workers and Peasants]." *Tempus*, 69 (1983), 18-19.

Walmsley, Anne. "Ngugi wa Thiong'o: No Licence for Musical." *Index on Censorship*, 12, 1 (1983), 22-24.

Vivan, Itala. "Intervista a Ngugi wa Thiong'o: Non mi tiro indietro." *Nigrizia*, September 1983, pp. 48-51.

** Wilkinson (Calé), Jane. "Intervista con Ngugi wa Thiong'o scrittore keniota in esilio: L'orgoglio di parlare africano." *Rinascita*,

23 September 1983, pp. 27-28; rpt. in English with additional material in *Talking with African Writers: Interviews with African Poets, Playwrights & Novelists*. Ed. Wilkinson. Rome: Bagatto Libri Soc. Coop, 1990; London: James Currey; Portsmouth NH: Heinemann, 1992. Pp. 123-35.

Breitinger, Eckhard. "Ein Fisch auf dem Trockenen: Gespräch mit Ngugi wa Thiong'o / Ein Kampf ums Publikum." *Stuttgarter Zeitung*, 29 November 1983, p. 26.

* Castley, Jerusha and Nick Barber. "[Interview with Mike Kirkwood, Ngugi wa Thiong'o, and Eldred Jones about Winners of Noma Award]." *BBC Arts and Africa*, 539 (1984), 1-5.

Frederikse, Julie. "[The Second Zimbabwe International Book Fair]." *BBC Arts and Africa*, 559 (1984), 1-5.

Lindquist, Bosse. "Boken, teatern, filmen—i Afrika blir allt till vapen [The Book, Theater, and the Film—in Africa Everything Becomes a Weapon]." *Arbetaren*, 24 (1984), 4.

----------. "Möte med afrikanska författare [A Meeting with African Writers]." *Afrikabulletinen*, 4 (1984), 12-13.

Schütt, Peter. "Kolonialismus und Bewusstsein: Ein Gespräch zwischen Peter Schütt und Ngugi wa Thiong'o." *Nommo*, 2-3 (1984), 68-74.

* Warner-Lewis, Maureen. "[Interview with Ngugi wa Thiong'o]." *World Marxist Review* (London), 27, 2 (1984), 103-06.

Bryce, Jane. "Ngugi wa Thiong'o: Forging Theatrical Links." *New African*, January 1984, p. 44.

Lindquist, Bosse. "Vi måste tjäna folket [We Have to Serve the People]." *Aftonbladet*, 17 March 1984.

* Whatiri, Raina, and John Timmins. "An Interview with Ngugi wa Thiong'o." *Span*, 19 (1984), 26-34; first published in *Kia Ora*, 7 August 1984.

Green, John. "Past Tale and Present Reality of Struggle against Imperialism." *Morning Star* (London), 18 October 1984, p. 2.

Wilson, Amrit. "Playwright in Exile." *New Statesman*, 23 November 1984, p. 22.

* Darah, G.G. "To Choose a Language Is to Choose a Class: Interview with Ngugi wa Thiong'o for *Isala*." *Ife Studies in African Literature and the Arts*, 3 (1985), 20-40.

Eyoh, Hansel Ndumbe. "Language as Carrier of Peoples' Culture: An Interview with Ngugi wa Thiong'o." *Nytt från Nordiska Afrikainstitutet*,16 (1985), 26-28; *Ufahamu*, 14, 3 (1985), 156-60; *Journal of Commonwealth Literature*, 21,1 (1986), 162-66; *African Theatre Review*, 1,2 (1986), 110-14; *Union of African Performing Artists News*, 10 (1986), 19-21; rpt. in *Beyond the Theatre: Interviews*. Ed. Eyoh. Bonn: German Foundation for International Development (DSE), Education, Science and Documentation Centre (ZED), 1991. Pp. 142-48.

Desai, Gaurav. "Conversation with Ngugi wa Thiong'o." Evanston, IL.: Northwestern University, [1986]. [Mimeographed.]

Onwordi, Ike. "Breaking the Vicious Circle." *African Concord*, 14 August 1986, pp. 21-22.

* Owusu, Kwesi. "A Political Choice." *West Africa*, 18 August 1986, pp. 1734-35.

Brooke, James. "African Writers Note Hazards of the Trade." *New York Times*, 9 November 1986, p. 18.

Anon. "The RW Interview: Ngugi wa Thiong'o." *Revolutionary Worker*, 15 December 1986, pp. 8-10.

Mchunu, Vusi D. "Impressions of the 6th Book Fair of Radical Black and Third World Books." *Awa-Finnaba*, 10 (1987), 3-7.

Petersen, Kirsten Holst, ed. [Ngugi Discussing Black South African Writing]. *Criticism and Ideology: Second African Writers' Conference, Stockholm 1986*. Uppsala: Scandinavian Institute of African Studies, 1988. Pp. 203-04.

Herzberger-Fofana, Pierrette. "We Should Increasingly Exploit the Resources of Our Own Languages: An Interview with Kenyan Writer Ngugi wa Thiong'o." *Zeitschrift für Kulturaustausch*, 38 (1988), 189-92; *Isivivane*, 1 (1990), 23-26.

* Meli, Francis, Essop Pahad, and Mandla Langa. "The Role of Culture in the African Revolution: Ngugi wa Thiong'o and Mongane Wally Serote in a Round-Table Discussion." *African Communist*, 113 (1988), 31-48.

* Jaggi, Maya. "Ngugi wa Thiong'o: *Matigari* as Myth and History: An Interview." *Third World Quarterly*, 11 (1989), 241-51.

van Niekerk, Phillip. "Ten Millionaires and 10 Million Poor." *Weekly Mail* (Johannesburg), 30 June 1989, pp. 1-2.

Acworth, William. "Interview with Ngugi wa Thiong'o." *Ufahamu*, 18,2 (1990), 41-46.

Anderson, Lanchester, and Oji Adisa. "Ngugi wa Thiong'o's Quest for Justice." *African Literature Association Bulletin*, 16, 3-4 (1990), 12-14; rpt. from *The Varsity* (U of Toronto), 18 October 1990, p. 11.

Andrewes, Georgina. "Timeless Traveller: Ngugi wa Thiongo." *Focus on Africa*, 1,1 (1990), 86.

* Schwerdt, Dianne. "An Interview with Ngugi at The Flinders University of South Australia, September 1990." *CRNLE Reviews Journal*, 2 (1990), 1-9.

Anon. "Kenyan Writer Ngugi wa Thiong'o: Activist Artist." *West Africa*, 6-12 August 1990, p. 2233.

* During, Simon, and Jenny Lee. "The Third World Mainstream: Ngugi wa Thiong'o in Conversation with Simon During and Jenny Lee." *Meanjin*, 50, 1 (1991), 53-62.

* Jussawalla, Feroza. "The Language of Struggle: Ngugi wa Thiong'o on the Prisonhouse of Language," *Transition*, 54 (1991), 142-54; rpt. in *Interviews with Writers of the Post-Colonial World*. Ed. Jussawalla and Reed Way Dasenbrock. Jackson, MS, and London: University Press of Mississippi, 1992. Pp. 24-41; and in *Daily Times* (Lagos), 28 August 1993, pp. 6,11.

Anon. "A Question of Language." *New Nation*, 23 August 1991, p. 11.

Memela, Sandile. "Putting Africa in Perspective." *City Press* (Johannesburg), 25 August 1991, p. 15.

* Msimang, Nonqaba. "Ngugi: In His Own Words." *Tribute*, September 1991, pp. 26-28.

Abu, Eugenia. "Ngugi, See You Again." *Timesweek*, 11 November 1991, p. 9.

Bini, Obi. "Entrevista com Ngugi wa Thiong'o: 'Intellectual Africano deve servir a causa do seu povo.'" *Domingo*, 24 November 1991, p. 5.

Anon. "Mwakenya's Stand." *Africa Events*, 8, 2 (1992), 30-31.

* Alpert, Tami. "Ngugi by Telephone." *Paintbrush*, 20, 39-40 (1993), 229-32; rpt. in *The World of Ngugi wa Thiong'o*. Ed. Charles Cantalupo. Trenton, NJ: Africa World Press, 1995. Pp. 229-32.

* Cantalupo, Charles. "'Moving the Center': An Interview by Charles Cantalupo." *Paintbrush*, 20, 39-40 (1993), 207-27; rpt. in

The World of Ngugi wa Thiong'o. Ed. Cantalupo. Trenton, NJ: Africa World Press, 1995. Pp. 207-27.

Mwagiru, Ciugu. "A Conversation with Ngugi wa Thiong'o." *Sunday Nation Lifestyle*, 28 March 1993, p. 13.

Chege wa Gachamba. "[Ngugi wa] Thiong'o on the Threshold of a New Career." *Daily Nation*, 2 April 1993, pp. 6-7.

Kelley, Kevin J. "Ngugi Denounces Repression of Writers as Undemocratic." *Daily Nation Weekender*, 30 July 1993, p. 10.

Anselmi, Ines. "Exil und Engagement: Begegnung mit dem kenyanischen Autor Ngugi wa Thiong'o." *Neue Züricher Zeitung*, 18 April 1994, p. 19.

Agyeman-Duah, Ivor. "Ngugi wa Thiong'o as a Reformist." *Some African Voices of Our Time*. Accra: Anansesem Publications, 1995. Pp. 7-14.

Mbugua, Martin. "Why I Advance African Languages." *Daily Nation Weekender Magazine* (Nairobi), 13 January 1995, p. 6.

* Ali, Trayo A. "'The Strength of Our People Is My Inspiration.'" *West Africa*, 6-12 November 1995, pp. 1734-36.

Kumar, T. Vijay. "The Writer as Activist: An Interview with Ngugi wa Thiong'o." *Book Review*, 20, 5 (1996), 27-28; rpt. in *The Writer as Activist: South Asian Perspectives on Ngugi wa Thiong'o*. Ed. Bernth Lindfors and Bala Kothandaraman. Trenton, NJ: Africa World Press, 2001. Pp. 169-76.

* Nichols, Lee. "Lee Nichols's Interview of Ngugi wa Thiong'o, March 30 at Stony Brook." *African Literature Association Bulletin*, 22, 2 (1996), 21-25.

* Enekwe, Onuora Ossie. "'We Are All Learning from History': Interview with Ngugi wa Thiong'o." *Glendora Review*, 1, 3 (1996), 12-19; *Sunday Times* (Lagos), 14 July 1996, p.14; partially rpt. as

"Interview with Ngugi wa Thiong'o" in *Okike*, 35 (1997), 99-115.

Legodi, Tlou. "Ngugi Visits Wits." *Wits Student* (U of the Witwatersrand), 49, 6 (1997), 18.

Large, Jerry. "Peasant-Playwright Gives Voice to Value of Self-Respect." *Seattle Times*, 29 May 1997, p. E1.

Molakeng, Saint. "African Writer Ngugi Welcomes Open Talks." *Sowetan*, 28 July 1997, p. 1.

Gandhi, Lingaraja. "An Interview with Ngugi wa Thiong'o." *Literary Half-Yearly*, 39, 1 (1998), 109-12.

* Rao, D. Venkat. "A Conversation with Ngugi wa Thiong'o." *Research in African Literatures,* 30, 1 (1999), 162-68; rpt. in *The Writer as Activist: South Asian Perspectives on Ngugi wa Thiong'o.* Ed. Bernth Lindfors and Bala Kothandaraman. Trenton, NJ: Africa World Press, 2001. Pp. 157-67.

* Cantalupo, Charles. "Ngugi wa Thiong'o: *Penpoints, Gunpoints, and Dreams*: An Interview." *Left Curve*, 23 (1999), 30-35.

Na'Allah, Abdul-Rasheed. "African Languages and the Twenty-First Century: An Interview with Ngugi wa Thiong'o." *ALA Bulletin*, 27, 2 (2001), 53-69.

* Trivedi, Harish. "Ngugi wa Thiong'o in Conversation." *Wasafiri*, 40 (2003), 5-10.

Critical Studies of Ngũgĩ wa Thiong'o

Adegala, Kavetsa. *Wanja of* Petals of Blood*: The Woman Question and Imperialism in Kenya.* Nairobi: Derika Associates, 1985.

Amuzu, Koku. *Beyond Ideology: Literary Technique in Ngugi's* Petals of Blood *and* Devil on the Cross. Montreux, Switzerland; London; Washington, DC: Minerva Press, 1997.

Balogun, Fidelis Odun. *Ngugi and African Post-Colonial Narrative: The Novel as Oral Narrative in Multi-Genre Performance*. St. Hyacinthe, Quebec: World Heritage Press, 1997.

Bardolph, Jacqueline. *Ngugi wa Thiong'o: l'homme et l'oeuvre*. Paris: Présence Africaine, 1991.

Björkman, Ingrid. *"Mother, Sing for Me": People's Theatre in Kenya*. London; Atlantic Highlands, NJ: Zed Books, 1989.

Breidlid, Anders. *Resistance and Consciousness in Kenya and South Africa: Subalternity and Representation in the Novels of Ngugi wa Thiong'o and Alex La Guma*. Frankfurt; New York: P. Lang, 2002.

Cantalupo, Charles, ed. *Ngugi wa Thiong'o: Texts and Contexts*. Trenton, NJ: Africa World Press, 1995.

----------, ed. *The World of Ngugi wa Thiong'o*. Trenton, NJ: Africa World Press, 1995.

Cook, David and Michael Okenimkpe. *Ngugi wa Thiong'o: An Exploration of His Writings*. London & Exeter, NH: Heinemann, 1983.

Dramé, Kandioura. *The Novel as Transformation Myth: A Study of the Novels of Mongo Beti and Ngugi wa Thiong'o*. Syracuse, NY: Syracuse University, 1990.

Dusaidi, Claude. *Ngugi wa Thiong'o and the Development of Socially Committed Theatre in East Africa*. Ontario: African Human Rights Research Association, 1984.

Gikandi, Simon. *Ngugi wa Thiong'o*. Cambridge, UK; New York: Cambridge University Press, 2000.

Gugelberger, Georg. *Blake, Neruda and Ngugi wa Thiong'o: Towards a Definition of Third World Literature*. Ile-Ife: Department of Literature in English, University of Ife, 1983-84.

Indrasena Reddy, K. *The Novels of Achebe and Ngugi: A Study in the Dialectics of Commitment*. New Delhi: Prestige Books, 1994.

Killam, G. D., ed. *Critical Perspectives on Ngugi wa Thiong'o*. Washington: Three Continents Press, 1984.

----------. *An Introduction to the Writings of Ngugi*. London; Exeter, NH: Heinemann, 1980.

Lar, Isaac B. and Taiwo I. Ogundare. *Conflicting Symbols in the Novels of Ngugi wa Thiong'o*. Jos, Nigeria: Deka Publications, 1998.

Lebdaï, Benaouda. *Post-Independence African Literature: Case Study—Boujedra/Ngugi*. Algiers: Office des Publications Universitaires, 1992.

Lindfors, Bernth and Bala Kothandaraman, eds. *The Writer as Activist: South Asian Perspectives on Ngugi wa Thiong'o*. Trenton, NJ: Africa World Press, 2001.

Lovesey, Oliver. *Ngugi wa Thiong'o*. New York: Twayne Publishers, 2000.

Meyer, Herta. *"Justice for the Oppressed—": The Political Dimension in the Language Use of Ngugi wa Thiong'o*. Essen: Verlag Die Blaue Eule, 1991.

Mugo, Micere Githae. *Visions of Africa: The Fiction of Chinua Achebe, Margaret Laurence, Elspeth Huxley and Ngugi wa Thiong'o*. Nairobi: Kenya Literature Bureau, 1978.

Narang, Harish. *Politics as Fiction: The Novels of Ngugi wa Thiong'o*. New Delhi: Creative Books, 1995.

Nazareth, Peter, ed. *Critical Essays on Ngugi wa Thiong'o*. New York: Twayne Publishers, 2000.

Nwankwo, Chimalum Moses. *The Works of Ngugi wa Thiong'o: Towards the Kingdom of Woman and Man*. Ikeja: Longman, Nigeria, 1992.

O'Callaghan, Helen. *Women in the Writings of Ngugi wa Thiong'o*. Cork: Department of Sociology, University College, Cork, 1992.

Ogude, James. *Ngugi's Novels and African History: Narrating the Nation*. London; Sterling, VA: Pluto, 1999.

Onyeberechi, Sydney E. *Critical Essays: Achebe, Baldwin, Cullen, Ngugi, and Tutuola*. Hyattsville, MD: Rising Star Publishers, 1999.

Palmer, Eustace. *An Introduction to the African Novel: A Critical Study of Twelve Books by Chinua Achebe, James Ngugi, Camara Laye, Elechi Amadi, Ayi Kwei Armah, Mongo Beti and Gabriel Okara*. London: Heinemann; New York: Africana, 1972.

Parker, Michael and Roger Starkey, eds. *Postcolonial Literatures: Achebe, Ngugi, Desai, Walcott*. Basingstoke: Macmillan; New York: St. Martin's Press, 1995.

Peicke, Sigrid. *In den Frauen liegt die Zukunft: Frauengestalten im Werk des kenianischen Schriftstellers Ngugi wa Thiong'o*. Frankfurt: Nexus, 1981.

Richard, René. *History and Literature: Narration and Time in* Petals of Blood *by Ngugi wa Thiong'o*. Montpellier: Centre d'Etudes et de Recherches sur les Pays d'Afrique Noire Anglophones, Université Paul Valéry de Montpellier, n. d.

Robson, Clifford B. *Ngugi wa Thiong'o*. London: Macmillan; New York: St. Martin's Press, 1979.

Sicherman, Carol. *Ngugi wa Thiong'o: A Bibliography of Primary and Secondary Sources, 1957-1987*. London; New York: H. Zell Publishers, 1989.

----------. *Ngugi wa Thiong'o: The Making of a Rebel: A Source Book in Kenyan Literature and Resistance*. London; New York: H. Zell Publishers, 1990.

Stotesbury, John. *The Logic of Ngugi's Use of Biblical and Christian References in* A Grain of Wheat. Joensuu, Finland: Faculty of Arts, University of Joensuu, 1985.

Trigona, Prospero. *Ngugi wa Thiong'o da fede a rivoluzione*. Naples: Edizioni Scientifiche Italiane, 1991.

Tsabedze, Clara. *African Independence from Francophone and Anglophone Voices: A Comparative Study of the Post-Independence Novels by Ngugi and Sembène*. New York: P. Lang, 1994.

Vol'pe, M. L. *Ngugi wa Thiong'o: S Dumoi o Kenii.* Moscow: Nauka, 1989.

Wilkinson, Jane. *Orpheus in Africa: Fragmentation and Renewal in the Work of Four African Writers*. Roma: Bulzoni editore, 1990.

Williams, Patrick. *Ngugi wa Thiong'o*. Manchester; New York: Manchester University Press, 1999.

Index